MW01078003

SCIENCE FICTION *Classics*

Graphic Classics® Volume Seventeen

2009

Edited by Tom Pomplun

EUREKA PRODUCTIONS
8778 Oak Grove Road, Mount Horeb, Wisconsin 53572
www.graphicclassics.com

ILLUSTRATION ©2009 GEORGE SELLAS

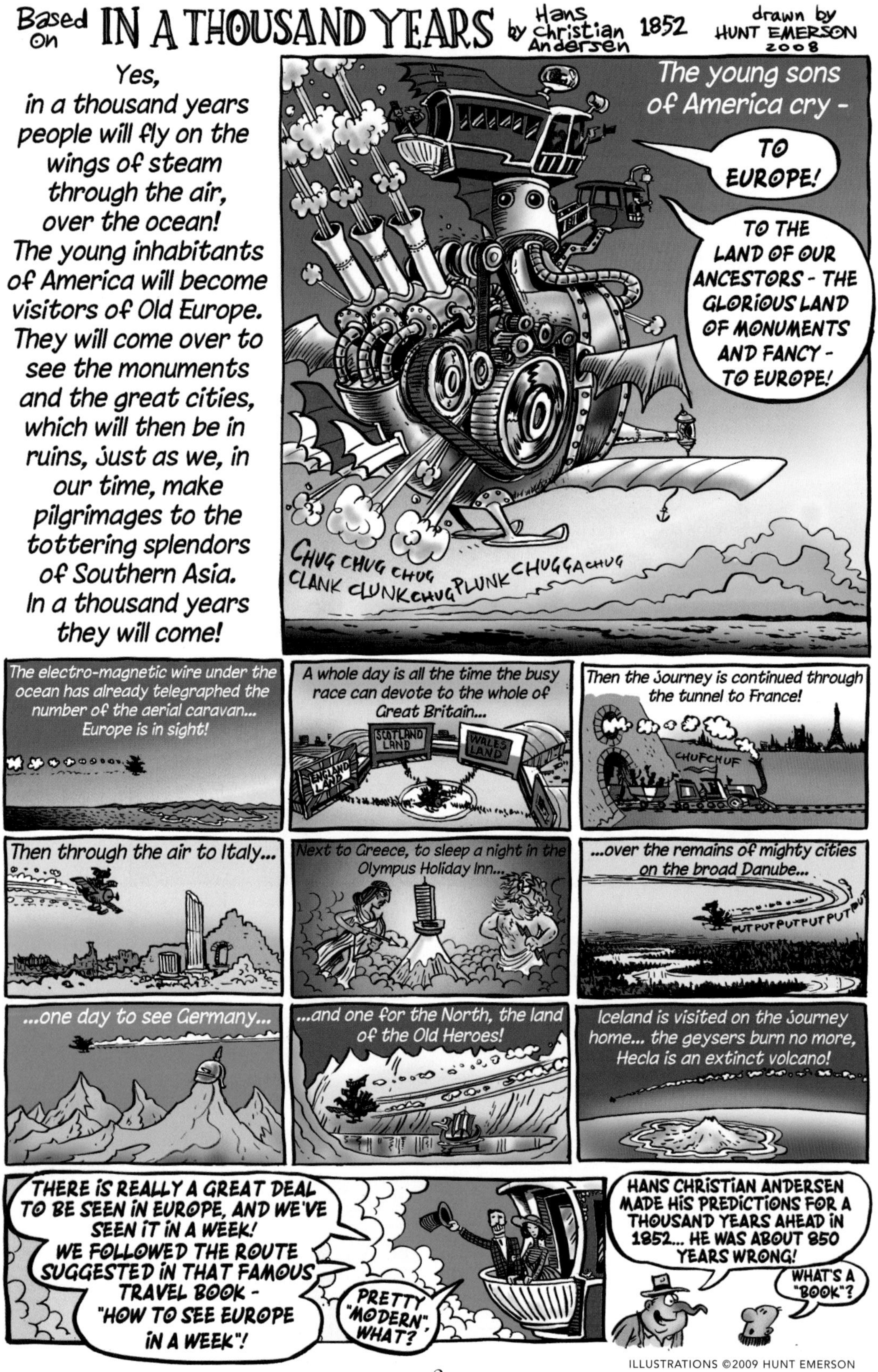
Based on IN A THOUSAND YEARS by Hans Christian Andersen 1852
drawn by HUNT EMERSON 2008
Yes, in a thousand years people will fly on the wings of steam through the air, over the ocean! The young inhabitants of America will become visitors of Old Europe. They will come over to see the monuments and the great cities, which will then be in ruins, just as we, in our time, make pilgrimages to the tottering splendors of Southern Asia. In a thousand years they will come!
The young sons of America cry -
TO EUROPE!
TO THE LAND OF OUR ANCESTORS - THE GLORIOUS LAND OF MONUMENTS AND FANCY - TO EUROPE!
CHUG CHUG CHUG CLANK CLUNK CHUG PLUNK CHUGGA CHUG
The electro-magnetic wire under the ocean has already telegraphed the number of the aerial caravan... Europe is in sight!
A whole day is all the time the busy race can devote to the whole of Great Britain...
ENGLAND LAND
SCOTLAND LAND
WALES LAND
Then the journey is continued through the tunnel to France!
CHUFCHUF
Then through the air to Italy...
Next to Greece, to sleep a night in the Olympus Holiday Inn...
...over the remains of mighty cities on the broad Danube...
PUT PUT PUT PUT PUT PUT PUT
...one day to see Germany...
...and one for the North, the land of the Old Heroes!
Iceland is visited on the journey home... the geysers burn no more, Hecla is an extinct volcano!
THERE IS REALLY A GREAT DEAL TO BE SEEN IN EUROPE, AND WE'VE SEEN IT IN A WEEK! WE FOLLOWED THE ROUTE SUGGESTED IN THAT FAMOUS TRAVEL BOOK - "HOW TO SEE EUROPE IN A WEEK"!
PRETTY "MODERN", WHAT?
HANS CHRISTIAN ANDERSEN MADE HIS PREDICTIONS FOR A THOUSAND YEARS AHEAD IN 1852... HE WAS ABOUT 850 YEARS WRONG!
WHAT'S A "BOOK"?

CONTENTS

SCIENCE FICTION *Classics*

Graphic Classics® Volume Seventeen

Cover illustration by Micah Farritor
Back cover illustration by George Sellas

ILLUSTRATION ©2009 ROGER LANGRIDGE

Science Fiction Classics: Graphic Classics Volume Seventeen / ISBN 978-0-9787919-7-1 is published by Eureka Productions. Price US $17.95, CAN $22.50. Available from Eureka Productions, 8778 Oak Grove Road, Mount Horeb, WI 53572. Tom Pomplun, designer and publisher, tom@graphicclassics.com. Eileen Fitzgerald, editorial assistant. *The Disintegration Machine* ©1996 Sir Arthur Conan Doyle Copyright Holders. Printed with permission of Jonathan Clowes Ltd., London, on behalf of Andrea Plunket, administrator of the Conan Doyle copyrights. Compilation and all original works ©2009 Eureka Productions. Graphic Classics is a registered trademark of Eureka Productions. For ordering information and previews of upcoming volumes visit the Graphic Classics website at http://www.graphicclassics.com. Printed in Canada.

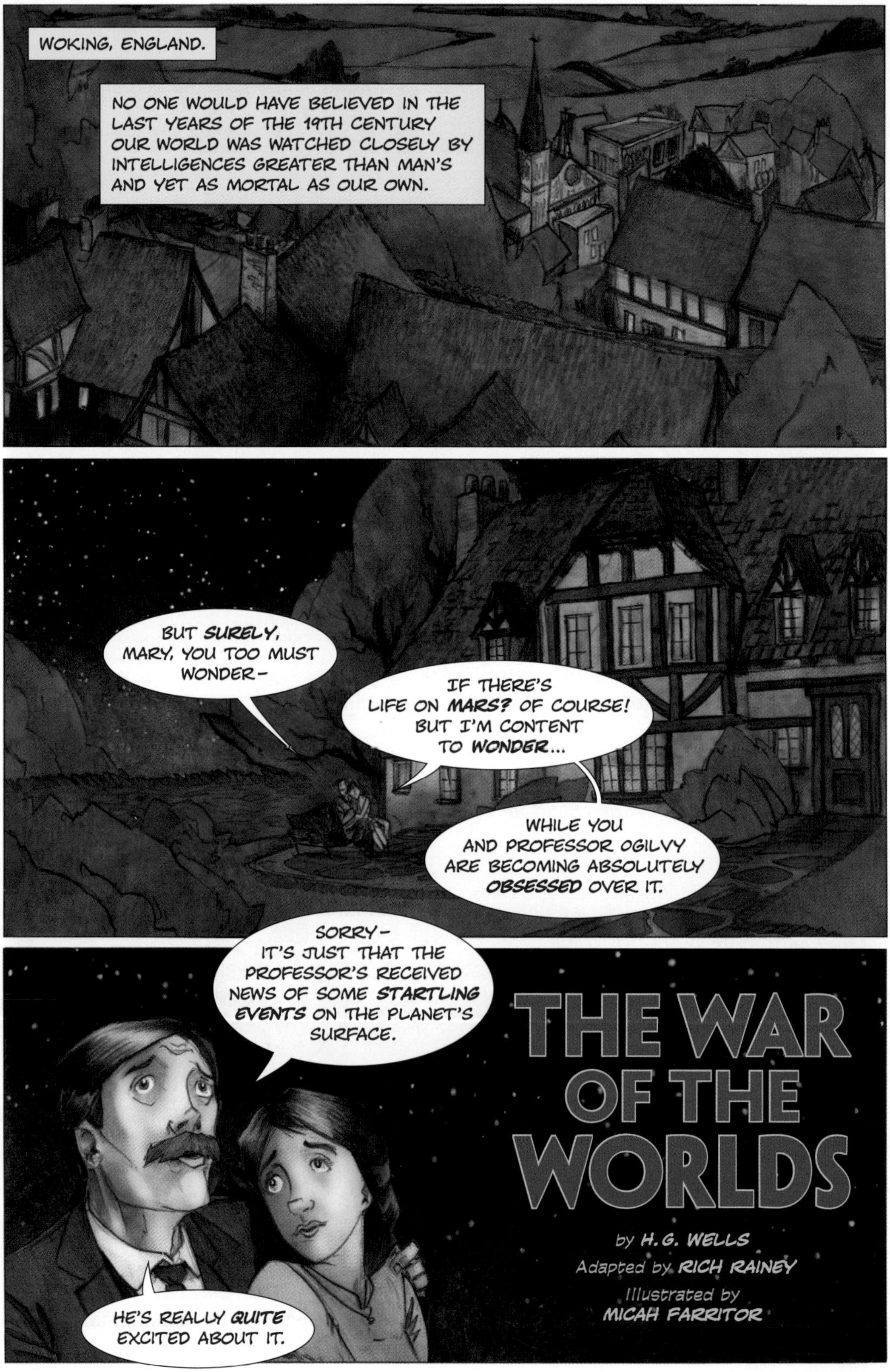
WOKING, ENGLAND.
NO ONE WOULD HAVE BELIEVED IN THE LAST YEARS OF THE 19TH CENTURY OUR WORLD WAS WATCHED CLOSELY BY INTELLIGENCES GREATER THAN MAN'S AND YET AS MORTAL AS OUR OWN.
BUT SURELY, MARY, YOU TOO MUST WONDER-
IF THERE'S LIFE ON MARS? OF COURSE! BUT I'M CONTENT TO WONDER...
WHILE YOU AND PROFESSOR OGILVY ARE BECOMING ABSOLUTELY OBSESSED OVER IT.
SORRY- IT'S JUST THAT THE PROFESSOR'S RECEIVED NEWS OF SOME STARTLING EVENTS ON THE PLANET'S SURFACE.
HE'S REALLY QUITE EXCITED ABOUT IT.
THE WAR OF THE WORLDS
by H.G. WELLS
Adapted by RICH RAINEY
Illustrated by MICAH FARRITOR

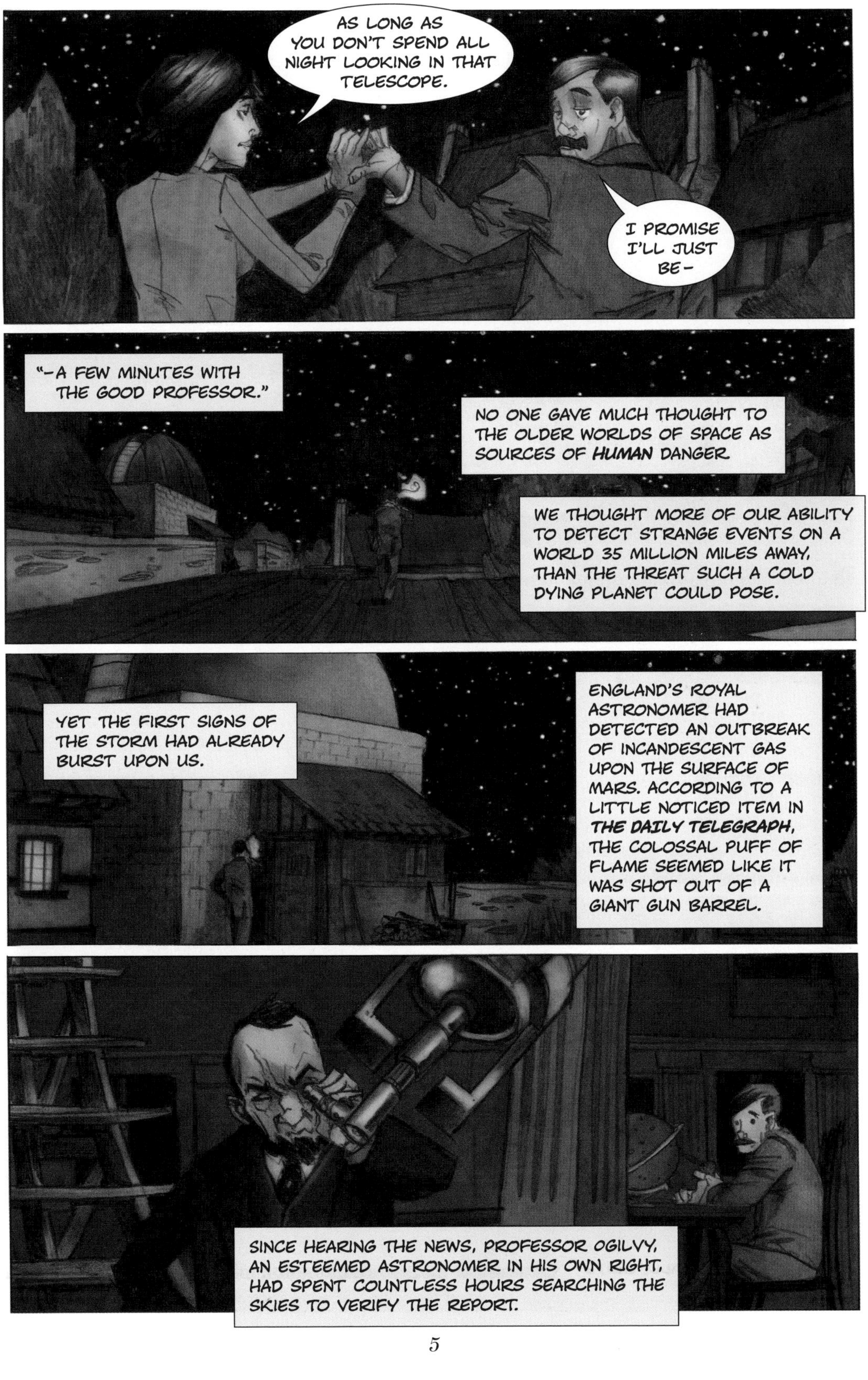
AS LONG AS YOU DON'T SPEND ALL NIGHT LOOKING IN THAT TELESCOPE.
I PROMISE I'LL JUST BE–
"–A FEW MINUTES WITH THE GOOD PROFESSOR."
NO ONE GAVE MUCH THOUGHT TO THE OLDER WORLDS OF SPACE AS SOURCES OF **HUMAN** DANGER.
WE THOUGHT MORE OF OUR ABILITY TO DETECT STRANGE EVENTS ON A WORLD 35 MILLION MILES AWAY, THAN THE THREAT SUCH A COLD DYING PLANET COULD POSE.
YET THE FIRST SIGNS OF THE STORM HAD ALREADY BURST UPON US.
ENGLAND'S ROYAL ASTRONOMER HAD DETECTED AN OUTBREAK OF INCANDESCENT GAS UPON THE SURFACE OF MARS. ACCORDING TO A LITTLE NOTICED ITEM IN ***THE DAILY TELEGRAPH***, THE COLOSSAL PUFF OF FLAME SEEMED LIKE IT WAS SHOT OUT OF A GIANT GUN BARREL.
SINCE HEARING THE NEWS, PROFESSOR OGILVY, AN ESTEEMED ASTRONOMER IN HIS OWN RIGHT, HAD SPENT COUNTLESS HOURS SEARCHING THE SKIES TO VERIFY THE REPORT.

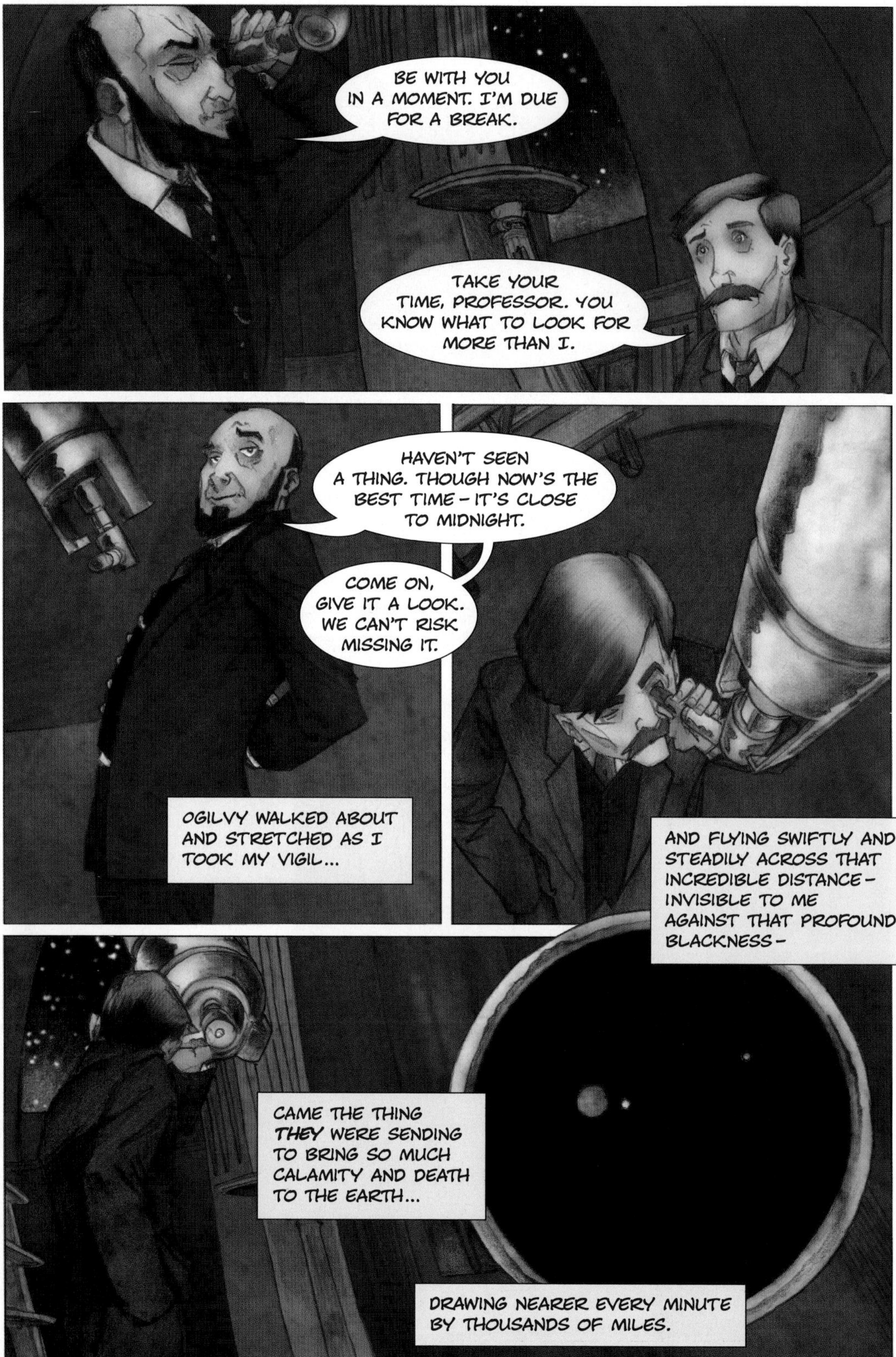
BE WITH YOU IN A MOMENT. I'M DUE FOR A BREAK.
TAKE YOUR TIME, PROFESSOR. YOU KNOW WHAT TO LOOK FOR MORE THAN I.
HAVEN'T SEEN A THING. THOUGH NOW'S THE BEST TIME – IT'S CLOSE TO MIDNIGHT.
COME ON, GIVE IT A LOOK. WE CAN'T RISK MISSING IT.
OGILVY WALKED ABOUT AND STRETCHED AS I TOOK MY VIGIL...
AND FLYING SWIFTLY AND STEADILY ACROSS THAT INCREDIBLE DISTANCE – INVISIBLE TO ME AGAINST THAT PROFOUND BLACKNESS –
CAME THE THING *THEY* WERE SENDING TO BRING SO MUCH CALAMITY AND DEATH TO THE EARTH...
DRAWING NEARER EVERY MINUTE BY THOUSANDS OF MILES.

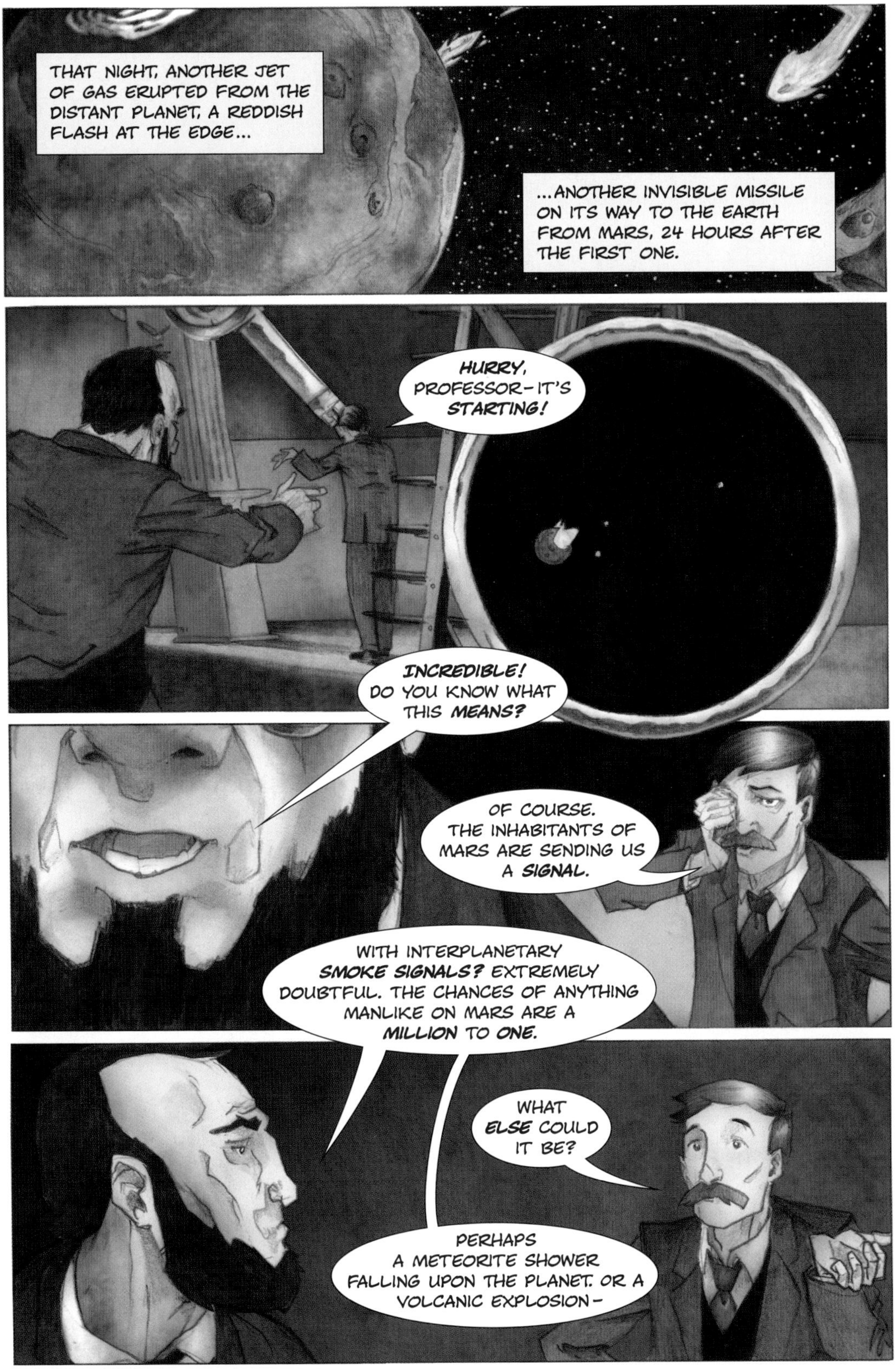
THAT NIGHT, ANOTHER JET OF GAS ERUPTED FROM THE DISTANT PLANET, A REDDISH FLASH AT THE EDGE...
...ANOTHER INVISIBLE MISSILE ON ITS WAY TO THE EARTH FROM MARS, 24 HOURS AFTER THE FIRST ONE.
HURRY, PROFESSOR–IT'S STARTING!
INCREDIBLE! DO YOU KNOW WHAT THIS MEANS?
OF COURSE. THE INHABITANTS OF MARS ARE SENDING US A SIGNAL.
WITH INTERPLANETARY SMOKE SIGNALS? EXTREMELY DOUBTFUL. THE CHANCES OF ANYTHING MANLIKE ON MARS ARE A MILLION TO ONE.
WHAT ELSE COULD IT BE?
PERHAPS A METEORITE SHOWER FALLING UPON THE PLANET. OR A VOLCANIC EXPLOSION–

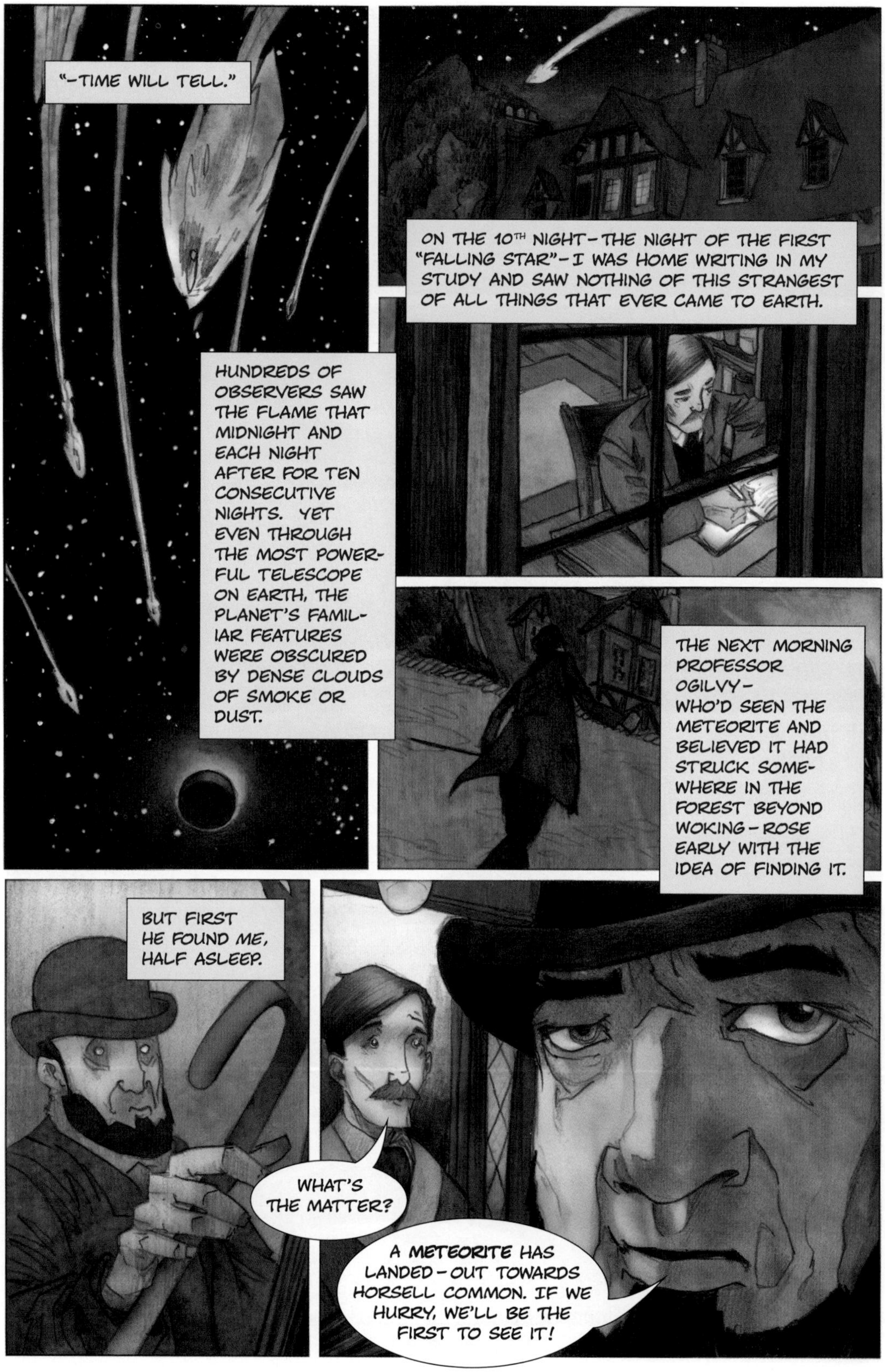
"–TIME WILL TELL."
HUNDREDS OF OBSERVERS SAW THE FLAME THAT MIDNIGHT AND EACH NIGHT AFTER FOR TEN CONSECUTIVE NIGHTS. YET EVEN THROUGH THE MOST POWERFUL TELESCOPE ON EARTH, THE PLANET'S FAMILIAR FEATURES WERE OBSCURED BY DENSE CLOUDS OF SMOKE OR DUST.
ON THE 10TH NIGHT–THE NIGHT OF THE FIRST "FALLING STAR"–I WAS HOME WRITING IN MY STUDY AND SAW NOTHING OF THIS STRANGEST OF ALL THINGS THAT EVER CAME TO EARTH.
THE NEXT MORNING PROFESSOR OGILVY– WHO'D SEEN THE METEORITE AND BELIEVED IT HAD STRUCK SOMEWHERE IN THE FOREST BEYOND WOKING–ROSE EARLY WITH THE IDEA OF FINDING IT.
BUT FIRST HE FOUND ME, HALF ASLEEP.
WHAT'S THE MATTER?
A **METEORITE** HAS LANDED–OUT TOWARDS HORSELL COMMON. IF WE HURRY, WE'LL BE THE FIRST TO SEE IT!

THERE WAS LITTLE DOUBT ABOUT FINDING THE WAY— WE JUST FOLLOWED THE SCENT OF BRIMSTONE FLOATING THROUGH THE FOREST.

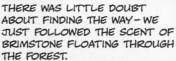

OH, MY GOD!

WHAT IS IT?

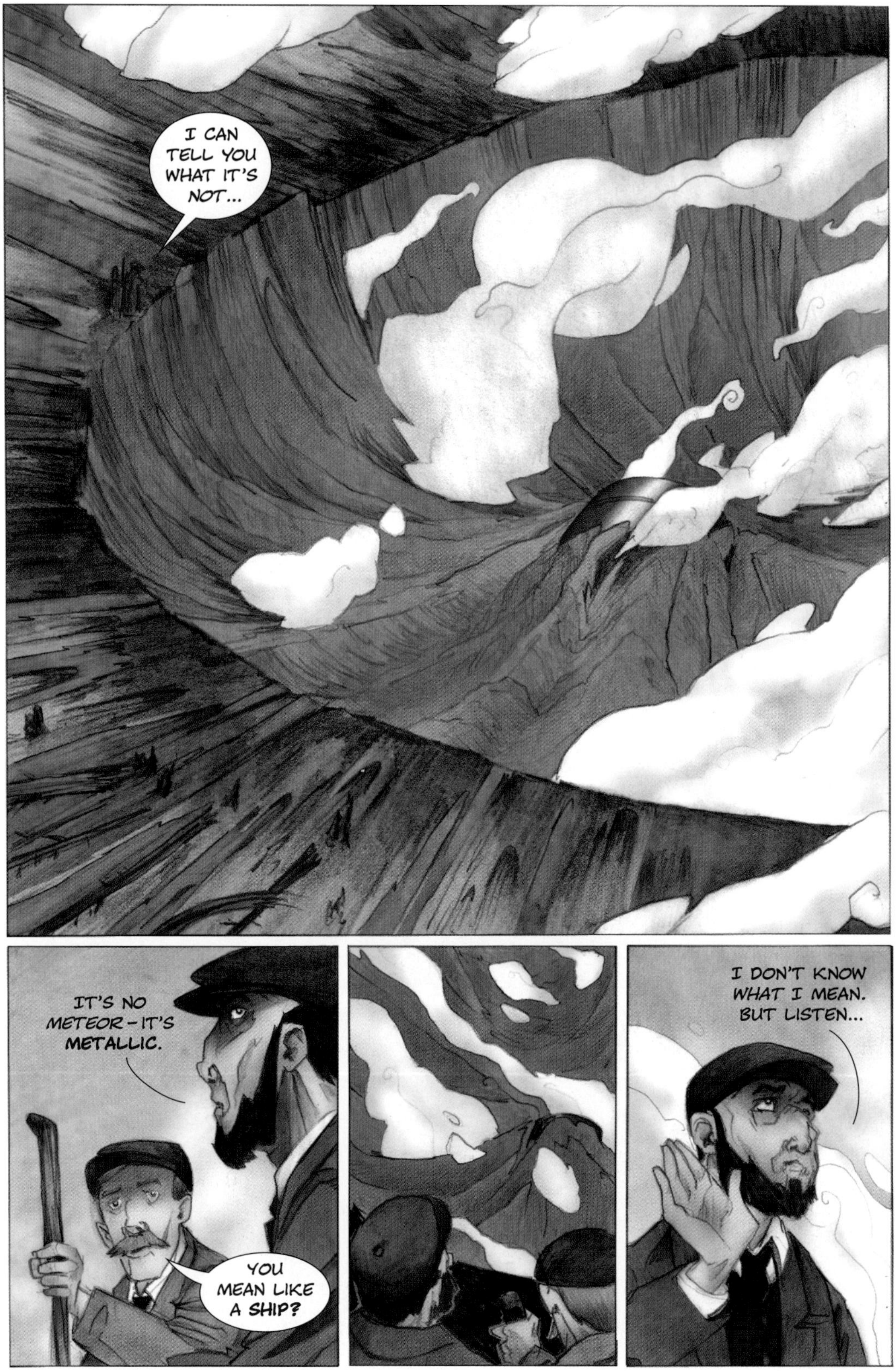
I CAN TELL YOU WHAT IT'S NOT...
IT'S NO METEOR – IT'S METALLIC.
YOU MEAN LIKE A SHIP?
I DON'T KNOW WHAT I MEAN. BUT LISTEN...

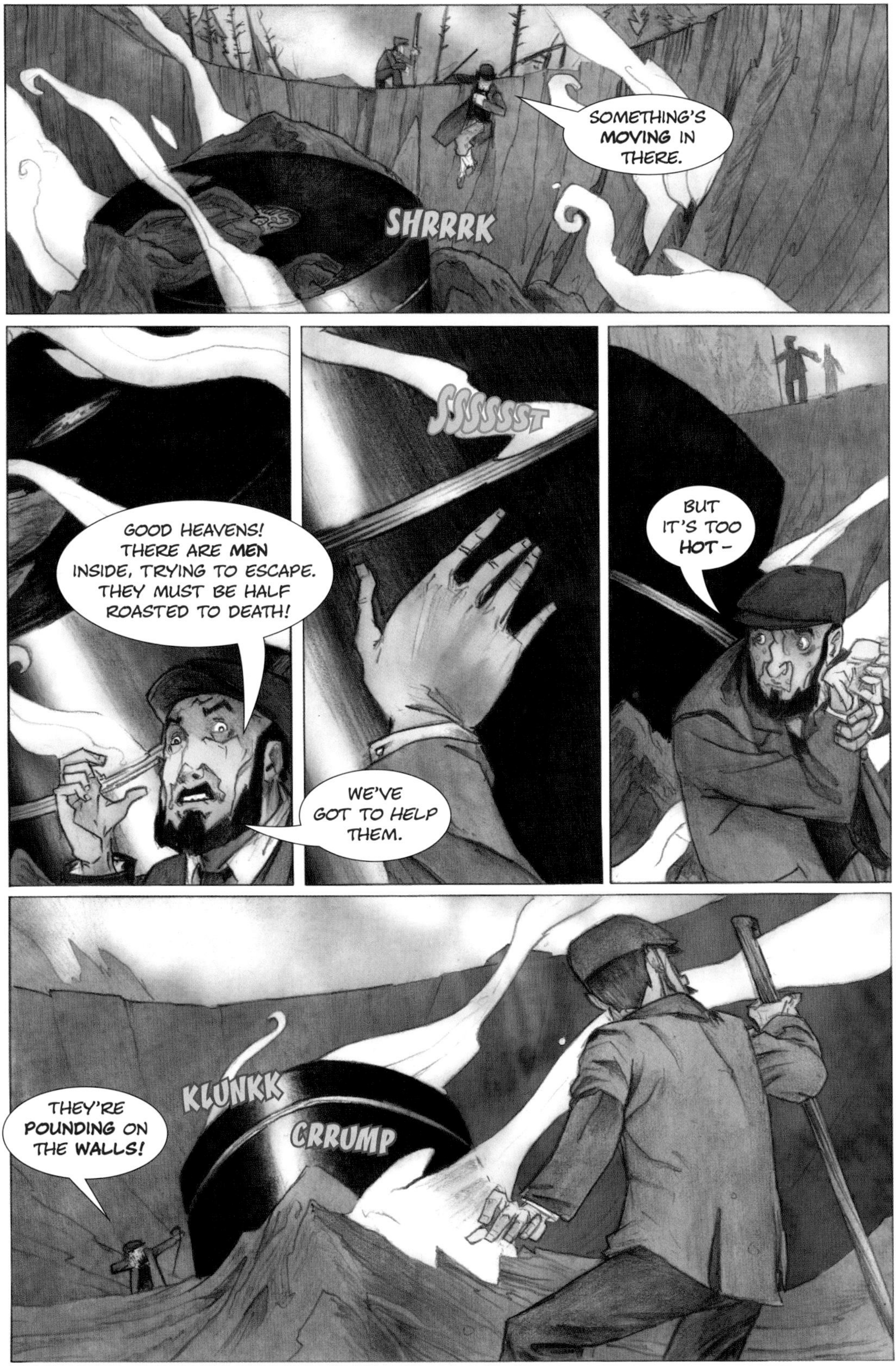
SOMETHING'S MOVING IN THERE.
SHRRRK
GOOD HEAVENS! THERE ARE MEN INSIDE, TRYING TO ESCAPE. THEY MUST BE HALF ROASTED TO DEATH!
SSSSSSST
WE'VE GOT TO HELP THEM.
BUT IT'S TOO HOT -
KLUNKK
CRRUMP
THEY'RE POUNDING ON THE WALLS!

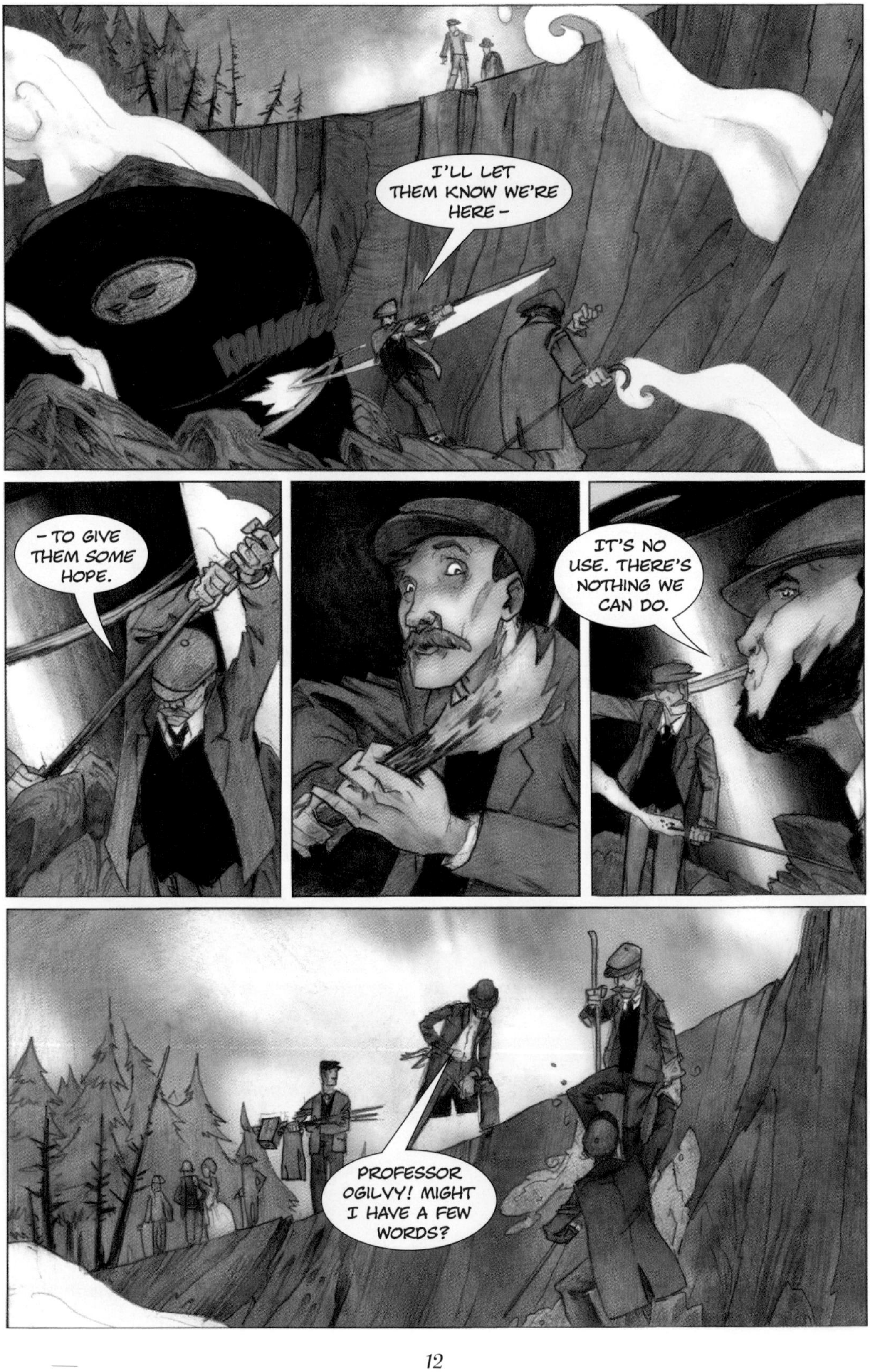
I'LL LET THEM KNOW WE'RE HERE –
– TO GIVE THEM SOME HOPE.
IT'S NO USE. THERE'S NOTHING WE CAN DO.
PROFESSOR OGILVY! MIGHT I HAVE A FEW WORDS?

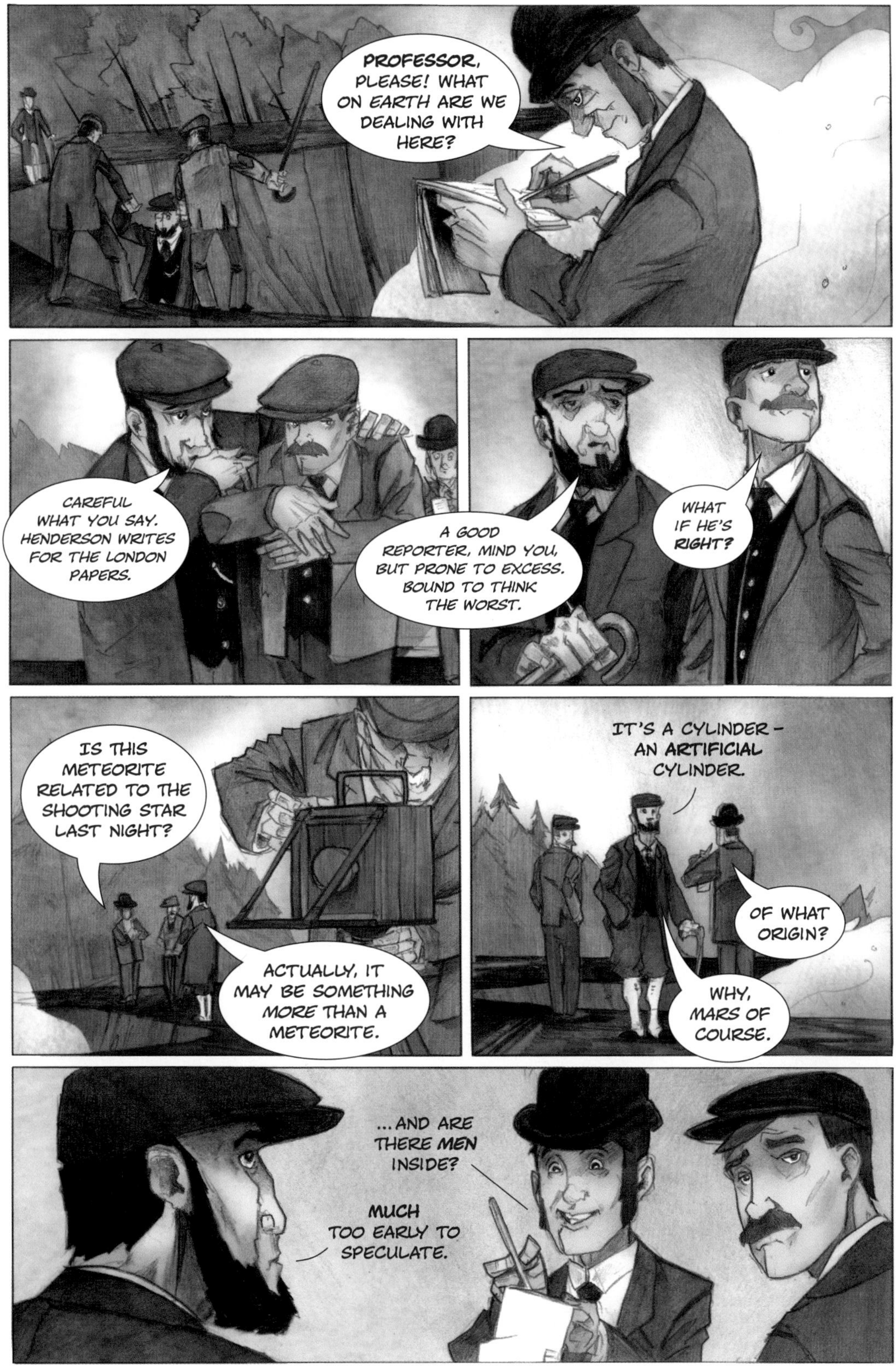
PROFESSOR, PLEASE! WHAT ON EARTH ARE WE DEALING WITH HERE?
CAREFUL WHAT YOU SAY. HENDERSON WRITES FOR THE LONDON PAPERS.
A GOOD REPORTER, MIND YOU, BUT PRONE TO EXCESS. BOUND TO THINK THE WORST.
WHAT IF HE'S RIGHT?
IS THIS METEORITE RELATED TO THE SHOOTING STAR LAST NIGHT?
ACTUALLY, IT MAY BE SOMETHING MORE THAN A METEORITE.
IT'S A CYLINDER – AN ARTIFICIAL CYLINDER.
OF WHAT ORIGIN?
WHY, MARS OF COURSE.
...AND ARE THERE MEN INSIDE?
MUCH TOO EARLY TO SPECULATE.

AFTER A FEW MORE FRUITLESS HOURS WATCHING THE CYLINDER, I WENT HOME TO TELL MY WIFE WHAT HAPPENED AT HORSELL COMMON.

BY THE TIME I RETURNED, THE EARLY EDITIONS OF THE EVENING PAPERS HAD REACHED THE SURROUNDING VILLAGES. HENDERSON HAD GONE TO WOKING STATION TO TELEGRAPH HIS STORY TO LONDON BEFORE COMING BACK TO SEE FURTHER DEVELOPMENTS.
IN ADDITION, OGILVY'S WIRE TO THE ASTRONOMICAL EXCHANGE ROUSED EVERY OBSERVATORY IN THE COUNTRY.

LONDON OBSERVER
DEAD MEN FROM MARS

THE DAILY CHRONICLE
EXTRA-TERRESTRIAL
EXPEDITION
LANDS AT HORSELL COMMON

THE EVENING JOURNAL
MESSAGE RECEIVED FROM MARS

MANY BELIEVED IT WAS SOME KIND OF SIGNAL FROM THE MARTIANS. OTHERS THOUGHT THERE WERE MEN INSIDE THE CYLINDER AND WERE TRAPPED THERE.

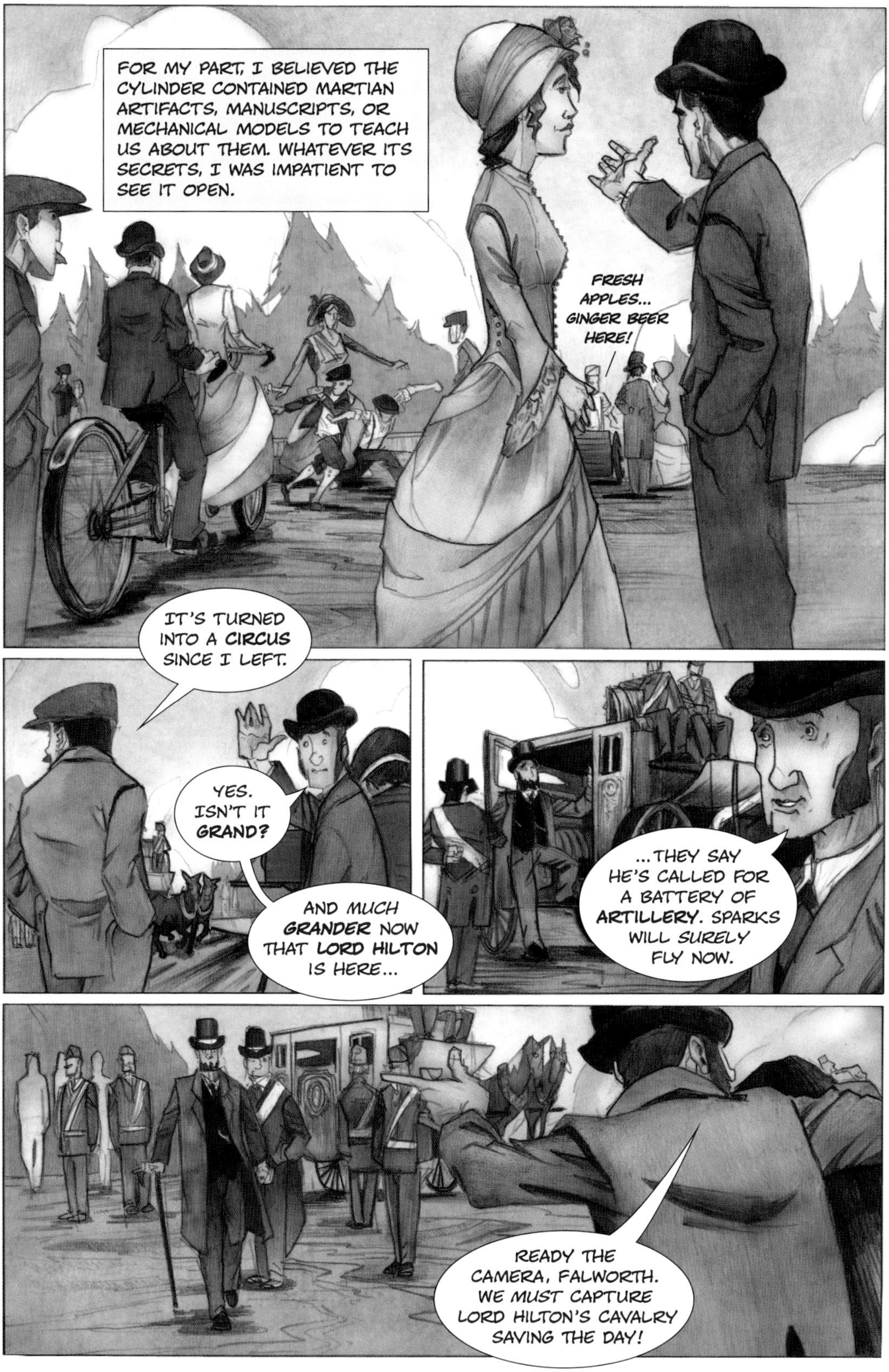
FOR MY PART, I BELIEVED THE CYLINDER CONTAINED MARTIAN ARTIFACTS, MANUSCRIPTS, OR MECHANICAL MODELS TO TEACH US ABOUT THEM. WHATEVER ITS SECRETS, I WAS IMPATIENT TO SEE IT OPEN.
FRESH APPLES... GINGER BEER HERE!
IT'S TURNED INTO A CIRCUS SINCE I LEFT.
YES. ISN'T IT GRAND?
AND MUCH GRANDER NOW THAT LORD HILTON IS HERE...
...THEY SAY HE'S CALLED FOR A BATTERY OF ARTILLERY. SPARKS WILL SURELY FLY NOW.
READY THE CAMERA, FALWORTH. WE MUST CAPTURE LORD HILTON'S CAVALRY SAVING THE DAY!

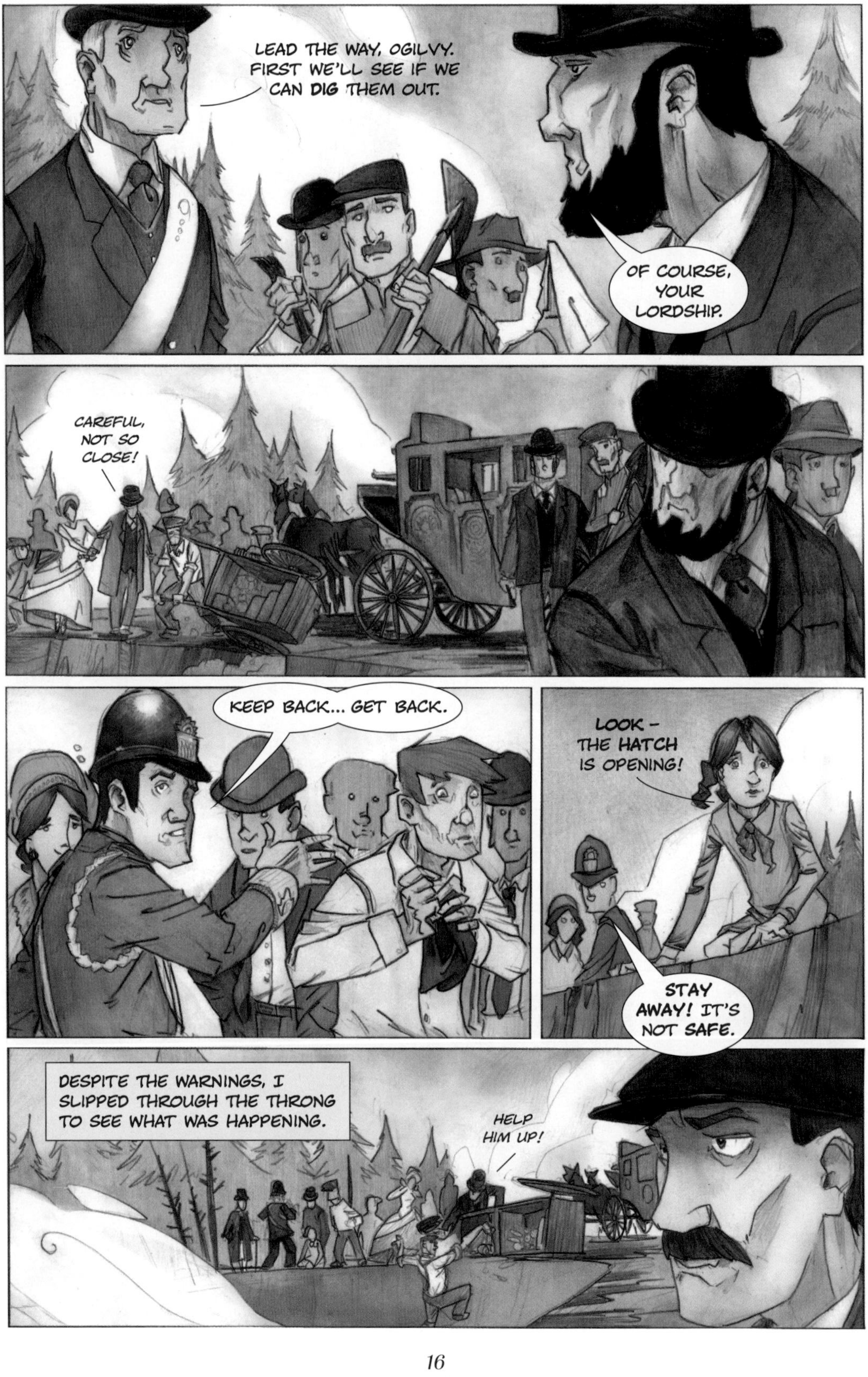
LEAD THE WAY, OGILVY. FIRST WE'LL SEE IF WE CAN DIG THEM OUT.
OF COURSE, YOUR LORDSHIP.
CAREFUL, NOT SO CLOSE!
KEEP BACK... GET BACK.
LOOK – THE HATCH IS OPENING!
STAY AWAY! IT'S NOT SAFE.
DESPITE THE WARNINGS, I SLIPPED THROUGH THE THRONG TO SEE WHAT WAS HAPPENING.
HELP HIM UP!

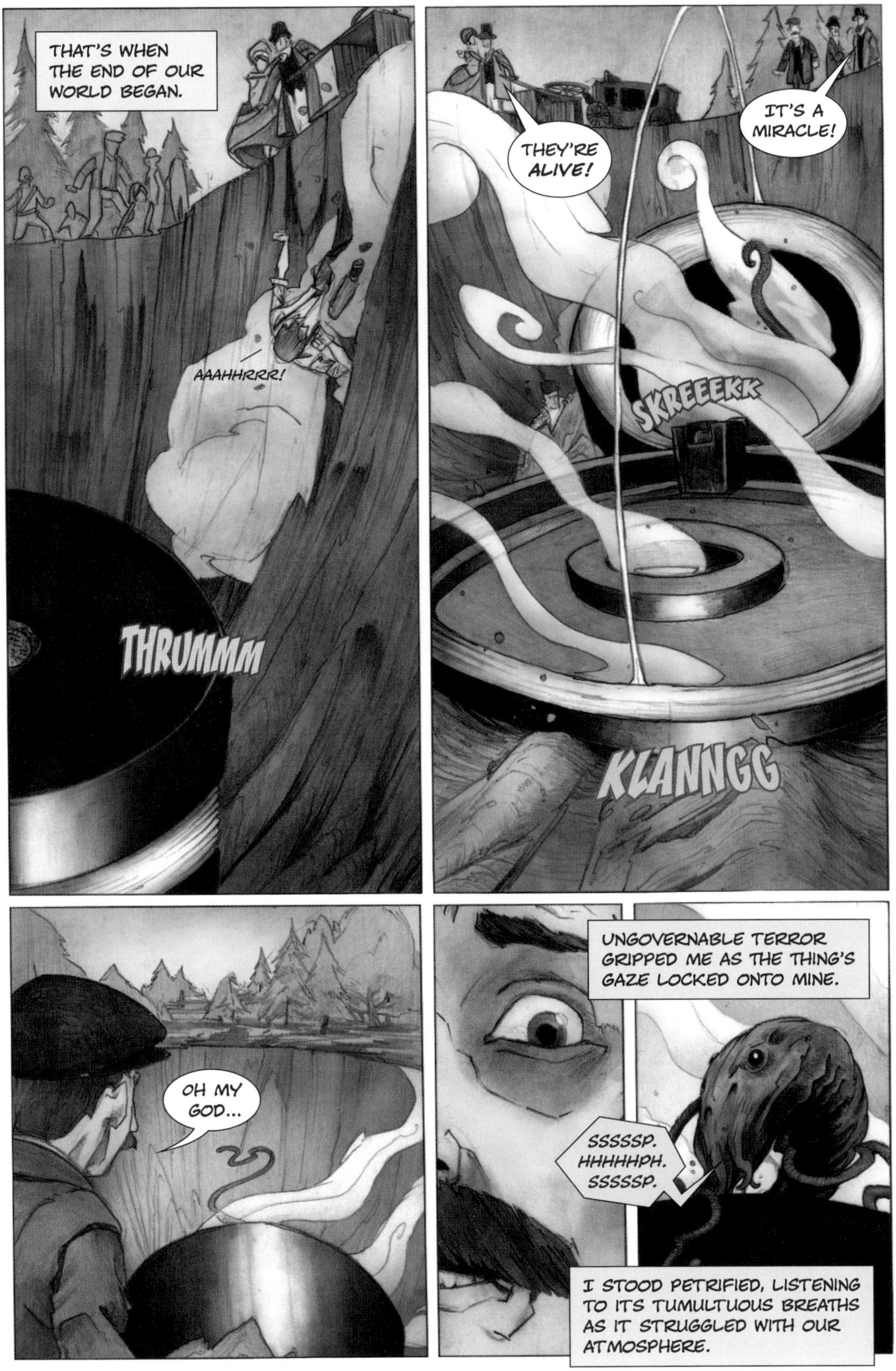
THAT'S WHEN THE END OF OUR WORLD BEGAN.
AAAHHRRR!
THRUMMM
THEY'RE ALIVE!
IT'S A MIRACLE!
SKREEEKK
KLANNGG
OH MY GOD...
UNGOVERNABLE TERROR GRIPPED ME AS THE THING'S GAZE LOCKED ONTO MINE.
SSSSSP. HHHHHPH. SSSSSP.
I STOOD PETRIFIED, LISTENING TO ITS TUMULTUOUS BREATHS AS IT STRUGGLED WITH OUR ATMOSPHERE.

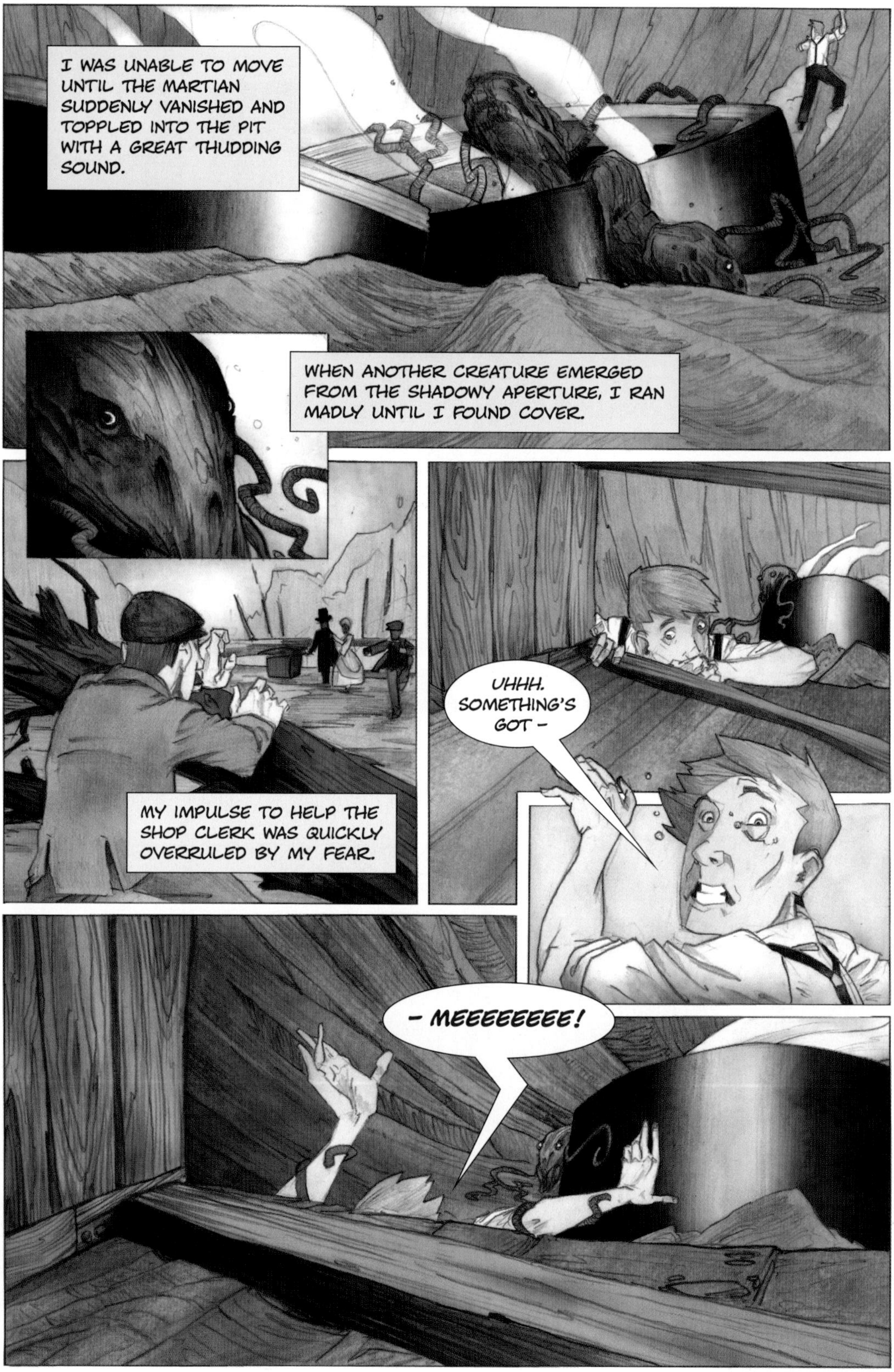
I WAS UNABLE TO MOVE UNTIL THE MARTIAN SUDDENLY VANISHED AND TOPPLED INTO THE PIT WITH A GREAT THUDDING SOUND.
WHEN ANOTHER CREATURE EMERGED FROM THE SHADOWY APERTURE, I RAN MADLY UNTIL I FOUND COVER.
MY IMPULSE TO HELP THE SHOP CLERK WAS QUICKLY OVERRULED BY MY FEAR.
UHHH. SOMETHING'S GOT –
– MEEEEEEEE!

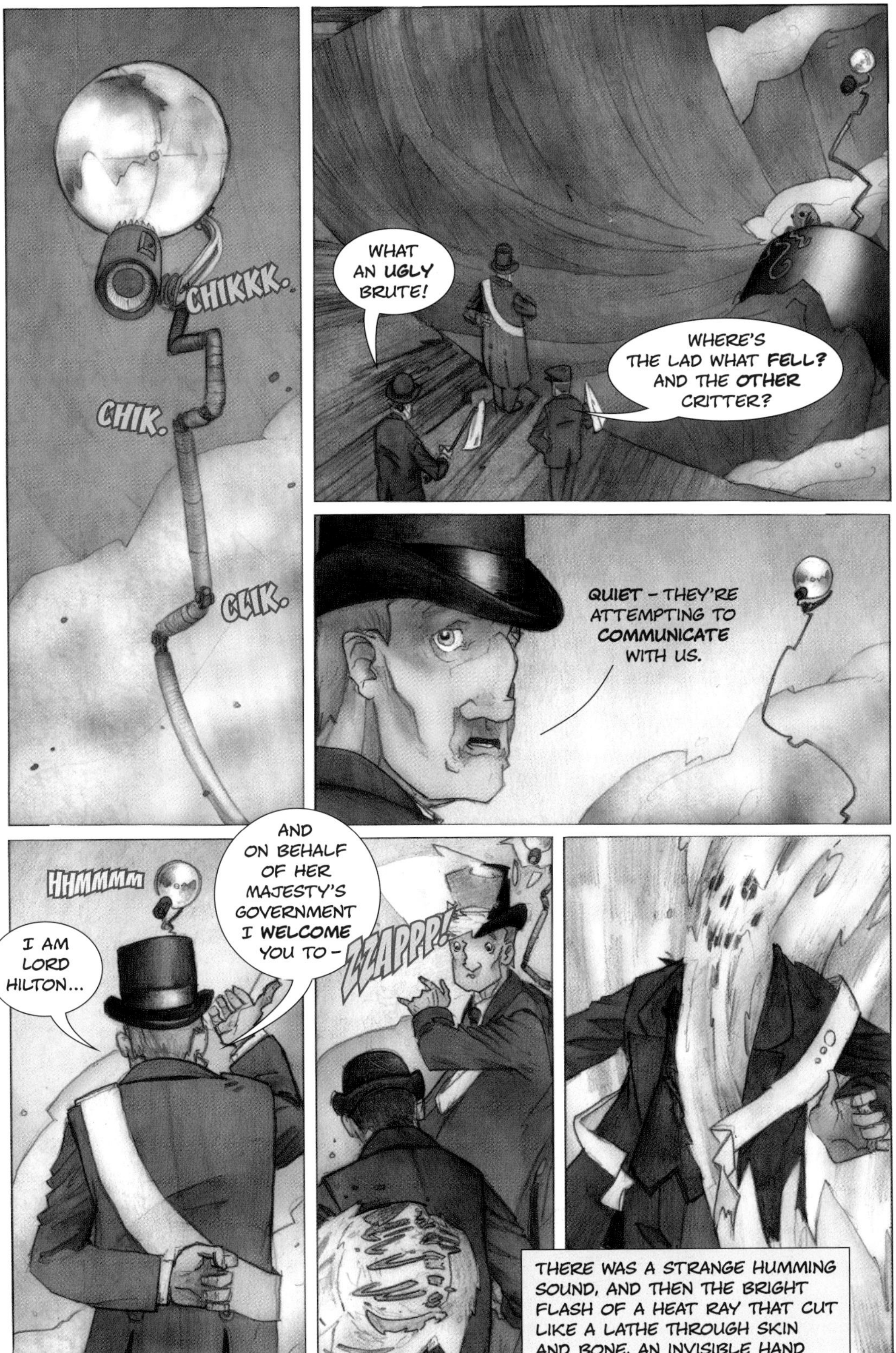
CHIKKK.
CHIK.
CLIK.
WHAT AN UGLY BRUTE!
WHERE'S THE LAD WHAT FELL? AND THE OTHER CRITTER?
QUIET – THEY'RE ATTEMPTING TO COMMUNICATE WITH US.
HHMMMM
I AM LORD HILTON...
AND ON BEHALF OF HER MAJESTY'S GOVERNMENT I WELCOME YOU TO –
ZZAPPP!
THERE WAS A STRANGE HUMMING SOUND, AND THEN THE BRIGHT FLASH OF A HEAT RAY THAT CUT LIKE A LATHE THROUGH SKIN AND BONE, AN INVISIBLE HAND THAT STRUCK AGAIN AND AGAIN.

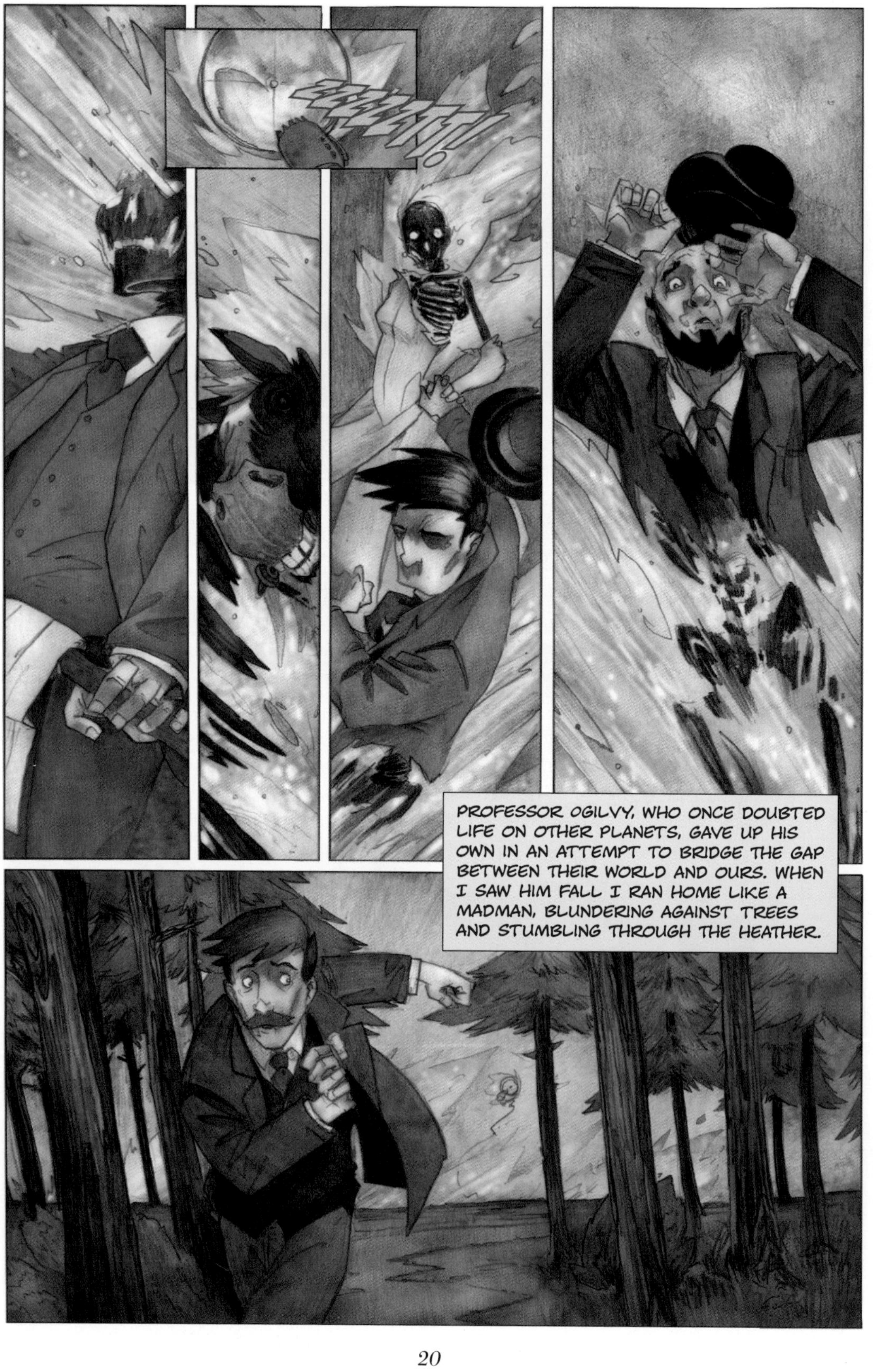
PROFESSOR OGILVY, WHO ONCE DOUBTED LIFE ON OTHER PLANETS, GAVE UP HIS OWN IN AN ATTEMPT TO BRIDGE THE GAP BETWEEN THEIR WORLD AND OURS. WHEN I SAW HIM FALL I RAN HOME LIKE A MADMAN, BLUNDERING AGAINST TREES AND STUMBLING THROUGH THE HEATHER.

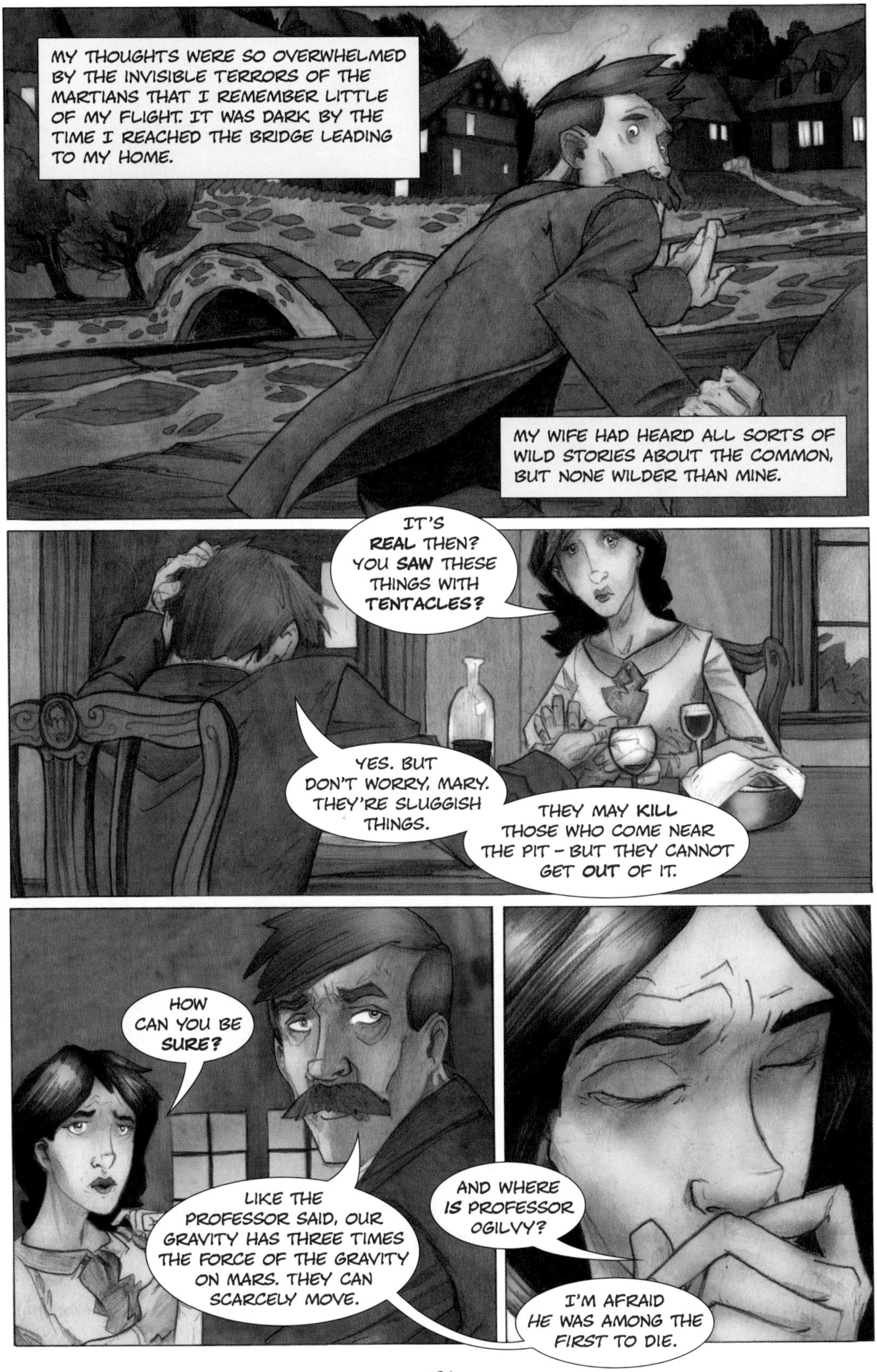
MY THOUGHTS WERE SO OVERWHELMED BY THE INVISIBLE TERRORS OF THE MARTIANS THAT I REMEMBER LITTLE OF MY FLIGHT. IT WAS DARK BY THE TIME I REACHED THE BRIDGE LEADING TO MY HOME.
MY WIFE HAD HEARD ALL SORTS OF WILD STORIES ABOUT THE COMMON, BUT NONE WILDER THAN MINE.
IT'S **REAL** THEN? YOU **SAW** THESE THINGS WITH **TENTACLES?**
YES. BUT DON'T WORRY, MARY. THEY'RE SLUGGISH THINGS.
THEY MAY **KILL** THOSE WHO COME NEAR THE PIT – BUT THEY CANNOT GET **OUT** OF IT.
HOW CAN YOU BE **SURE?**
LIKE THE PROFESSOR SAID, OUR GRAVITY HAS THREE TIMES THE FORCE OF THE GRAVITY ON MARS. THEY CAN SCARCELY MOVE.
AND WHERE *IS* PROFESSOR OGILVY?
I'M AFRAID HE WAS AMONG THE FIRST TO DIE.

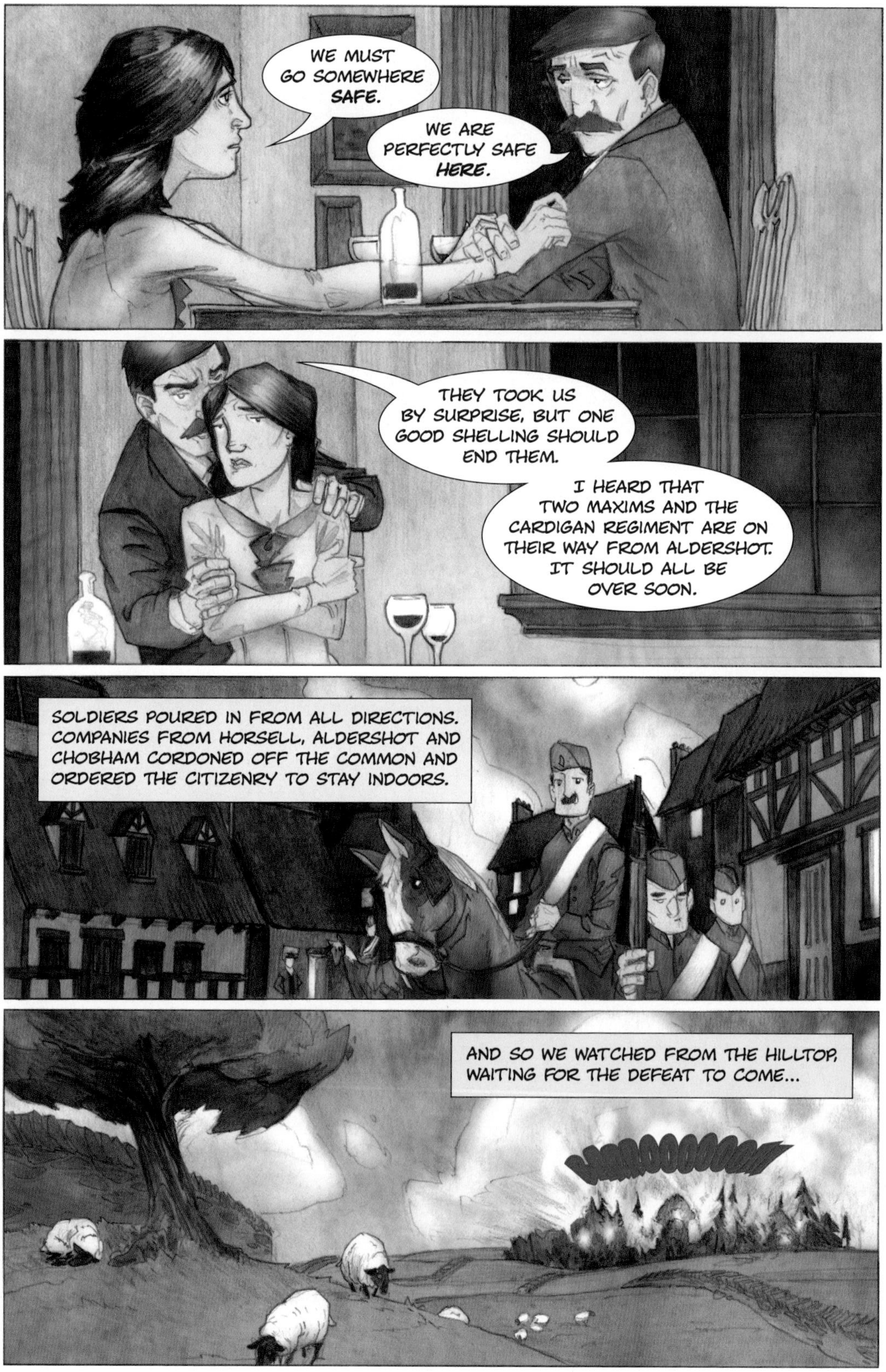
WE MUST GO SOMEWHERE SAFE.
WE ARE PERFECTLY SAFE HERE.
THEY TOOK US BY SURPRISE, BUT ONE GOOD SHELLING SHOULD END THEM.
I HEARD THAT TWO MAXIMS AND THE CARDIGAN REGIMENT ARE ON THEIR WAY FROM ALDERSHOT. IT SHOULD ALL BE OVER SOON.
SOLDIERS POURED IN FROM ALL DIRECTIONS. COMPANIES FROM HORSELL, ALDERSHOT AND CHOBHAM CORDONED OFF THE COMMON AND ORDERED THE CITIZENRY TO STAY INDOORS.
AND SO WE WATCHED FROM THE HILLTOP, WAITING FOR THE DEFEAT TO COME...

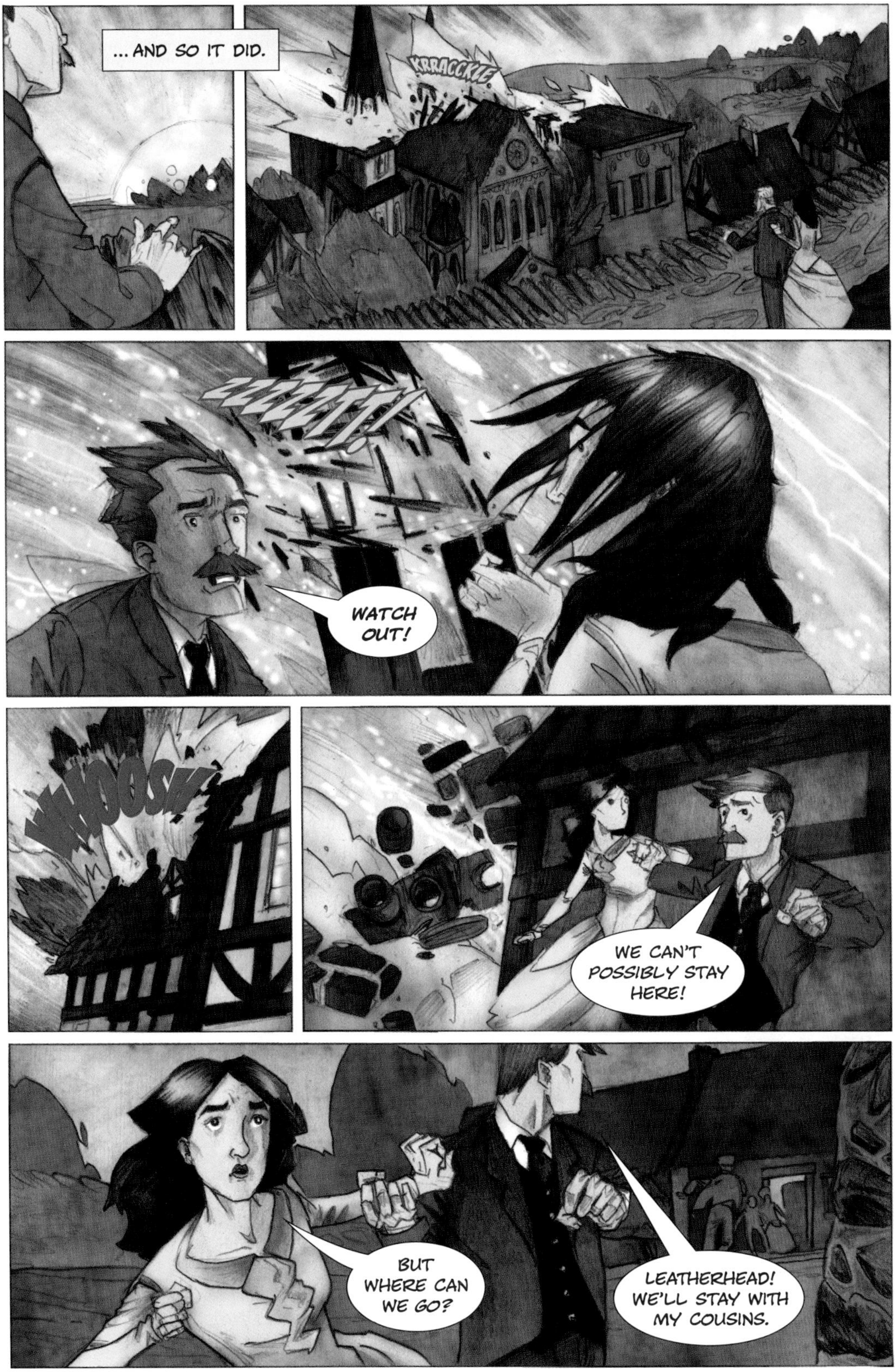
... AND SO IT DID.
KRRACCKLE
ZZZZZTT!
WATCH OUT!
WHOOSH
WE CAN'T POSSIBLY STAY HERE!
BUT WHERE CAN WE GO?
LEATHERHEAD! WE'LL STAY WITH MY COUSINS.

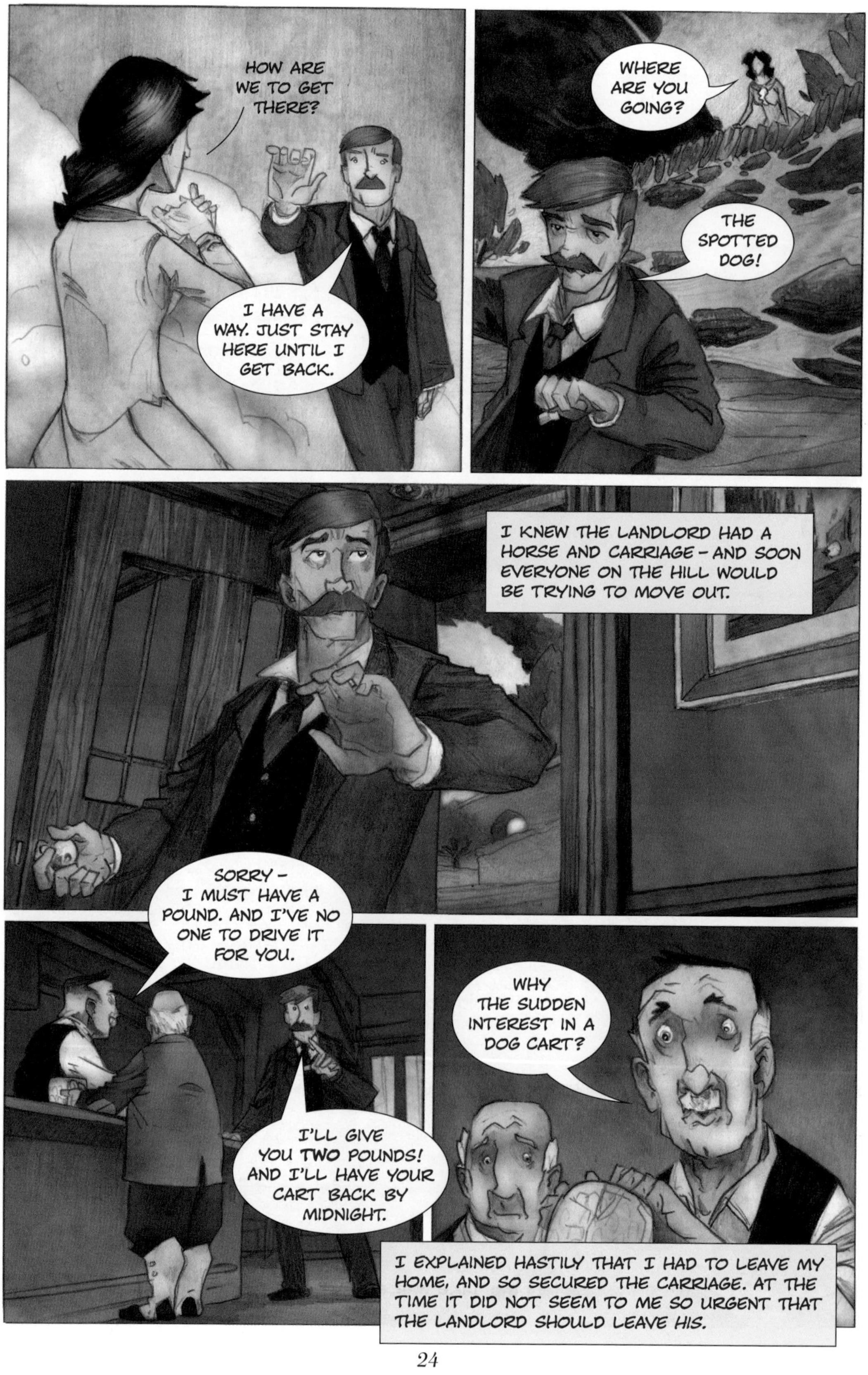
HOW ARE WE TO GET THERE?
I HAVE A WAY. JUST STAY HERE UNTIL I GET BACK.
WHERE ARE YOU GOING?
THE SPOTTED DOG!
I KNEW THE LANDLORD HAD A HORSE AND CARRIAGE - AND SOON EVERYONE ON THE HILL WOULD BE TRYING TO MOVE OUT.
SORRY - I MUST HAVE A POUND. AND I'VE NO ONE TO DRIVE IT FOR YOU.
I'LL GIVE YOU **TWO** POUNDS! AND I'LL HAVE YOUR CART BACK BY MIDNIGHT.
WHY THE SUDDEN INTEREST IN A DOG CART?
I EXPLAINED HASTILY THAT I HAD TO LEAVE MY HOME, AND SO SECURED THE CARRIAGE. AT THE TIME IT DID NOT SEEM TO ME SO URGENT THAT THE LANDLORD SHOULD LEAVE HIS.

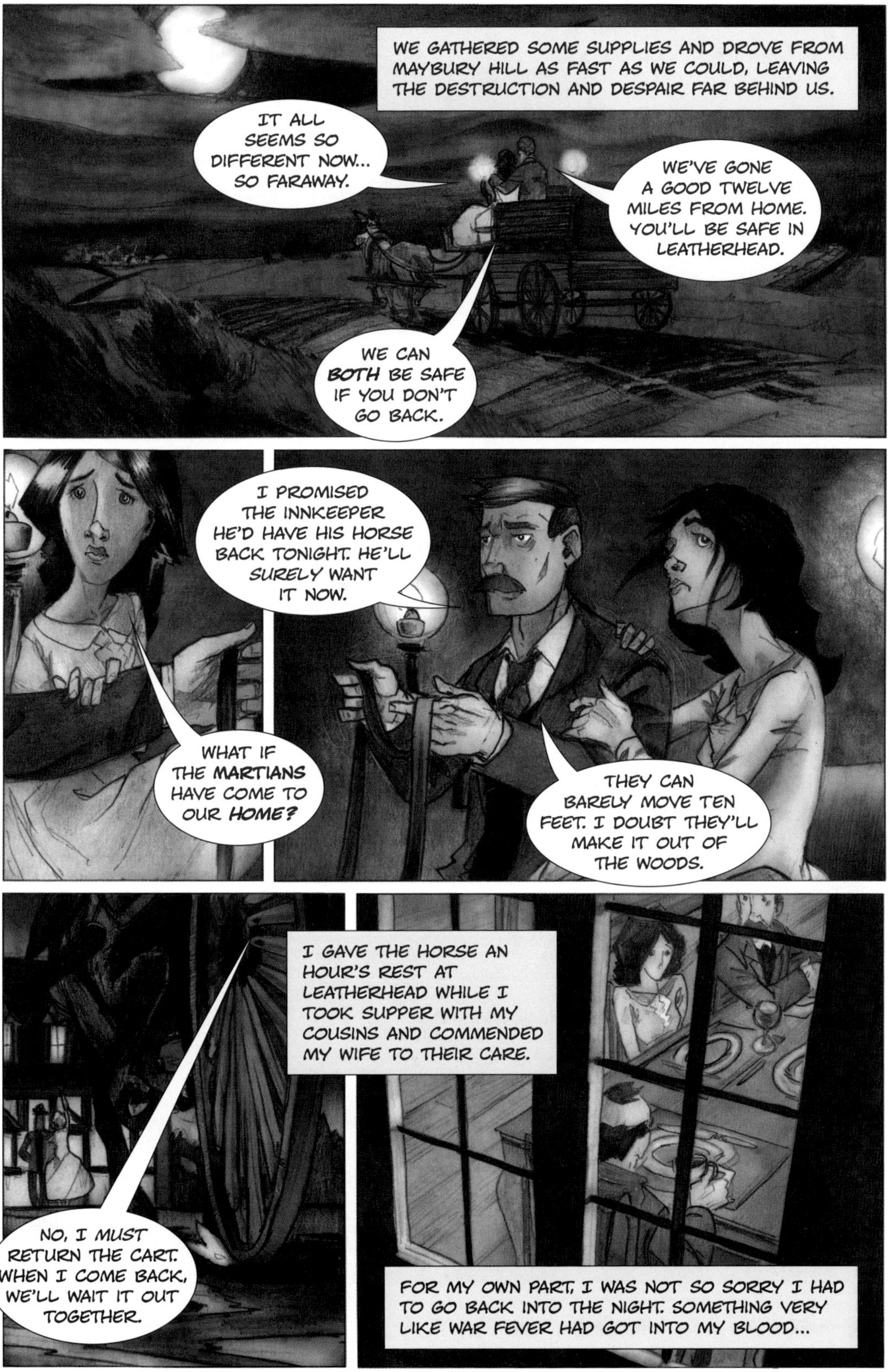
WE GATHERED SOME SUPPLIES AND DROVE FROM MAYBURY HILL AS FAST AS WE COULD, LEAVING THE DESTRUCTION AND DESPAIR FAR BEHIND US.
IT ALL SEEMS SO DIFFERENT NOW... SO FARAWAY.
WE'VE GONE A GOOD TWELVE MILES FROM HOME. YOU'LL BE SAFE IN LEATHERHEAD.
WE CAN BOTH BE SAFE IF YOU DON'T GO BACK.
I PROMISED THE INNKEEPER HE'D HAVE HIS HORSE BACK TONIGHT. HE'LL SURELY WANT IT NOW.
WHAT IF THE MARTIANS HAVE COME TO OUR HOME?
THEY CAN BARELY MOVE TEN FEET. I DOUBT THEY'LL MAKE IT OUT OF THE WOODS.
I GAVE THE HORSE AN HOUR'S REST AT LEATHERHEAD WHILE I TOOK SUPPER WITH MY COUSINS AND COMMENDED MY WIFE TO THEIR CARE.
NO, I MUST RETURN THE CART. WHEN I COME BACK, WE'LL WAIT IT OUT TOGETHER.
FOR MY OWN PART, I WAS NOT SO SORRY I HAD TO GO BACK INTO THE NIGHT. SOMETHING VERY LIKE WAR FEVER HAD GOT INTO MY BLOOD...

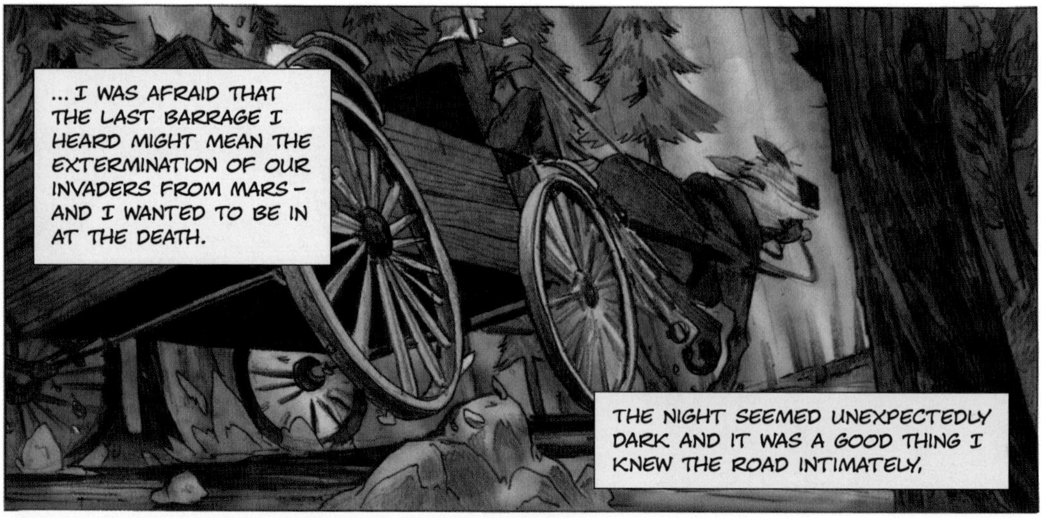
... I WAS AFRAID THAT THE LAST BARRAGE I HEARD MIGHT MEAN THE EXTERMINATION OF OUR INVADERS FROM MARS – AND I WANTED TO BE IN AT THE DEATH.
THE NIGHT SEEMED UNEXPECTEDLY DARK AND IT WAS A GOOD THING I KNEW THE ROAD INTIMATELY,

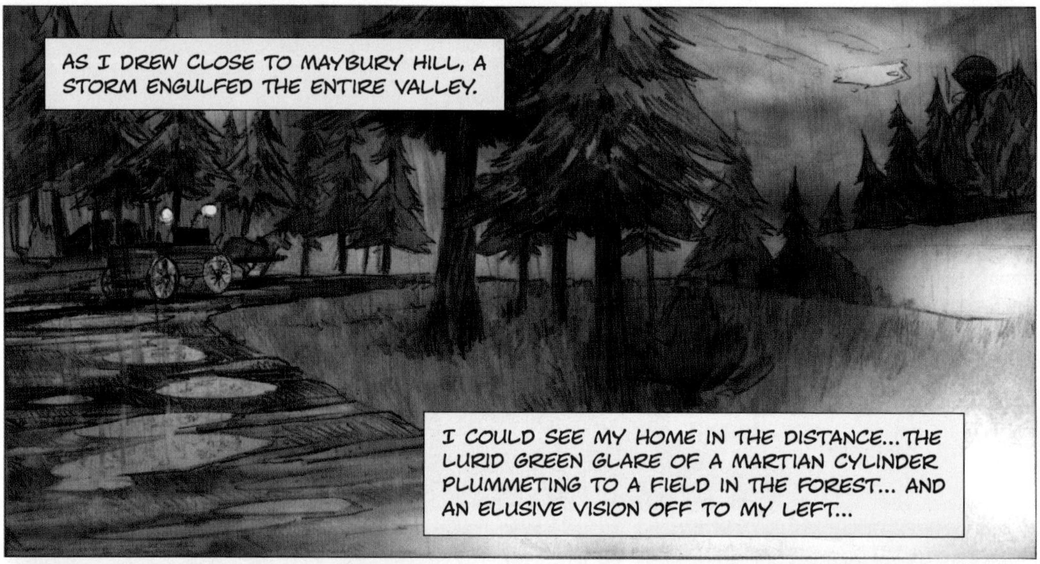
AS I DREW CLOSE TO MAYBURY HILL, A STORM ENGULFED THE ENTIRE VALLEY.
I COULD SEE MY HOME IN THE DISTANCE... THE LURID GREEN GLARE OF A MARTIAN CYLINDER PLUMMETING TO A FIELD IN THE FOREST... AND AN ELUSIVE VISION OFF TO MY LEFT...

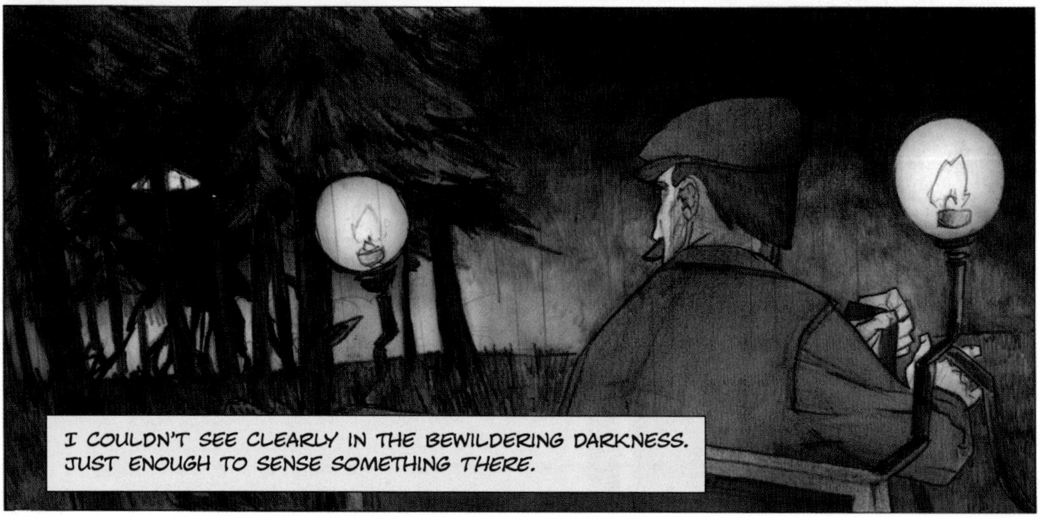
I COULDN'T SEE CLEARLY IN THE BEWILDERING DARKNESS. JUST ENOUGH TO SENSE SOMETHING THERE.

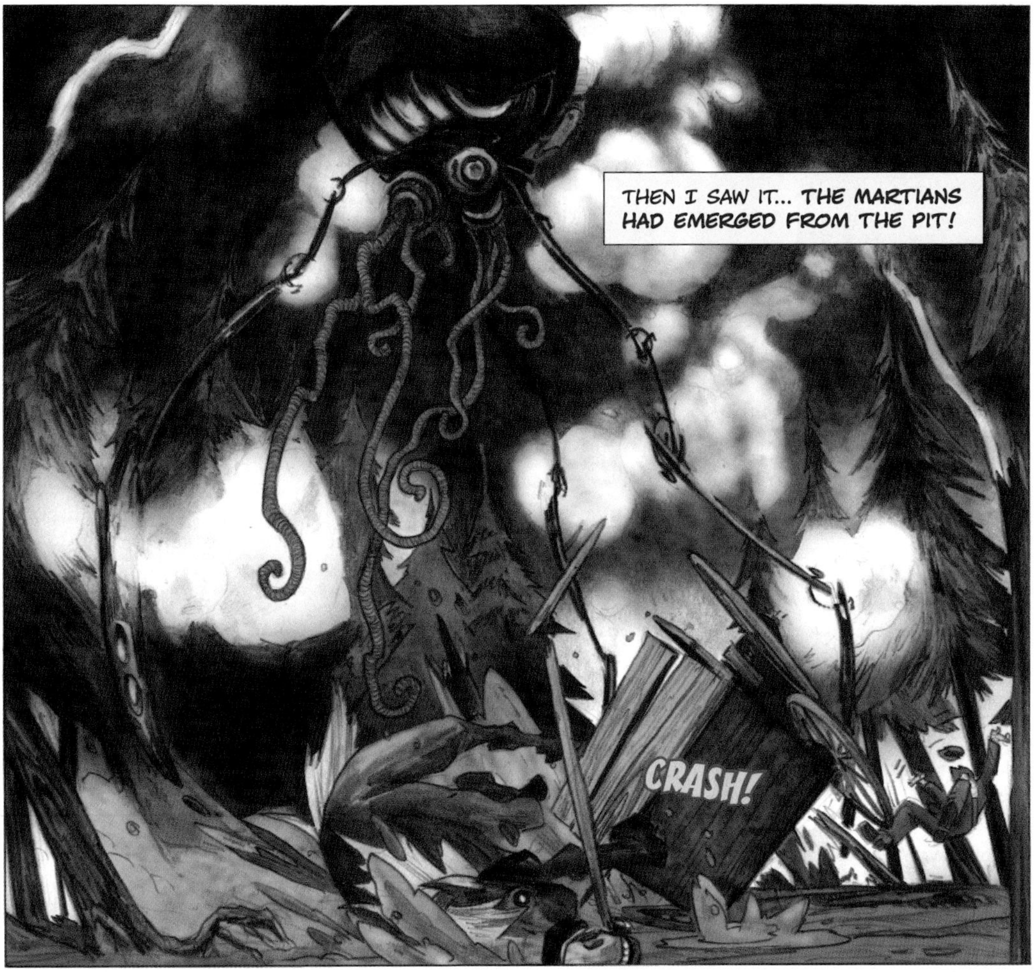
THEN I SAW IT... THE MARTIANS HAD EMERGED FROM THE PIT!
CRASH!

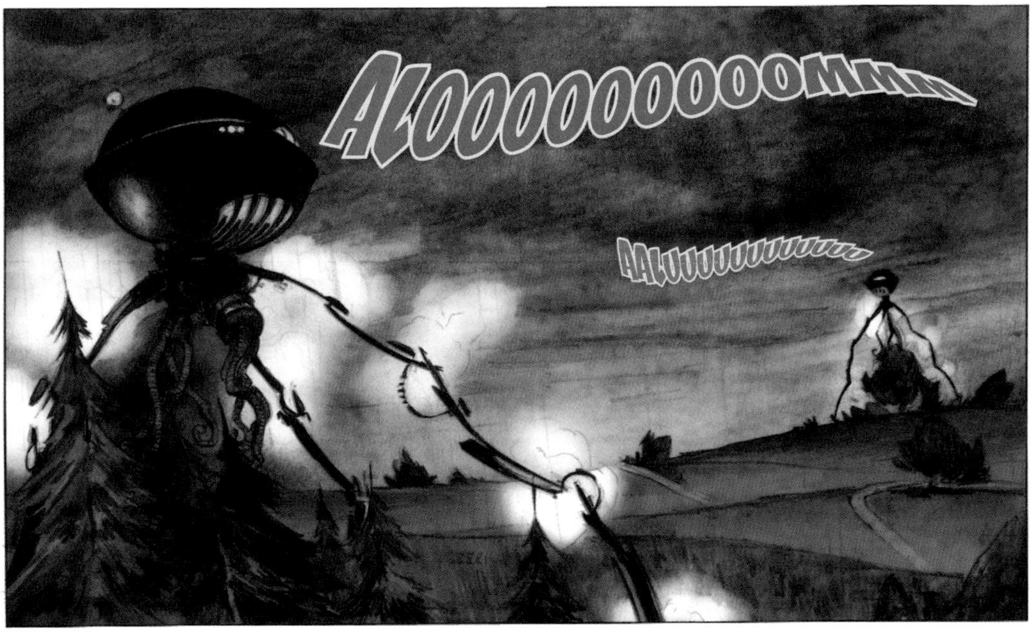
ALOOOOOOOOOMMM
AALUUUUUUUUUUUU

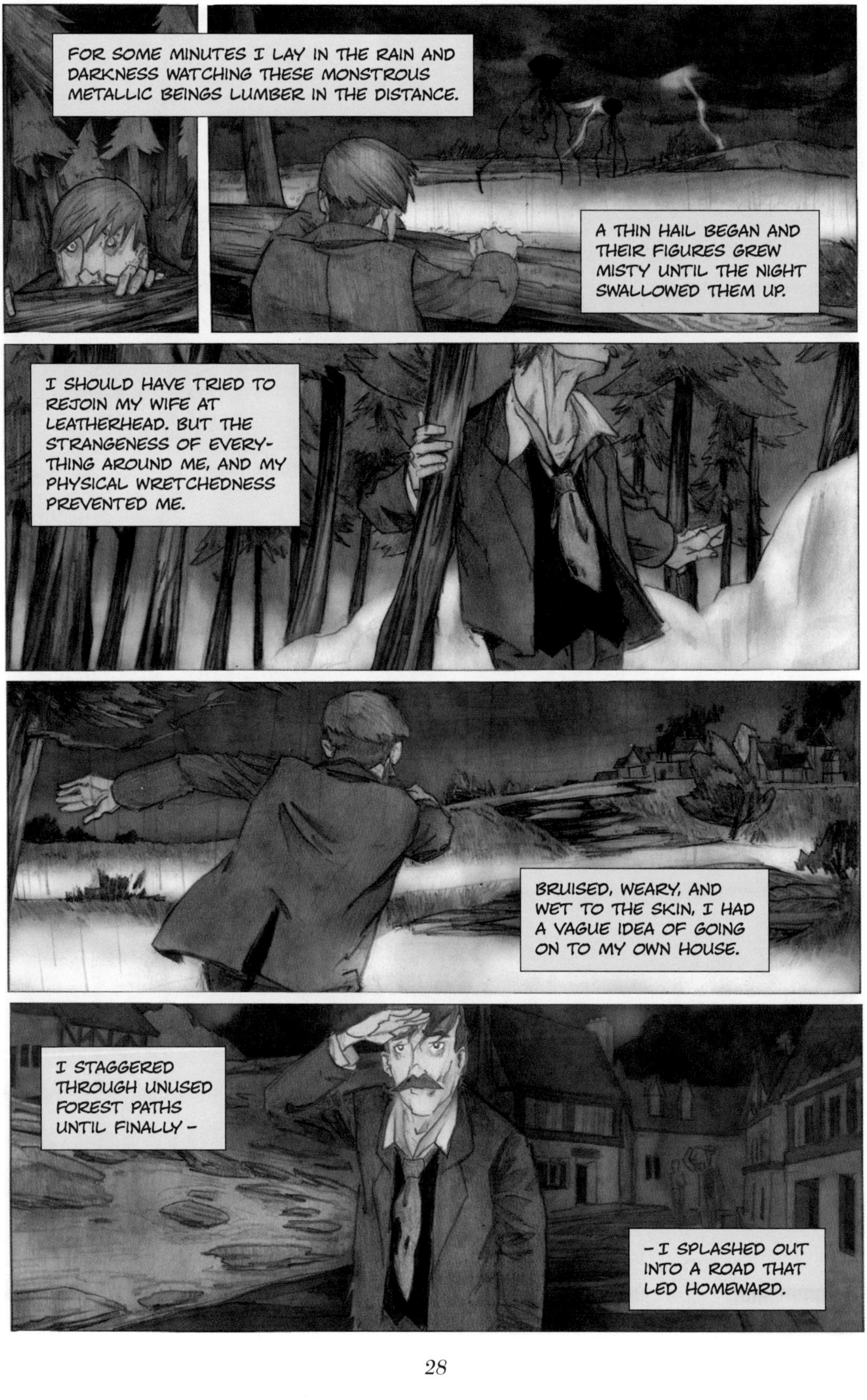
FOR SOME MINUTES I LAY IN THE RAIN AND DARKNESS WATCHING THESE MONSTROUS METALLIC BEINGS LUMBER IN THE DISTANCE.
A THIN HAIL BEGAN AND THEIR FIGURES GREW MISTY UNTIL THE NIGHT SWALLOWED THEM UP.
I SHOULD HAVE TRIED TO REJOIN MY WIFE AT LEATHERHEAD. BUT THE STRANGENESS OF EVERY-THING AROUND ME, AND MY PHYSICAL WRETCHEDNESS PREVENTED ME.
BRUISED, WEARY, AND WET TO THE SKIN, I HAD A VAGUE IDEA OF GOING ON TO MY OWN HOUSE.
I STAGGERED THROUGH UNUSED FOREST PATHS UNTIL FINALLY –
– I SPLASHED OUT INTO A ROAD THAT LED HOMEWARD.

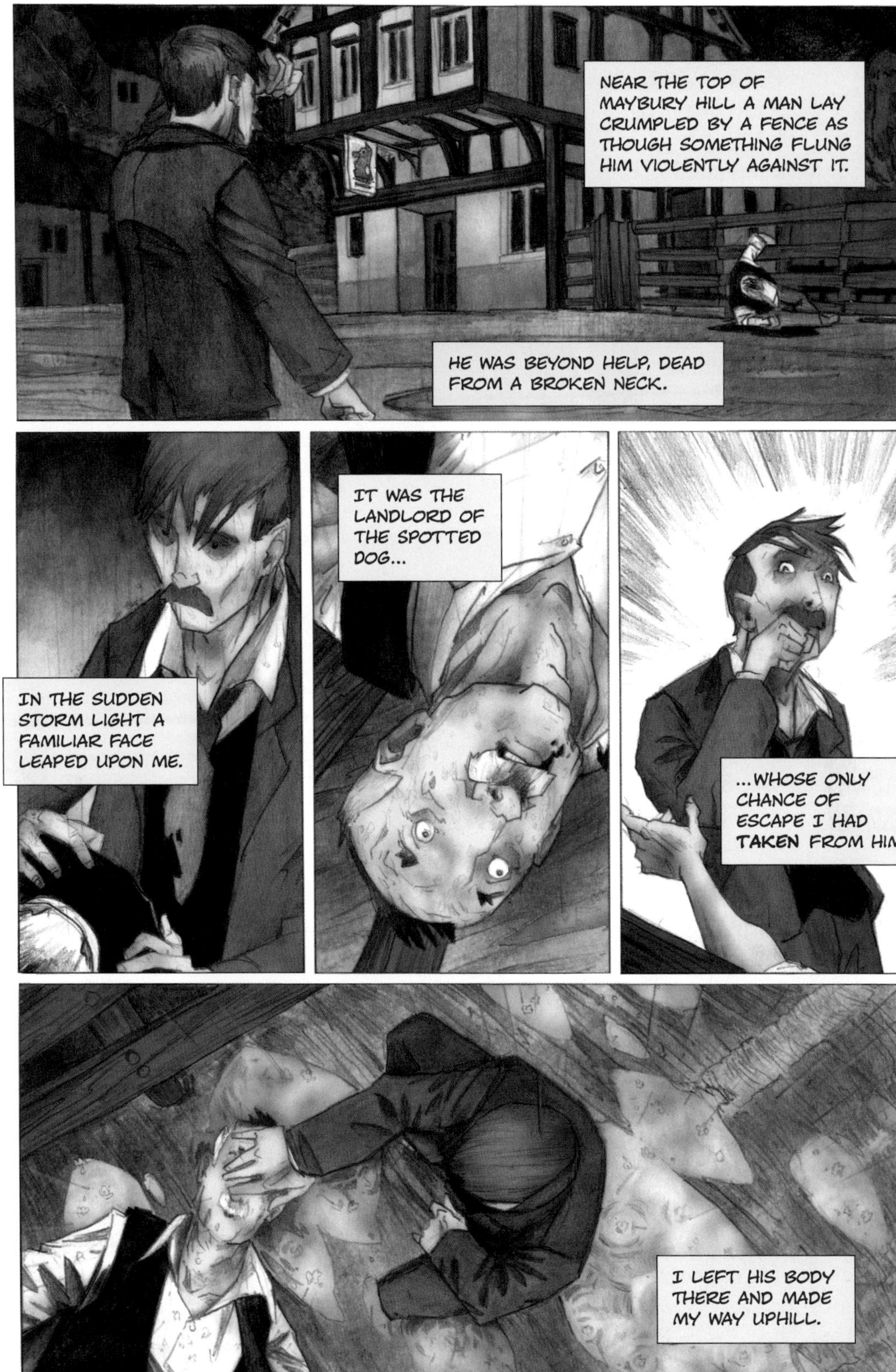
NEAR THE TOP OF MAYBURY HILL A MAN LAY CRUMPLED BY A FENCE AS THOUGH SOMETHING FLUNG HIM VIOLENTLY AGAINST IT.
HE WAS BEYOND HELP, DEAD FROM A BROKEN NECK.
IN THE SUDDEN STORM LIGHT A FAMILIAR FACE LEAPED UPON ME.
IT WAS THE LANDLORD OF THE SPOTTED DOG...
...WHOSE ONLY CHANCE OF ESCAPE I HAD TAKEN FROM HIM.
I LEFT HIS BODY THERE AND MADE MY WAY UPHILL.

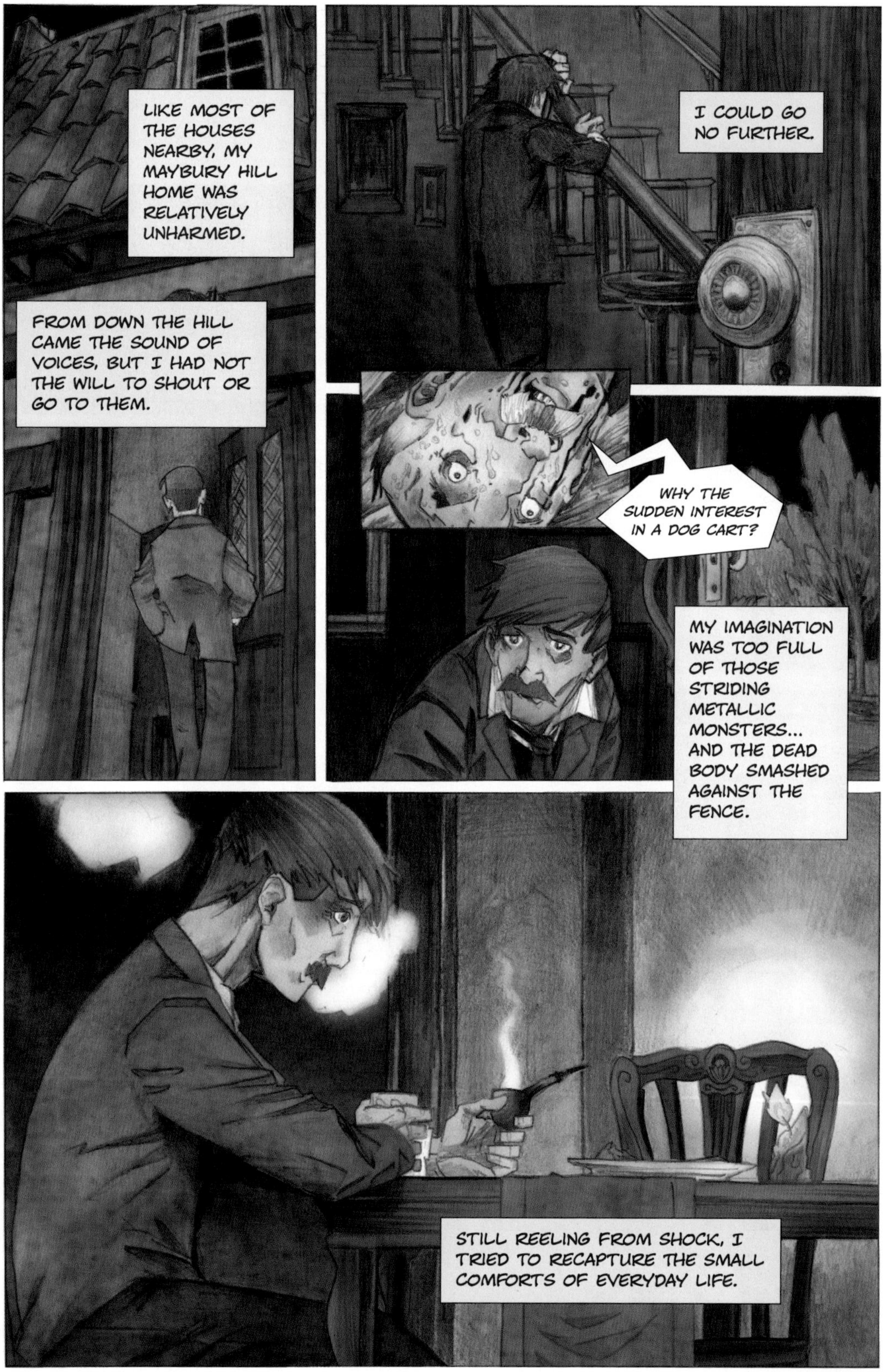
LIKE MOST OF THE HOUSES NEARBY, MY MAYBURY HILL HOME WAS RELATIVELY UNHARMED.
FROM DOWN THE HILL CAME THE SOUND OF VOICES, BUT I HAD NOT THE WILL TO SHOUT OR GO TO THEM.
I COULD GO NO FURTHER.
WHY THE SUDDEN INTEREST IN A DOG CART?
MY IMAGINATION WAS TOO FULL OF THOSE STRIDING METALLIC MONSTERS... AND THE DEAD BODY SMASHED AGAINST THE FENCE.
STILL REELING FROM SHOCK, I TRIED TO RECAPTURE THE SMALL COMFORTS OF EVERYDAY LIFE.

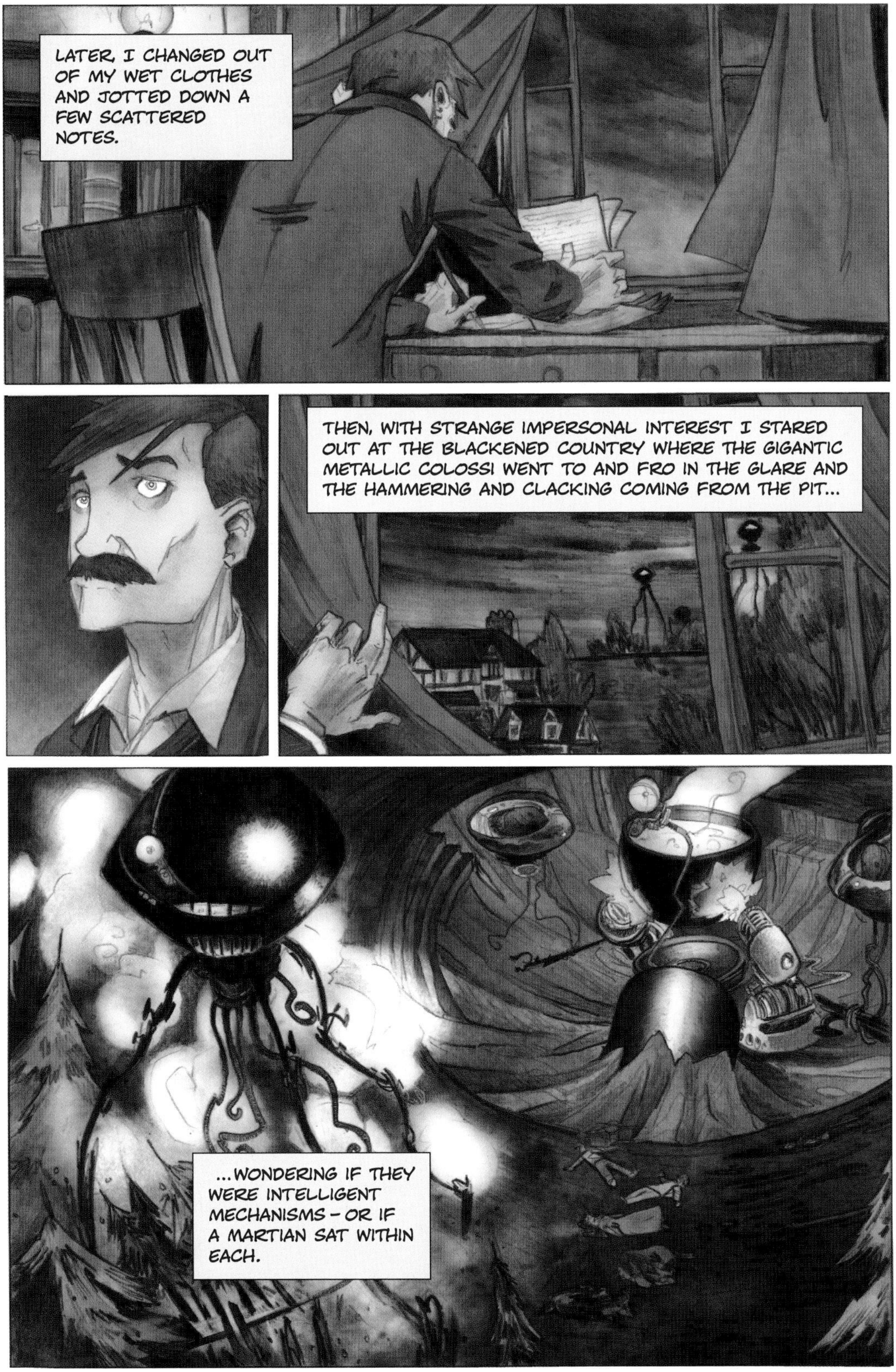
LATER, I CHANGED OUT OF MY WET CLOTHES AND JOTTED DOWN A FEW SCATTERED NOTES.
THEN, WITH STRANGE IMPERSONAL INTEREST I STARED OUT AT THE BLACKENED COUNTRY WHERE THE GIGANTIC METALLIC COLOSSI WENT TO AND FRO IN THE GLARE AND THE HAMMERING AND CLACKING COMING FROM THE PIT...
...WONDERING IF THEY WERE INTELLIGENT MECHANISMS – OR IF A MARTIAN SAT WITHIN EACH.

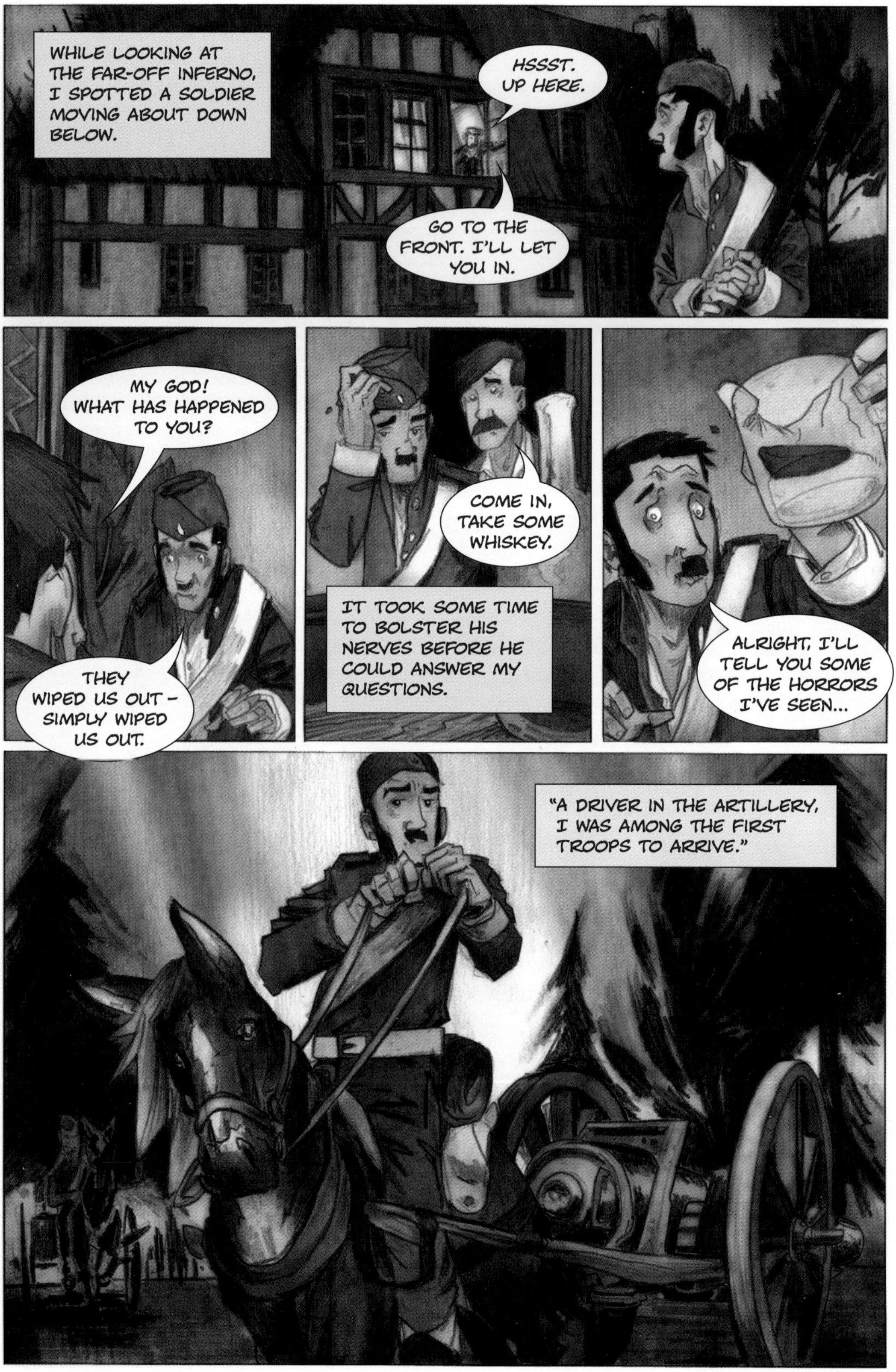
WHILE LOOKING AT THE FAR-OFF INFERNO, I SPOTTED A SOLDIER MOVING ABOUT DOWN BELOW.
HSSST. UP HERE.
GO TO THE FRONT. I'LL LET YOU IN.
MY GOD! WHAT HAS HAPPENED TO YOU?
THEY WIPED US OUT - SIMPLY WIPED US OUT.
COME IN, TAKE SOME WHISKEY.
IT TOOK SOME TIME TO BOLSTER HIS NERVES BEFORE HE COULD ANSWER MY QUESTIONS.
ALRIGHT, I'LL TELL YOU SOME OF THE HORRORS I'VE SEEN...
"A DRIVER IN THE ARTILLERY, I WAS AMONG THE FIRST TROOPS TO ARRIVE."

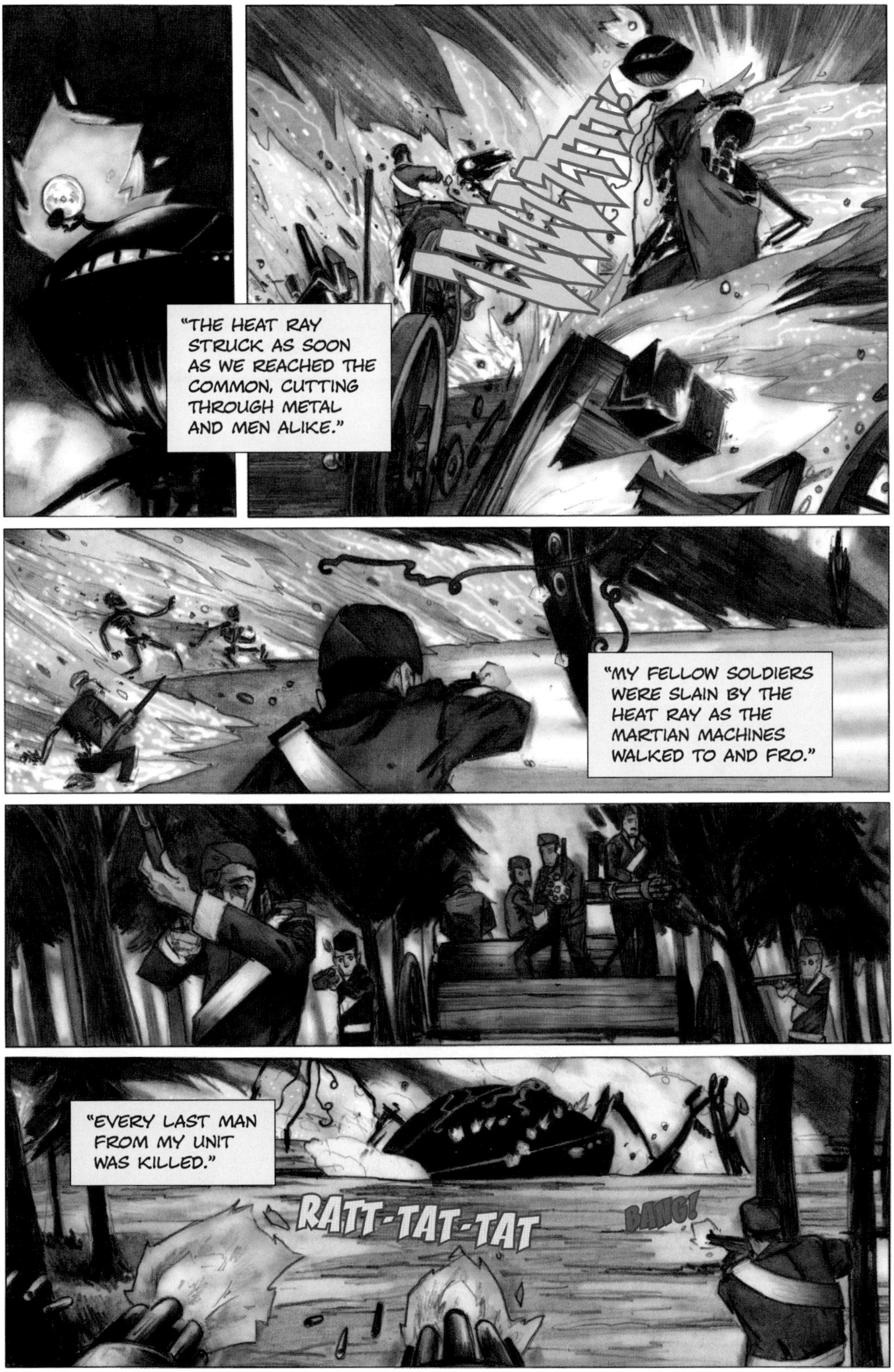
"THE HEAT RAY STRUCK AS SOON AS WE REACHED THE COMMON, CUTTING THROUGH METAL AND MEN ALIKE."
"MY FELLOW SOLDIERS WERE SLAIN BY THE HEAT RAY AS THE MARTIAN MACHINES WALKED TO AND FRO."
"EVERY LAST MAN FROM MY UNIT WAS KILLED."
RATT-TAT-TAT
BANG!

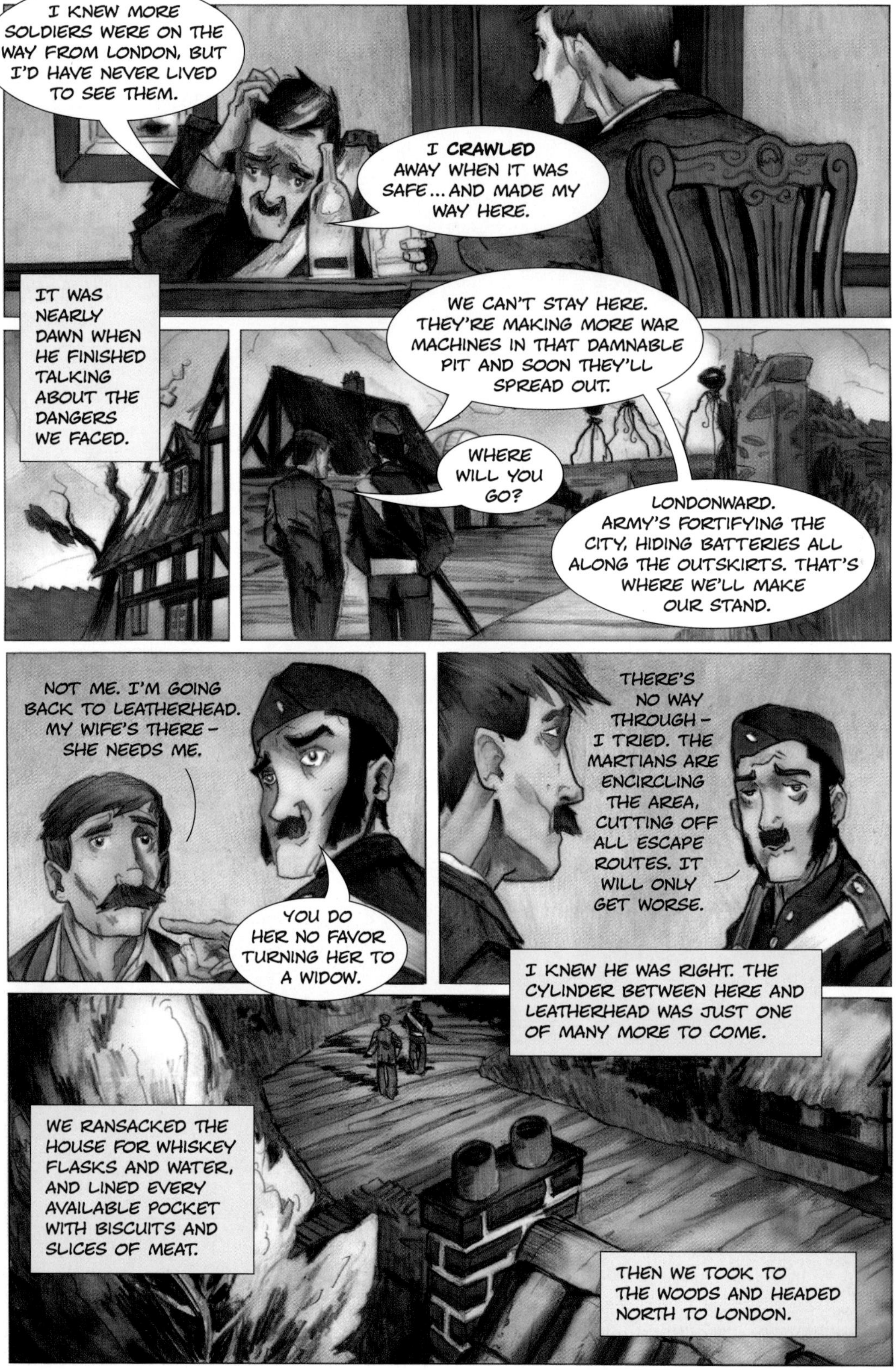
I KNEW MORE SOLDIERS WERE ON THE WAY FROM LONDON, BUT I'D HAVE NEVER LIVED TO SEE THEM.
I CRAWLED AWAY WHEN IT WAS SAFE... AND MADE MY WAY HERE.
IT WAS NEARLY DAWN WHEN HE FINISHED TALKING ABOUT THE DANGERS WE FACED.
WE CAN'T STAY HERE. THEY'RE MAKING MORE WAR MACHINES IN THAT DAMNABLE PIT AND SOON THEY'LL SPREAD OUT.
WHERE WILL YOU GO?
LONDONWARD. ARMY'S FORTIFYING THE CITY, HIDING BATTERIES ALL ALONG THE OUTSKIRTS. THAT'S WHERE WE'LL MAKE OUR STAND.
NOT ME. I'M GOING BACK TO LEATHERHEAD. MY WIFE'S THERE - SHE NEEDS ME.
YOU DO HER NO FAVOR TURNING HER TO A WIDOW.
THERE'S NO WAY THROUGH - I TRIED. THE MARTIANS ARE ENCIRCLING THE AREA, CUTTING OFF ALL ESCAPE ROUTES. IT WILL ONLY GET WORSE.
I KNEW HE WAS RIGHT. THE CYLINDER BETWEEN HERE AND LEATHERHEAD WAS JUST ONE OF MANY MORE TO COME.
WE RANSACKED THE HOUSE FOR WHISKEY FLASKS AND WATER, AND LINED EVERY AVAILABLE POCKET WITH BISCUITS AND SLICES OF MEAT.
THEN WE TOOK TO THE WOODS AND HEADED NORTH TO LONDON.

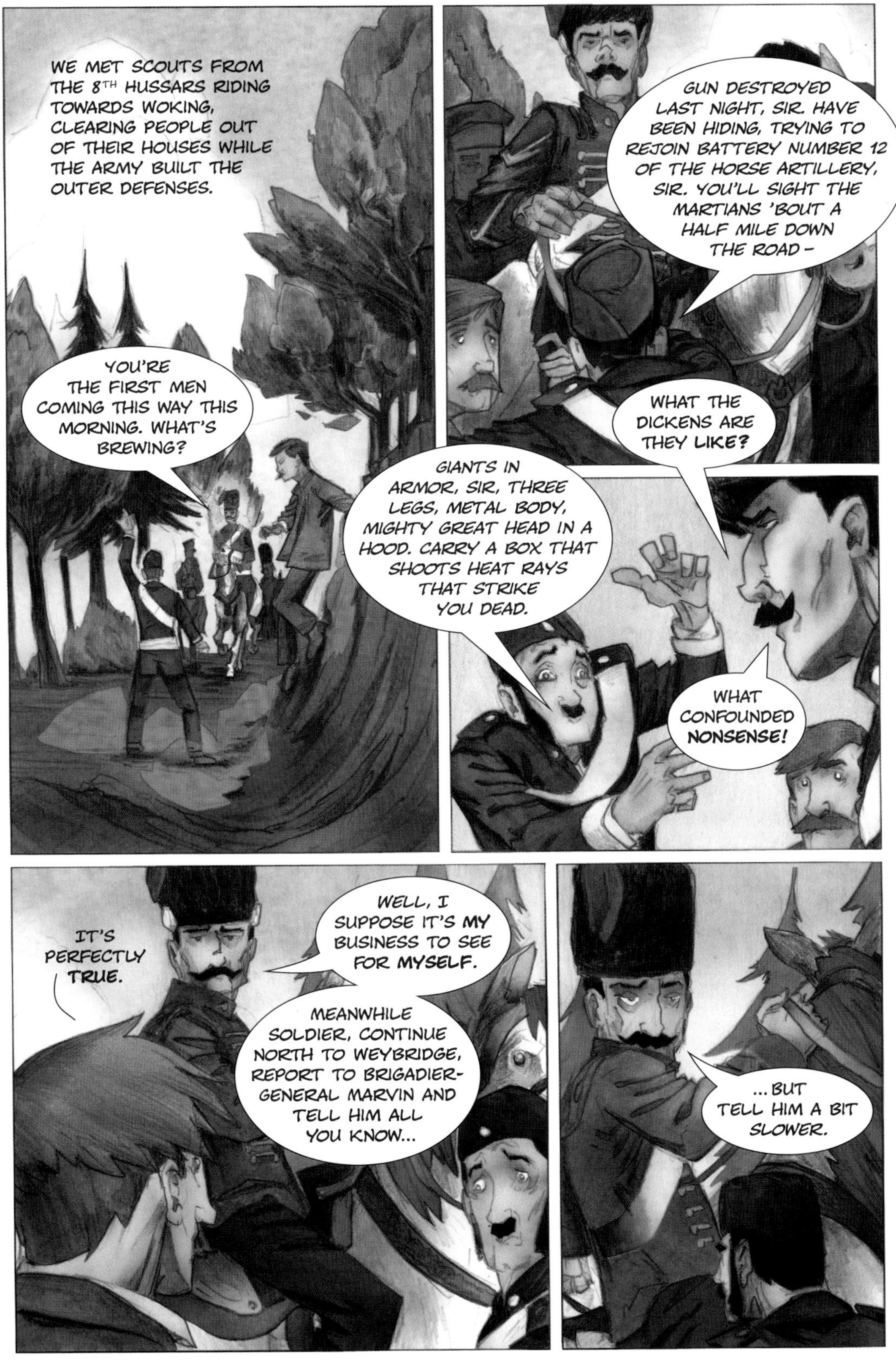
WE MET SCOUTS FROM THE 8TH HUSSARS RIDING TOWARDS WOKING, CLEARING PEOPLE OUT OF THEIR HOUSES WHILE THE ARMY BUILT THE OUTER DEFENSES.
YOU'RE THE FIRST MEN COMING THIS WAY THIS MORNING. WHAT'S BREWING?
GUN DESTROYED LAST NIGHT, SIR. HAVE BEEN HIDING, TRYING TO REJOIN BATTERY NUMBER 12 OF THE HORSE ARTILLERY, SIR. YOU'LL SIGHT THE MARTIANS 'BOUT A HALF MILE DOWN THE ROAD –
WHAT THE DICKENS ARE THEY LIKE?
GIANTS IN ARMOR, SIR, THREE LEGS, METAL BODY, MIGHTY GREAT HEAD IN A HOOD. CARRY A BOX THAT SHOOTS HEAT RAYS THAT STRIKE YOU DEAD.
WHAT CONFOUNDED NONSENSE!
IT'S PERFECTLY TRUE.
WELL, I SUPPOSE IT'S MY BUSINESS TO SEE FOR MYSELF.
MEANWHILE SOLDIER, CONTINUE NORTH TO WEYBRIDGE, REPORT TO BRIGADIER-GENERAL MARVIN AND TELL HIM ALL YOU KNOW...
...BUT TELL HIM A BIT SLOWER.

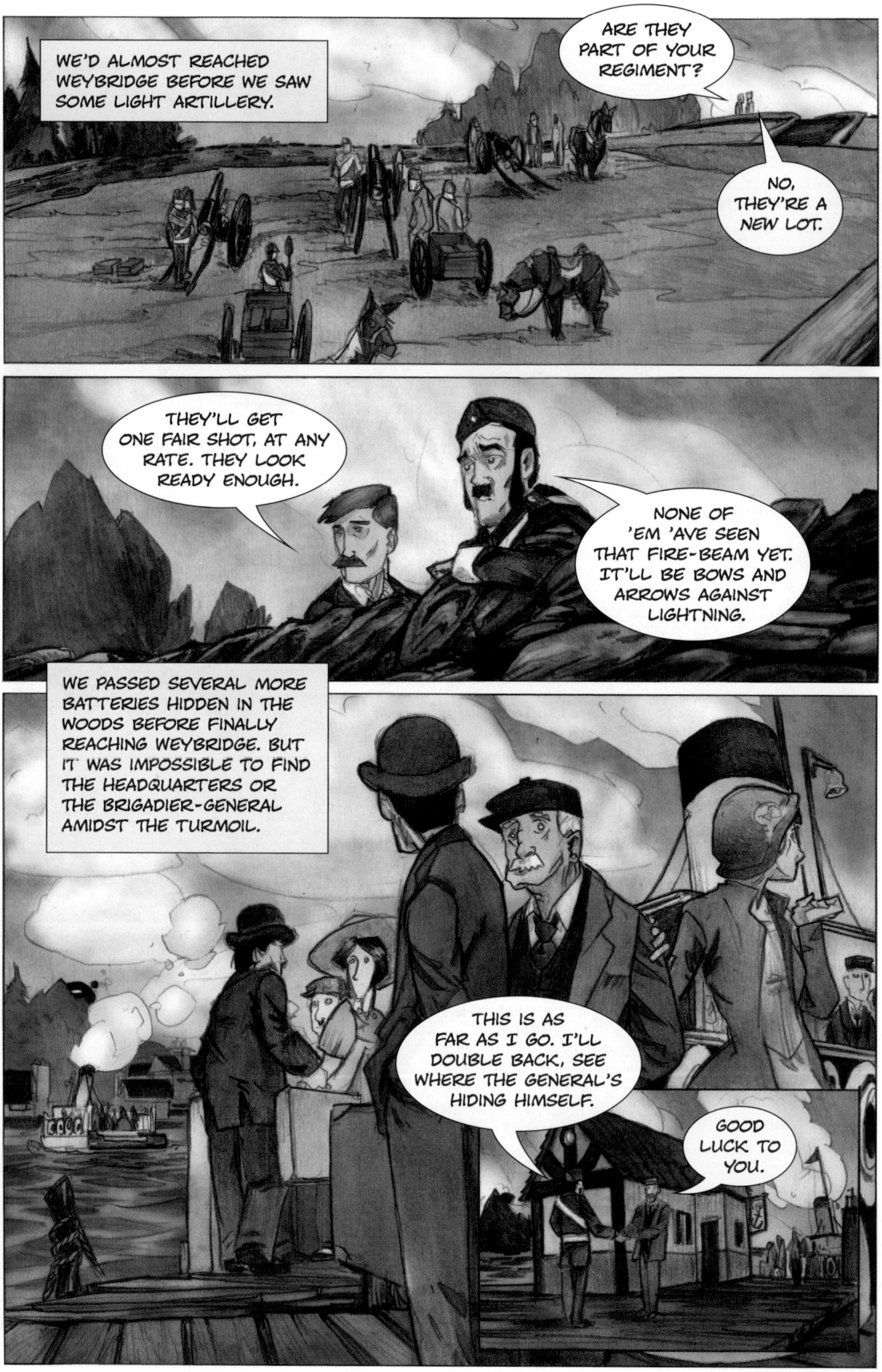
WE'D ALMOST REACHED WEYBRIDGE BEFORE WE SAW SOME LIGHT ARTILLERY.
ARE THEY PART OF YOUR REGIMENT?
NO, THEY'RE A NEW LOT.
THEY'LL GET ONE FAIR SHOT, AT ANY RATE. THEY LOOK READY ENOUGH.
NONE OF 'EM 'AVE SEEN THAT FIRE-BEAM YET. IT'LL BE BOWS AND ARROWS AGAINST LIGHTNING.
WE PASSED SEVERAL MORE BATTERIES HIDDEN IN THE WOODS BEFORE FINALLY REACHING WEYBRIDGE. BUT IT WAS IMPOSSIBLE TO FIND THE HEADQUARTERS OR THE BRIGADIER-GENERAL AMIDST THE TURMOIL.
THIS IS AS FAR AS I GO. I'LL DOUBLE BACK, SEE WHERE THE GENERAL'S HIDING HIMSELF.
GOOD LUCK TO YOU.

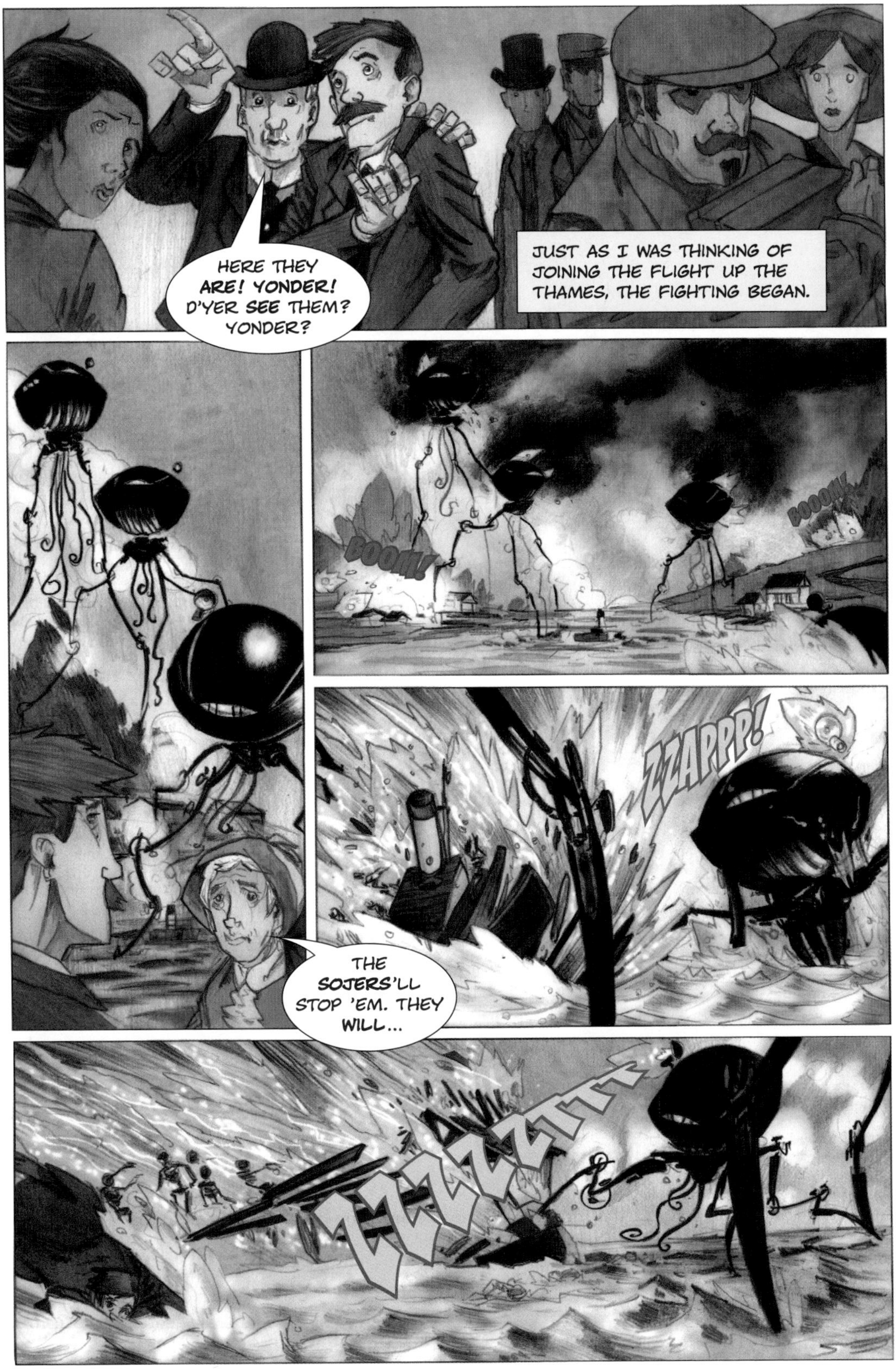
HERE THEY ARE! YONDER! D'YER SEE THEM? YONDER?
JUST AS I WAS THINKING OF JOINING THE FLIGHT UP THE THAMES, THE FIGHTING BEGAN.
BOOOM!
BOOOM!
ZZAPPP!
THE SOJERS'LL STOP 'EM. THEY WILL...
ZZZZZTTTT

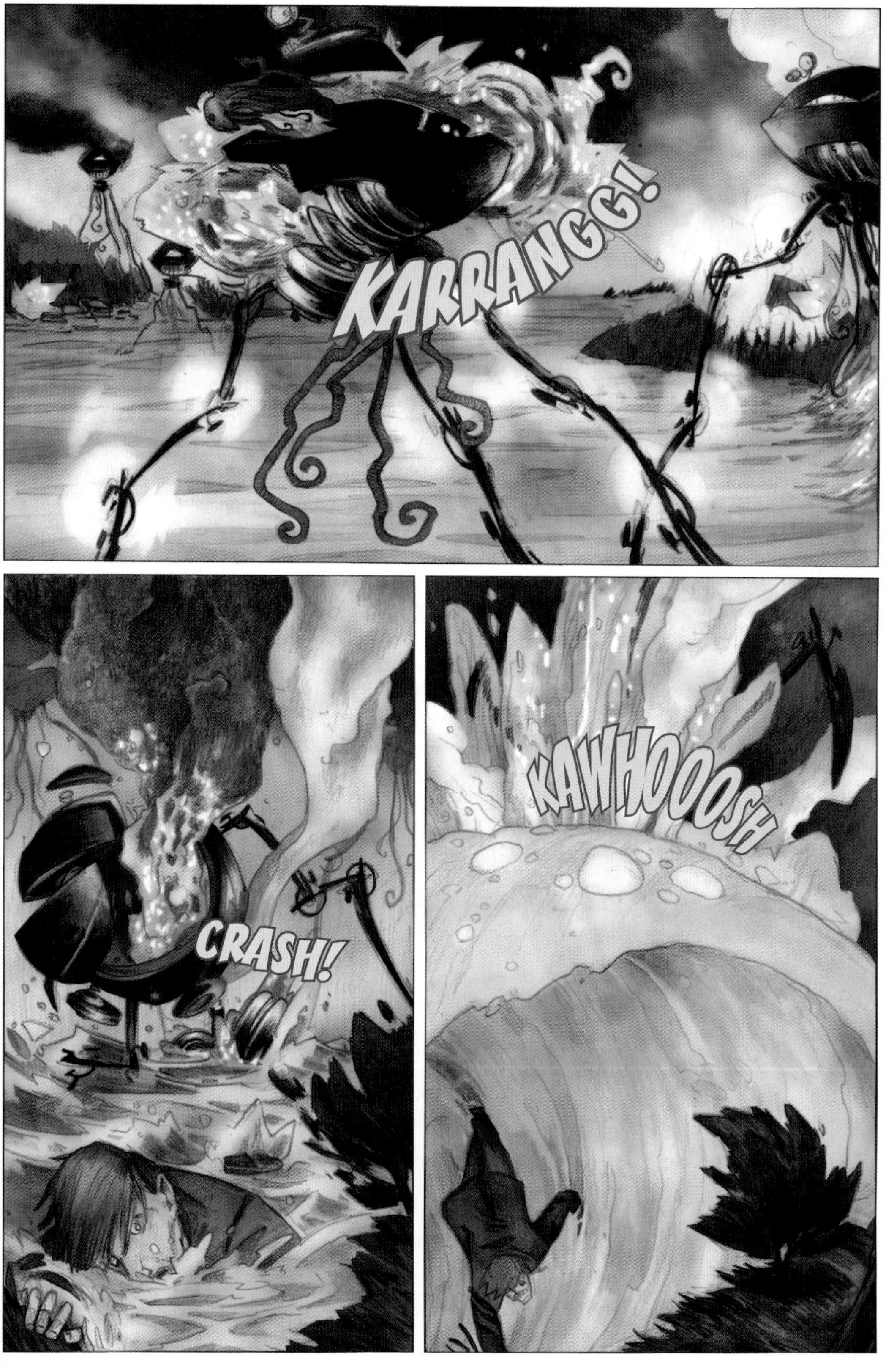
KARRANGG!
CRASH!
KAWHOOOOSH

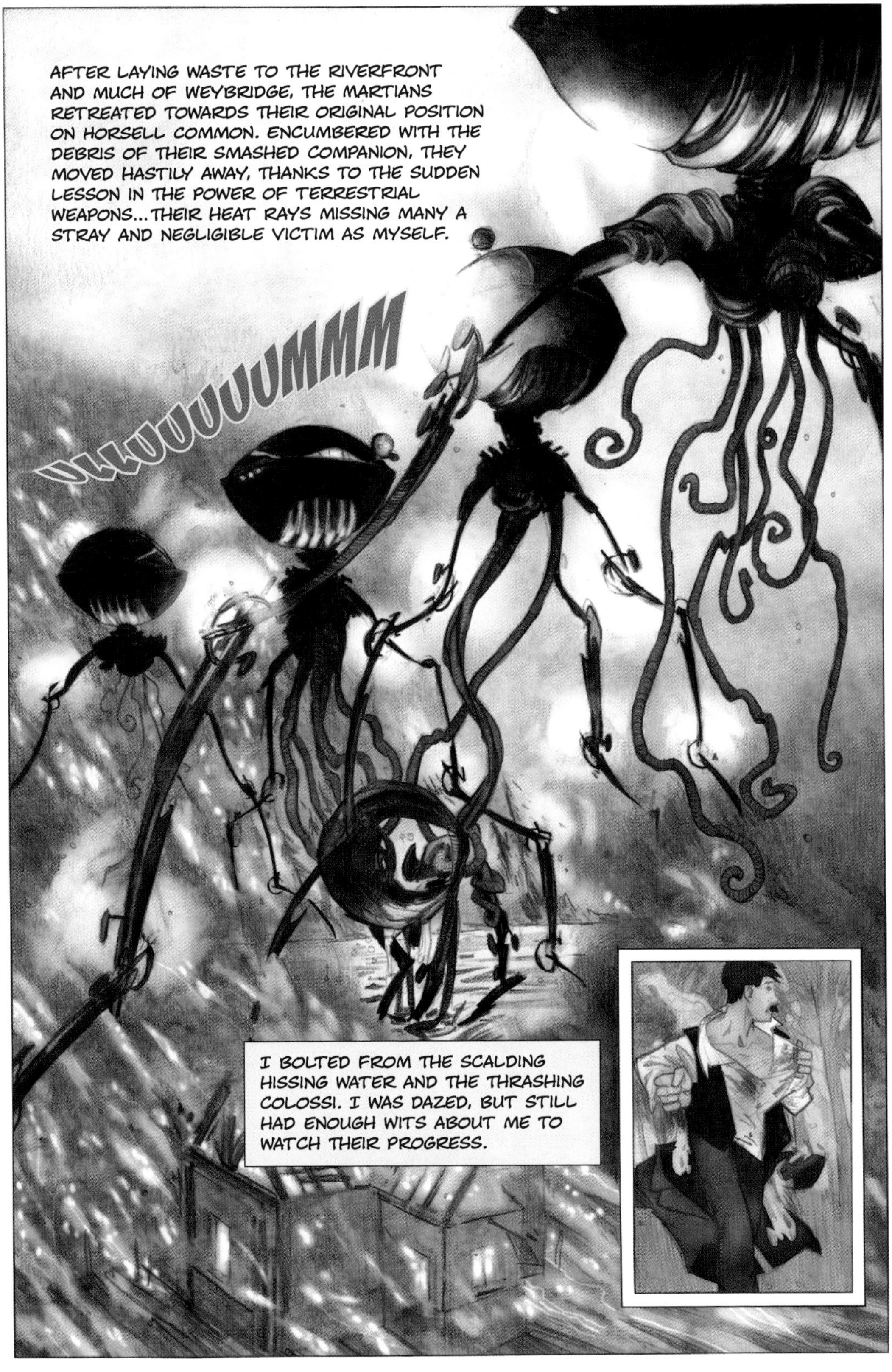
AFTER LAYING WASTE TO THE RIVERFRONT AND MUCH OF WEYBRIDGE, THE MARTIANS RETREATED TOWARDS THEIR ORIGINAL POSITION ON HORSELL COMMON. ENCUMBERED WITH THE DEBRIS OF THEIR SMASHED COMPANION, THEY MOVED HASTILY AWAY, THANKS TO THE SUDDEN LESSON IN THE POWER OF TERRESTRIAL WEAPONS...THEIR HEAT RAYS MISSING MANY A STRAY AND NEGLIGIBLE VICTIM AS MYSELF.
ULLUUUUUMMM
I BOLTED FROM THE SCALDING HISSING WATER AND THE THRASHING COLOSSI. I WAS DAZED, BUT STILL HAD ENOUGH WITS ABOUT ME TO WATCH THEIR PROGRESS.

I STUMBLED INTO THE WILDERNESS OUTSIDE WEYBRIDGE, THEN LAY DOWN FEVERISH AND EXHAUSTED.

WHEN I WOKE SEVERAL HOURS LATER THE CURATE WAS THERE, ADRIFT FROM HIS SANCTUARY.

H-HELLO? ...HAVE YOU ANY WATER?

SORRY. MY ANSWER REMAINS THE SAME.

I DON'T UNDERSTAND.

YOU HAVE BEEN ASKING FOR WATER FOR THE LAST HOUR. THERE IS NONE.

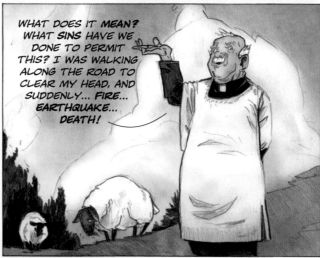

WHAT DOES IT MEAN? WHAT SINS HAVE WE DONE TO PERMIT THIS? I WAS WALKING ALONG THE ROAD TO CLEAR MY HEAD, AND SUDDENLY... FIRE... EARTHQUAKE... DEATH!

WHAT ARE THESE MARTIANS WHO CAN WREAK SUCH HAVOC ON US... WITHOUT EVEN THINKING TWICE?

WE ARE AS ANTS TO THEM. AND WE TRAMPLE ANTS WITHOUT THOUGHT.

BUT MY CHURCH – REBUILT JUST THREE YEARS AGO – IS GONE. SWEPT OUT OF EXISTENCE. WHY?...

"...THE SMOKE OF HER BURNING GOETH UP FOR EVER AND EVER!

"IT IS THE BEGINNING OF THE END. WE MUST HIDE FROM THE FACE OF HIM THAT SITTITH UPON THE THRONE!"

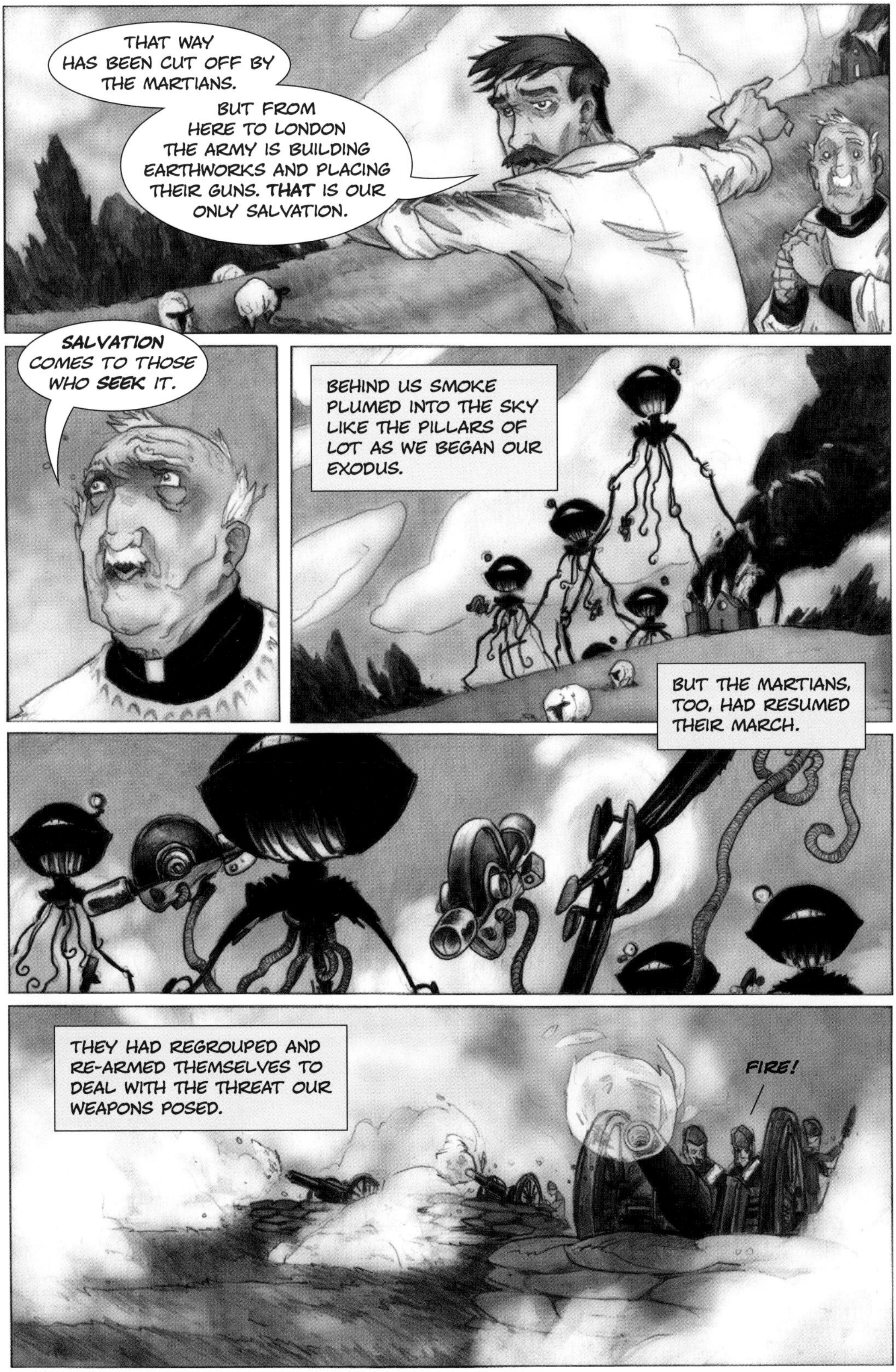
THAT WAY HAS BEEN CUT OFF BY THE MARTIANS.
BUT FROM HERE TO LONDON THE ARMY IS BUILDING EARTHWORKS AND PLACING THEIR GUNS. THAT IS OUR ONLY SALVATION.
SALVATION COMES TO THOSE WHO SEEK IT.
BEHIND US SMOKE PLUMED INTO THE SKY LIKE THE PILLARS OF LOT AS WE BEGAN OUR EXODUS.
BUT THE MARTIANS, TOO, HAD RESUMED THEIR MARCH.
THEY HAD REGROUPED AND RE-ARMED THEMSELVES TO DEAL WITH THE THREAT OUR WEAPONS POSED.
FIRE!

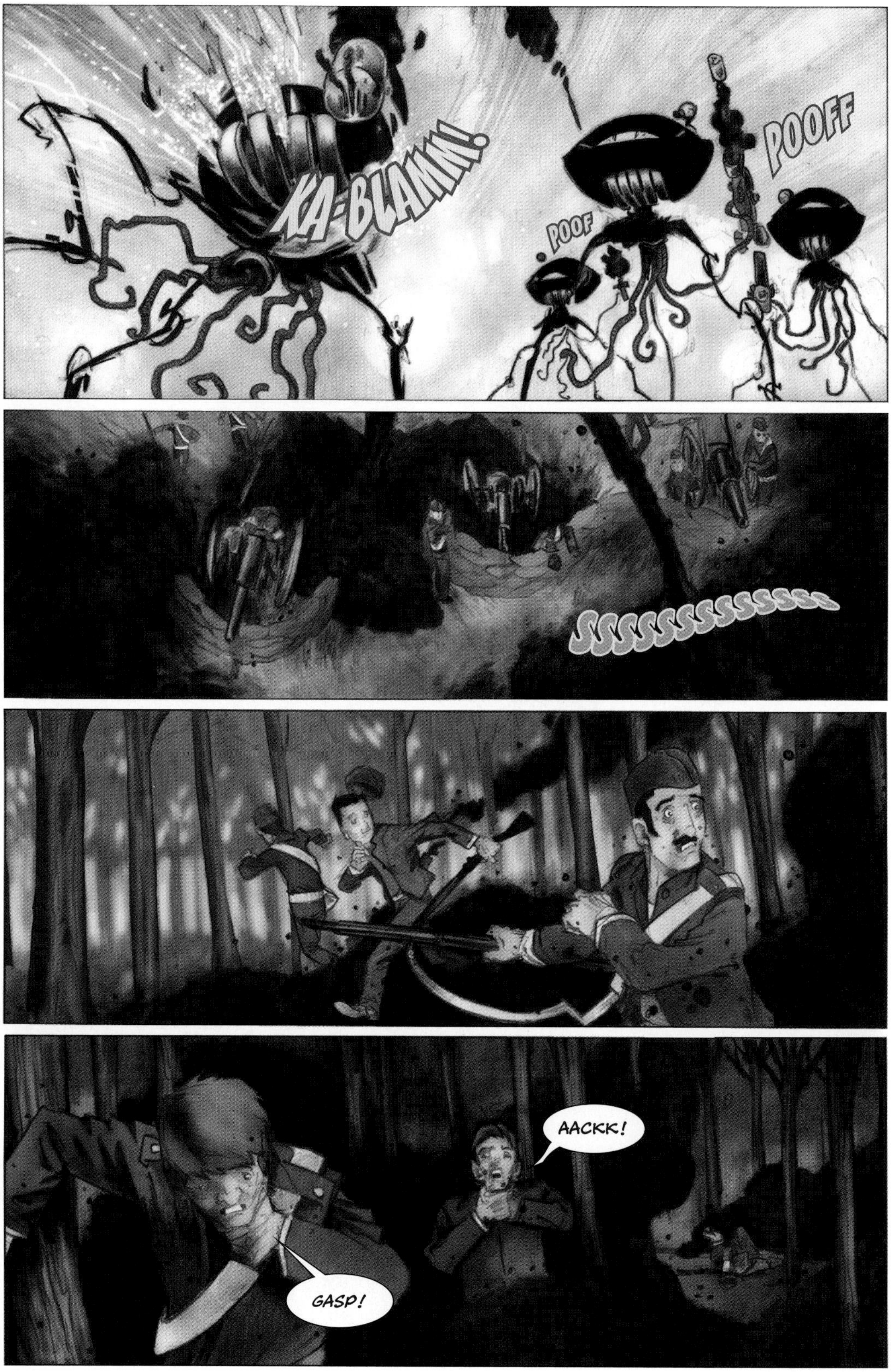
KA-BLAMM!
POOF
POOFF
SSSSSSSSSSSSS
AACKK!
GASP!

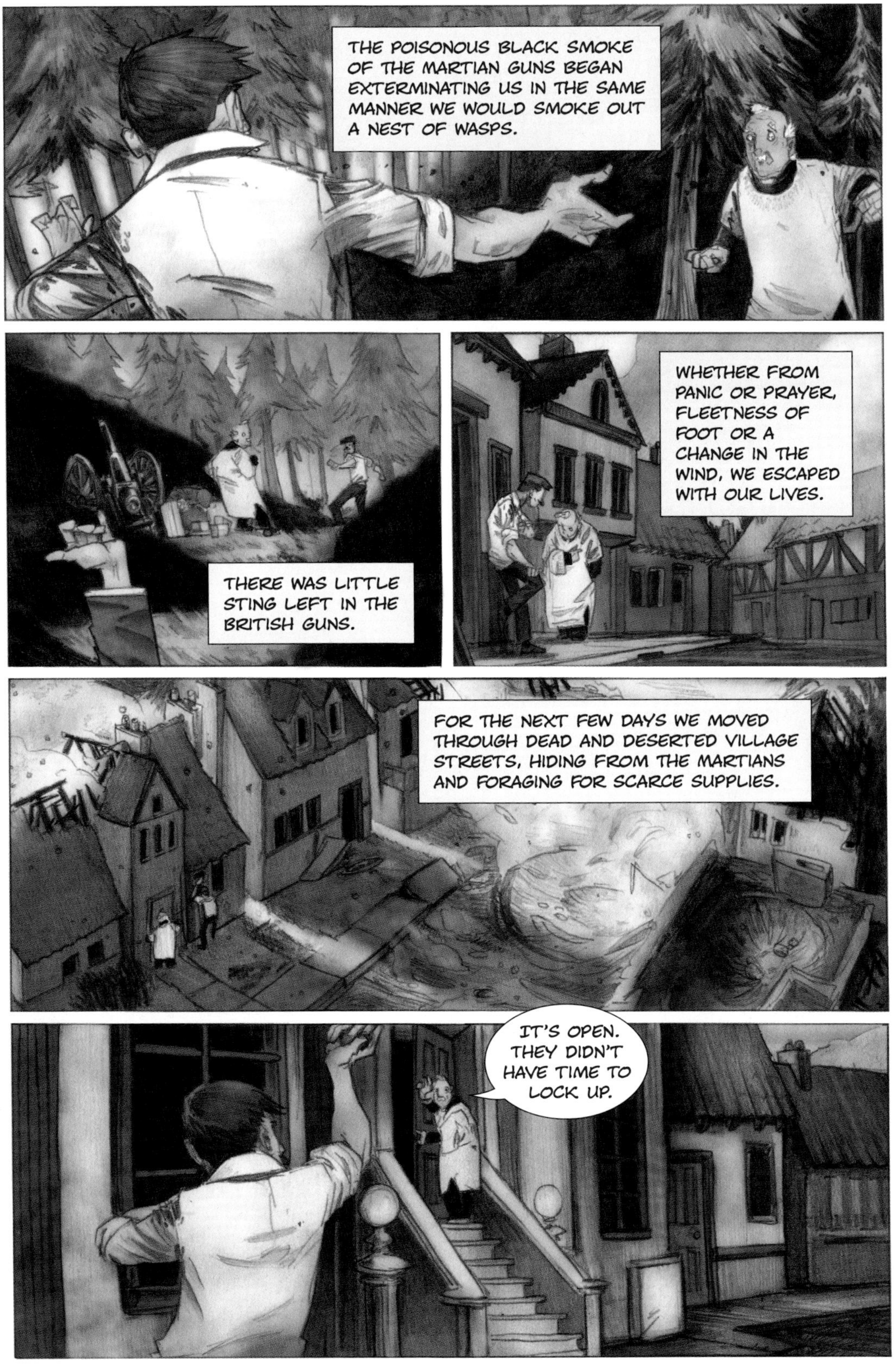
THE POISONOUS BLACK SMOKE OF THE MARTIAN GUNS BEGAN EXTERMINATING US IN THE SAME MANNER WE WOULD SMOKE OUT A NEST OF WASPS.
THERE WAS LITTLE STING LEFT IN THE BRITISH GUNS.
WHETHER FROM PANIC OR PRAYER, FLEETNESS OF FOOT OR A CHANGE IN THE WIND, WE ESCAPED WITH OUR LIVES.
FOR THE NEXT FEW DAYS WE MOVED THROUGH DEAD AND DESERTED VILLAGE STREETS, HIDING FROM THE MARTIANS AND FORAGING FOR SCARCE SUPPLIES.
IT'S OPEN. THEY DIDN'T HAVE TIME TO LOCK UP.

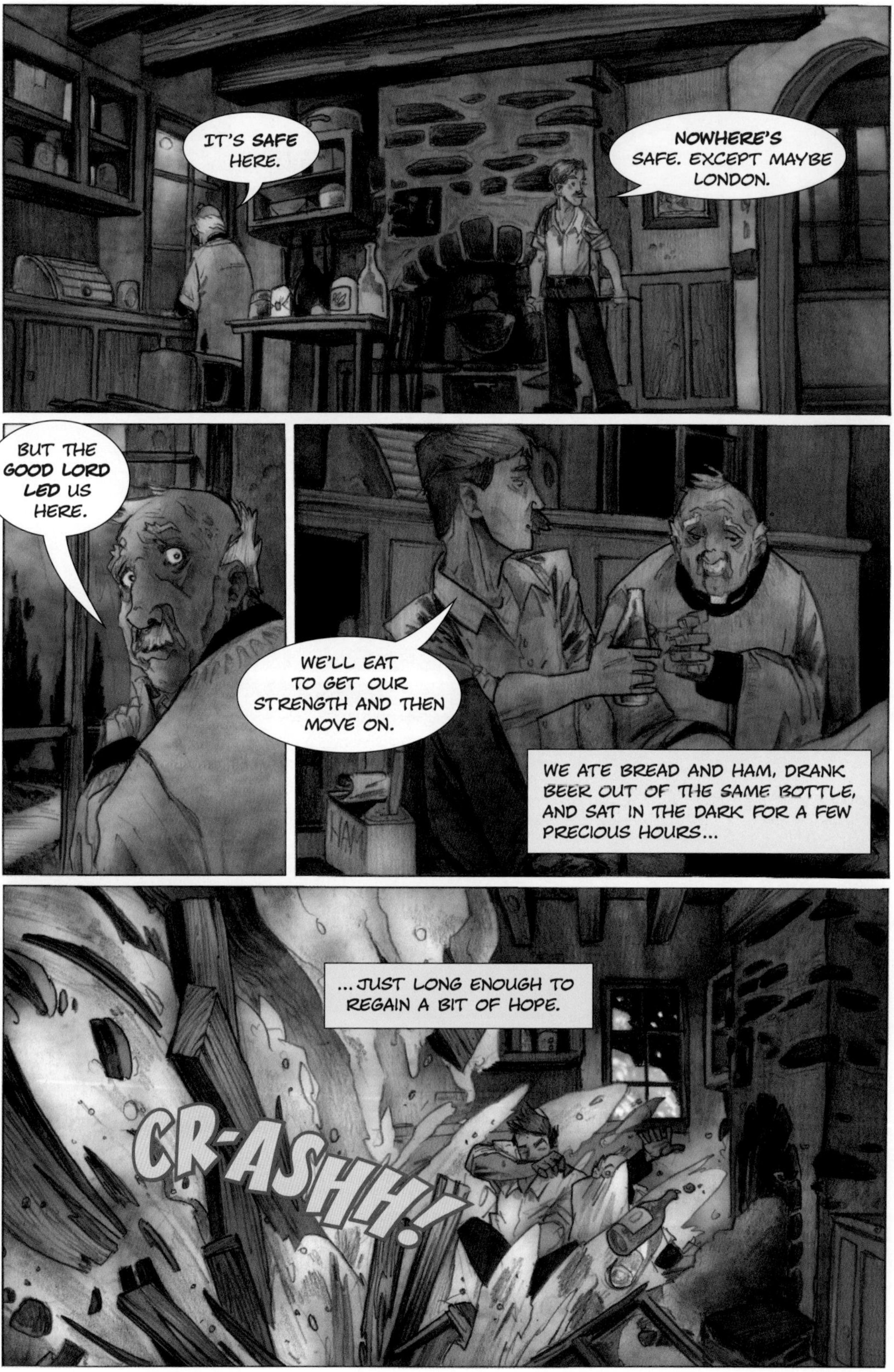
IT'S SAFE HERE.
NOWHERE'S SAFE. EXCEPT MAYBE LONDON.
BUT THE GOOD LORD LED US HERE.
WE'LL EAT TO GET OUR STRENGTH AND THEN MOVE ON.
WE ATE BREAD AND HAM, DRANK BEER OUT OF THE SAME BOTTLE, AND SAT IN THE DARK FOR A FEW PRECIOUS HOURS...
...JUST LONG ENOUGH TO REGAIN A BIT OF HOPE.
CR-ASHH!

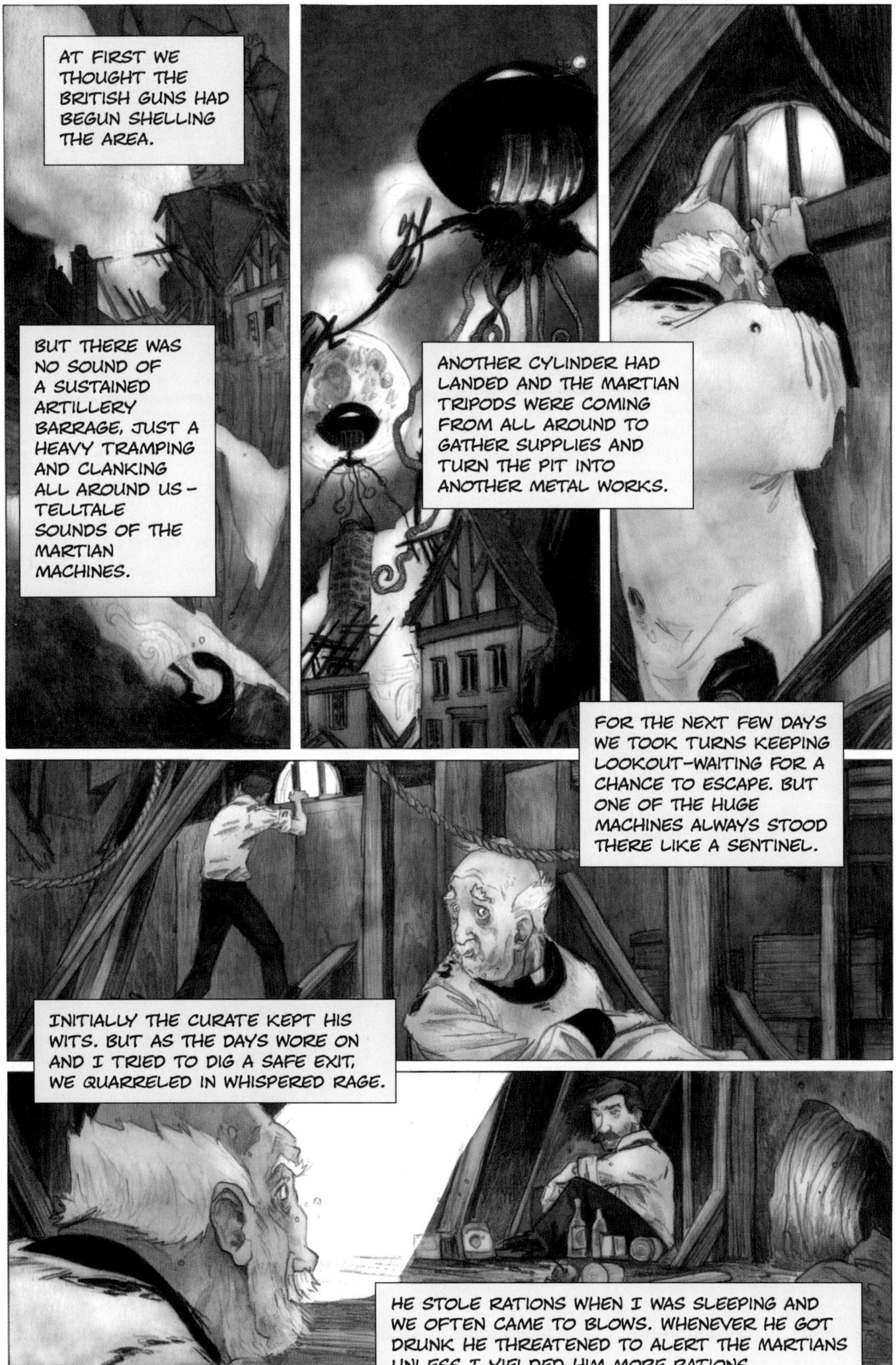
AT FIRST WE THOUGHT THE BRITISH GUNS HAD BEGUN SHELLING THE AREA.
BUT THERE WAS NO SOUND OF A SUSTAINED ARTILLERY BARRAGE, JUST A HEAVY TRAMPING AND CLANKING ALL AROUND US– TELLTALE SOUNDS OF THE MARTIAN MACHINES.
ANOTHER CYLINDER HAD LANDED AND THE MARTIAN TRIPODS WERE COMING FROM ALL AROUND TO GATHER SUPPLIES AND TURN THE PIT INTO ANOTHER METAL WORKS.
FOR THE NEXT FEW DAYS WE TOOK TURNS KEEPING LOOKOUT–WAITING FOR A CHANCE TO ESCAPE. BUT ONE OF THE HUGE MACHINES ALWAYS STOOD THERE LIKE A SENTINEL.
INITIALLY THE CURATE KEPT HIS WITS. BUT AS THE DAYS WORE ON AND I TRIED TO DIG A SAFE EXIT, WE QUARRELED IN WHISPERED RAGE.
HE STOLE RATIONS WHEN I WAS SLEEPING AND WE OFTEN CAME TO BLOWS. WHENEVER HE GOT DRUNK HE THREATENED TO ALERT THE MARTIANS UNLESS I YIELDED HIM MORE RATIONS.

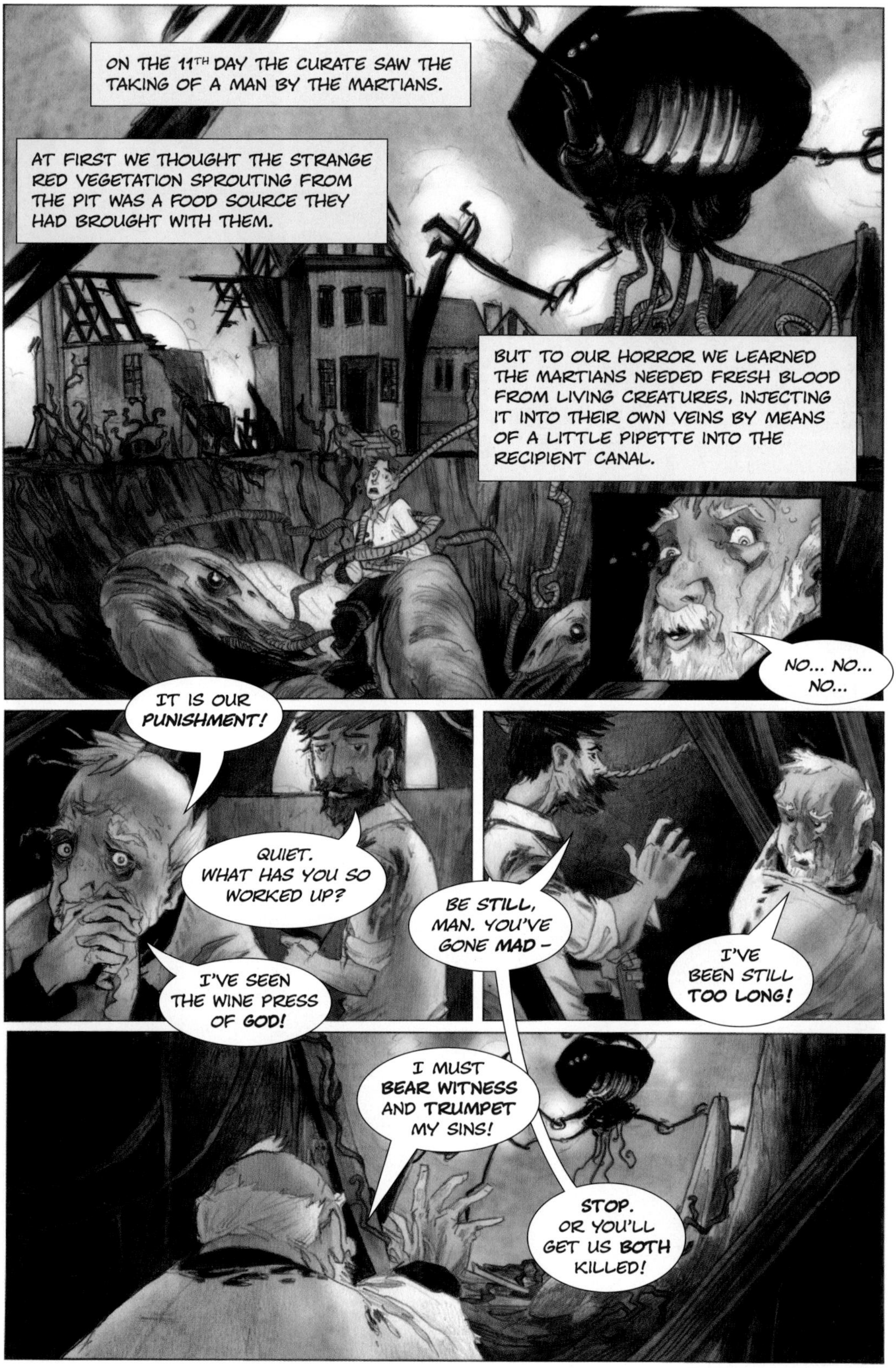
ON THE 11TH DAY THE CURATE SAW THE TAKING OF A MAN BY THE MARTIANS.
AT FIRST WE THOUGHT THE STRANGE RED VEGETATION SPROUTING FROM THE PIT WAS A FOOD SOURCE THEY HAD BROUGHT WITH THEM.
BUT TO OUR HORROR WE LEARNED THE MARTIANS NEEDED FRESH BLOOD FROM LIVING CREATURES, INJECTING IT INTO THEIR OWN VEINS BY MEANS OF A LITTLE PIPETTE INTO THE RECIPIENT CANAL.
NO... NO... NO...
IT IS OUR PUNISHMENT!
QUIET. WHAT HAS YOU SO WORKED UP?
I'VE SEEN THE WINE PRESS OF GOD!
BE STILL, MAN. YOU'VE GONE MAD –
I'VE BEEN STILL TOO LONG!
I MUST BEAR WITNESS AND TRUMPET MY SINS!
STOP. OR YOU'LL GET US BOTH KILLED!

WOE! WOE! WOE TO THE INHABITANTS OF THE EARTH!
I SAID BE...
QUIET!
WAPP
CRASH!
I WAITED FOR HOURS, MAYBE DAYS, WITHOUT MAKING A SOUND. ONLY WHEN I BECAME AWARE OF A STILLNESS – THE LACK OF SOUNDS FROM THAT HORRID PIT – DID I REALIZE THE MARTIANS HAD MOVED ON.

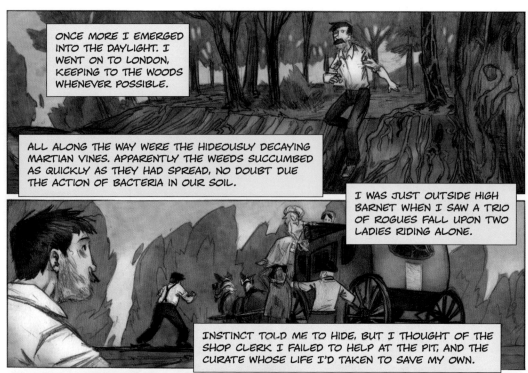

ONCE MORE I EMERGED INTO THE DAYLIGHT. I WENT ON TO LONDON, KEEPING TO THE WOODS WHENEVER POSSIBLE.

ALL ALONG THE WAY WERE THE HIDEOUSLY DECAYING MARTIAN VINES. APPARENTLY THE WEEDS SUCCUMBED AS QUICKLY AS THEY HAD SPREAD, NO DOUBT DUE THE ACTION OF BACTERIA IN OUR SOIL.

I WAS JUST OUTSIDE HIGH BARNET WHEN I SAW A TRIO OF ROGUES FALL UPON TWO LADIES RIDING ALONE.

INSTINCT TOLD ME TO HIDE, BUT I THOUGHT OF THE SHOP CLERK I FAILED TO HELP AT THE PIT, AND THE CURATE WHOSE LIFE I'D TAKEN TO SAVE MY OWN.

LET US BE!

KWAPP!

AND I THOUGHT OF WHAT WOULD HAPPEN TO MY WIFE IF SHE WERE ATTACKED AND NO ONE STEPPED FORWARD.

UHHHHN!

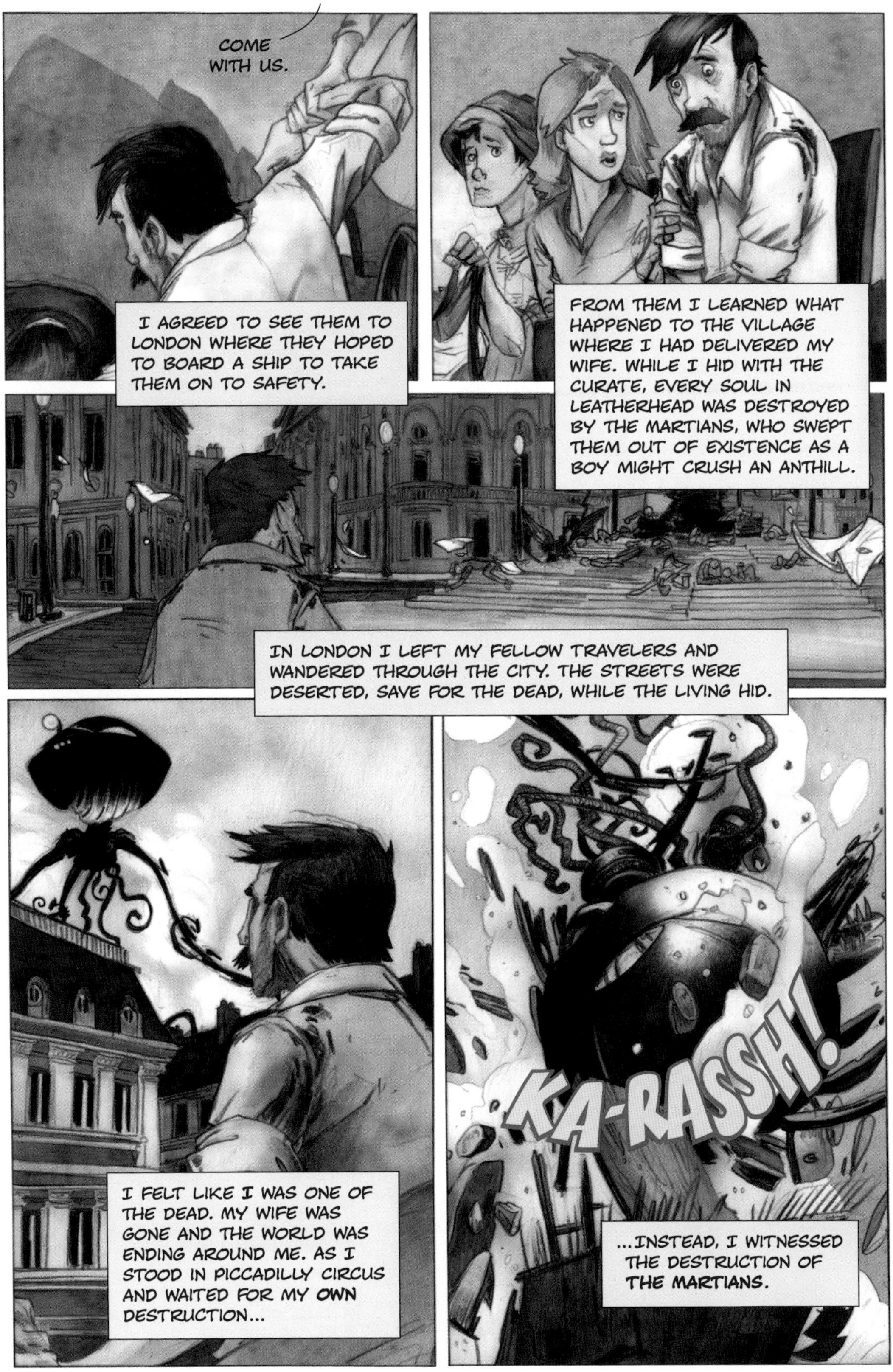
COME WITH US.
I AGREED TO SEE THEM TO LONDON WHERE THEY HOPED TO BOARD A SHIP TO TAKE THEM ON TO SAFETY.
FROM THEM I LEARNED WHAT HAPPENED TO THE VILLAGE WHERE I HAD DELIVERED MY WIFE. WHILE I HID WITH THE CURATE, EVERY SOUL IN LEATHERHEAD WAS DESTROYED BY THE MARTIANS, WHO SWEPT THEM OUT OF EXISTENCE AS A BOY MIGHT CRUSH AN ANTHILL.
IN LONDON I LEFT MY FELLOW TRAVELERS AND WANDERED THROUGH THE CITY. THE STREETS WERE DESERTED, SAVE FOR THE DEAD, WHILE THE LIVING HID.
I FELT LIKE I WAS ONE OF THE DEAD. MY WIFE WAS GONE AND THE WORLD WAS ENDING AROUND ME. AS I STOOD IN PICCADILLY CIRCUS AND WAITED FOR MY OWN DESTRUCTION...
KA-RASSH!
...INSTEAD, I WITNESSED THE DESTRUCTION OF THE MARTIANS.

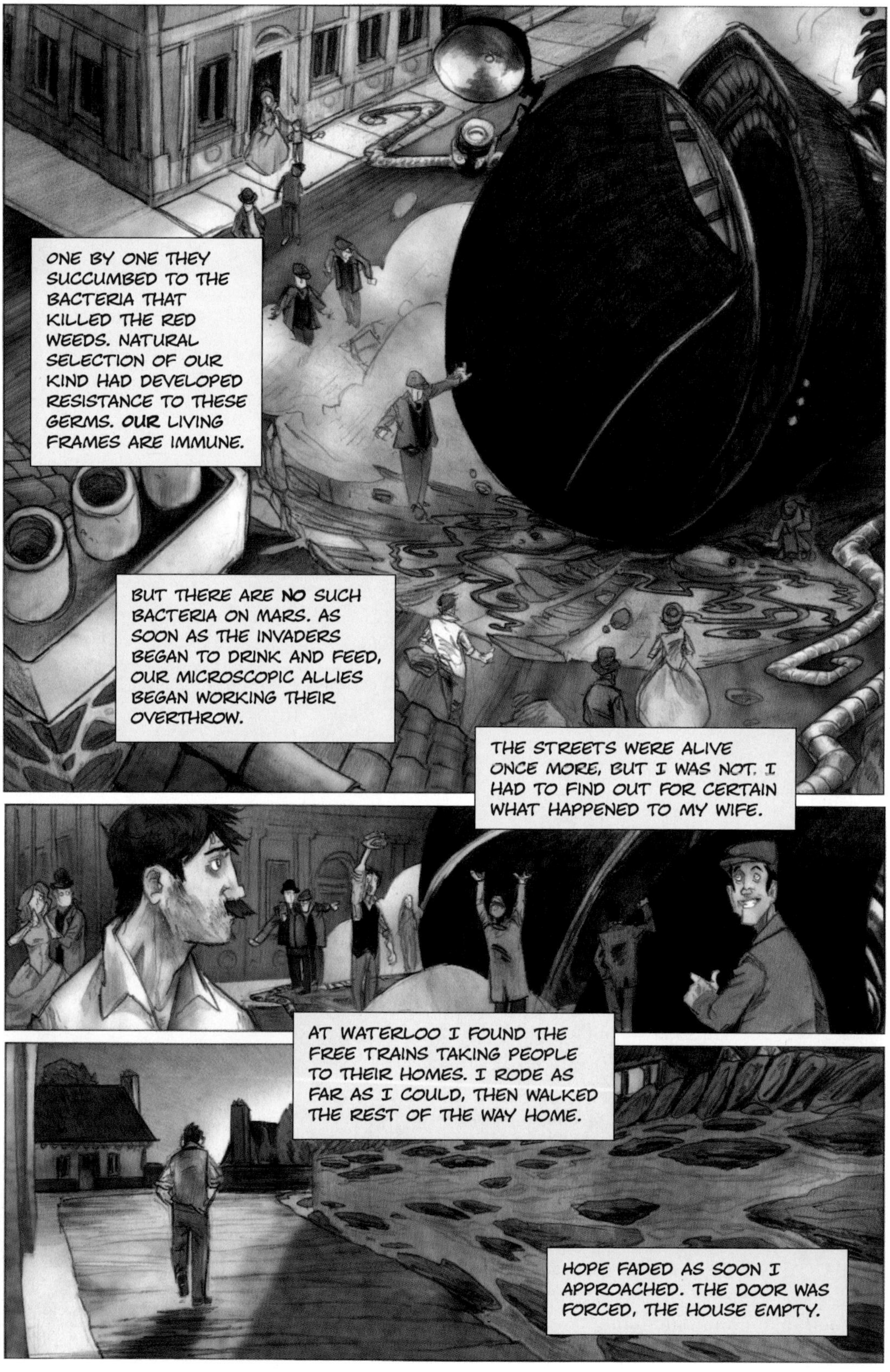
ONE BY ONE THEY SUCCUMBED TO THE BACTERIA THAT KILLED THE RED WEEDS. NATURAL SELECTION OF OUR KIND HAD DEVELOPED RESISTANCE TO THESE GERMS. **OUR** LIVING FRAMES ARE IMMUNE.
BUT THERE ARE **NO** SUCH BACTERIA ON MARS. AS SOON AS THE INVADERS BEGAN TO DRINK AND FEED, OUR MICROSCOPIC ALLIES BEGAN WORKING THEIR OVERTHROW.
THE STREETS WERE ALIVE ONCE MORE, BUT I WAS NOT. I HAD TO FIND OUT FOR CERTAIN WHAT HAPPENED TO MY WIFE.
AT WATERLOO I FOUND THE FREE TRAINS TAKING PEOPLE TO THEIR HOMES. I RODE AS FAR AS I COULD, THEN WALKED THE REST OF THE WAY HOME.
HOPE FADED AS SOON I APPROACHED. THE DOOR WAS FORCED, THE HOUSE EMPTY.

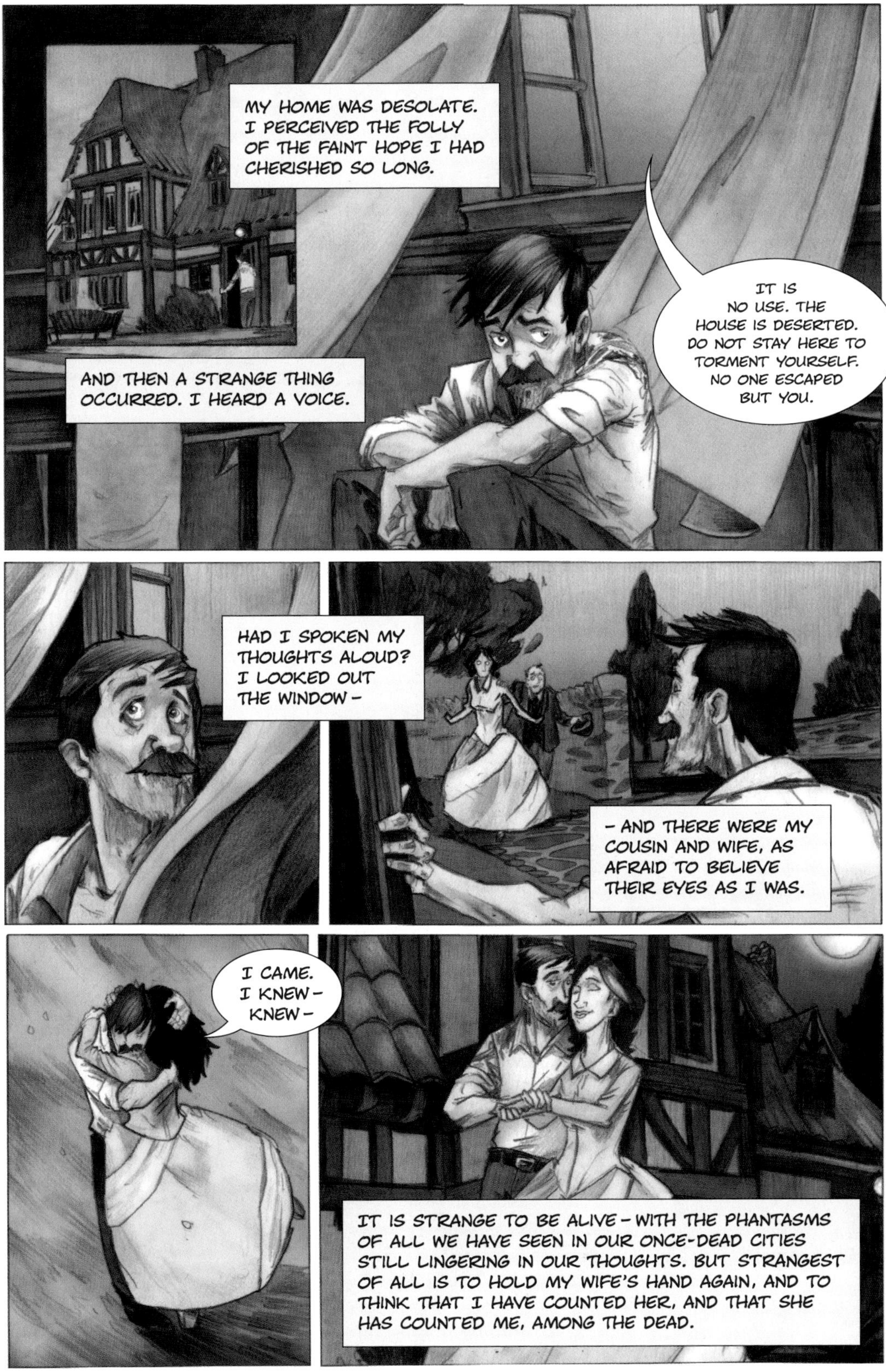
MY HOME WAS DESOLATE. I PERCEIVED THE FOLLY OF THE FAINT HOPE I HAD CHERISHED SO LONG.
AND THEN A STRANGE THING OCCURRED. I HEARD A VOICE.
IT IS NO USE. THE HOUSE IS DESERTED. DO NOT STAY HERE TO TORMENT YOURSELF. NO ONE ESCAPED BUT YOU.
HAD I SPOKEN MY THOUGHTS ALOUD? I LOOKED OUT THE WINDOW –
– AND THERE WERE MY COUSIN AND WIFE, AS AFRAID TO BELIEVE THEIR EYES AS I WAS.
I CAME. I KNEW – KNEW –
IT IS STRANGE TO BE ALIVE – WITH THE PHANTASMS OF ALL WE HAVE SEEN IN OUR ONCE-DEAD CITIES STILL LINGERING IN OUR THOUGHTS. BUT STRANGEST OF ALL IS TO HOLD MY WIFE'S HAND AGAIN, AND TO THINK THAT I HAVE COUNTED HER, AND THAT SHE HAS COUNTED ME, AMONG THE DEAD.

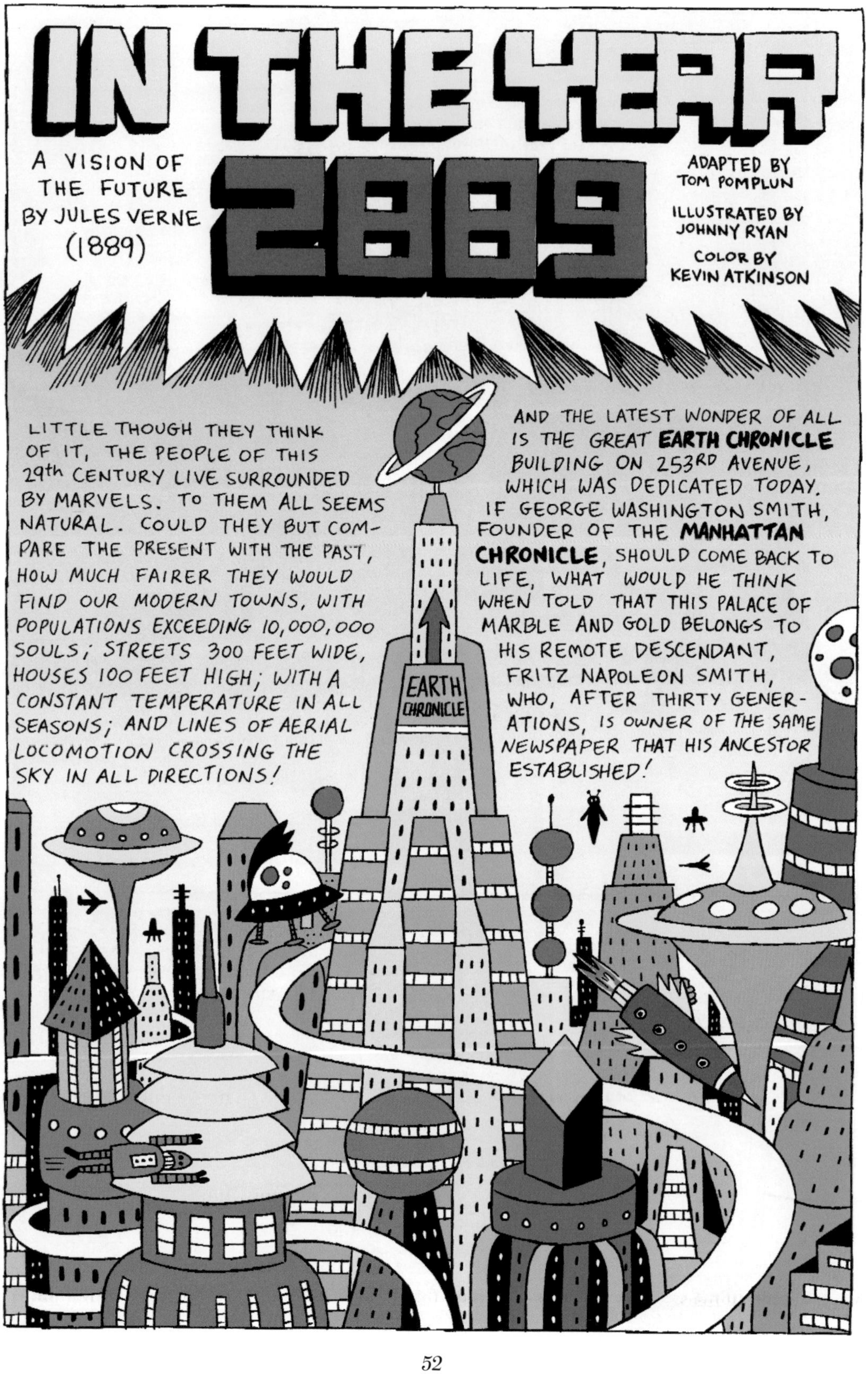
IN THE YEAR 2889
A VISION OF THE FUTURE BY JULES VERNE (1889)
ADAPTED BY TOM POMPLUN
ILLUSTRATED BY JOHNNY RYAN
COLOR BY KEVIN ATKINSON
LITTLE THOUGH THEY THINK OF IT, THE PEOPLE OF THIS 29th CENTURY LIVE SURROUNDED BY MARVELS. TO THEM ALL SEEMS NATURAL. COULD THEY BUT COMPARE THE PRESENT WITH THE PAST, HOW MUCH FAIRER THEY WOULD FIND OUR MODERN TOWNS, WITH POPULATIONS EXCEEDING 10,000,000 SOULS; STREETS 300 FEET WIDE, HOUSES 100 FEET HIGH; WITH A CONSTANT TEMPERATURE IN ALL SEASONS; AND LINES OF AERIAL LOCOMOTION CROSSING THE SKY IN ALL DIRECTIONS!
AND THE LATEST WONDER OF ALL IS THE GREAT EARTH CHRONICLE BUILDING ON 253RD AVENUE, WHICH WAS DEDICATED TODAY. IF GEORGE WASHINGTON SMITH, FOUNDER OF THE MANHATTAN CHRONICLE, SHOULD COME BACK TO LIFE, WHAT WOULD HE THINK WHEN TOLD THAT THIS PALACE OF MARBLE AND GOLD BELONGS TO HIS REMOTE DESCENDANT, FRITZ NAPOLEON SMITH, WHO, AFTER THIRTY GENERATIONS, IS OWNER OF THE SAME NEWSPAPER THAT HIS ANCESTOR ESTABLISHED!
EARTH CHRONICLE

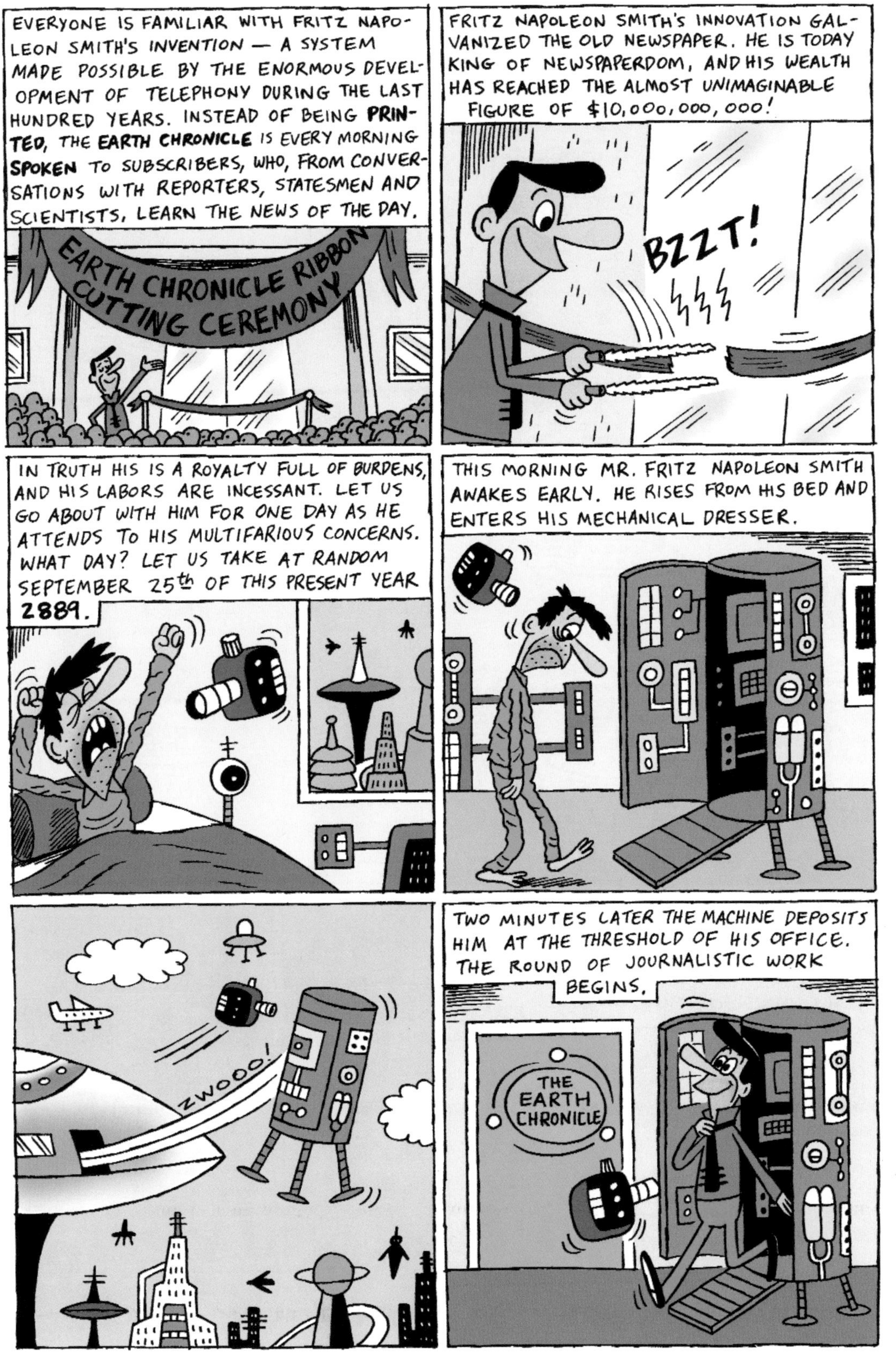
EVERYONE IS FAMILIAR WITH FRITZ NAPOLEON SMITH'S INVENTION — A SYSTEM MADE POSSIBLE BY THE ENORMOUS DEVELOPMENT OF TELEPHONY DURING THE LAST HUNDRED YEARS. INSTEAD OF BEING **PRINTED**, THE **EARTH CHRONICLE** IS EVERY MORNING **SPOKEN** TO SUBSCRIBERS, WHO, FROM CONVERSATIONS WITH REPORTERS, STATESMEN AND SCIENTISTS, LEARN THE NEWS OF THE DAY.
EARTH CHRONICLE RIBBON CUTTING CEREMONY
FRITZ NAPOLEON SMITH'S INNOVATION GALVANIZED THE OLD NEWSPAPER. HE IS TODAY KING OF NEWSPAPERDOM, AND HIS WEALTH HAS REACHED THE ALMOST UNIMAGINABLE FIGURE OF $10,000,000,000!
BZZT!
IN TRUTH HIS IS A ROYALTY FULL OF BURDENS, AND HIS LABORS ARE INCESSANT. LET US GO ABOUT WITH HIM FOR ONE DAY AS HE ATTENDS TO HIS MULTIFARIOUS CONCERNS. WHAT DAY? LET US TAKE AT RANDOM SEPTEMBER 25th OF THIS PRESENT YEAR **2889**.
THIS MORNING MR. FRITZ NAPOLEON SMITH AWAKES EARLY. HE RISES FROM HIS BED AND ENTERS HIS MECHANICAL DRESSER.
ZWOOO!
TWO MINUTES LATER THE MACHINE DEPOSITS HIM AT THE THRESHOLD OF HIS OFFICE. THE ROUND OF JOURNALISTIC WORK BEGINS.
THE EARTH CHRONICLE

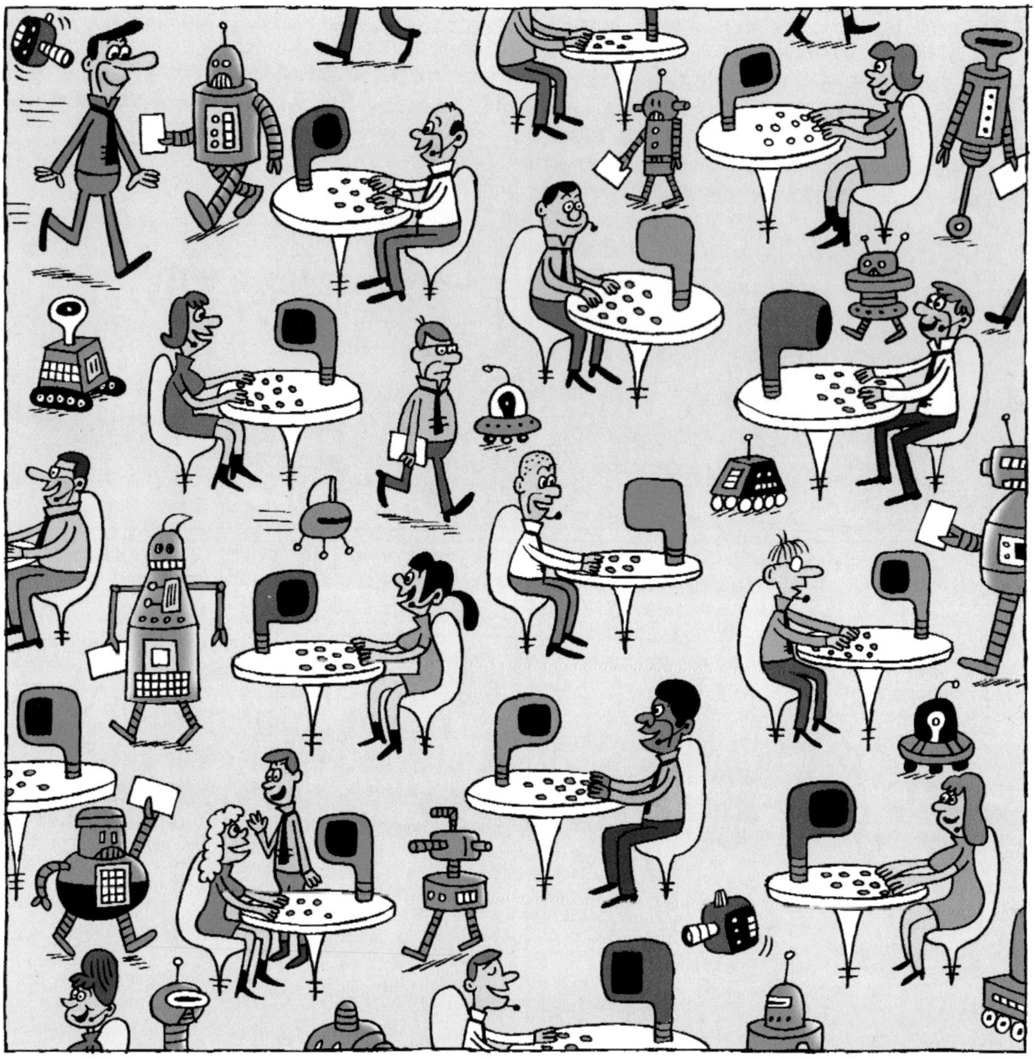

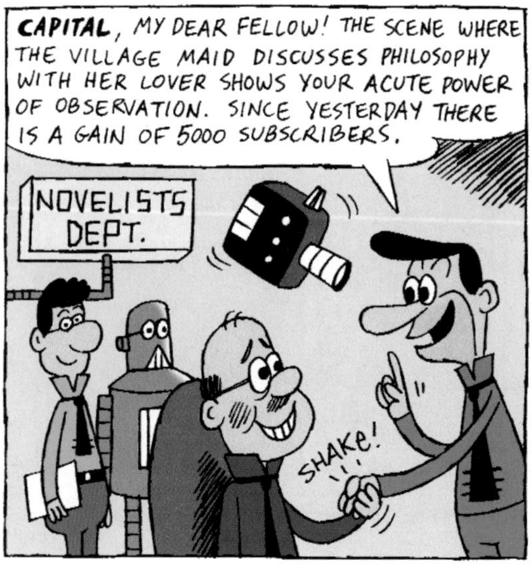
CAPITAL, MY DEAR FELLOW! THE SCENE WHERE THE VILLAGE MAID DISCUSSES PHILOSOPHY WITH HER LOVER SHOWS YOUR ACUTE POWER OF OBSERVATION. SINCE YESTERDAY THERE IS A GAIN OF 5000 SUBSCRIBERS.
NOVELISTS DEPT.
SHAKE!

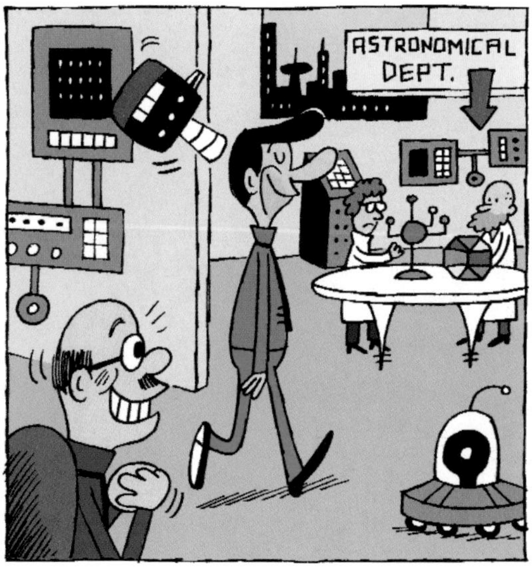
ASTRONOMICAL DEPT.

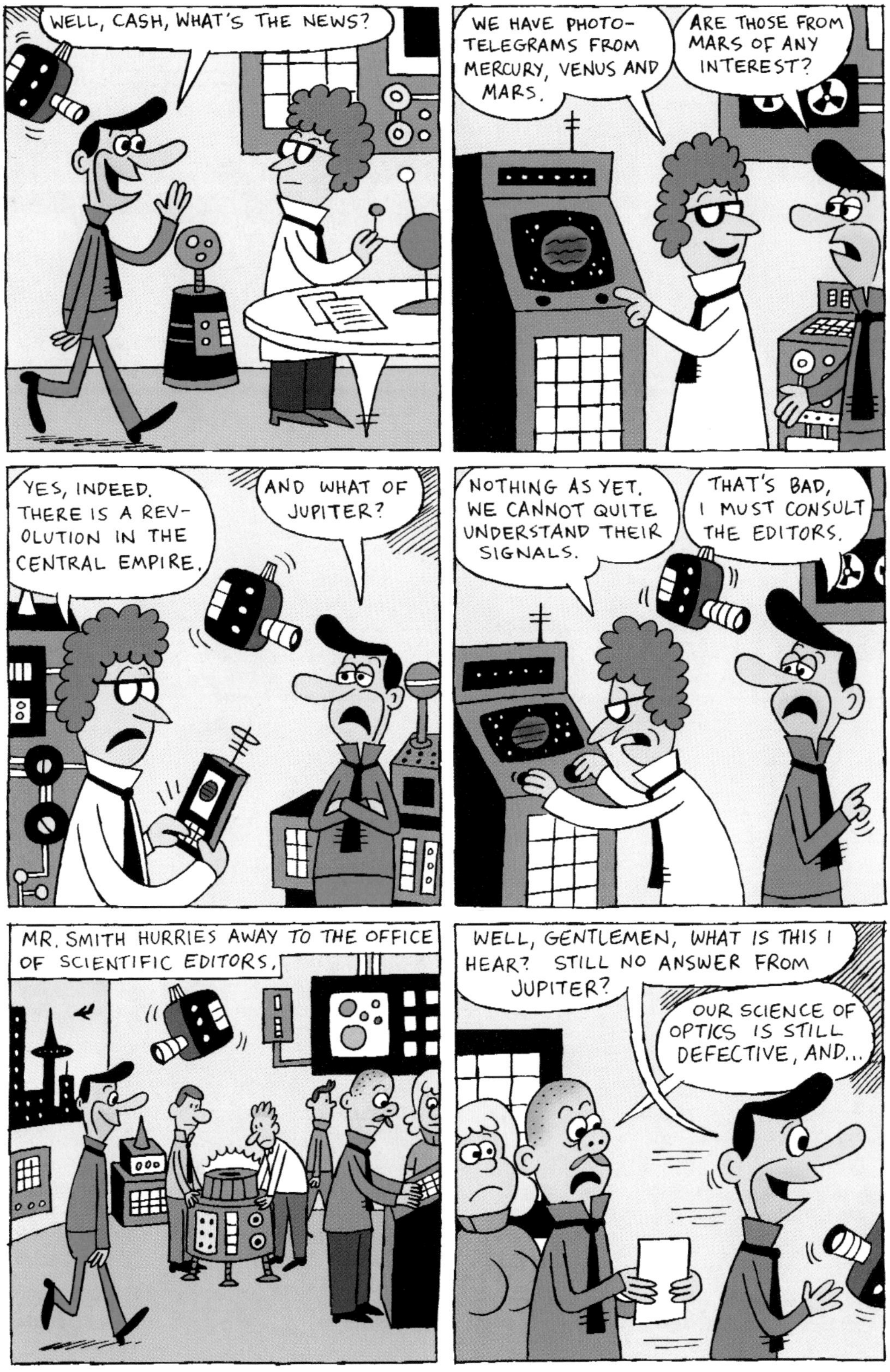
WELL, CASH, WHAT'S THE NEWS?
WE HAVE PHOTO-TELEGRAMS FROM MERCURY, VENUS AND MARS.
ARE THOSE FROM MARS OF ANY INTEREST?
YES, INDEED. THERE IS A REVOLUTION IN THE CENTRAL EMPIRE.
AND WHAT OF JUPITER?
NOTHING AS YET. WE CANNOT QUITE UNDERSTAND THEIR SIGNALS.
THAT'S BAD, I MUST CONSULT THE EDITORS.
MR. SMITH HURRIES AWAY TO THE OFFICE OF SCIENTIFIC EDITORS.
WELL, GENTLEMEN, WHAT IS THIS I HEAR? STILL NO ANSWER FROM JUPITER?
OUR SCIENCE OF OPTICS IS STILL DEFECTIVE, AND...

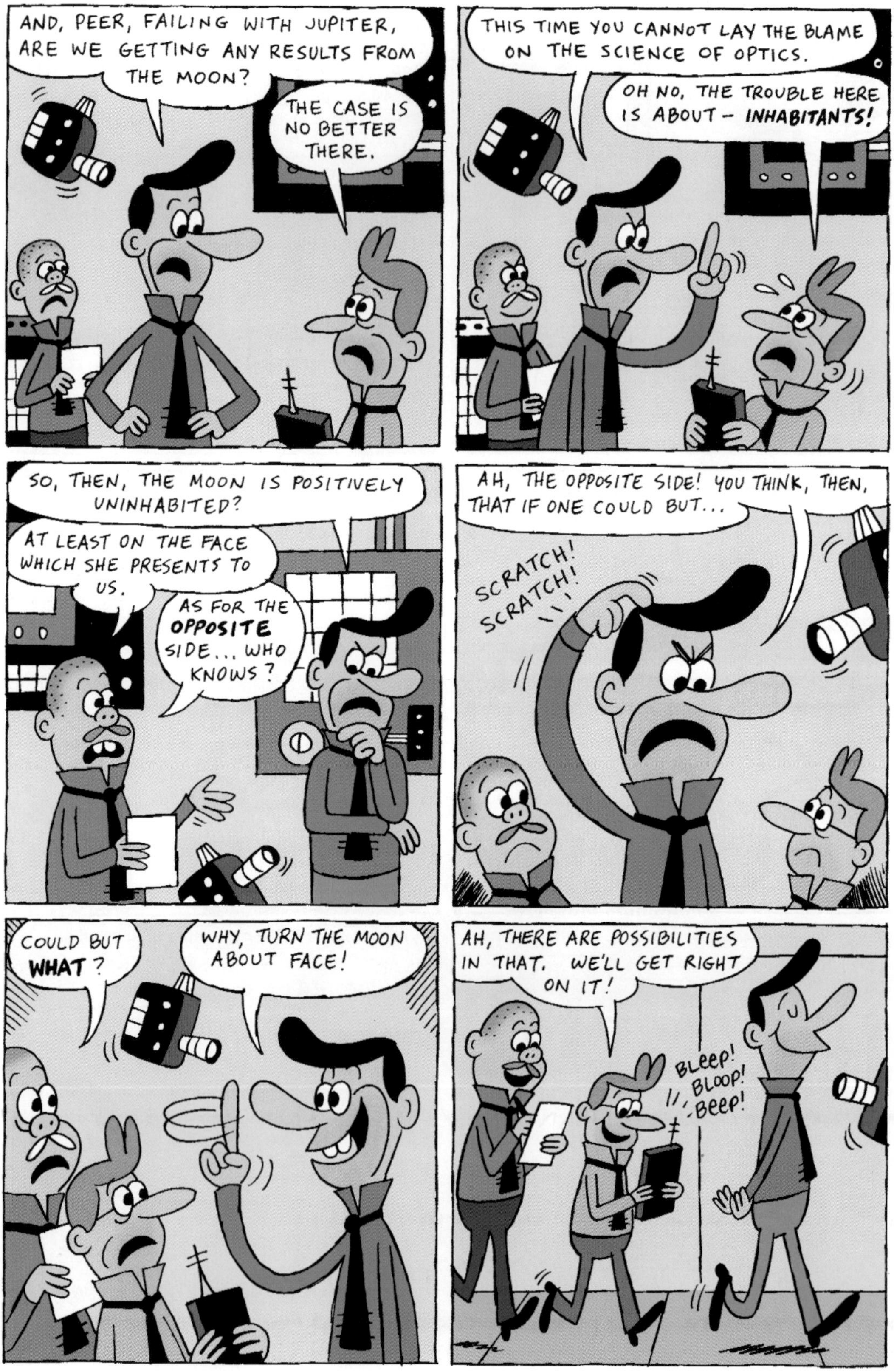
AND, PEER, FAILING WITH JUPITER, ARE WE GETTING ANY RESULTS FROM THE MOON?
THE CASE IS NO BETTER THERE.
THIS TIME YOU CANNOT LAY THE BLAME ON THE SCIENCE OF OPTICS.
OH NO, THE TROUBLE HERE IS ABOUT - **INHABITANTS!**
SO, THEN, THE MOON IS POSITIVELY UNINHABITED?
AT LEAST ON THE FACE WHICH SHE PRESENTS TO US.
AS FOR THE **OPPOSITE** SIDE... WHO KNOWS?
AH, THE OPPOSITE SIDE! YOU THINK, THEN, THAT IF ONE COULD BUT...
SCRATCH! SCRATCH!
COULD BUT **WHAT**?
WHY, TURN THE MOON ABOUT FACE!
AH, THERE ARE POSSIBILITIES IN THAT. WE'LL GET RIGHT ON IT!
BLEEP! BLOOP! BEEP!

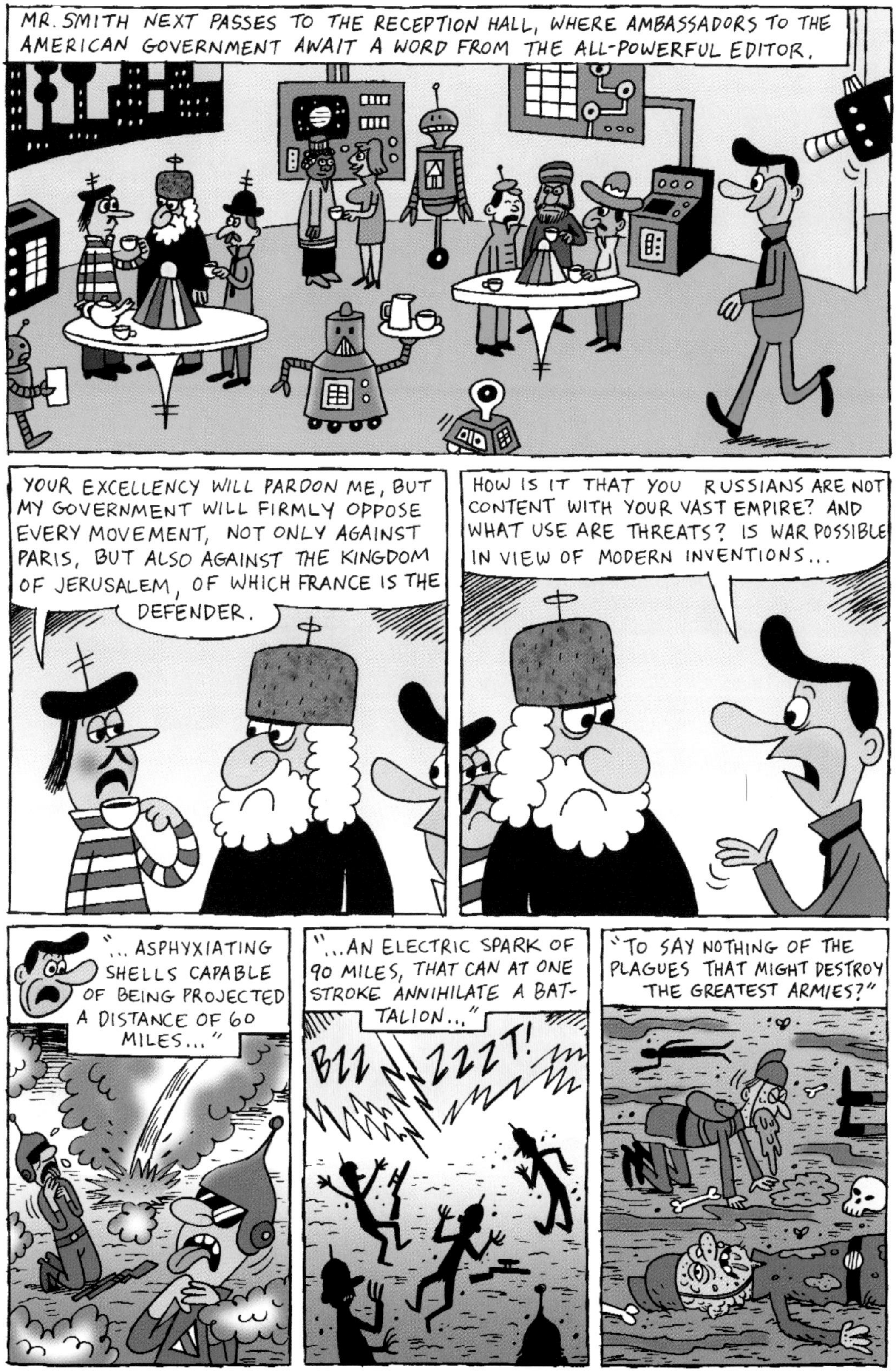
MR. SMITH NEXT PASSES TO THE RECEPTION HALL, WHERE AMBASSADORS TO THE AMERICAN GOVERNMENT AWAIT A WORD FROM THE ALL-POWERFUL EDITOR.
YOUR EXCELLENCY WILL PARDON ME, BUT MY GOVERNMENT WILL FIRMLY OPPOSE EVERY MOVEMENT, NOT ONLY AGAINST PARIS, BUT ALSO AGAINST THE KINGDOM OF JERUSALEM, OF WHICH FRANCE IS THE DEFENDER.
HOW IS IT THAT YOU RUSSIANS ARE NOT CONTENT WITH YOUR VAST EMPIRE? AND WHAT USE ARE THREATS? IS WAR POSSIBLE IN VIEW OF MODERN INVENTIONS...
"... ASPHYXIATING SHELLS CAPABLE OF BEING PROJECTED A DISTANCE OF 60 MILES..."
"...AN ELECTRIC SPARK OF 90 MILES, THAT CAN AT ONE STROKE ANNIHILATE A BATTALION..."
BZZ ZZZT!
"TO SAY NOTHING OF THE PLAGUES THAT MIGHT DESTROY THE GREATEST ARMIES?"

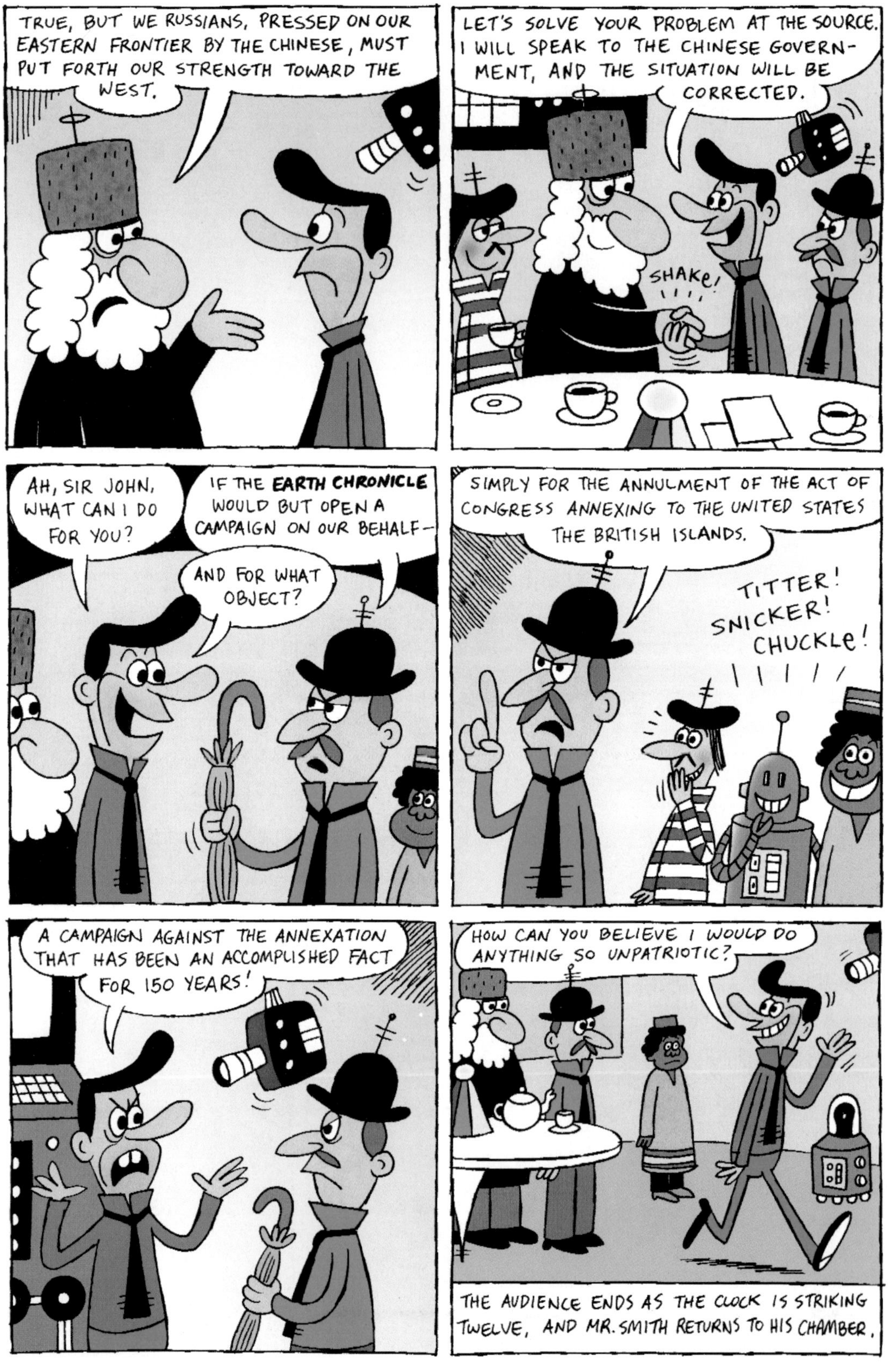
TRUE, BUT WE RUSSIANS, PRESSED ON OUR EASTERN FRONTIER BY THE CHINESE, MUST PUT FORTH OUR STRENGTH TOWARD THE WEST.
LET'S SOLVE YOUR PROBLEM AT THE SOURCE. I WILL SPEAK TO THE CHINESE GOVERNMENT, AND THE SITUATION WILL BE CORRECTED.
SHAKE!
AH, SIR JOHN, WHAT CAN I DO FOR YOU?
IF THE EARTH CHRONICLE WOULD BUT OPEN A CAMPAIGN ON OUR BEHALF—
AND FOR WHAT OBJECT?
SIMPLY FOR THE ANNULMENT OF THE ACT OF CONGRESS ANNEXING TO THE UNITED STATES THE BRITISH ISLANDS.
TITTER!
SNICKER!
CHUCKLE!
A CAMPAIGN AGAINST THE ANNEXATION THAT HAS BEEN AN ACCOMPLISHED FACT FOR 150 YEARS!
HOW CAN YOU BELIEVE I WOULD DO ANYTHING SO UNPATRIOTIC?
THE AUDIENCE ENDS AS THE CLOCK IS STRIKING TWELVE, AND MR. SMITH RETURNS TO HIS CHAMBER.

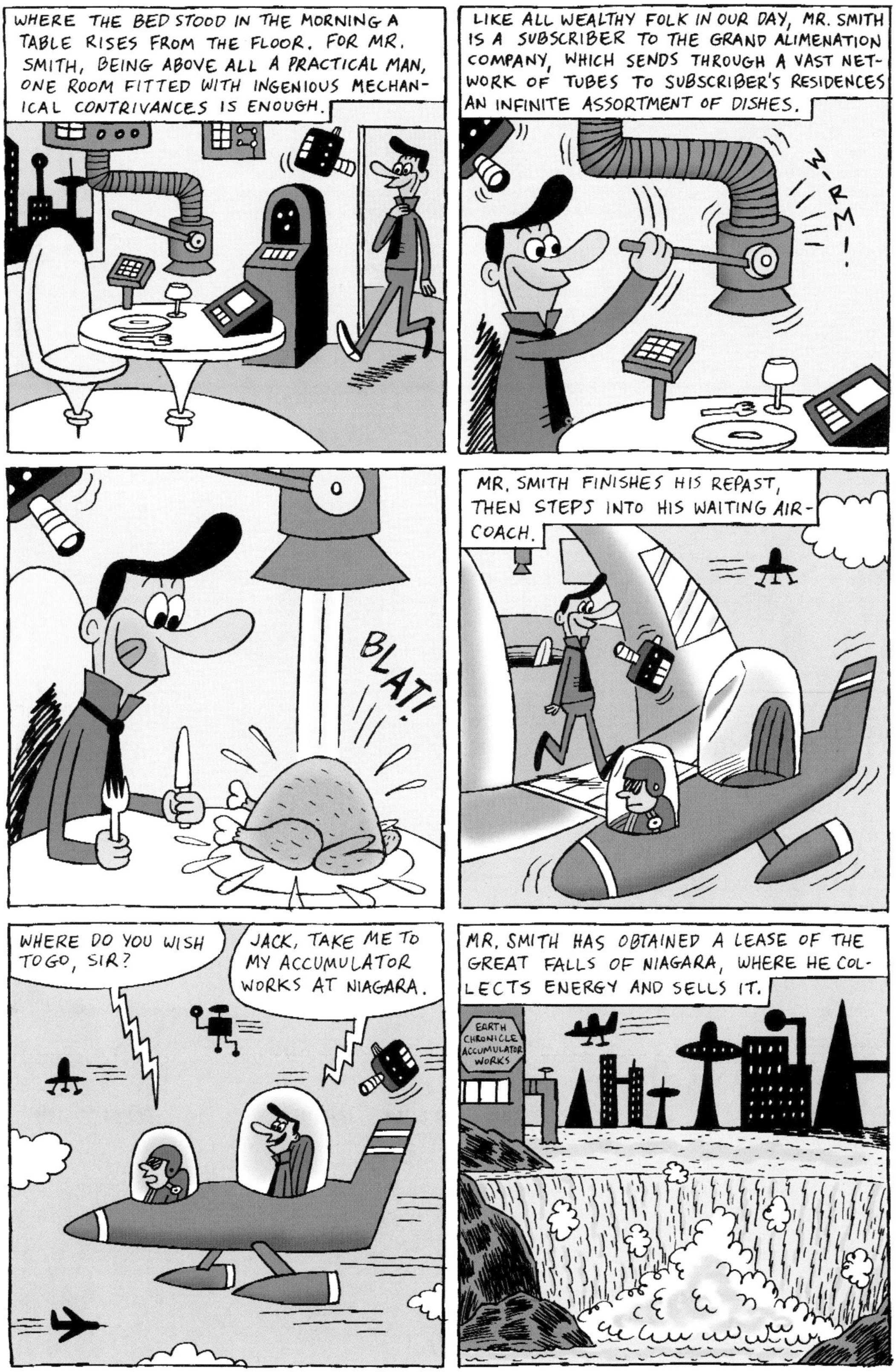
WHERE THE BED STOOD IN THE MORNING A TABLE RISES FROM THE FLOOR. FOR MR. SMITH, BEING ABOVE ALL A PRACTICAL MAN, ONE ROOM FITTED WITH INGENIOUS MECHANICAL CONTRIVANCES IS ENOUGH.
LIKE ALL WEALTHY FOLK IN OUR DAY, MR. SMITH IS A SUBSCRIBER TO THE GRAND ALIMENATION COMPANY, WHICH SENDS THROUGH A VAST NETWORK OF TUBES TO SUBSCRIBER'S RESIDENCES AN INFINITE ASSORTMENT OF DISHES.
W-R-M!
BLAT!
MR. SMITH FINISHES HIS REPAST, THEN STEPS INTO HIS WAITING AIR-COACH.
WHERE DO YOU WISH TO GO, SIR?
JACK, TAKE ME TO MY ACCUMULATOR WORKS AT NIAGARA.
MR. SMITH HAS OBTAINED A LEASE OF THE GREAT FALLS OF NIAGARA, WHERE HE COLLECTS ENERGY AND SELLS IT.
EARTH CHRONICLE ACCUMULATOR WORKS

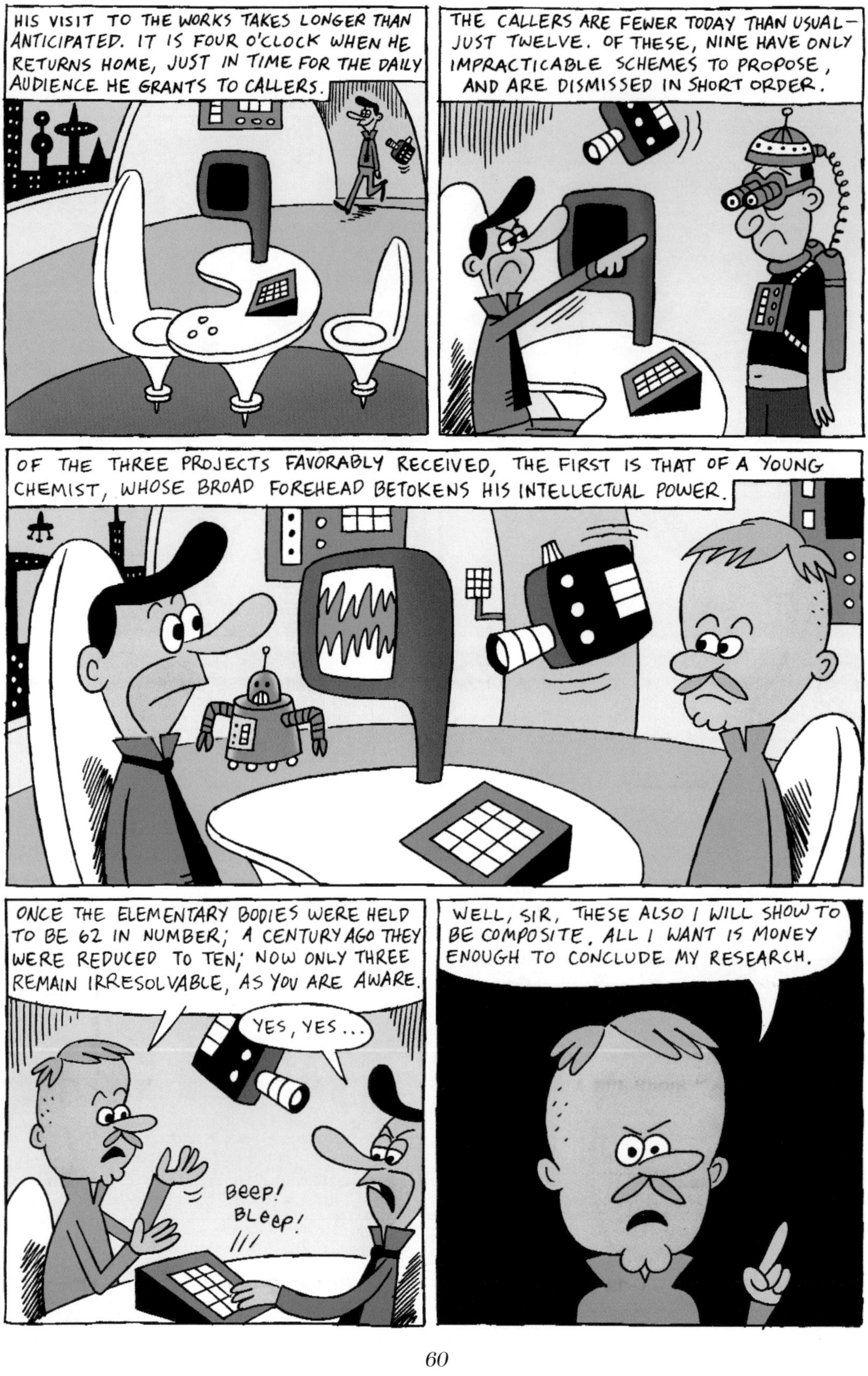
HIS VISIT TO THE WORKS TAKES LONGER THAN ANTICIPATED. IT IS FOUR O'CLOCK WHEN HE RETURNS HOME, JUST IN TIME FOR THE DAILY AUDIENCE HE GRANTS TO CALLERS.
THE CALLERS ARE FEWER TODAY THAN USUAL— JUST TWELVE. OF THESE, NINE HAVE ONLY IMPRACTICABLE SCHEMES TO PROPOSE, AND ARE DISMISSED IN SHORT ORDER.
OF THE THREE PROJECTS FAVORABLY RECEIVED, THE FIRST IS THAT OF A YOUNG CHEMIST, WHOSE BROAD FOREHEAD BETOKENS HIS INTELLECTUAL POWER.
ONCE THE ELEMENTARY BODIES WERE HELD TO BE 62 IN NUMBER; A CENTURY AGO THEY WERE REDUCED TO TEN; NOW ONLY THREE REMAIN IRRESOLVABLE, AS YOU ARE AWARE.
YES, YES...
BEEP! BLEEP!
WELL, SIR, THESE ALSO I WILL SHOW TO BE COMPOSITE. ALL I WANT IS MONEY ENOUGH TO CONCLUDE MY RESEARCH.

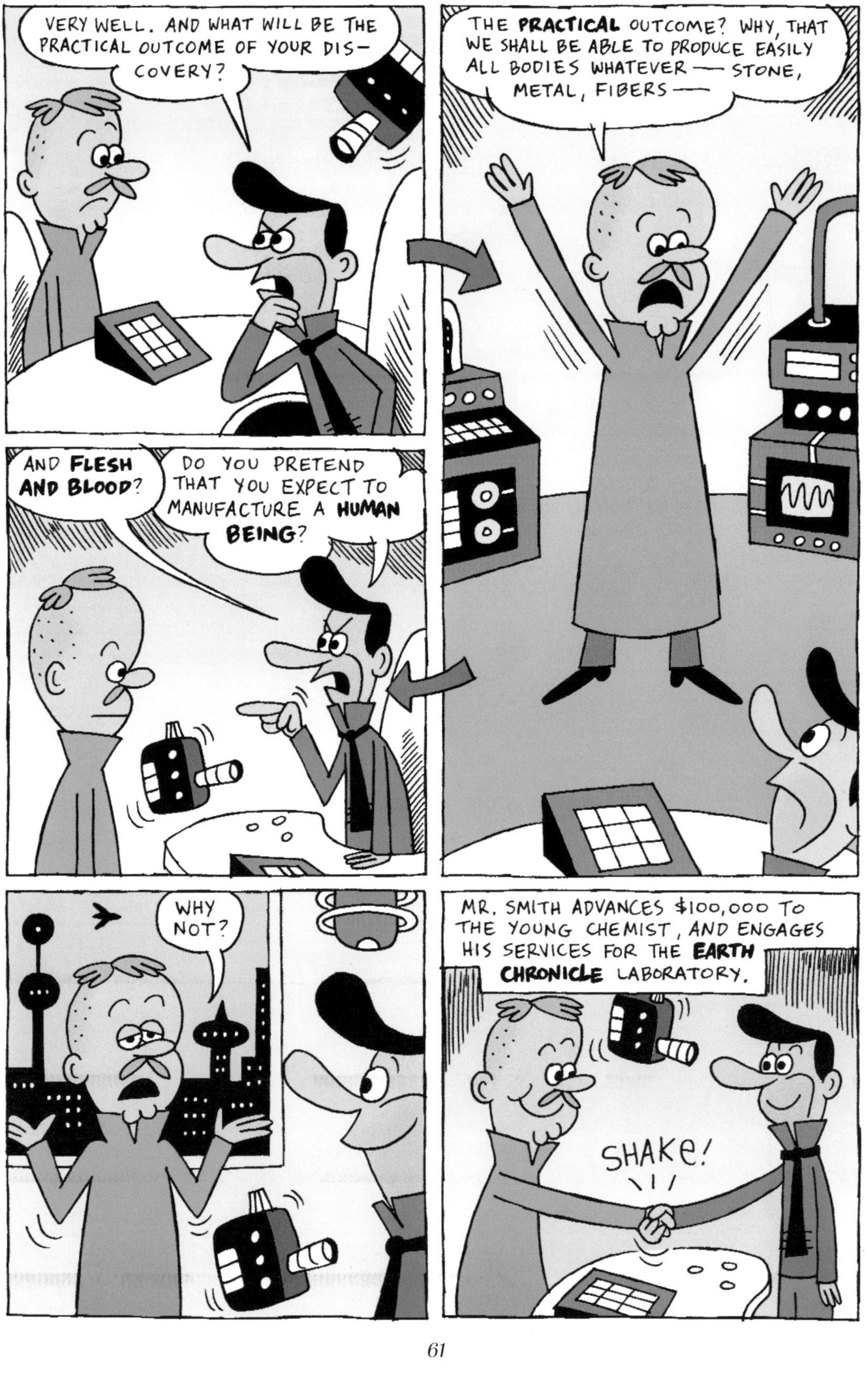
VERY WELL. AND WHAT WILL BE THE PRACTICAL OUTCOME OF YOUR DISCOVERY?
THE PRACTICAL OUTCOME? WHY, THAT WE SHALL BE ABLE TO PRODUCE EASILY ALL BODIES WHATEVER — STONE, METAL, FIBERS —
AND FLESH AND BLOOD?
DO YOU PRETEND THAT YOU EXPECT TO MANUFACTURE A HUMAN BEING?
WHY NOT?
MR. SMITH ADVANCES $100,000 TO THE YOUNG CHEMIST, AND ENGAGES HIS SERVICES FOR THE EARTH CHRONICLE LABORATORY.
SHAKE!

THE SECOND APPLICANT HAS CONCEIVED THE IDEA OF MOVING AN ENTIRE CITY FROM ONE PLACE TO ANOTHER. HIS PARTICULAR INTEREST IS THE CITY OF GRANTON, SOME 15 MILES INLAND...

HE PROPOSES TRANSPORTING THE CITY ON RAILS, AND TURNING IT INTO A BEACHFRONT RESORT. THE PROFIT, OF COURSE, WOULD BE ENORMOUS. MR. SMITH BUYS A HALF-INTEREST IN THE SCHEME.

FINALLY, THE LAST APPLICANT, PROFESSOR DRAKE, ANNOUNCES THE IMMINENT SOLUTION OF A WEIGHTY SCIENTIFIC PROBLEM. EVERYONE REMEMBERS THE BOLD EXPERIMENT MADE 100 YEARS AGO BY DR. NATHANIEL FAITHBURN.

THE DOCTOR, BEING A BELIEVER IN THE POSSIBILITY OF HUMAN HIBERNATION, RESOLVED TO SUBJECT THE THEORY TO A PRACTICAL TEST.

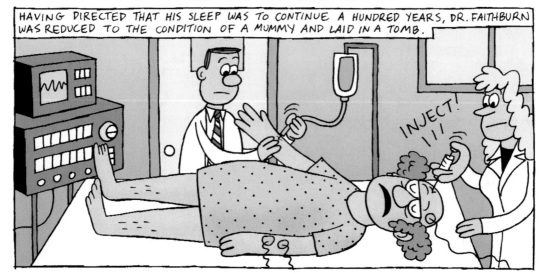

HAVING DIRECTED THAT HIS SLEEP WAS TO CONTINUE A HUNDRED YEARS, DR. FAITHBURN WAS REDUCED TO THE CONDITION OF A MUMMY AND LAID IN A TOMB.

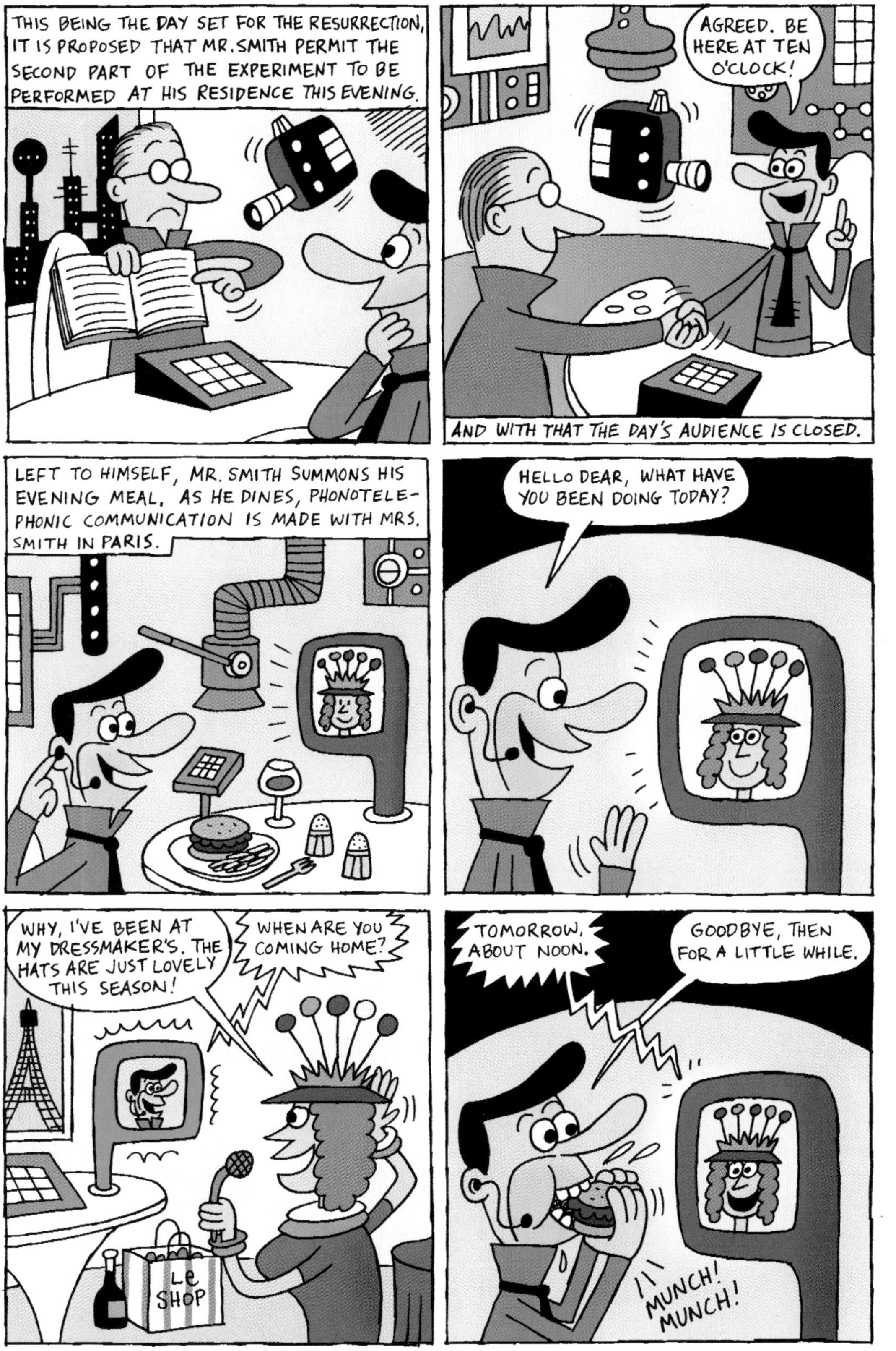
THIS BEING THE DAY SET FOR THE RESURRECTION, IT IS PROPOSED THAT MR. SMITH PERMIT THE SECOND PART OF THE EXPERIMENT TO BE PERFORMED AT HIS RESIDENCE THIS EVENING.
AGREED. BE HERE AT TEN O'CLOCK!
AND WITH THAT THE DAY'S AUDIENCE IS CLOSED.
LEFT TO HIMSELF, MR. SMITH SUMMONS HIS EVENING MEAL. AS HE DINES, PHONOTELEPHONIC COMMUNICATION IS MADE WITH MRS. SMITH IN PARIS.
HELLO DEAR, WHAT HAVE YOU BEEN DOING TODAY?
WHY, I'VE BEEN AT MY DRESSMAKER'S. THE HATS ARE JUST LOVELY THIS SEASON!
WHEN ARE YOU COMING HOME?
LE SHOP
TOMORROW, ABOUT NOON.
GOODBYE, THEN FOR A LITTLE WHILE.
MUNCH! MUNCH!

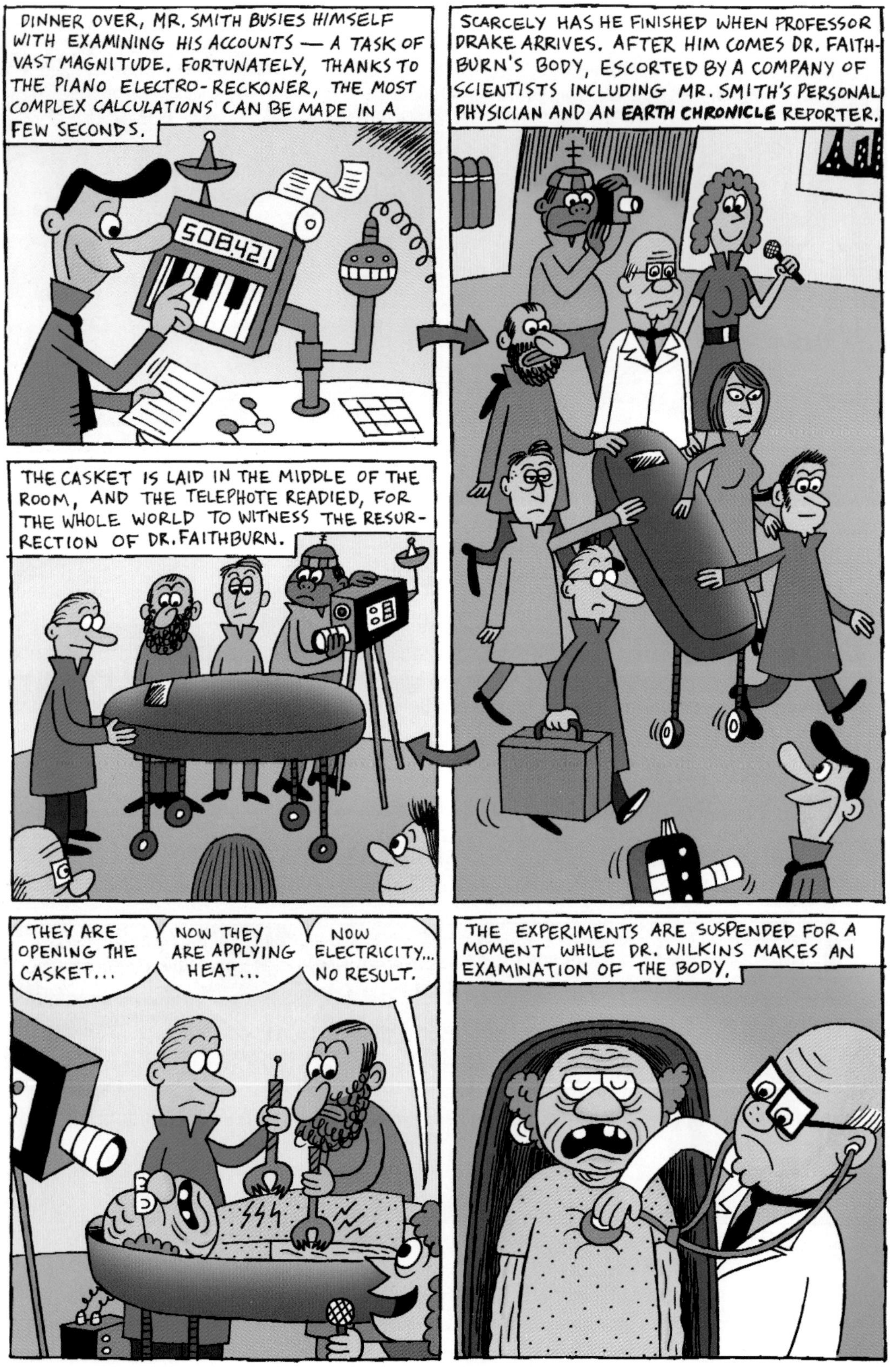
DINNER OVER, MR. SMITH BUSIES HIMSELF WITH EXAMINING HIS ACCOUNTS — A TASK OF VAST MAGNITUDE. FORTUNATELY, THANKS TO THE PIANO ELECTRO-RECKONER, THE MOST COMPLEX CALCULATIONS CAN BE MADE IN A FEW SECONDS.
508.421
SCARCELY HAS HE FINISHED WHEN PROFESSOR DRAKE ARRIVES. AFTER HIM COMES DR. FAITHBURN'S BODY, ESCORTED BY A COMPANY OF SCIENTISTS INCLUDING MR. SMITH'S PERSONAL PHYSICIAN AND AN EARTH CHRONICLE REPORTER.
THE CASKET IS LAID IN THE MIDDLE OF THE ROOM, AND THE TELEPHOTE READIED, FOR THE WHOLE WORLD TO WITNESS THE RESURRECTION OF DR. FAITHBURN.
THEY ARE OPENING THE CASKET...
NOW THEY ARE APPLYING HEAT...
NOW ELECTRICITY... NO RESULT.
THE EXPERIMENTS ARE SUSPENDED FOR A MOMENT WHILE DR. WILKINS MAKES AN EXAMINATION OF THE BODY.

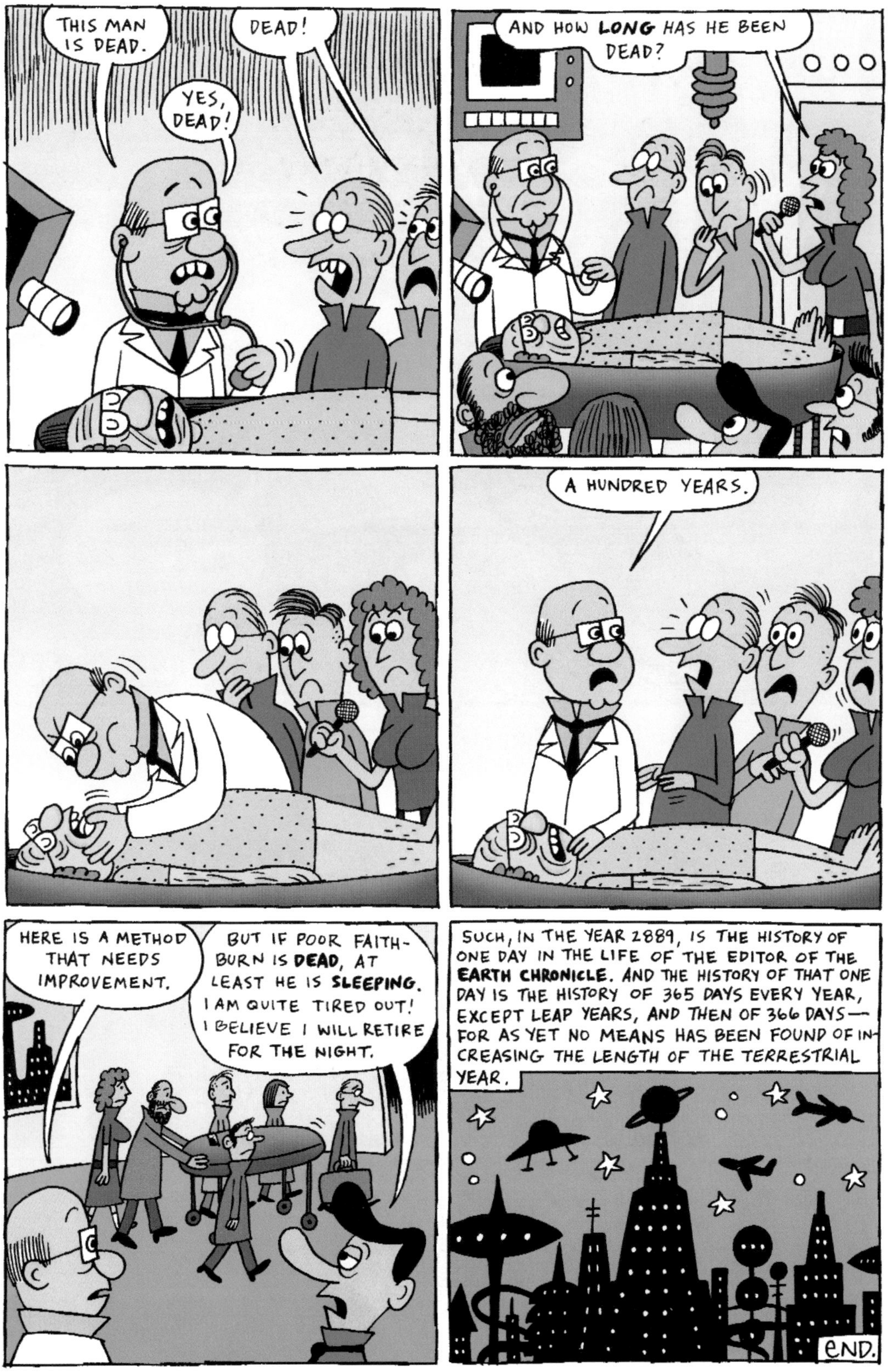
THIS MAN IS DEAD.
YES, DEAD!
DEAD!
AND HOW LONG HAS HE BEEN DEAD?
A HUNDRED YEARS.
HERE IS A METHOD THAT NEEDS IMPROVEMENT.
BUT IF POOR FAITHBURN IS DEAD, AT LEAST HE IS SLEEPING. I AM QUITE TIRED OUT! I BELIEVE I WILL RETIRE FOR THE NIGHT.
SUCH, IN THE YEAR 2889, IS THE HISTORY OF ONE DAY IN THE LIFE OF THE EDITOR OF THE EARTH CHRONICLE. AND THE HISTORY OF THAT ONE DAY IS THE HISTORY OF 365 DAYS EVERY YEAR, EXCEPT LEAP YEARS, AND THEN OF 366 DAYS— FOR AS YET NO MEANS HAS BEEN FOUND OF INCREASING THE LENGTH OF THE TERRESTRIAL YEAR.
END.

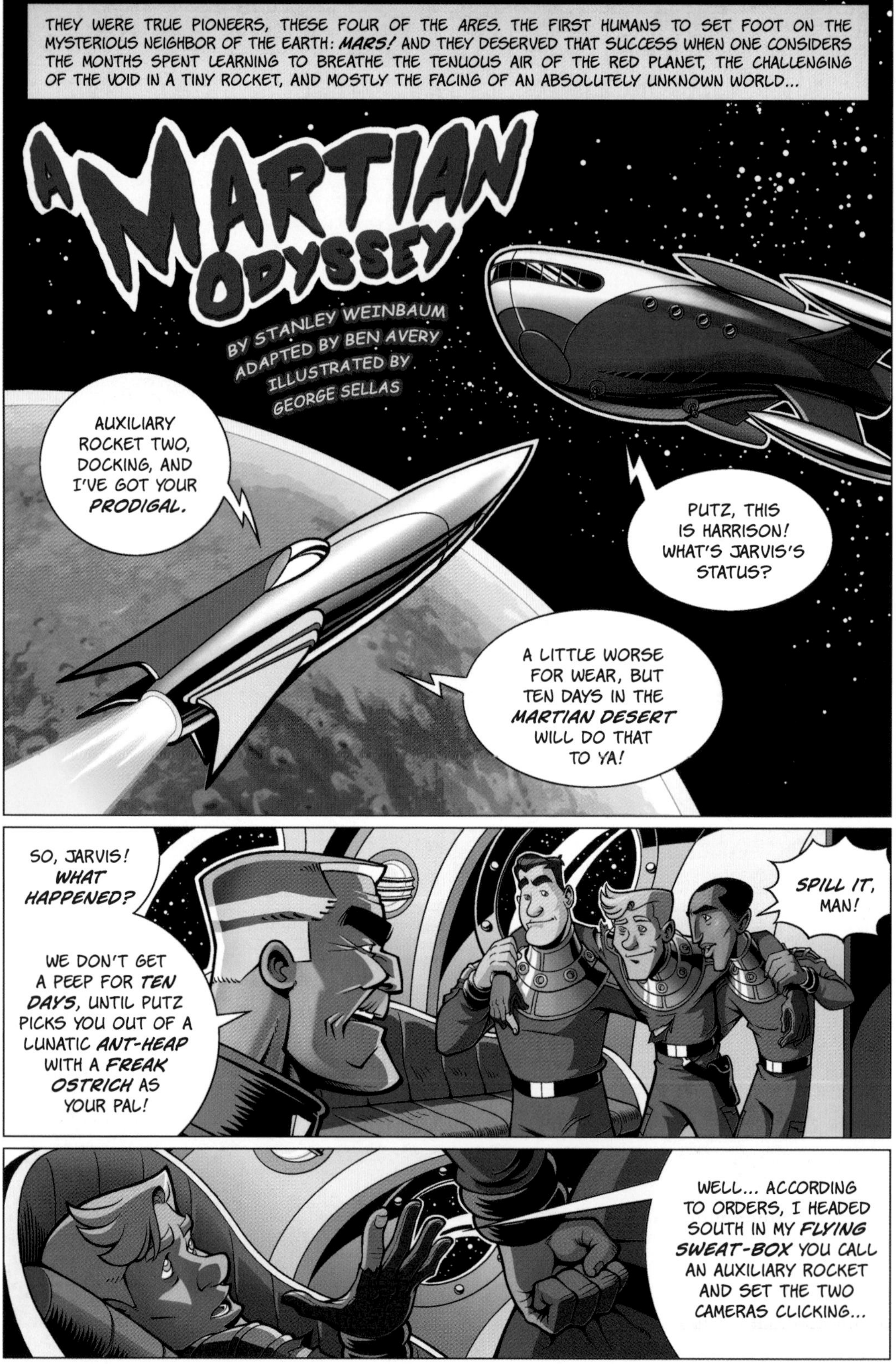
THEY WERE TRUE PIONEERS, THESE FOUR OF THE ARES. THE FIRST HUMANS TO SET FOOT ON THE MYSTERIOUS NEIGHBOR OF THE EARTH: MARS! AND THEY DESERVED THAT SUCCESS WHEN ONE CONSIDERS THE MONTHS SPENT LEARNING TO BREATHE THE TENUOUS AIR OF THE RED PLANET, THE CHALLENGING OF THE VOID IN A TINY ROCKET, AND MOSTLY THE FACING OF AN ABSOLUTELY UNKNOWN WORLD...
A MARTIAN ODYSSEY
BY STANLEY WEINBAUM
ADAPTED BY BEN AVERY
ILLUSTRATED BY GEORGE SELLAS
AUXILIARY ROCKET TWO, DOCKING, AND I'VE GOT YOUR PRODIGAL.
PUTZ, THIS IS HARRISON! WHAT'S JARVIS'S STATUS?
A LITTLE WORSE FOR WEAR, BUT TEN DAYS IN THE MARTIAN DESERT WILL DO THAT TO YA!
SO, JARVIS! WHAT HAPPENED?
WE DON'T GET A PEEP FOR TEN DAYS, UNTIL PUTZ PICKS YOU OUT OF A LUNATIC ANT-HEAP WITH A FREAK OSTRICH AS YOUR PAL!
SPILL IT, MAN!
WELL... ACCORDING TO ORDERS, I HEADED SOUTH IN MY FLYING SWEAT-BOX YOU CALL AN AUXILIARY ROCKET AND SET THE TWO CAMERAS CLICKING...

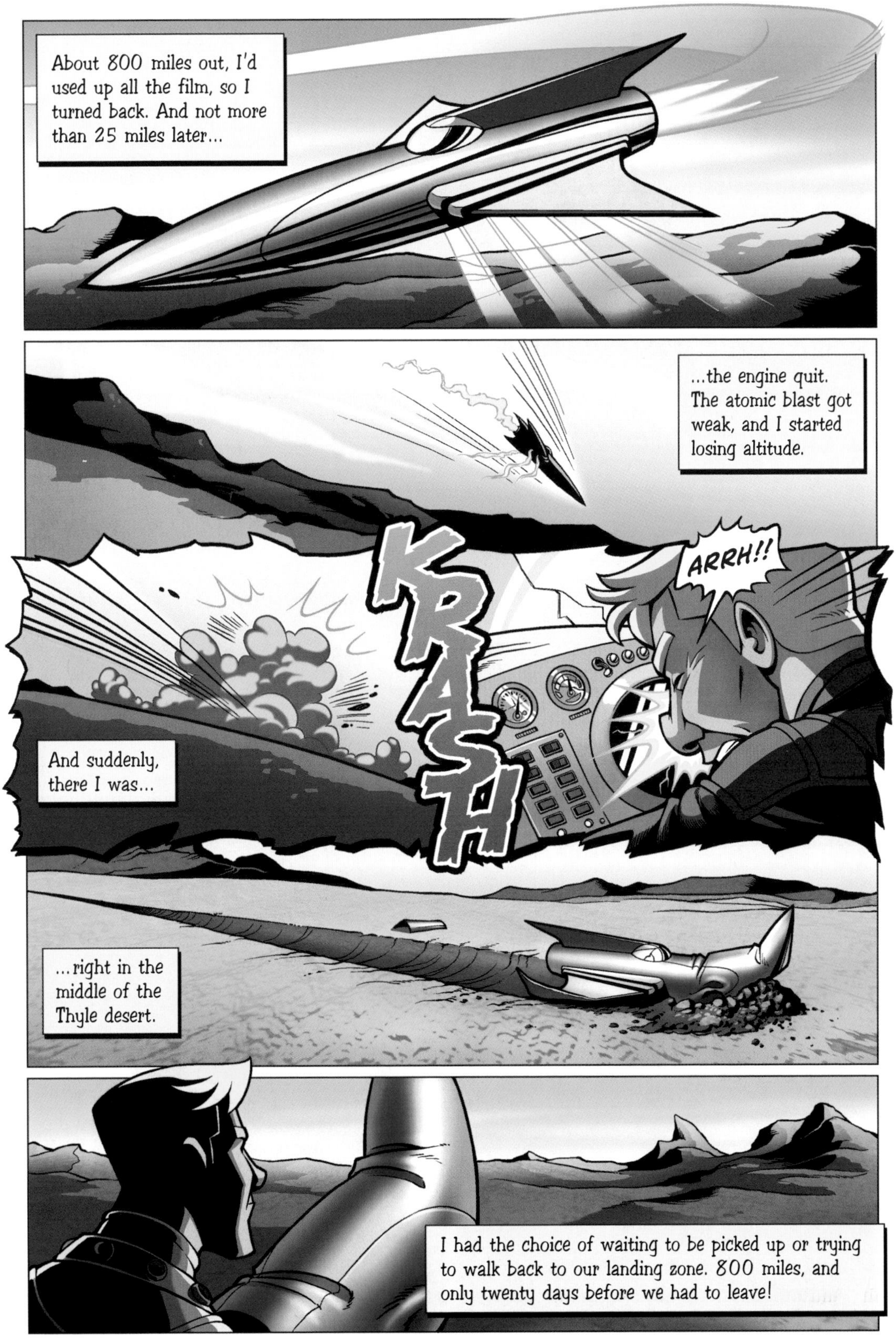
About 800 miles out, I'd used up all the film, so I turned back. And not more than 25 miles later...
...the engine quit. The atomic blast got weak, and I started losing altitude.
KRASH
ARRH!!
And suddenly, there I was...
...right in the middle of the Thyle desert.
I had the choice of waiting to be picked up or trying to walk back to our landing zone. 800 miles, and only twenty days before we had to leave!

I chose to walk. Just as much chance of being picked up, and it kept me busy.

The tank was 250 pounds earthweight. 85 here. At least, that's what I figured when I undertook the forty-mile daily stroll!

I rigged up a harness from some seat straps, put the water tank on my back, took a revolver and supplies, and started out.

I plugged along, cussing the sand that made the going so tiresome—

—cussing that cranky motor.

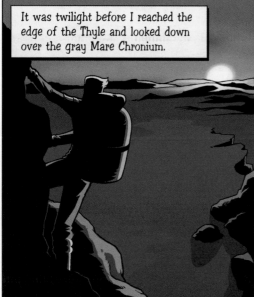

It was twilight before I reached the edge of the Thyle and looked down over the gray Mare Chronium.

75 miles of Mare Chronium lay ahead of me, followed by a couple hundred miles of that Xanthus desert, and about as much more Mare Cimmerium!

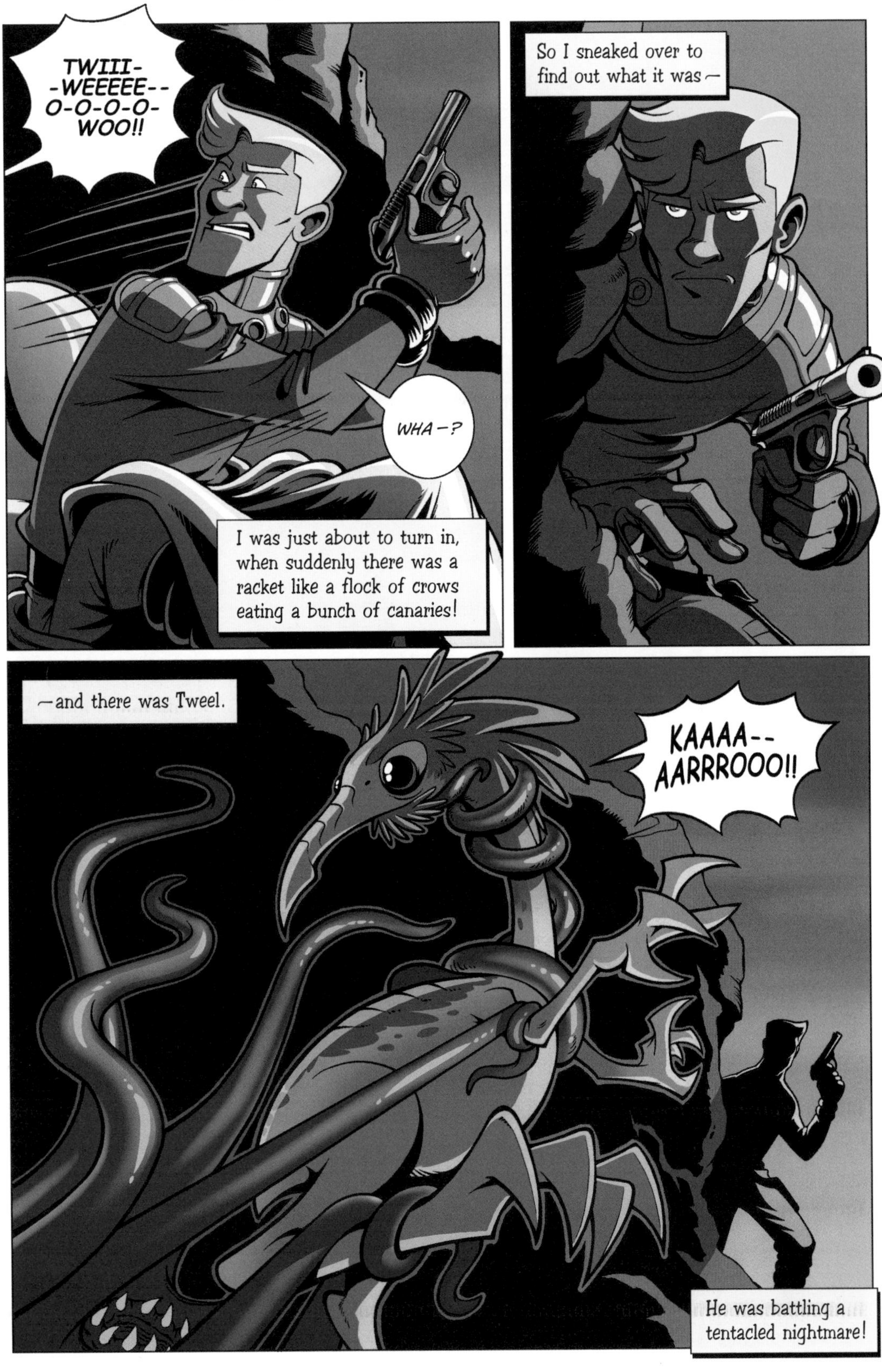
TWIII- -WEEEEE-- O-O-O-O- WOO!!
WHA-?
I was just about to turn in, when suddenly there was a racket like a flock of crows eating a bunch of canaries!
So I sneaked over to find out what it was—
—and there was Tweel.
KAAAA-- AARRROOO!!
He was battling a tentacled nightmare!

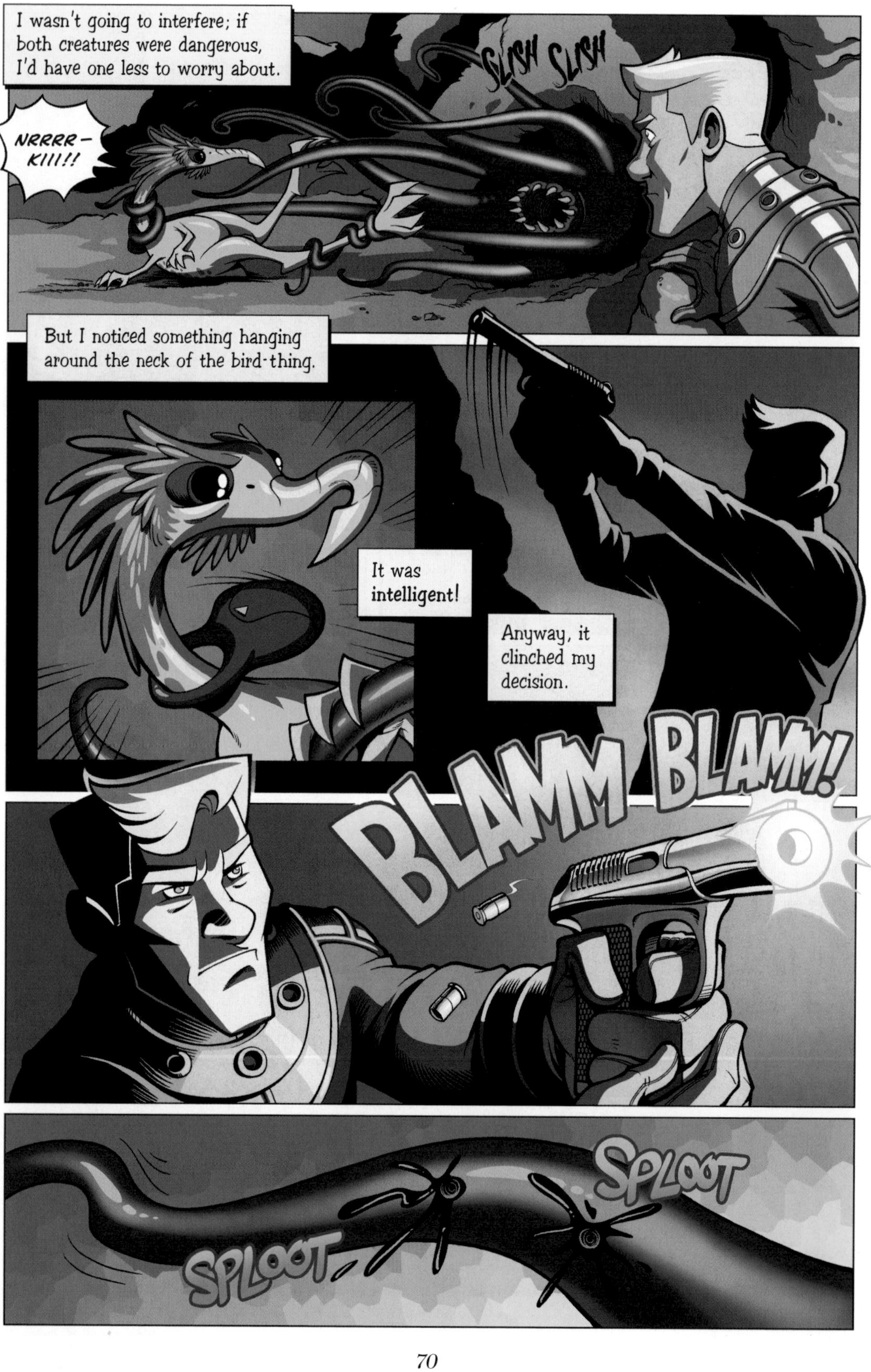
I wasn't going to interfere; if both creatures were dangerous, I'd have one less to worry about.
SLISH SLISH
NRRRR-KIII!!
But I noticed something hanging around the neck of the bird-thing.
It was intelligent!
Anyway, it clinched my decision.
BLAMM BLAMM!
SPLOOT
SPLOOT

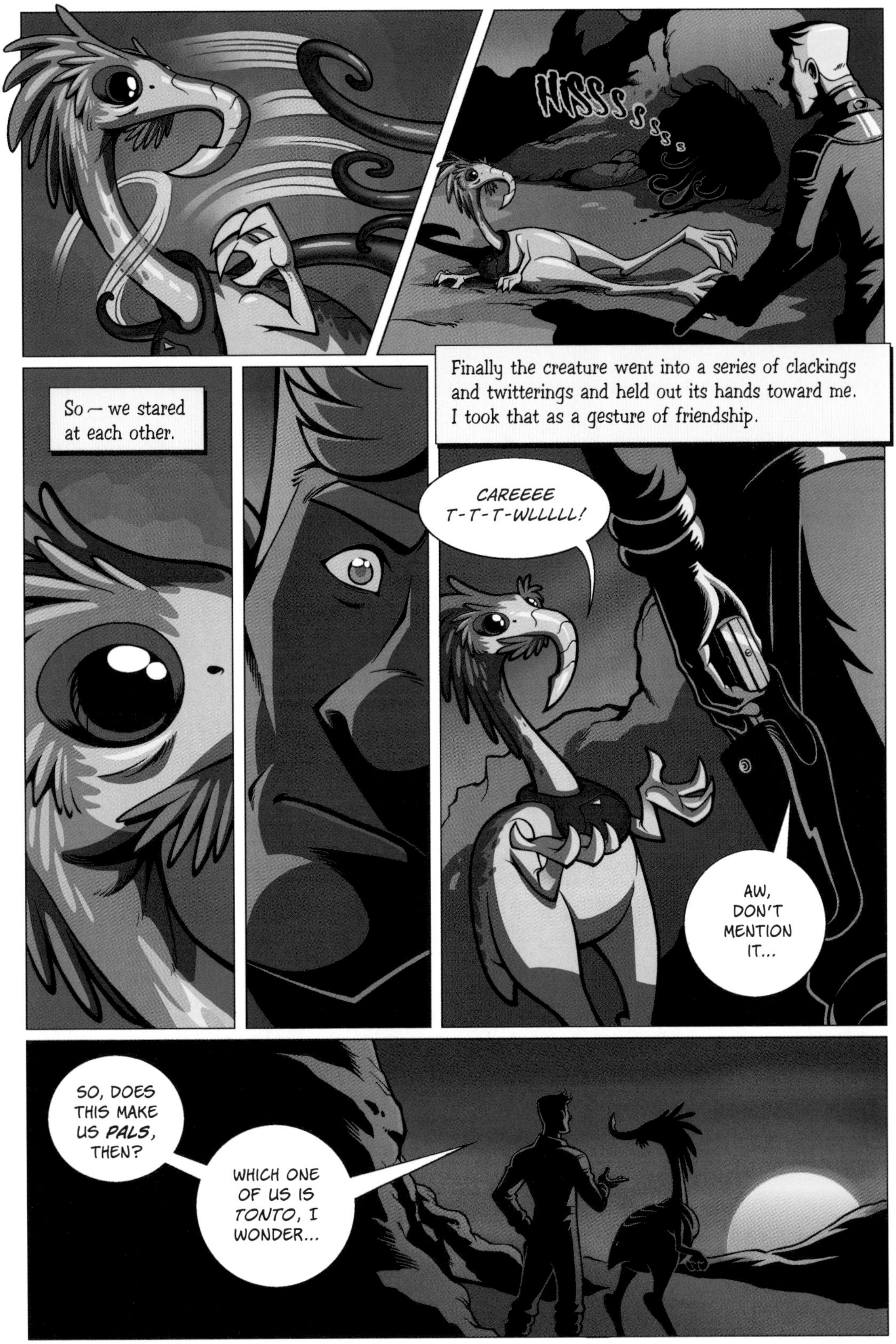
HISSSSSSS
So — we stared at each other.
Finally the creature went into a series of clackings and twitterings and held out its hands toward me. I took that as a gesture of friendship.
CAREEEE T-T-T-WLLLLL!
AW, DON'T MENTION IT...
SO, DOES THIS MAKE US *PALS*, THEN?
WHICH ONE OF US IS *TONTO*, I WONDER...

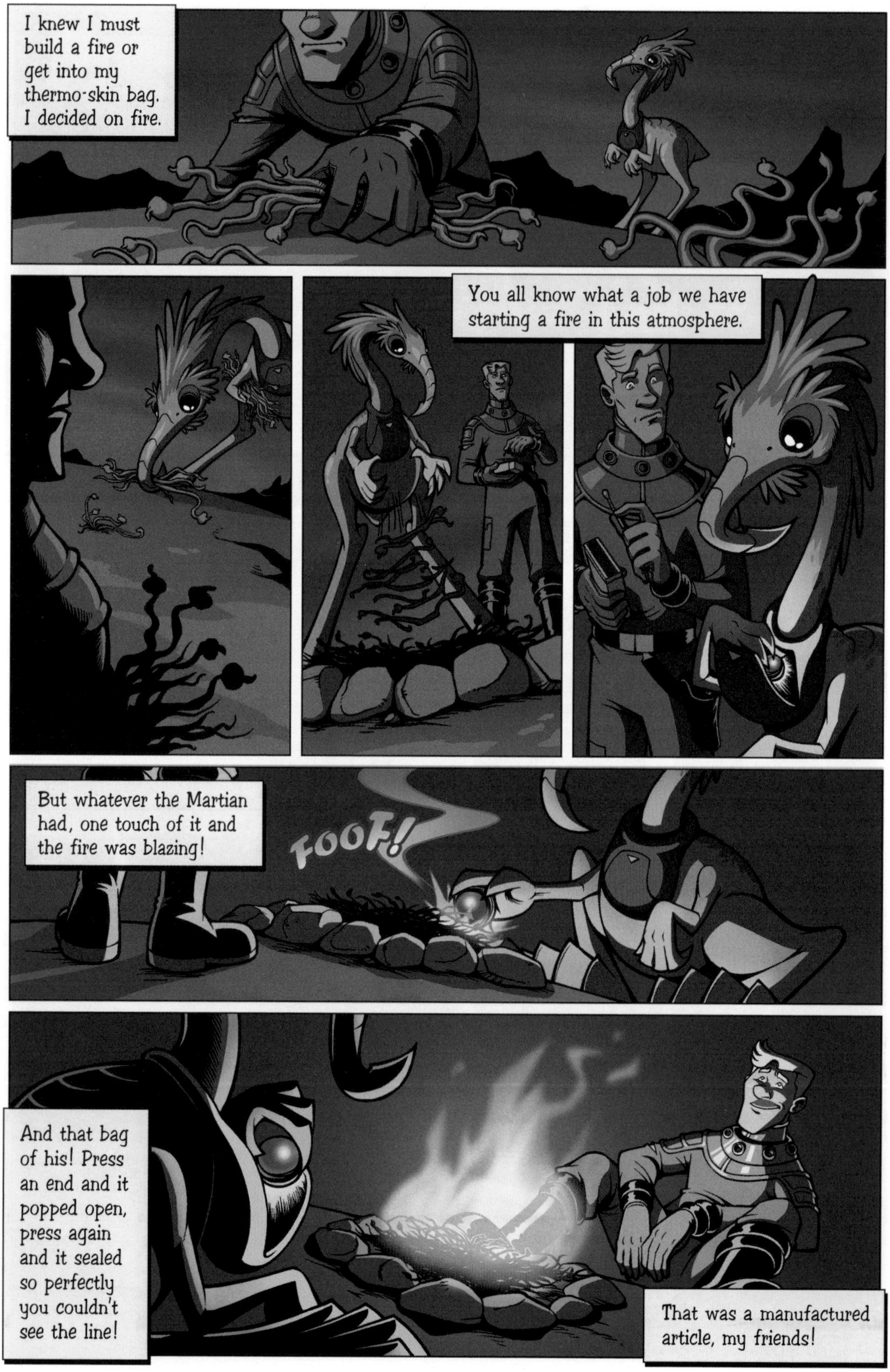
I knew I must build a fire or get into my thermo-skin bag. I decided on fire.
You all know what a job we have starting a fire in this atmosphere.
But whatever the Martian had, one touch of it and the fire was blazing!
FOOF!
And that bag of his! Press an end and it popped open, press again and it sealed so perfectly you couldn't see the line!
That was a manufactured article, my friends!

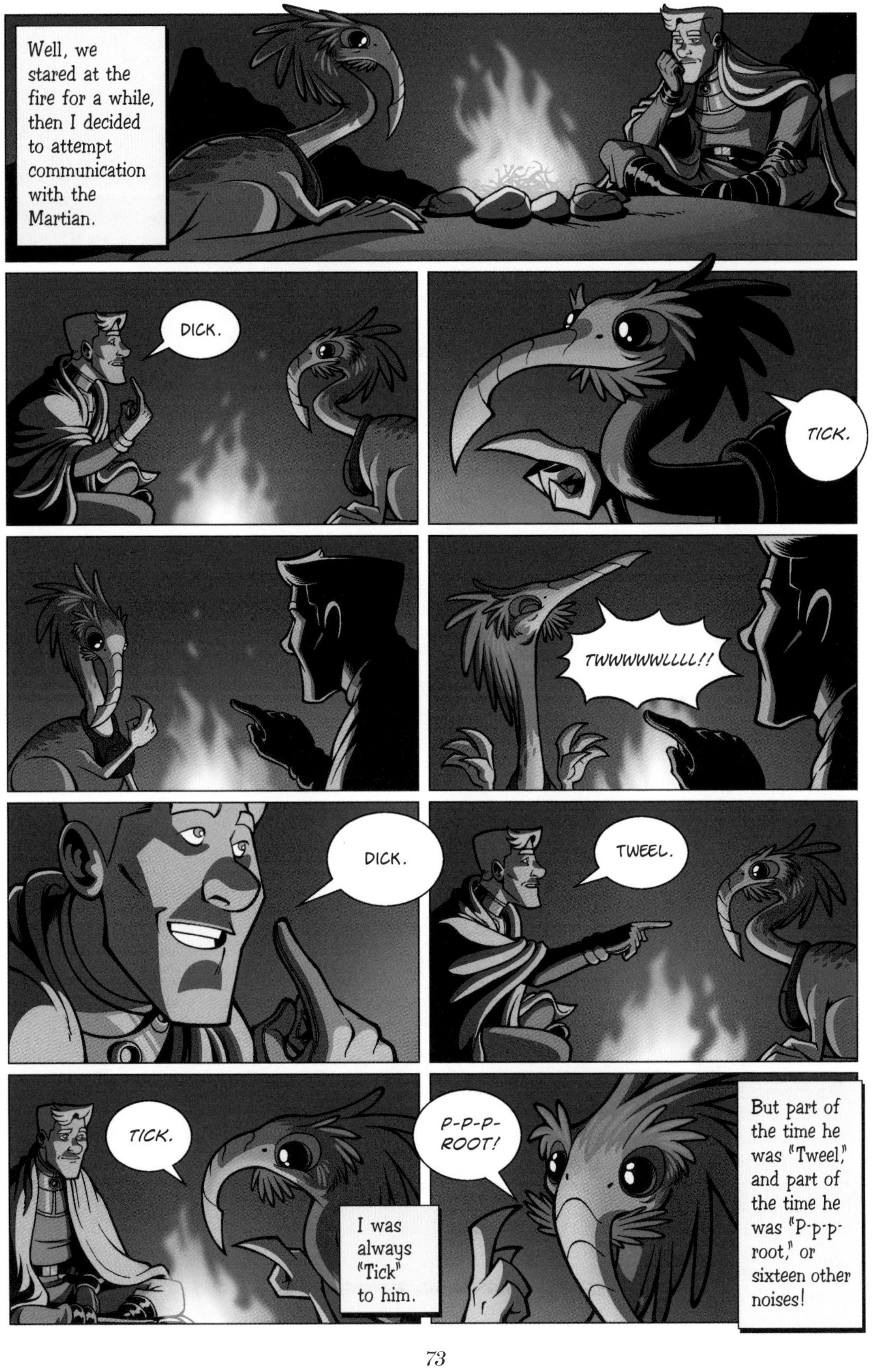

Well, we stared at the fire for a while, then I decided to attempt communication with the Martian.
DICK.
TICK.
TWWWWWLLLL!!
DICK.
TWEEL.
TICK.
I was always "Tick" to him.
P-P-P-ROOT!
But part of the time he was "Tweel," and part of the time he was "P-p-p-root," or sixteen other noises!

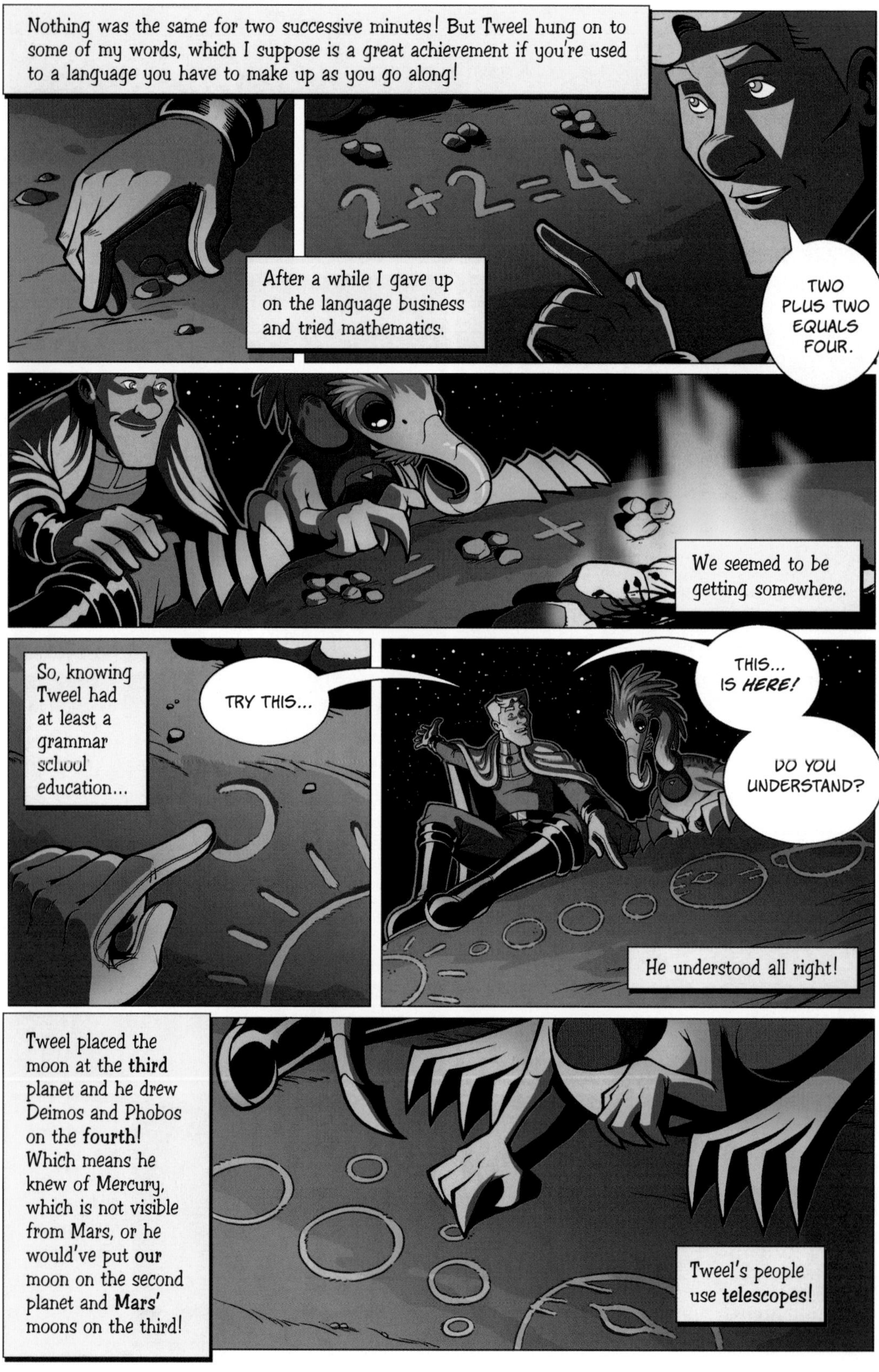
Nothing was the same for two successive minutes! But Tweel hung on to some of my words, which I suppose is a great achievement if you're used to a language you have to make up as you go along!
2+2=4
After a while I gave up on the language business and tried mathematics.
TWO PLUS TWO EQUALS FOUR.
We seemed to be getting somewhere.
So, knowing Tweel had at least a grammar school education...
TRY THIS...
THIS... IS ***HERE!***
DO YOU UNDERSTAND?
He understood all right!
Tweel placed the moon at the **third** planet and he drew Deimos and Phobos on the **fourth**! Which means he knew of Mercury, which is not visible from Mars, or he would've put **our** moon on the second planet and **Mars'** moons on the third!
Tweel's people use **telescopes**!

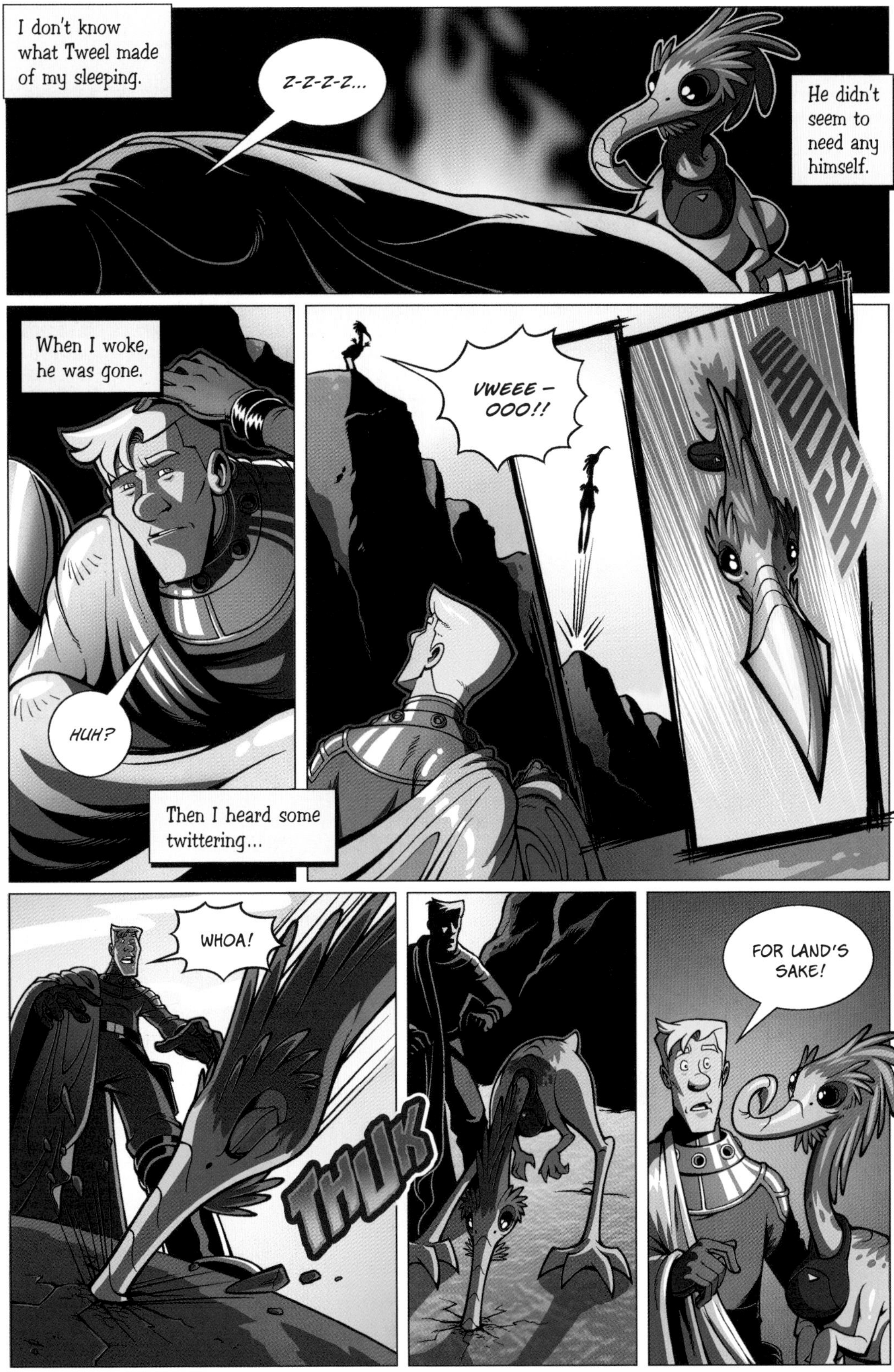
I don't know what Tweel made of my sleeping.
Z-Z-Z-Z...
He didn't seem to need any himself.
When I woke, he was gone.
HUH?
Then I heard some twittering...
VWEEE-OOO!!
WHOOSH
WHOA!
THUK
FOR LAND'S SAKE!

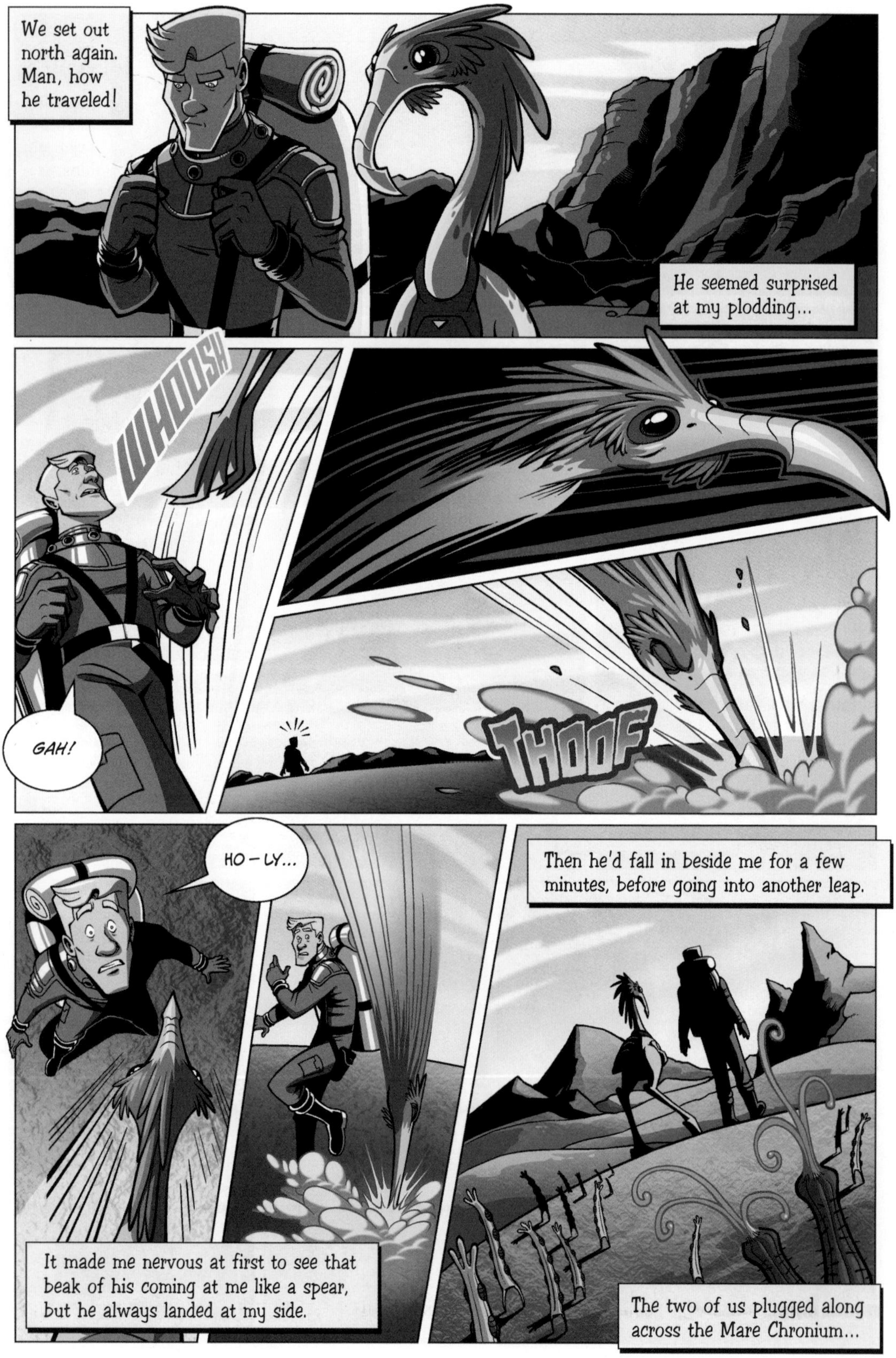
We set out north again. Man, how he traveled!
He seemed surprised at my plodding...
WHOOSH
GAH!
THOOF
HO-LY...
Then he'd fall in beside me for a few minutes, before going into another leap.
It made me nervous at first to see that beak of his coming at me like a spear, but he always landed at my side.
The two of us plugged along across the Mare Chronium...

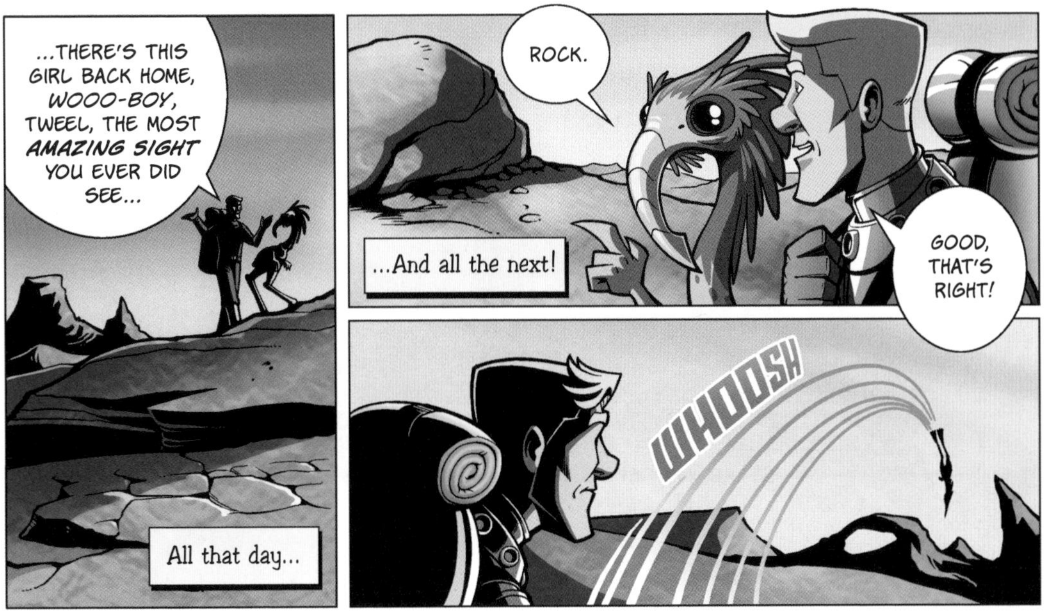
...THERE'S THIS GIRL BACK HOME, WOOO-BOY, TWEEL, THE MOST AMAZING SIGHT YOU EVER DID SEE...
All that day...
ROCK.
...And all the next!
GOOD, THAT'S RIGHT!
WHOOSH

I was fair worn out by the end of that march, but Tweel seemed as fresh as ever! I think he could've crossed the Mare Chronium in a couple hours with those nosedives of his, but he stuck along with me.

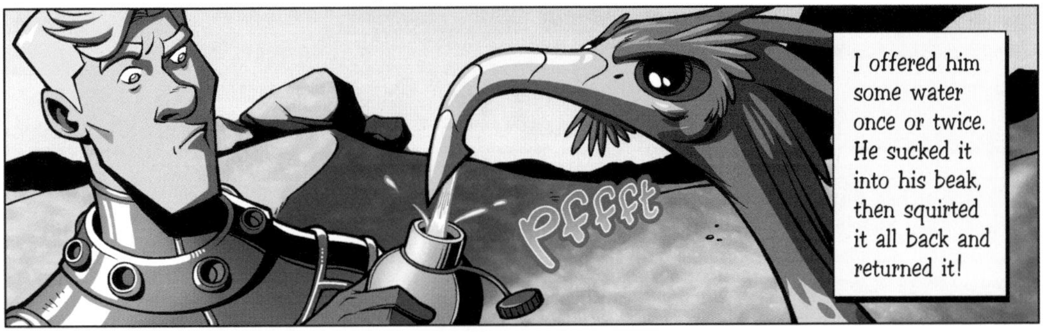
I offered him some water once or twice. He sucked it into his beak, then squirted it all back and returned it!
PFFFT

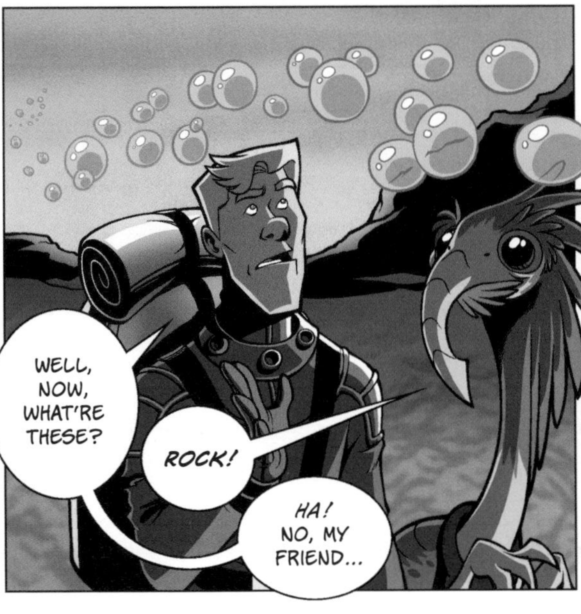
WELL, NOW, WHAT'RE THESE?
ROCK!
HA! NO, MY FRIEND...

We came to the bottom of the Xanthus cliffs. I decided to sleep on the plateau if possible...

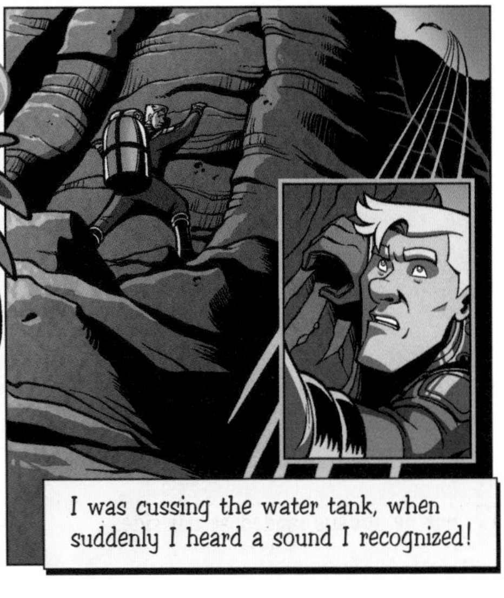
I was cussing the water tank, when suddenly I heard a sound I recognized!

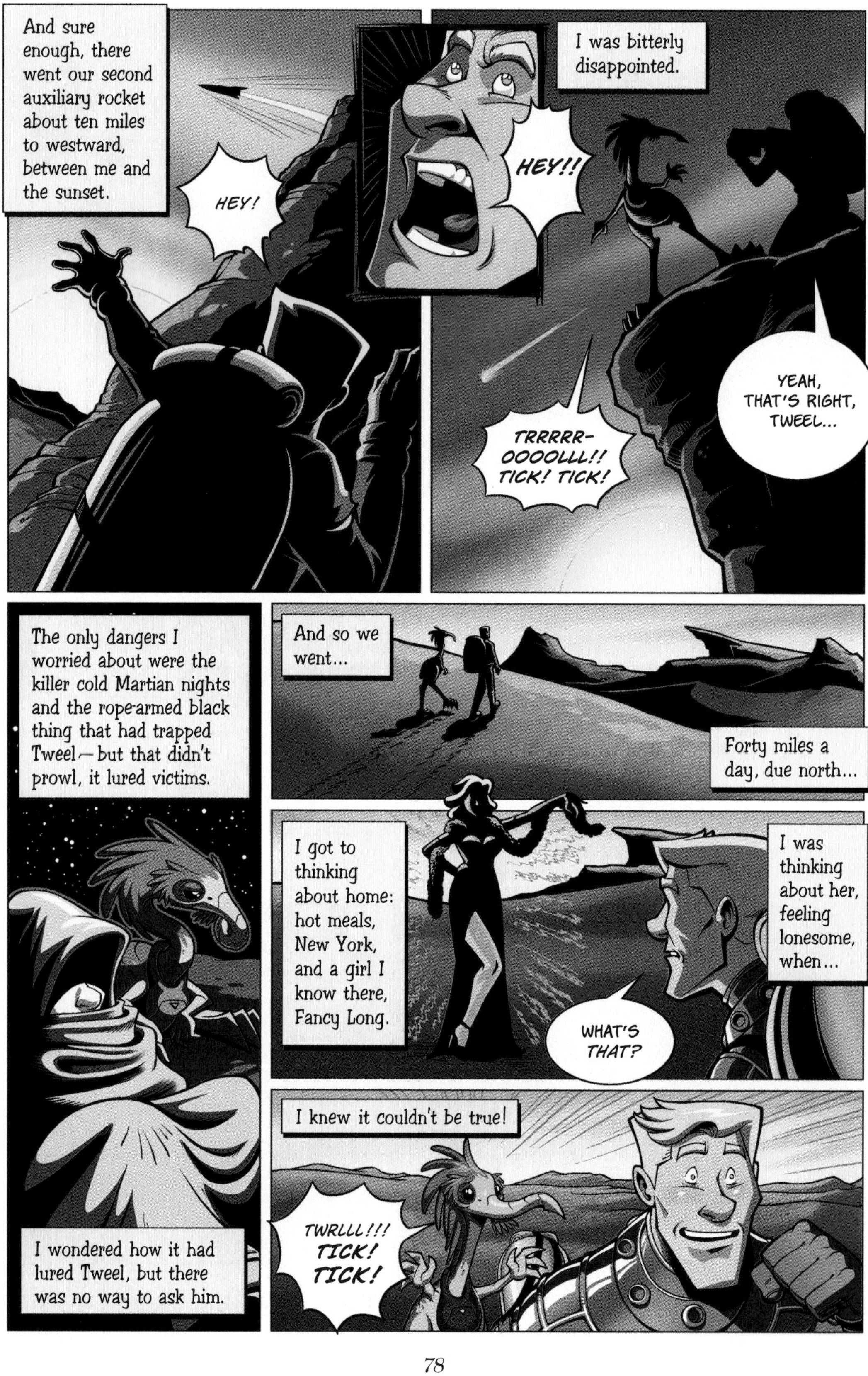
And sure enough, there went our second auxiliary rocket about ten miles to westward, between me and the sunset.
HEY!
HEY!!
I was bitterly disappointed.
TRRRRR-OOOOLLL!! TICK! TICK!
YEAH, THAT'S RIGHT, TWEEL...
The only dangers I worried about were the killer cold Martian nights and the rope-armed black thing that had trapped Tweel—but that didn't prowl, it lured victims.
I wondered how it had lured Tweel, but there was no way to ask him.
And so we went...
Forty miles a day, due north...
I got to thinking about home: hot meals, New York, and a girl I know there, Fancy Long.
I was thinking about her, feeling lonesome, when...
WHAT'S THAT?
I knew it couldn't be true!
TWRLLL!!! TICK! TICK!

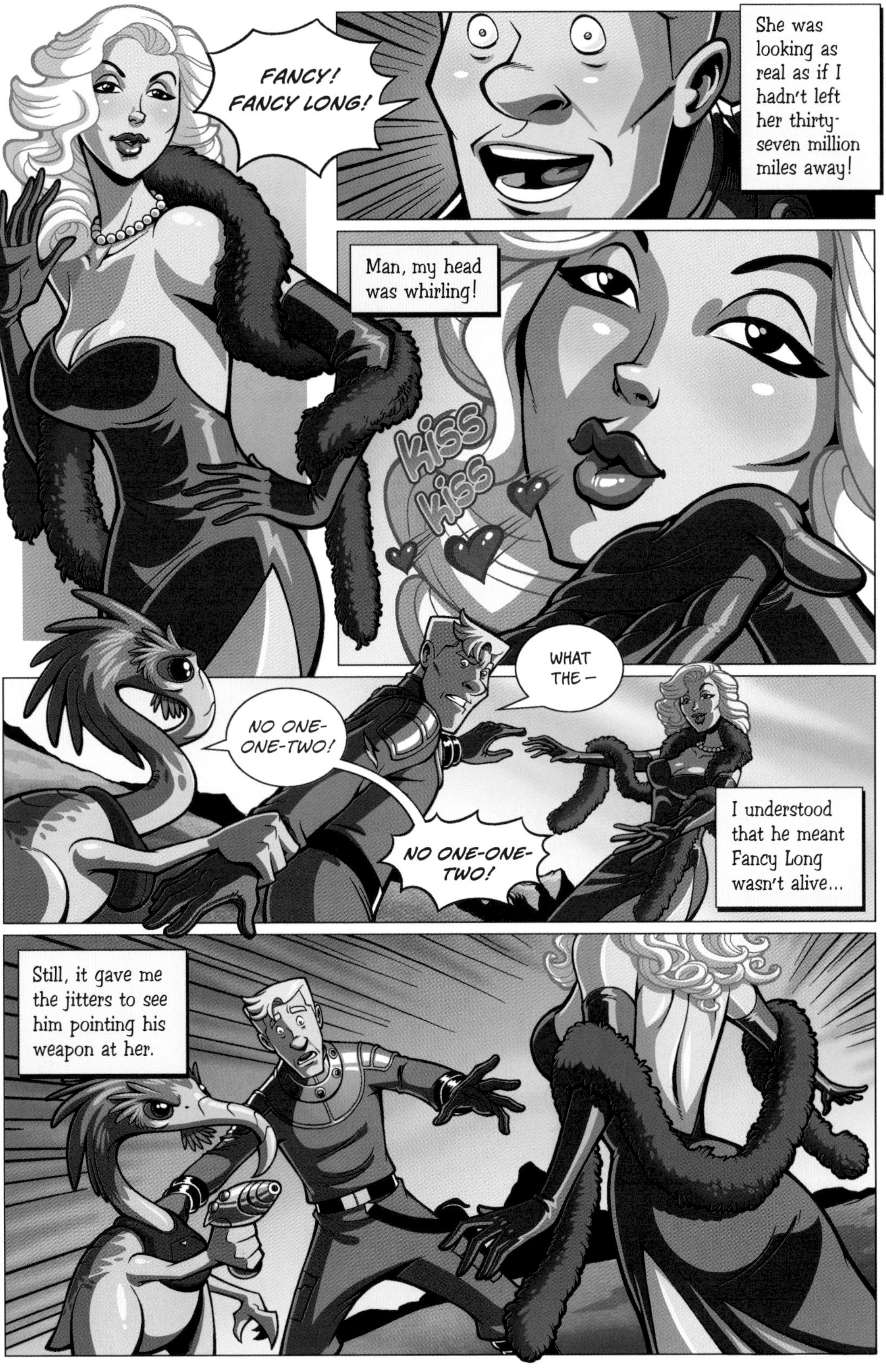
FANCY! FANCY LONG!
She was looking as real as if I hadn't left her thirty-seven million miles away!
Man, my head was whirling!
kiss kiss
WHAT THE—
NO ONE-ONE-TWO!
NO ONE-ONE-TWO!
I understood that he meant Fancy Long wasn't alive...
Still, it gave me the jitters to see him pointing his weapon at her.

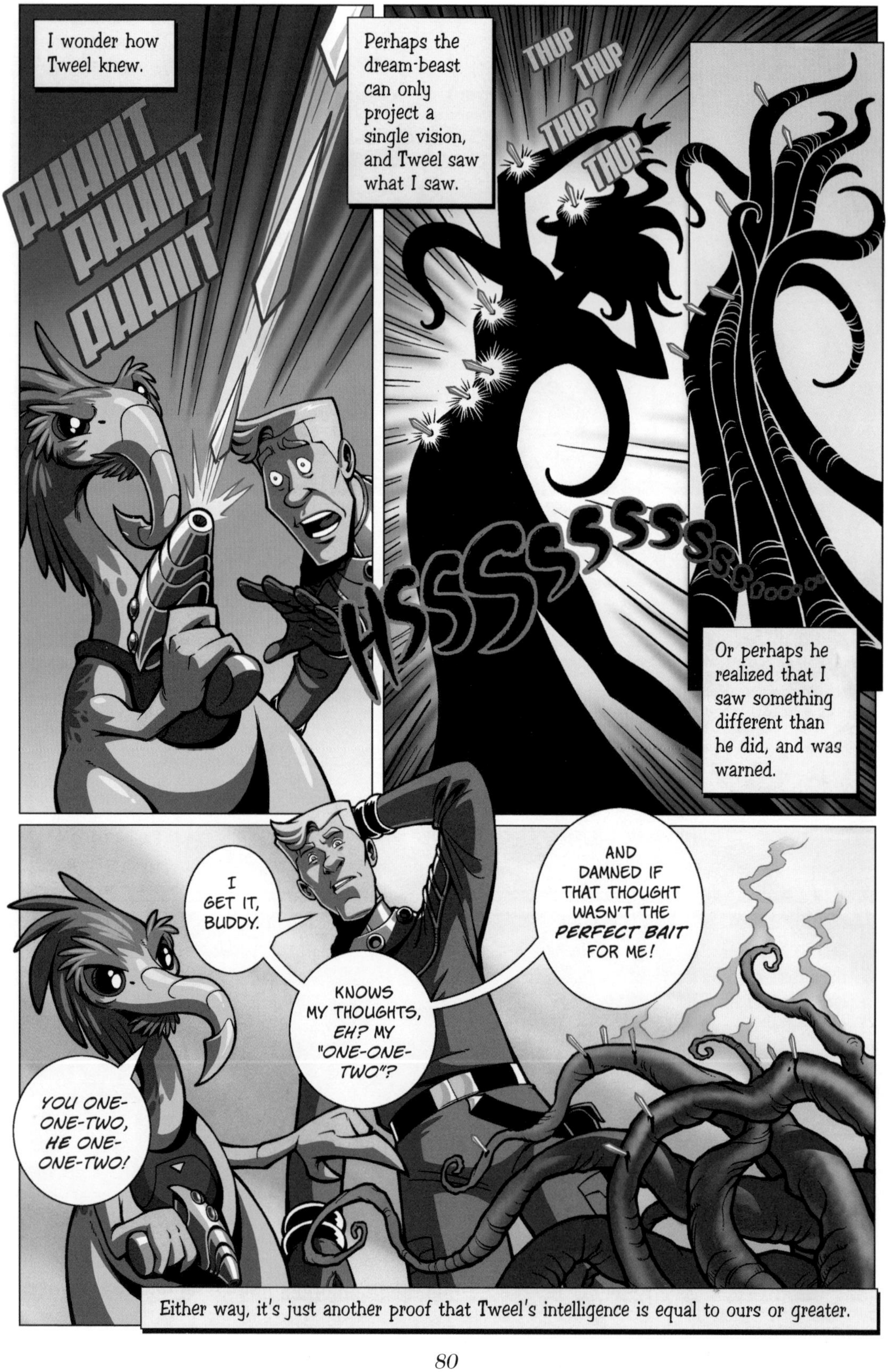
I wonder how Tweel knew.
PHHHT PHHHT PHHHT
Perhaps the dream-beast can only project a single vision, and Tweel saw what I saw.
THUP THUP THUP THUP
HSSSSSSSSSSSSS...
Or perhaps he realized that I saw something different than he did, and was warned.
I GET IT, BUDDY.
KNOWS MY THOUGHTS, EH? MY "ONE-ONE-TWO"?
AND DAMNED IF THAT THOUGHT WASN'T THE *PERFECT BAIT* FOR ME!
YOU ONE-ONE-TWO, **HE** ONE-ONE-TWO!
Either way, it's just another proof that Tweel's intelligence is equal to ours or greater.

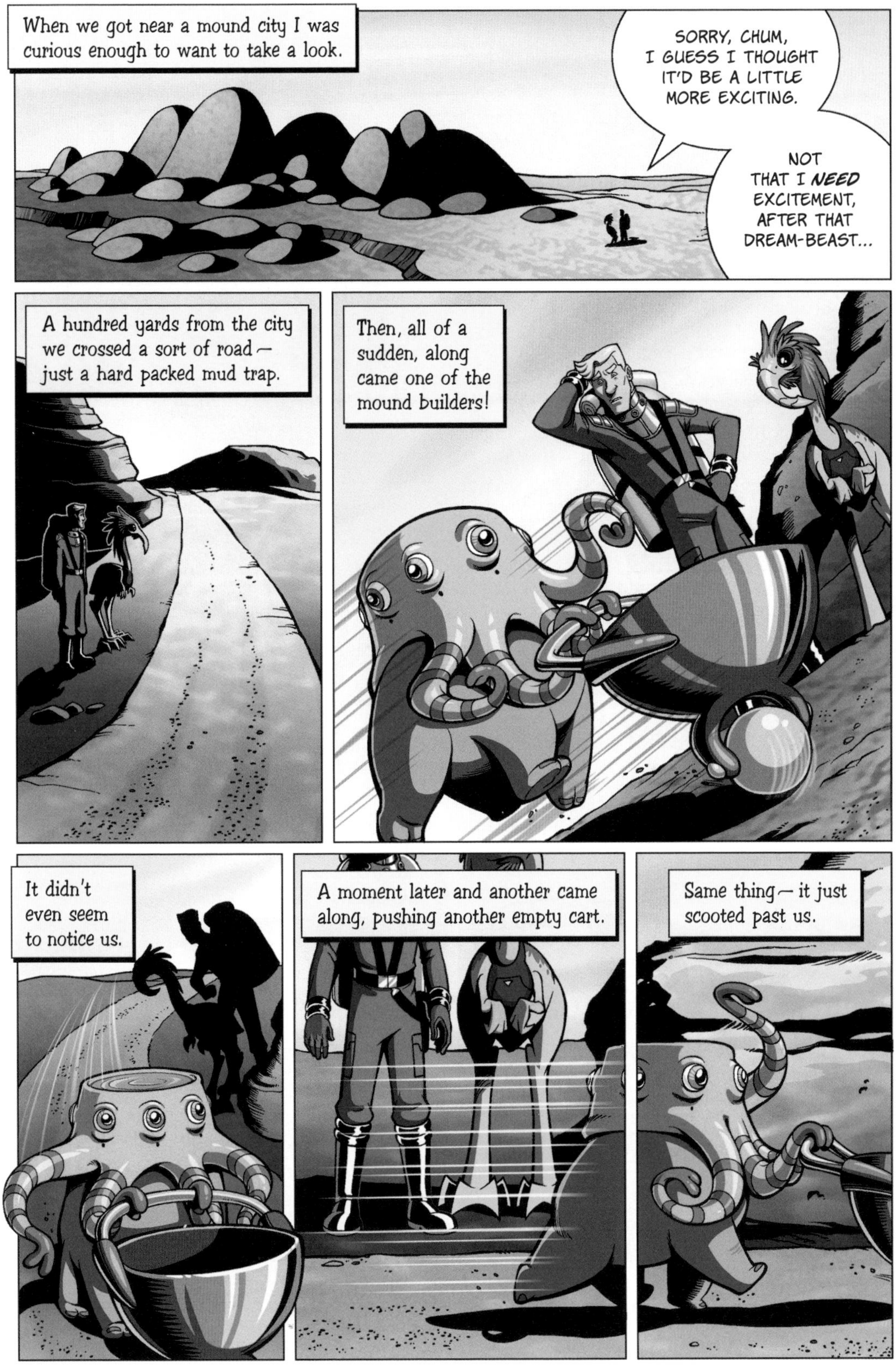
When we got near a mound city I was curious enough to want to take a look.
SORRY, CHUM, I GUESS I THOUGHT IT'D BE A LITTLE MORE EXCITING.
NOT THAT I *NEED* EXCITEMENT, AFTER THAT DREAM-BEAST...
A hundred yards from the city we crossed a sort of road— just a hard packed mud trap.
Then, all of a sudden, along came one of the mound builders!
It didn't even seem to notice us.
A moment later and another came along, pushing another empty cart.
Same thing— it just scooted past us.

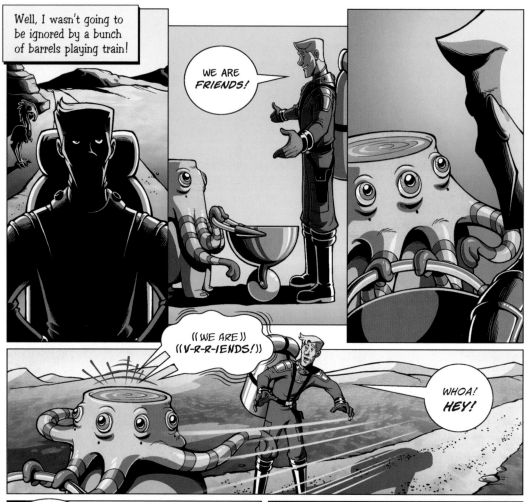

Well, I wasn't going to be ignored by a bunch of barrels playing train!

WE ARE *FRIENDS!*

((WE ARE))
((V-R-R-IENDS!))

WHOA!
HEY!

WELL, WHAT D'YA MAKE OUT OF *THAT?*

ONE-ONE-TWO—YES!

TWO-TWO-FOUR—NO!

The next one didn't pause, but simply drummed out:

((WE ARE))
((V-R-R-IENDS!))

How did it learn the phrase?

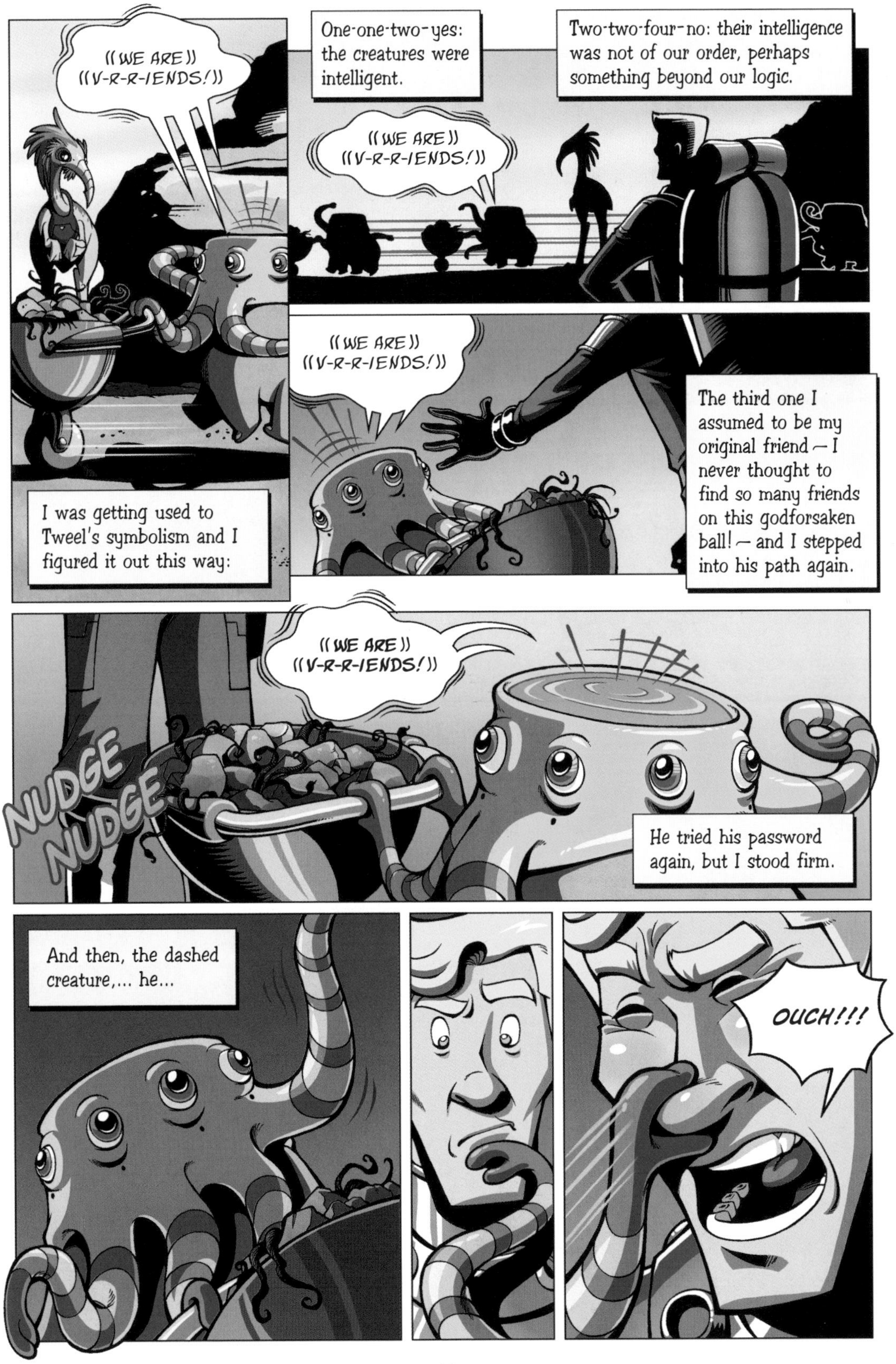
((WE ARE))
((V-R-R-IENDS!))
I was getting used to Tweel's symbolism and I figured it out this way:
One-one-two-yes: the creatures were intelligent.
Two-two-four-no: their intelligence was not of our order, perhaps something beyond our logic.
((WE ARE))
((V-R-R-IENDS!))
((WE ARE))
((V-R-R-IENDS!))
The third one I assumed to be my original friend — I never thought to find so many friends on this godforsaken ball! — and I stepped into his path again.
NUDGE
NUDGE
((WE ARE))
((V-R-R-IENDS!))
He tried his password again, but I stood firm.
And then, the dashed creature,... he...
OUCH!!!

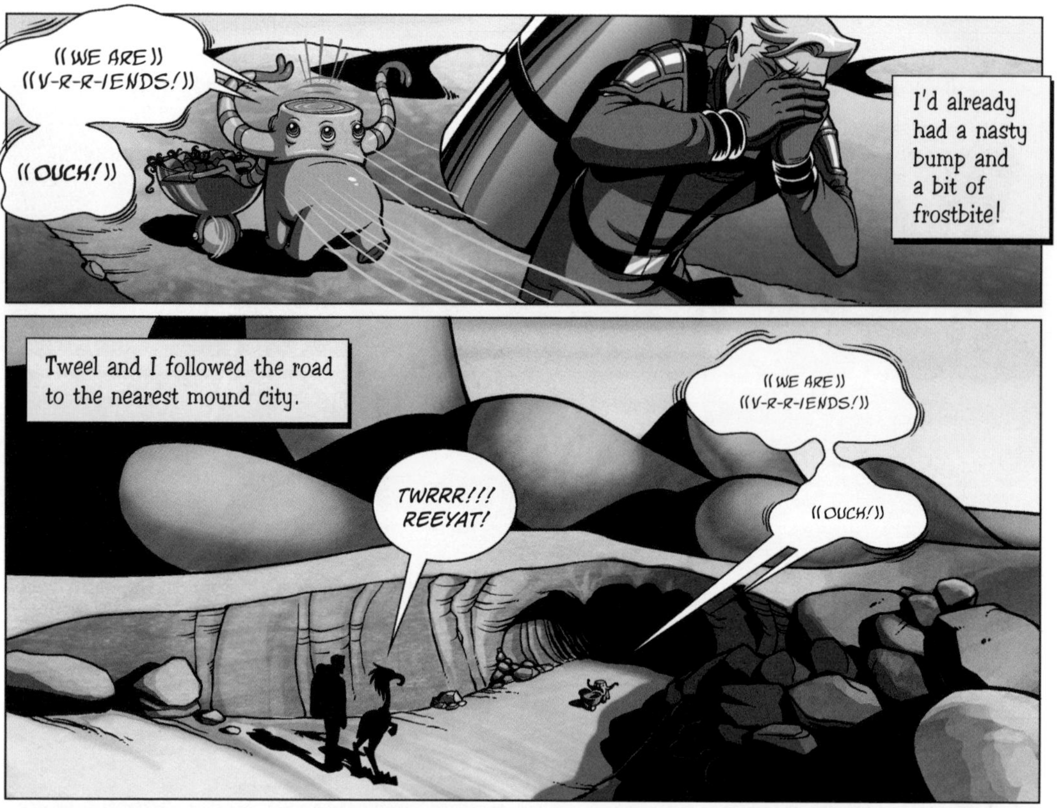
((WE ARE))
((V-R-R-IENDS!))
((OUCH!))
I'd already had a nasty bump and a bit of frostbite!
Tweel and I followed the road to the nearest mound city.
((WE ARE))
((V-R-R-IENDS!))
TWRRR!!! REEYAT!
((OUCH!))

A light came from the hole, and I thought I might get some clue as to the creatures' civilization.

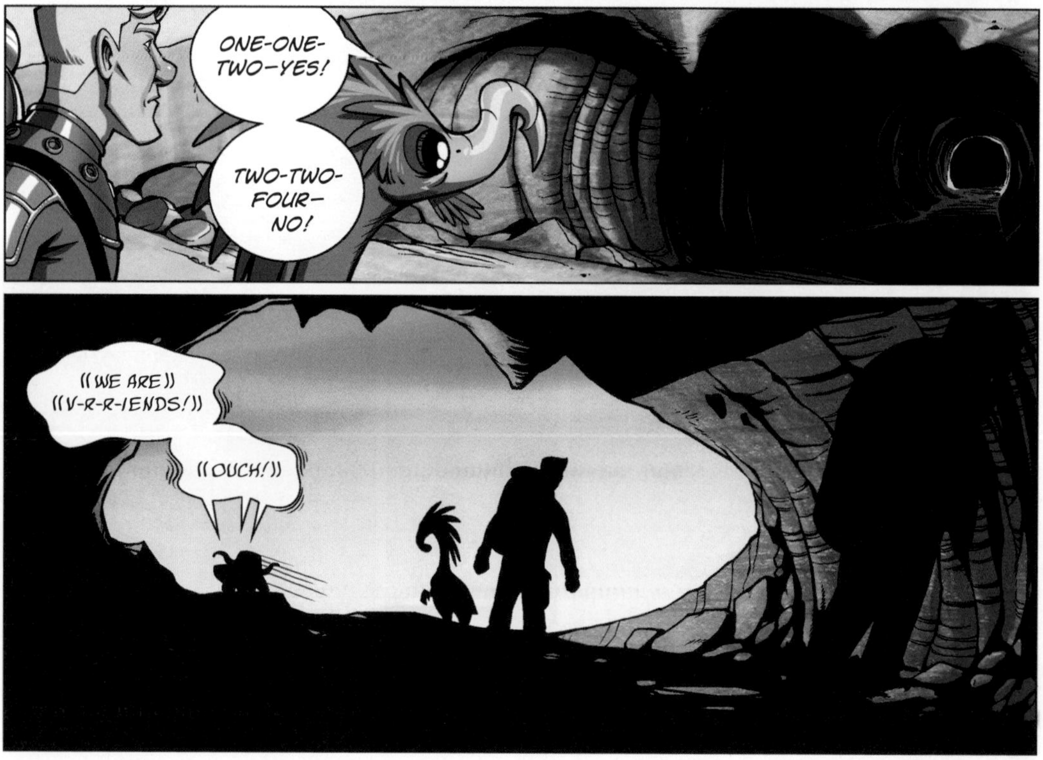
ONE-ONE-TWO—YES!
TWO-TWO-FOUR—NO!
((WE ARE))
((V-R-R-IENDS!))
((OUCH!))

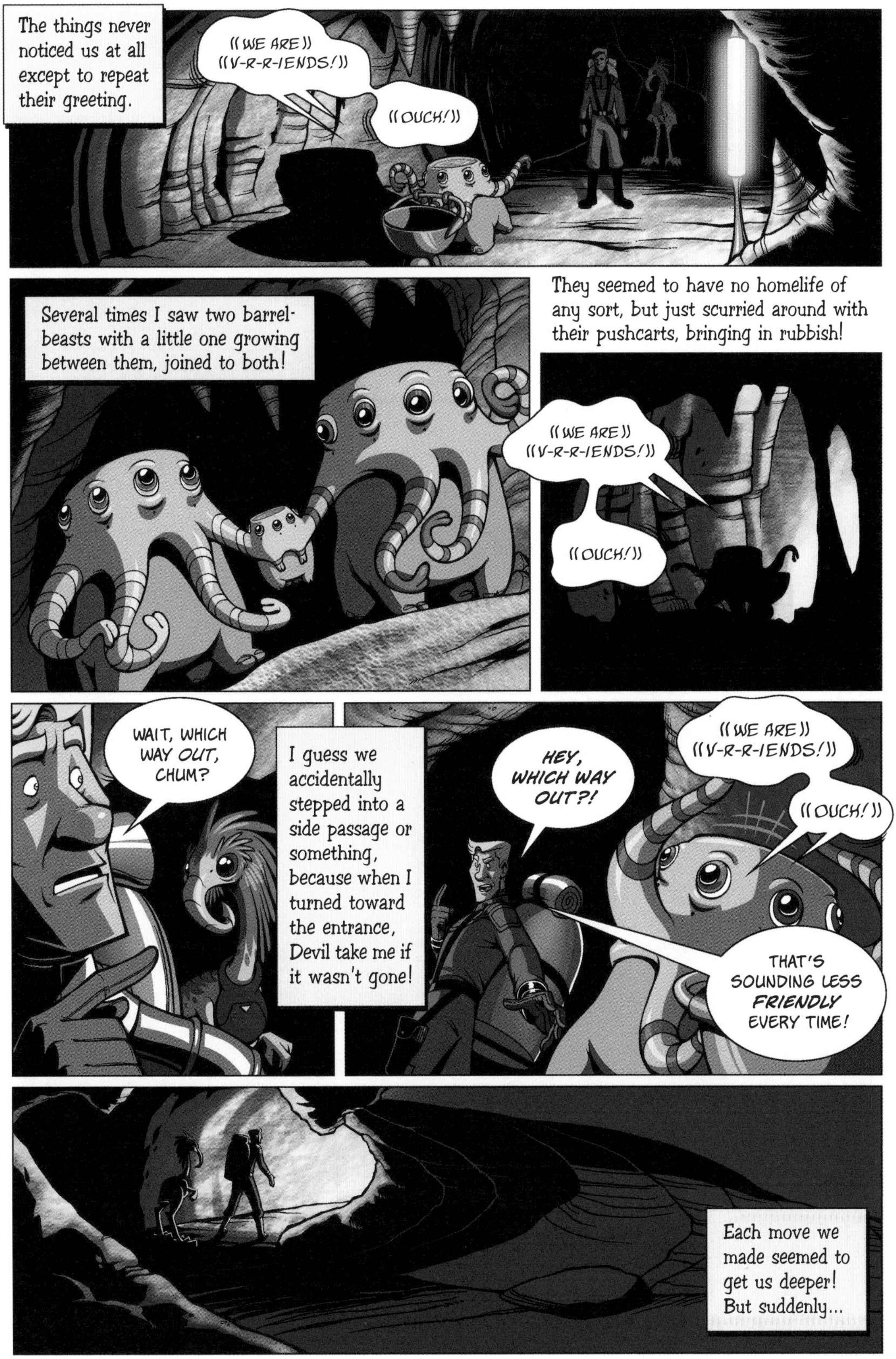
The things never noticed us at all except to repeat their greeting.
((WE ARE)) ((V-R-R-IENDS!))
((OUCH!))
Several times I saw two barrel-beasts with a little one growing between them, joined to both!
They seemed to have no homelife of any sort, but just scurried around with their pushcarts, bringing in rubbish!
((WE ARE)) ((V-R-R-IENDS!))
((OUCH!))
WAIT, WHICH WAY *OUT*, CHUM?
I guess we accidentally stepped into a side passage or something, because when I turned toward the entrance, Devil take me if it wasn't gone!
HEY, WHICH WAY OUT?!
((WE ARE)) ((V-R-R-IENDS!))
((OUCH!))
THAT'S SOUNDING LESS ***FRIENDLY*** EVERY TIME!
Each move we made seemed to get us deeper! But suddenly...

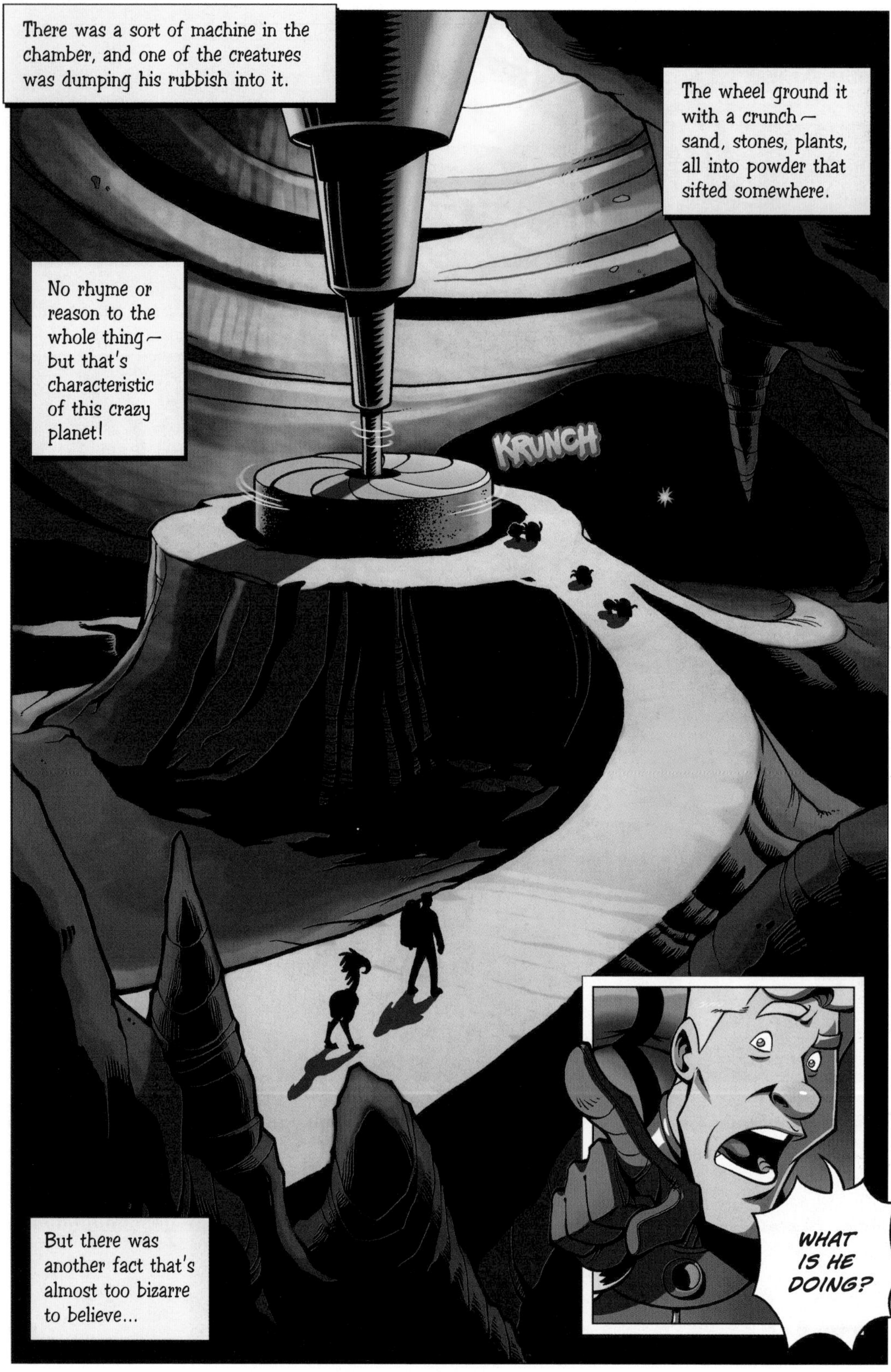
There was a sort of machine in the chamber, and one of the creatures was dumping his rubbish into it.
The wheel ground it with a crunch— sand, stones, plants, all into powder that sifted somewhere.
No rhyme or reason to the whole thing— but that's characteristic of this crazy planet!
KRUNCH
But there was another fact that's almost too bizarre to believe...
WHAT IS HE DOING?

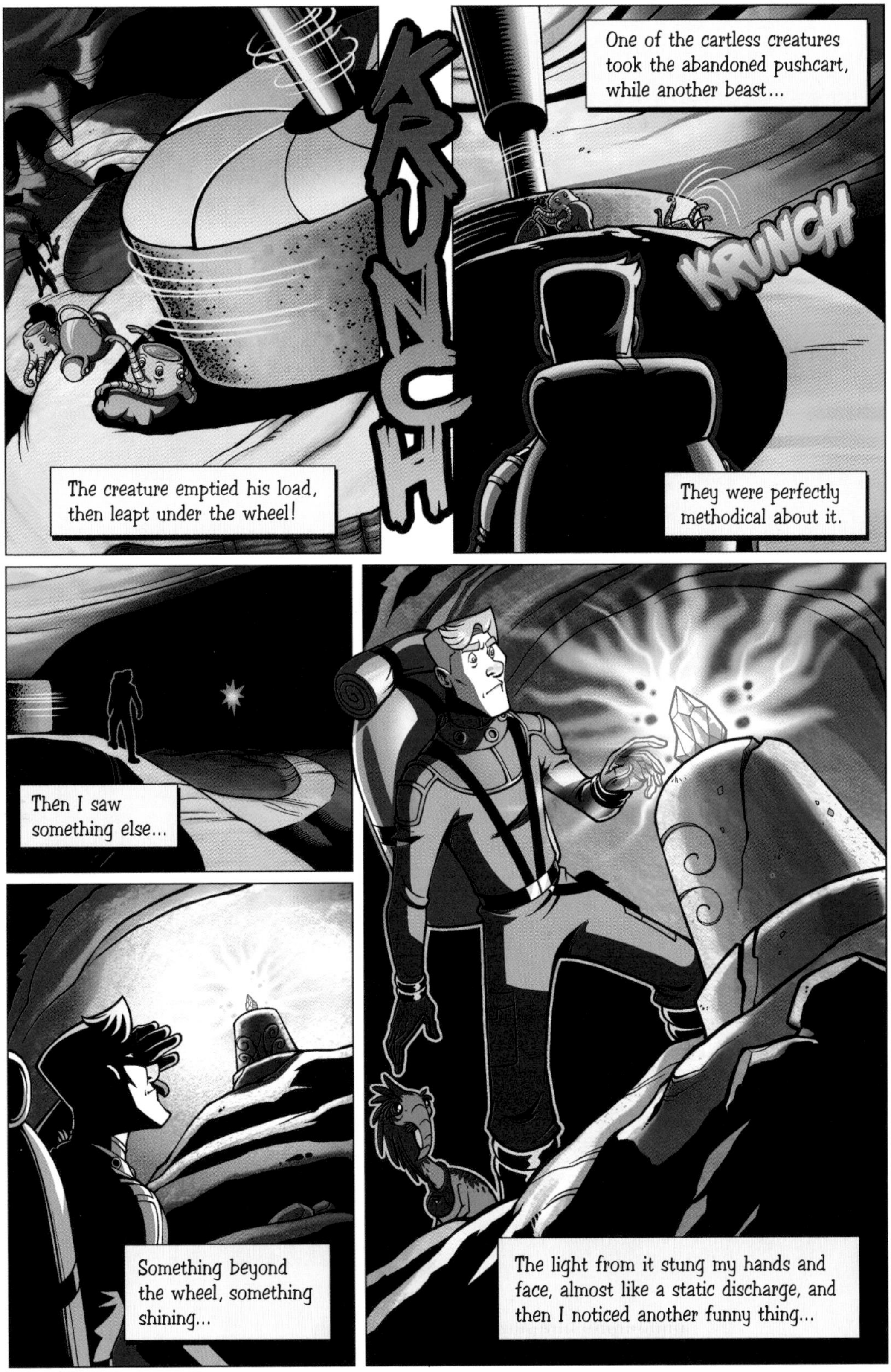
KRUNCH
The creature emptied his load, then leapt under the wheel!
One of the cartless creatures took the abandoned pushcart, while another beast...
KRUNCH
They were perfectly methodical about it.
Then I saw something else...
Something beyond the wheel, something shining...
The light from it stung my hands and face, almost like a static discharge, and then I noticed another funny thing...

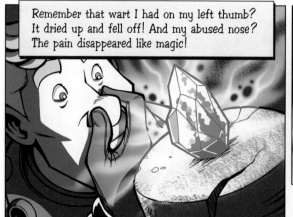

Remember that wart I had on my left thumb? It dried up and fell off! And my abused nose? The pain disappeared like magic!

The crystal's radiation destroyed diseased tissue and left healthy tissue unharmed!

I was thinking what a present that'd be to take back to Mother Earth when...

((WE ARE))
((V-R-R-IENDS!))
((OUCH!))

((WE ARE))
((V-R-R-IENDS!))
((OUCH!))

((WE ARE))
((V-R-R-IENDS!))
((OUCH!))

TWEEL, TIME FOR THE BETTER PART OF VALOR!...

I didn't like the "ouch!"— it was rather suggestive!

RUN!

Tweel had his gun out and I had mine. Though if we could get away without firing a shot, all the better; there wasn't any use in irritating these creatures!

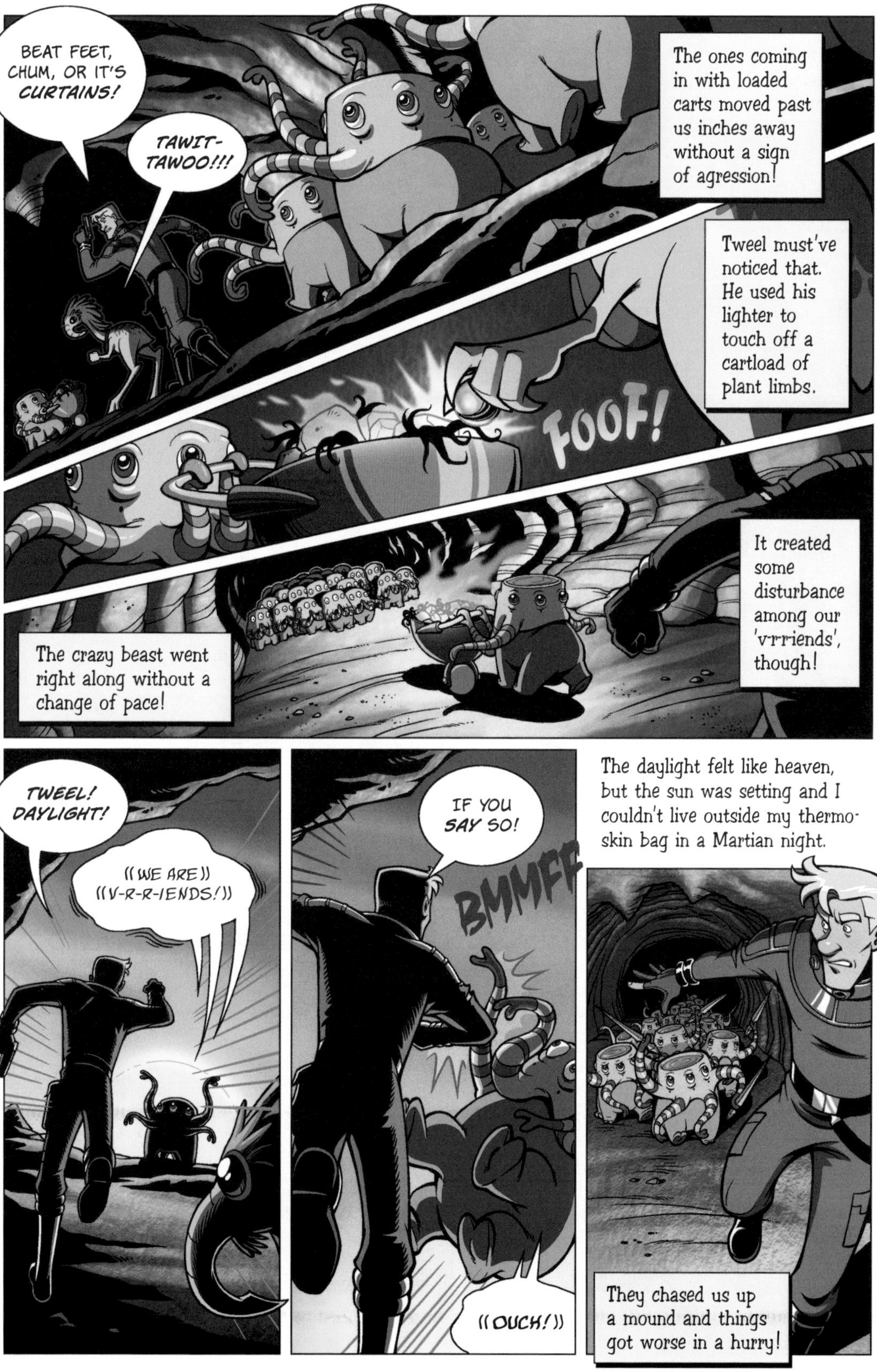
BEAT FEET, CHUM, OR IT'S CURTAINS!
TAWIT-TAWOO!!!
The ones coming in with loaded carts moved past us inches away without a sign of agression!
Tweel must've noticed that. He used his lighter to touch off a cartload of plant limbs.
FOOF!
The crazy beast went right along without a change of pace!
It created some disturbance among our 'v-r-riends', though!
TWEEL! DAYLIGHT!
((WE ARE)) ((V-R-R-IENDS!))
IF YOU SAY SO!
BMMFF
((OUCH!))
The daylight felt like heaven, but the sun was setting and I couldn't live outside my thermo-skin bag in a Martian night.
They chased us up a mound and things got worse in a hurry!

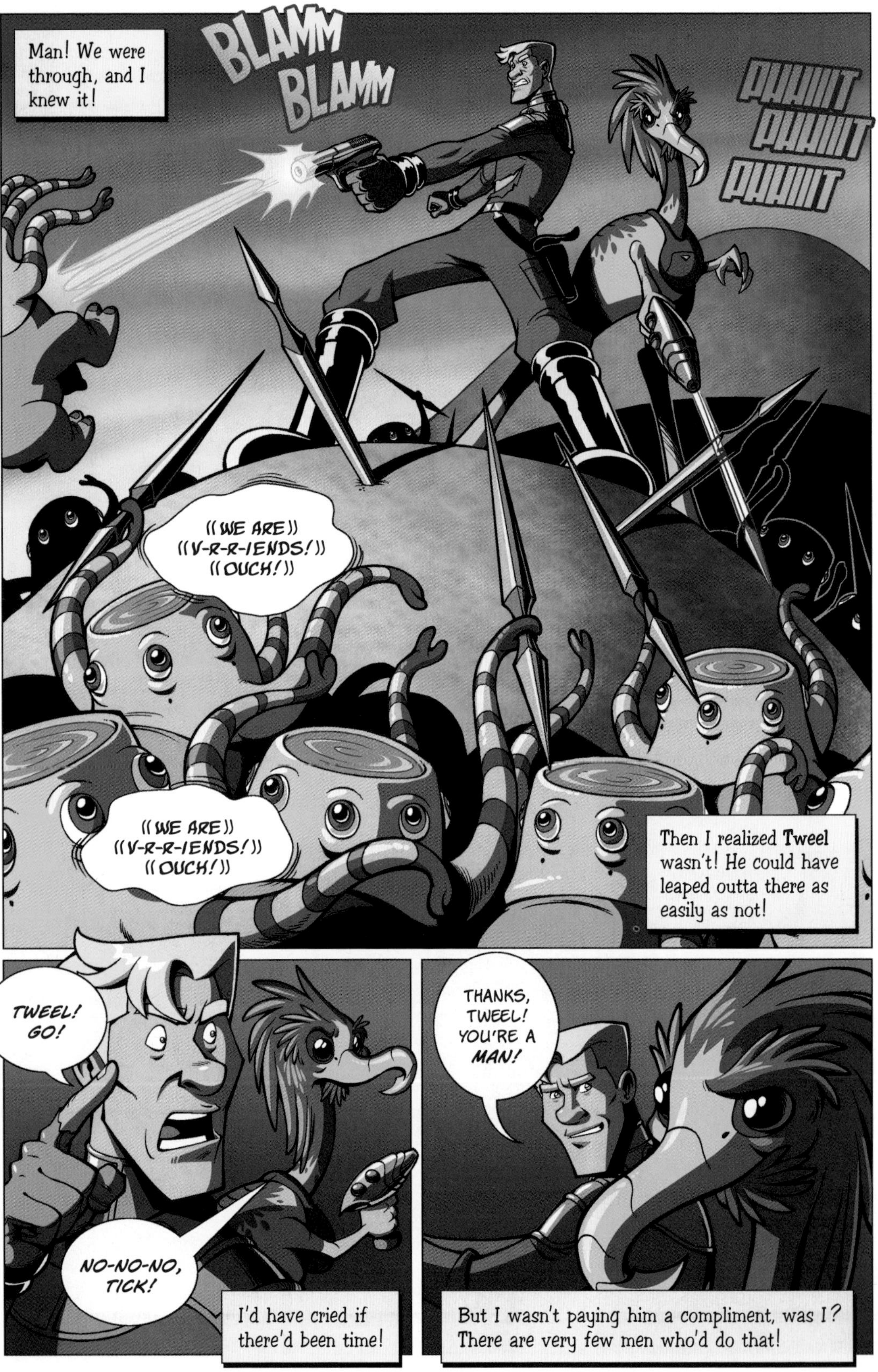
Man! We were through, and I knew it!
BLAMM BLAMM
PHHIIIT PHHIIIT PHHIIIT
((WE ARE)) ((V-R-R-IENDS!)) ((OUCH!))
((WE ARE)) ((V-R-R-IENDS!)) ((OUCH!))
Then I realized **Tweel** wasn't! He could have leaped outta there as easily as not!
TWEEL! GO!
NO-NO-NO, TICK!
I'd have cried if there'd been time!
THANKS, TWEEL! YOU'RE A *MAN!*
But I wasn't paying him a compliment, was I? There are very few men who'd do that!

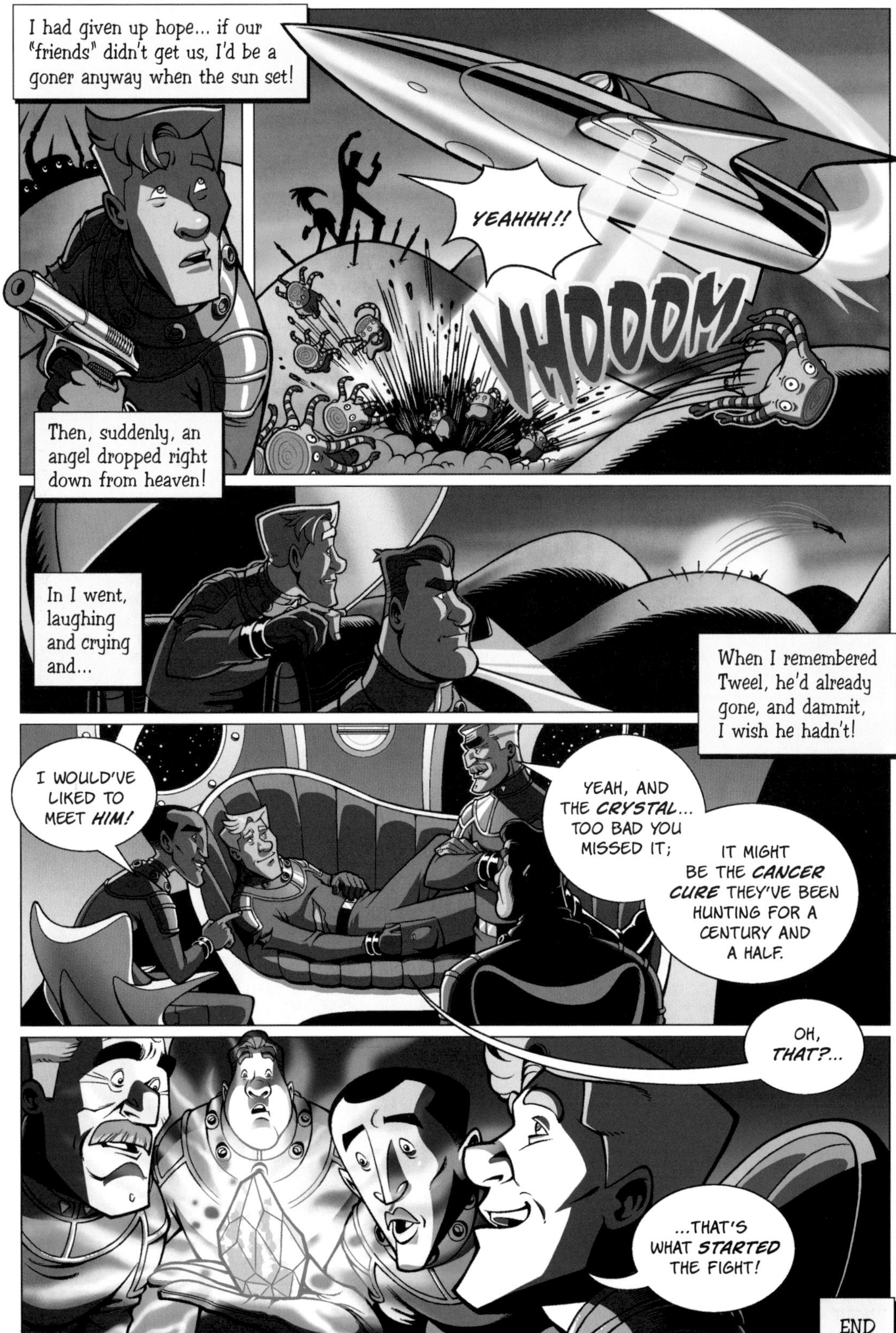
I had given up hope... if our "friends" didn't get us, I'd be a goner anyway when the sun set!
YEAHHH!!
VHOOOM
Then, suddenly, an angel dropped right down from heaven!
In I went, laughing and crying and...
When I remembered Tweel, he'd already gone, and dammit, I wish he hadn't!
I WOULD'VE LIKED TO MEET *HIM!*
YEAH, AND THE *CRYSTAL*... TOO BAD YOU MISSED IT;
IT MIGHT BE THE *CANCER CURE* THEY'VE BEEN HUNTING FOR A CENTURY AND A HALF.
OH, *THAT?*...
...THAT'S WHAT *STARTED* THE FIGHT!
END

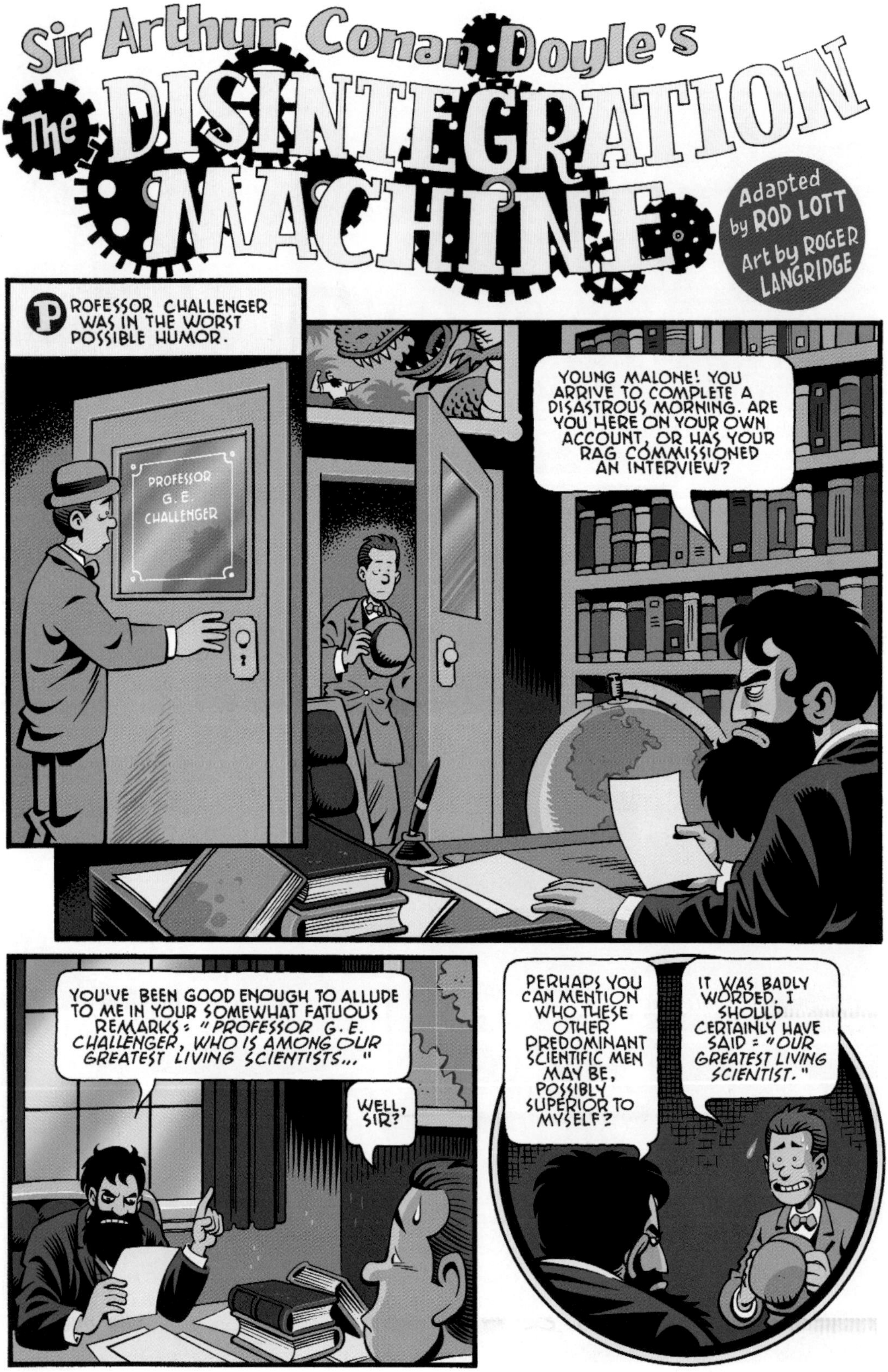
Sir Arthur Conan Doyle's
The DISINTEGRATION MACHINE
Adapted by ROD LOTT
Art by ROGER LANGRIDGE
PROFESSOR CHALLENGER WAS IN THE WORST POSSIBLE HUMOR.
PROFESSOR G. E. CHALLENGER
YOUNG MALONE! YOU ARRIVE TO COMPLETE A DISASTROUS MORNING. ARE YOU HERE ON YOUR OWN ACCOUNT, OR HAS YOUR RAG COMMISSIONED AN INTERVIEW?
YOU'VE BEEN GOOD ENOUGH TO ALLUDE TO ME IN YOUR SOMEWHAT FATUOUS REMARKS: "PROFESSOR G. E. CHALLENGER, WHO IS AMONG OUR GREATEST LIVING SCIENTISTS..."
WELL, SIR?
PERHAPS YOU CAN MENTION WHO THESE OTHER PREDOMINANT SCIENTIFIC MEN MAY BE, POSSIBLY SUPERIOR TO MYSELF?
IT WAS BADLY WORDED. I SHOULD CERTAINLY HAVE SAID: "OUR GREATEST LIVING SCIENTIST."

MY DEAR FRIEND, SIT! WHAT IS THE REASON FOR YOUR VISIT?

MAY I READ YOU SOMETHING, SIR? IT'S FROM McARDLE, MY EDITOR.

I REMEMBER THE MAN ~ NOT AN UNFAVORABLE SPECIMEN.

HE HAS A HIGH ADMIRATION FOR YOU. HE HAS TURNED TO YOU WHEN HE NEEDED THE HIGHEST QUALITIES IN SOME INVESTIGATION. THAT IS THE CASE NOW.

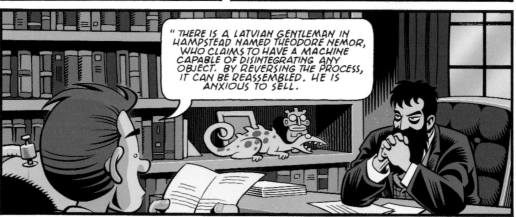

"THERE IS A LATVIAN GENTLEMAN IN HAMPSTEAD NAMED THEODORE NEMOR, WHO CLAIMS TO HAVE A MACHINE CAPABLE OF DISINTEGRATING ANY OBJECT. BY REVERSING THE PROCESS, IT CAN BE REASSEMBLED. HE IS ANXIOUS TO SELL.

"I NEED NOT ENLARGE UPON SUCH AN INVENTION'S POTENTIAL AS A WEAPON OF WAR. A FORCE LIKE THIS WOULD DOMINATE THE WORLD. I DESIRE YOU AND PROFESSOR CHALLENGER SHALL CALL UPON HIM, INSPECT HIS INVENTION AND WRITE A REPORT UPON ITS VALUE."

THERE ARE MY INSTRUCTIONS, PROFESSOR. I HOPE YOU WILL COME WITH ME, FOR HOW CAN I, WITH MY LIMITED CAPACITIES, ACT ALONE?

TRUE, MALONE, TRUE! THOUGH YOU ARE BY NO MEANS DESTITUTE OF INTELLIGENCE, I AGREE. I AM AT YOUR SERVICE!

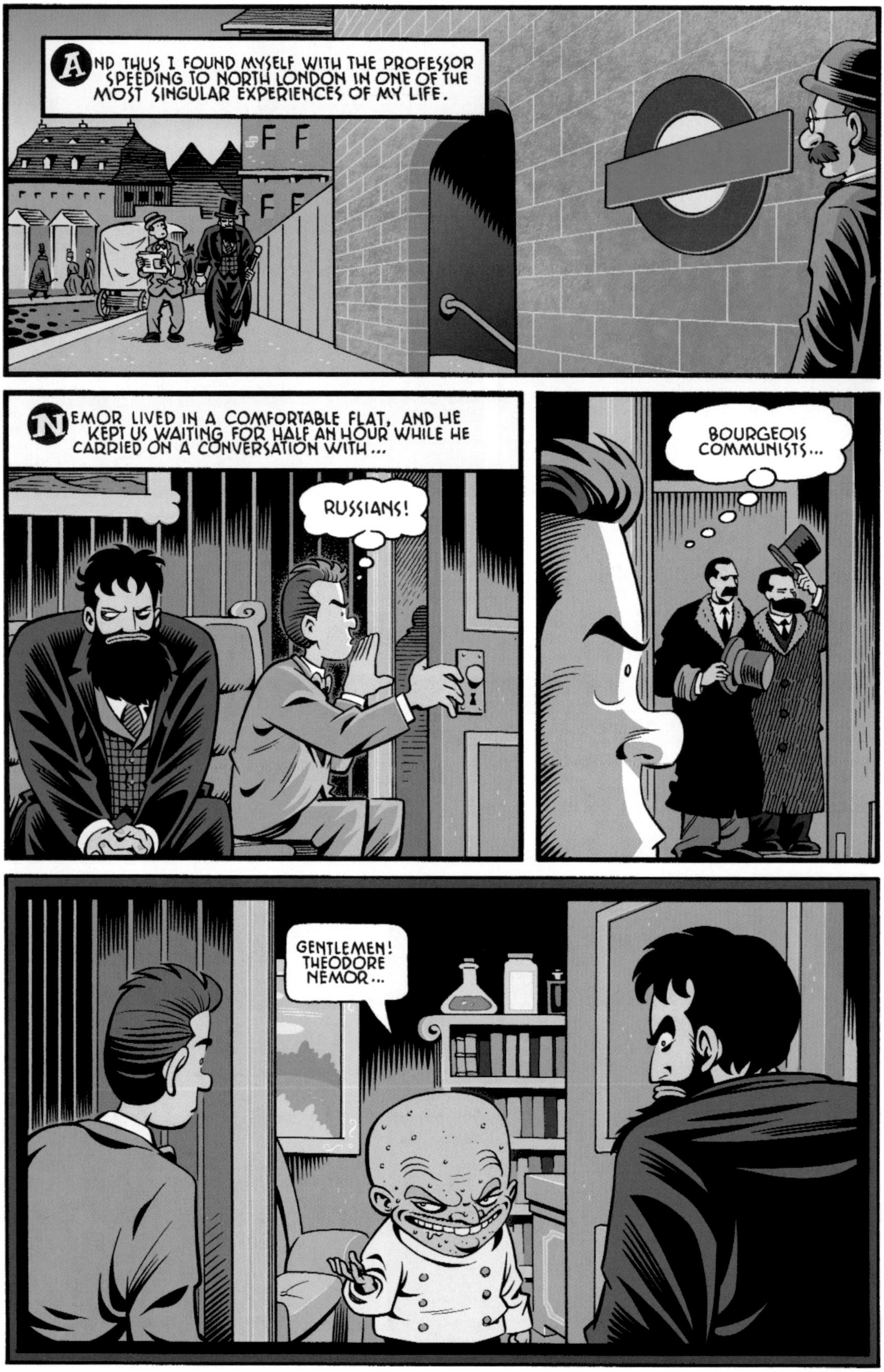
AND THUS I FOUND MYSELF WITH THE PROFESSOR SPEEDING TO NORTH LONDON IN ONE OF THE MOST SINGULAR EXPERIENCES OF MY LIFE.
NEMOR LIVED IN A COMFORTABLE FLAT, AND HE KEPT US WAITING FOR HALF AN HOUR WHILE HE CARRIED ON A CONVERSATION WITH...
RUSSIANS!
BOURGEOIS COMMUNISTS...
GENTLEMEN! THEODORE NEMOR...

YOU HAVE COME TO LEARN MORE OF THE NEMOR DISINTEGRATOR? DO YOU REPRESENT THE BRITISH GOVERNMENT?
NOT AT ALL. I AM A CORRESPONDENT OF THE GAZETTE, AND THIS IS PROFESSOR CHALLENGER.
I WAS ABOUT TO SAY THE BRITISH GOVERNMENT HAS LOST ITS CHANCE. I WAS PREPARED TO SELL TO THE FIRST GOVERNMENT WHICH GAVE ME MY PRICE.
IF IT HAS NOW FALLEN INTO HANDS OF WHICH YOU DISAPPROVE, YOU HAVE ONLY YOURSELVES TO BLAME.
YOU HAVE SOLD YOUR SECRET?
THIS IS THE SAFE IN WHICH THE SECRET IS SECURELY LOCKED. I'M NOT SO FOOLISH TO HAND OVER THE KNOWLEDGE UNTIL THE PRICE IS PAID. AFTER THAT, HISTORY WILL BE MADE.
EXCUSE ME, SIR, BUT I HAVE A REPUTATION TO SUSTAIN AS A MAN OF SCIENCE! CAUTION IS A SCIENTIFIC ATTRIBUTE, AND YOU MUST SHOW US YOUR PROOFS BEFORE WE CAN SERIOUSLY CONSIDER YOUR CLAIMS.
YOU LIVE UP TO YOUR REPUTATION, PROFESSOR, AS THE LAST MAN IN THE WORLD WHO COULD BE DECEIVED. YOU REALIZE THE DEVICE HERE IN MY LABORATORY IS A MERE MODEL.
MAY WE SEE THIS MODEL?
PROFESSOR, YOU WILL HAVE THE MOST CONCLUSIVE DEMONSTRATION POSSIBLE UPON YOUR OWN PERSON, IF YOU HAVE THE COURAGE.
IF! YOUR "IF" IS IN THE HIGHEST DEGREE OFFENSIVE!

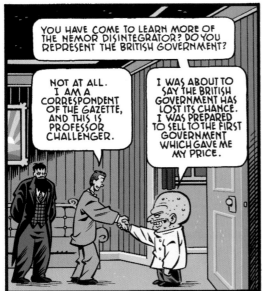

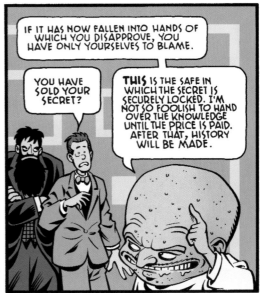

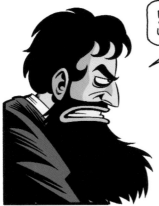

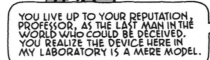

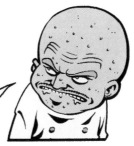

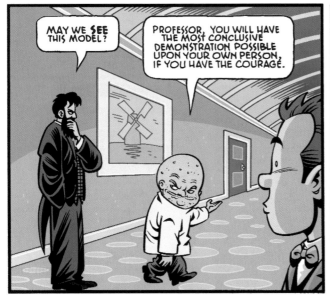

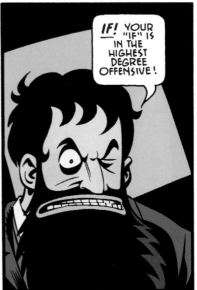

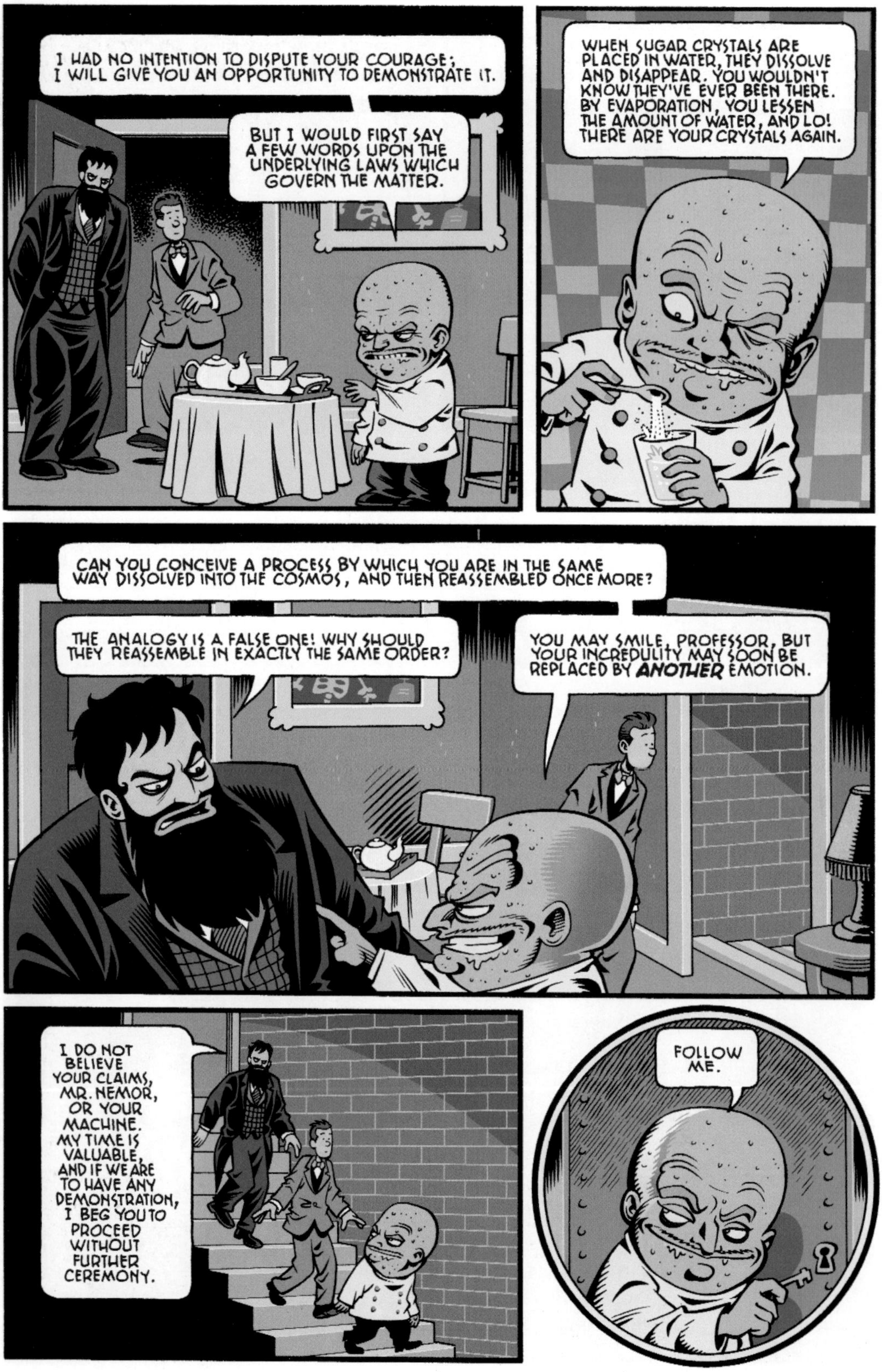
I HAD NO INTENTION TO DISPUTE YOUR COURAGE; I WILL GIVE YOU AN OPPORTUNITY TO DEMONSTRATE IT.
BUT I WOULD FIRST SAY A FEW WORDS UPON THE UNDERLYING LAWS WHICH GOVERN THE MATTER.
WHEN SUGAR CRYSTALS ARE PLACED IN WATER, THEY DISSOLVE AND DISAPPEAR. YOU WOULDN'T KNOW THEY'VE EVER BEEN THERE. BY EVAPORATION, YOU LESSEN THE AMOUNT OF WATER, AND LO! THERE ARE YOUR CRYSTALS AGAIN.
CAN YOU CONCEIVE A PROCESS BY WHICH YOU ARE IN THE SAME WAY DISSOLVED INTO THE COSMOS, AND THEN REASSEMBLED ONCE MORE?
THE ANALOGY IS A FALSE ONE! WHY SHOULD THEY REASSEMBLE IN EXACTLY THE SAME ORDER?
YOU MAY SMILE, PROFESSOR, BUT YOUR INCREDULITY MAY SOON BE REPLACED BY ANOTHER EMOTION.
I DO NOT BELIEVE YOUR CLAIMS, MR. NEMOR, OR YOUR MACHINE. MY TIME IS VALUABLE, AND IF WE ARE TO HAVE ANY DEMONSTRATION, I BEG YOU TO PROCEED WITHOUT FURTHER CEREMONY.
FOLLOW ME.

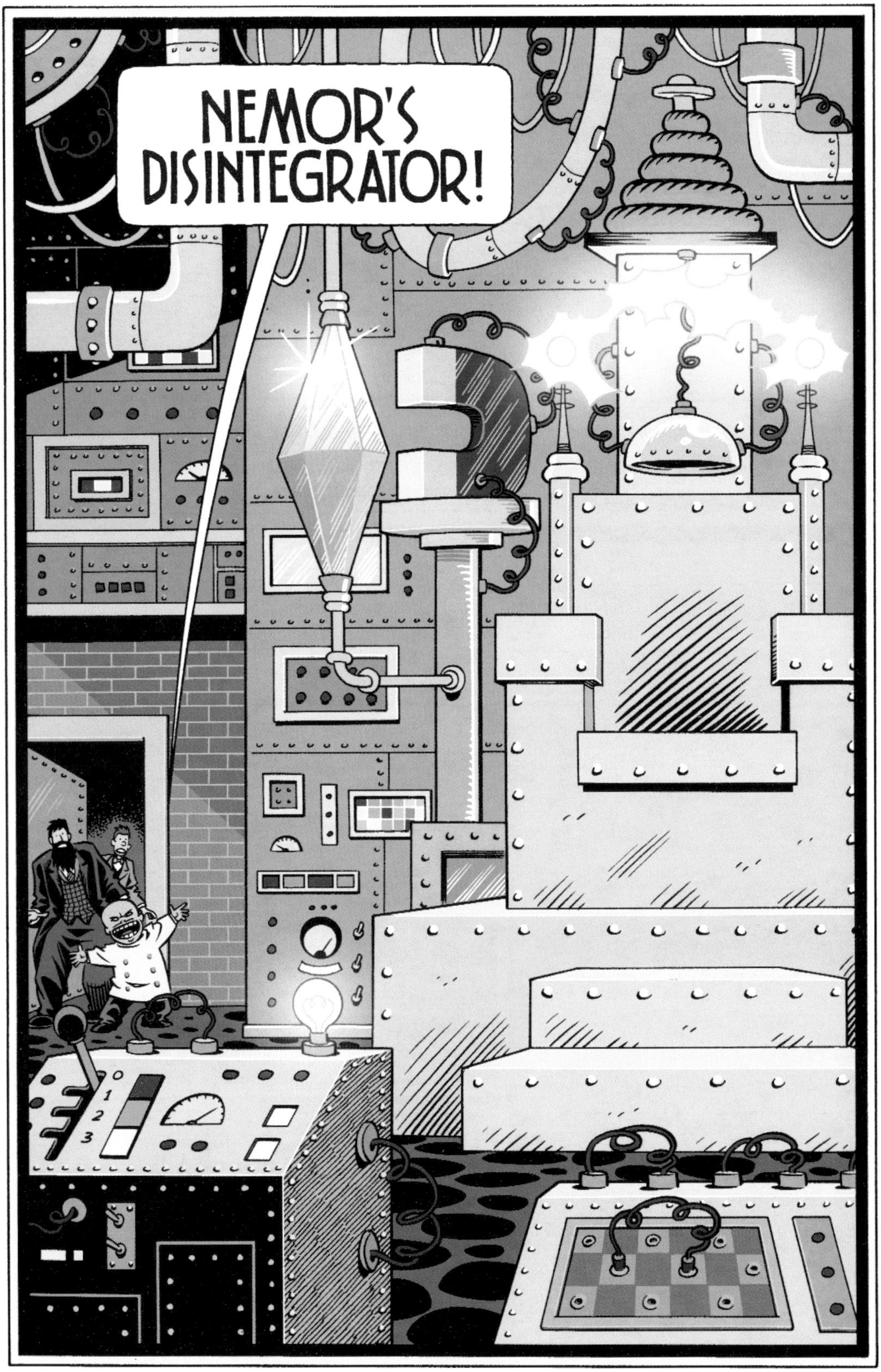
NEMOR'S DISINTEGRATOR!
0
1
2
3

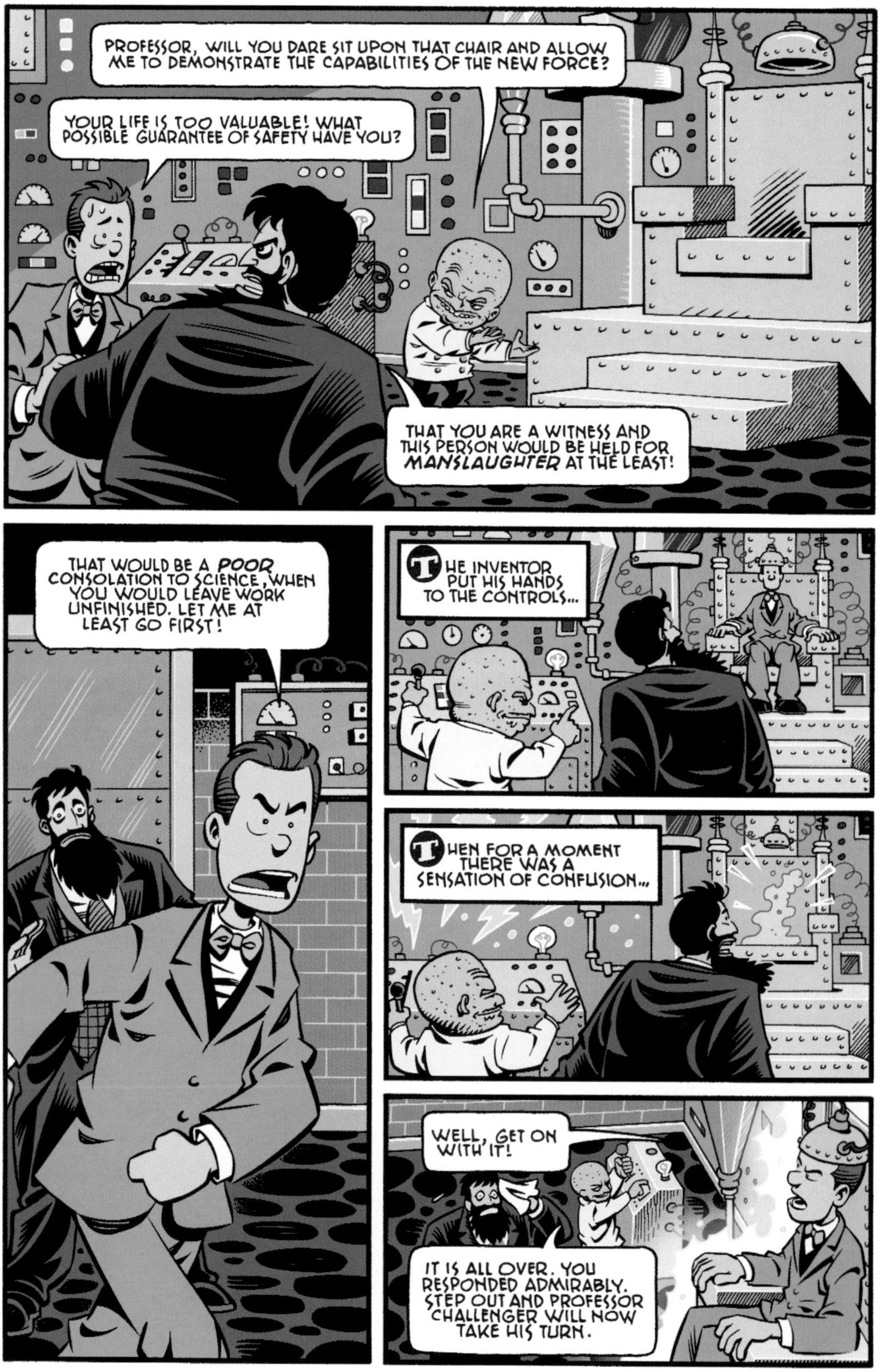
PROFESSOR, WILL YOU DARE SIT UPON THAT CHAIR AND ALLOW ME TO DEMONSTRATE THE CAPABILITIES OF THE NEW FORCE?
YOUR LIFE IS TOO VALUABLE! WHAT POSSIBLE GUARANTEE OF SAFETY HAVE YOU?
THAT YOU ARE A WITNESS AND THIS PERSON WOULD BE HELD FOR *MANSLAUGHTER* AT THE LEAST!
THAT WOULD BE A *POOR* CONSOLATION TO SCIENCE, WHEN YOU WOULD LEAVE WORK UNFINISHED. LET ME AT LEAST GO FIRST!
THE INVENTOR PUT HIS HANDS TO THE CONTROLS...
THEN FOR A MOMENT THERE WAS A SENSATION OF CONFUSION...
WELL, GET ON WITH IT!
IT IS ALL OVER. YOU RESPONDED ADMIRABLY. STEP OUT AND PROFESSOR CHALLENGER WILL NOW TAKE HIS TURN.

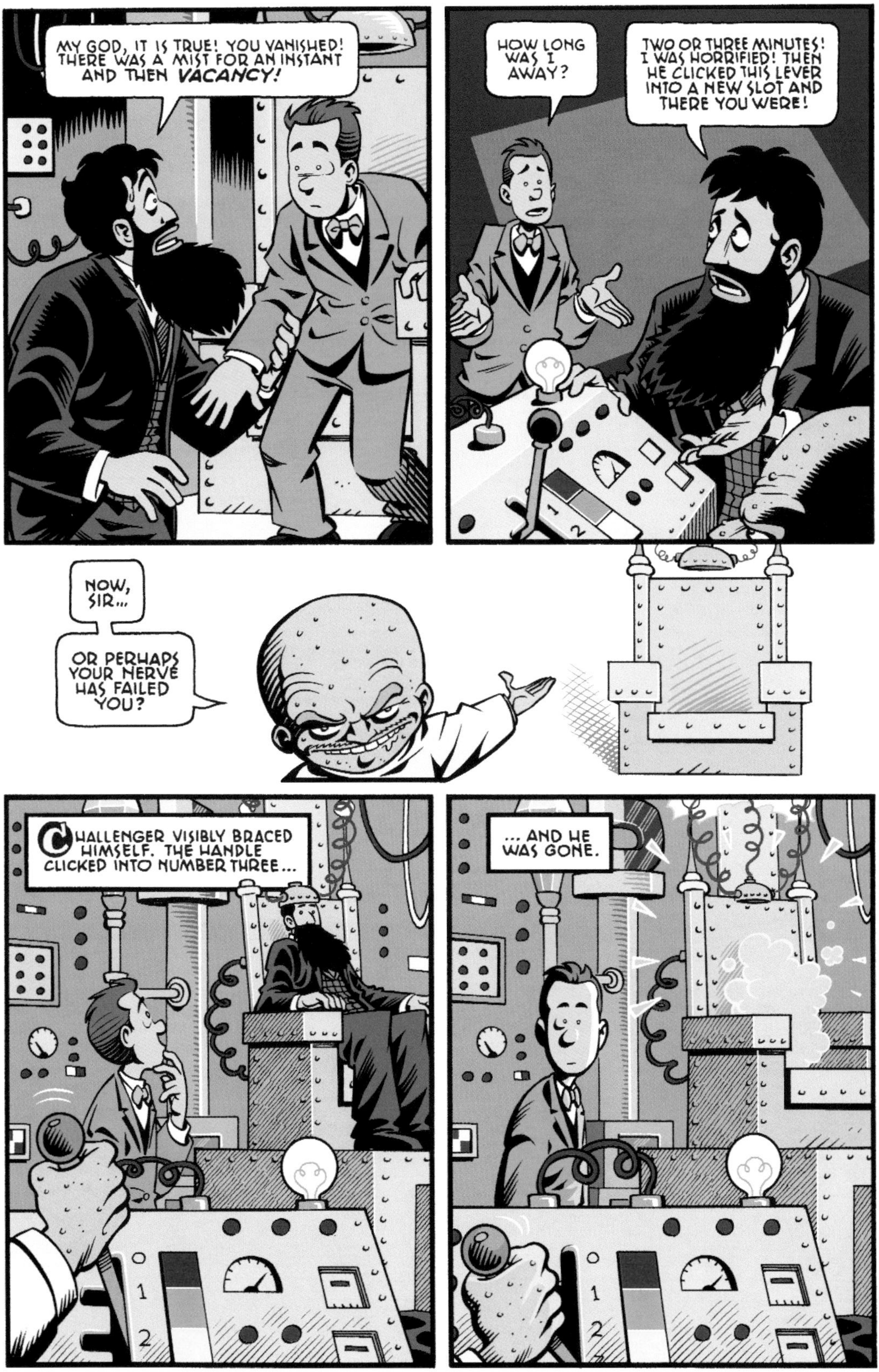
MY GOD, IT IS TRUE! YOU VANISHED! THERE WAS A MIST FOR AN INSTANT AND THEN VACANCY!
HOW LONG WAS I AWAY?
TWO OR THREE MINUTES! I WAS HORRIFIED! THEN HE CLICKED THIS LEVER INTO A NEW SLOT AND THERE YOU WERE!
NOW, SIR...
OR PERHAPS YOUR NERVE HAS FAILED YOU?
CHALLENGER VISIBLY BRACED HIMSELF. THE HANDLE CLICKED INTO NUMBER THREE...
... AND HE WAS GONE.

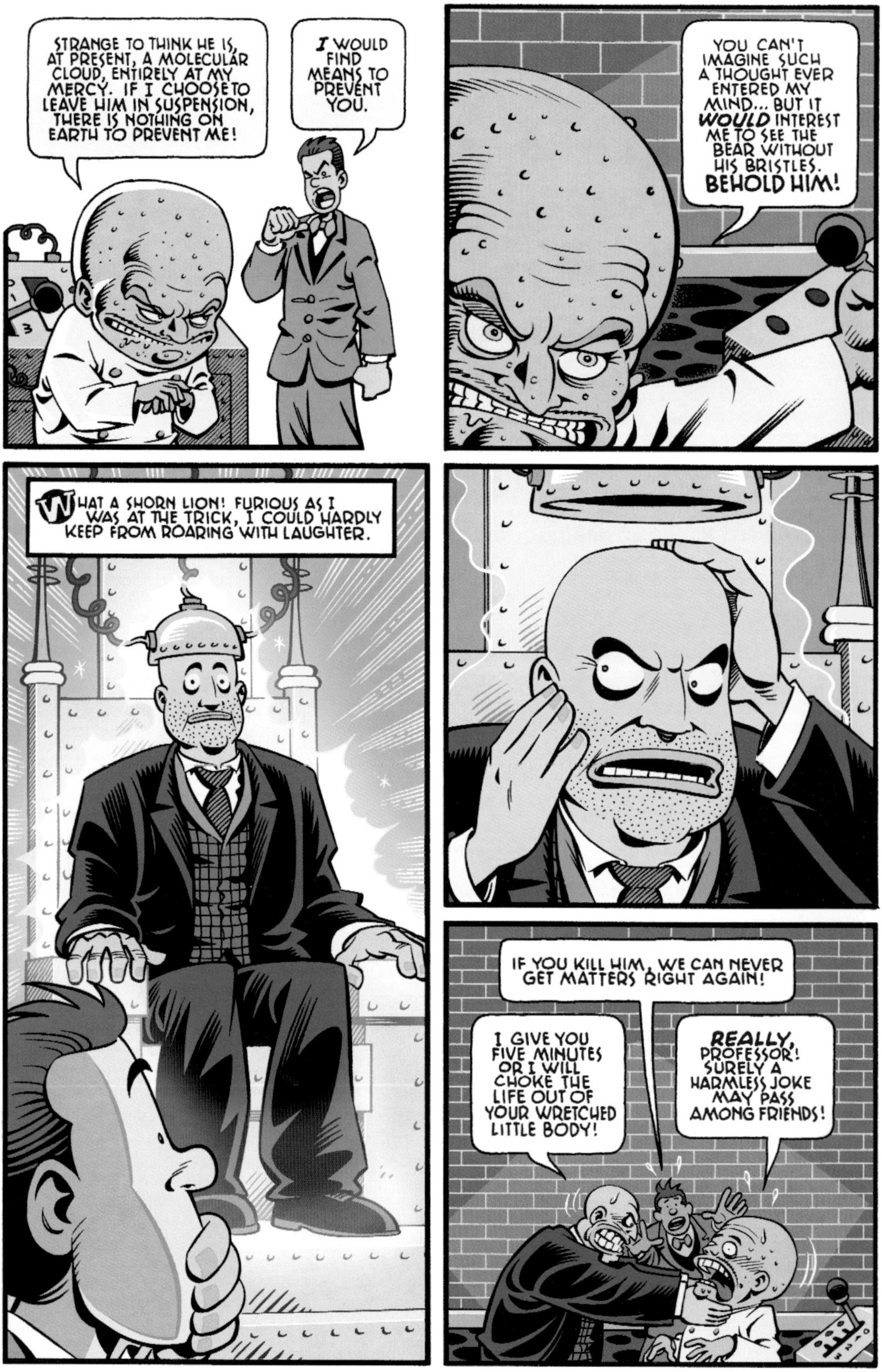
STRANGE TO THINK HE IS, AT PRESENT, A MOLECULAR CLOUD, ENTIRELY AT MY MERCY. IF I CHOOSE TO LEAVE HIM IN SUSPENSION, THERE IS NOTHING ON EARTH TO PREVENT ME!
I WOULD FIND MEANS TO PREVENT YOU.
YOU CAN'T IMAGINE SUCH A THOUGHT EVER ENTERED MY MIND... BUT IT WOULD INTEREST ME TO SEE THE BEAR WITHOUT HIS BRISTLES. BEHOLD HIM!
WHAT A SHORN LION! FURIOUS AS I WAS AT THE TRICK, I COULD HARDLY KEEP FROM ROARING WITH LAUGHTER.
IF YOU KILL HIM, WE CAN NEVER GET MATTERS RIGHT AGAIN!
I GIVE YOU FIVE MINUTES OR I WILL CHOKE THE LIFE OUT OF YOUR WRETCHED LITTLE BODY!
REALLY, PROFESSOR! SURELY A HARMLESS JOKE MAY PASS AMONG FRIENDS!

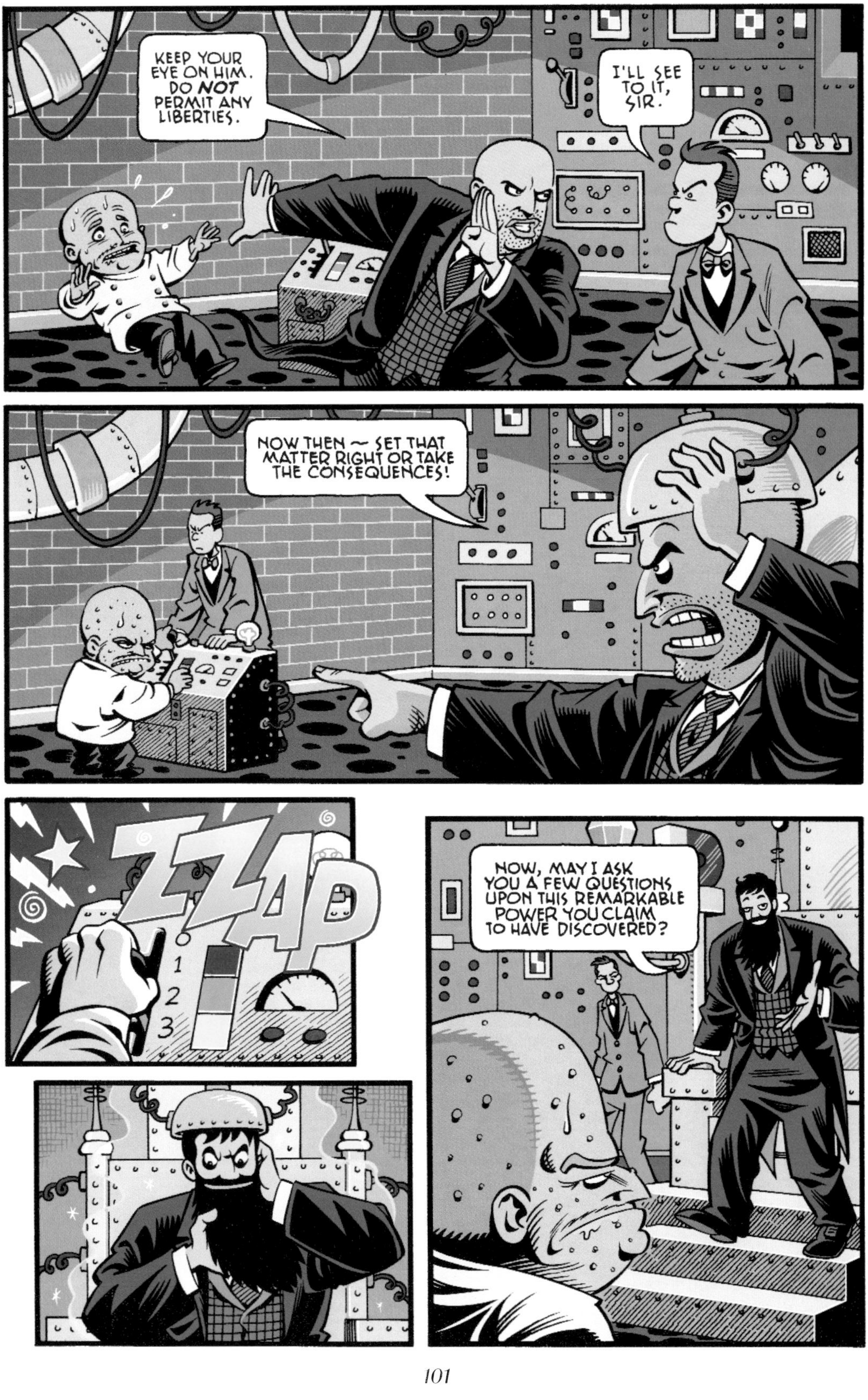
KEEP YOUR EYE ON HIM. DO NOT PERMIT ANY LIBERTIES.
I'LL SEE TO IT, SIR.
NOW THEN ~ SET THAT MATTER RIGHT OR TAKE THE CONSEQUENCES!
ZZAP
1
2
3
NOW, MAY I ASK YOU A FEW QUESTIONS UPON THIS REMARKABLE POWER YOU CLAIM TO HAVE DISCOVERED?

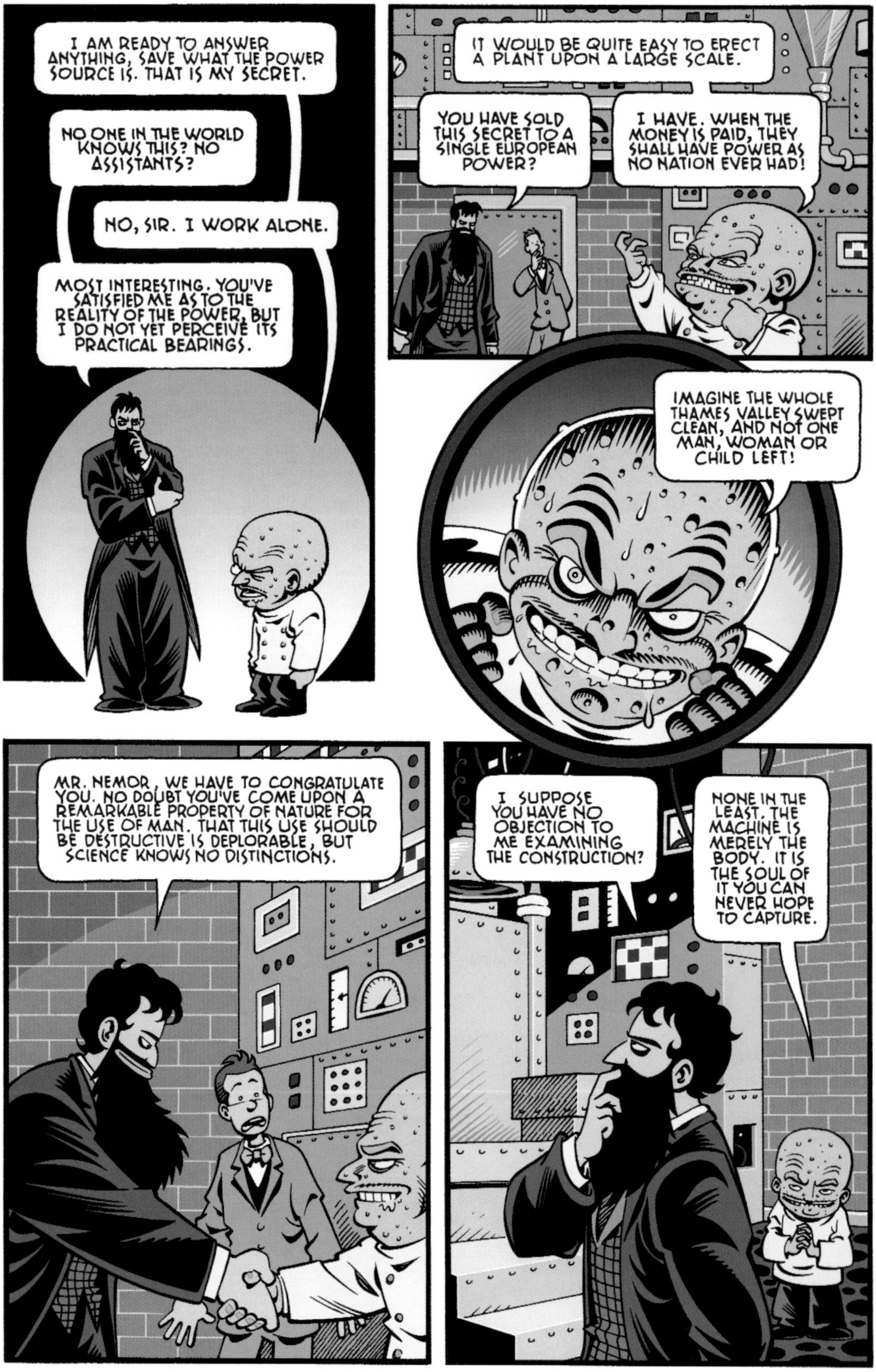
I AM READY TO ANSWER ANYTHING, SAVE WHAT THE POWER SOURCE IS. THAT IS MY SECRET.
NO ONE IN THE WORLD KNOWS THIS? NO ASSISTANTS?
NO, SIR. I WORK ALONE.
MOST INTERESTING. YOU'VE SATISFIED ME AS TO THE REALITY OF THE POWER, BUT I DO NOT YET PERCEIVE ITS PRACTICAL BEARINGS.
IT WOULD BE QUITE EASY TO ERECT A PLANT UPON A LARGE SCALE.
YOU HAVE SOLD THIS SECRET TO A SINGLE EUROPEAN POWER?
I HAVE. WHEN THE MONEY IS PAID, THEY SHALL HAVE POWER AS NO NATION EVER HAD!
IMAGINE THE WHOLE THAMES VALLEY SWEPT CLEAN, AND NOT ONE MAN, WOMAN OR CHILD LEFT!
MR. NEMOR, WE HAVE TO CONGRATULATE YOU. NO DOUBT YOU'VE COME UPON A REMARKABLE PROPERTY OF NATURE FOR THE USE OF MAN. THAT THIS USE SHOULD BE DESTRUCTIVE IS DEPLORABLE, BUT SCIENCE KNOWS NO DISTINCTIONS.
I SUPPOSE YOU HAVE NO OBJECTION TO ME EXAMINING THE CONSTRUCTION?
NONE IN THE LEAST. THE MACHINE IS MERELY THE BODY. IT IS THE SOUL OF IT YOU CAN NEVER HOPE TO CAPTURE.

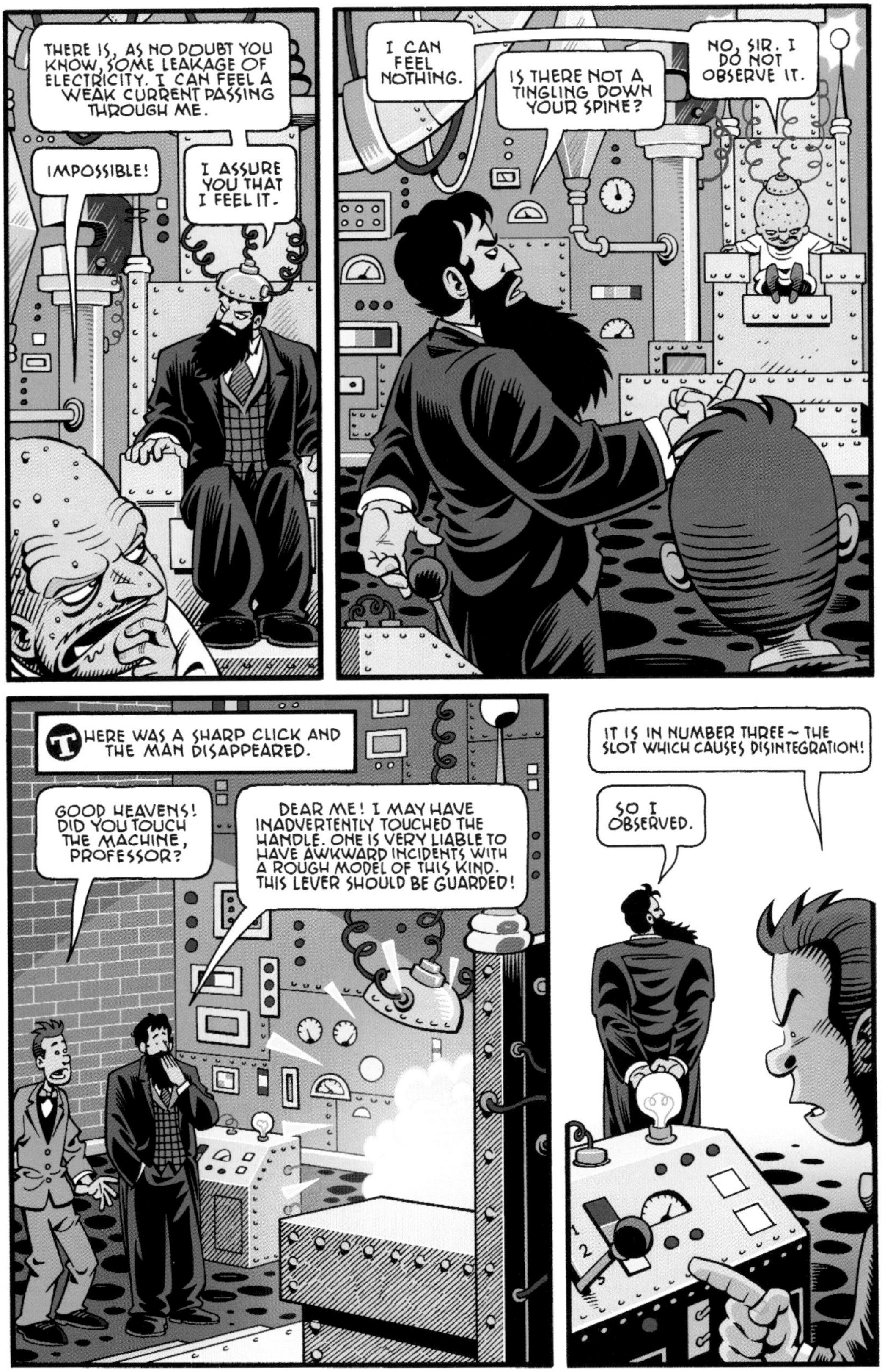
THERE IS, AS NO DOUBT YOU KNOW, SOME LEAKAGE OF ELECTRICITY. I CAN FEEL A WEAK CURRENT PASSING THROUGH ME.
IMPOSSIBLE!
I ASSURE YOU THAT I FEEL IT.
I CAN FEEL NOTHING.
IS THERE NOT A TINGLING DOWN YOUR SPINE?
NO, SIR. I DO NOT OBSERVE IT.
THERE WAS A SHARP CLICK AND THE MAN DISAPPEARED.
GOOD HEAVENS! DID YOU TOUCH THE MACHINE, PROFESSOR?
DEAR ME! I MAY HAVE INADVERTENTLY TOUCHED THE HANDLE. ONE IS VERY LIABLE TO HAVE AWKWARD INCIDENTS WITH A ROUGH MODEL OF THIS KIND. THIS LEVER SHOULD BE GUARDED!
IT IS IN NUMBER THREE ~ THE SLOT WHICH CAUSES DISINTEGRATION!
SO I OBSERVED.
1
2
3

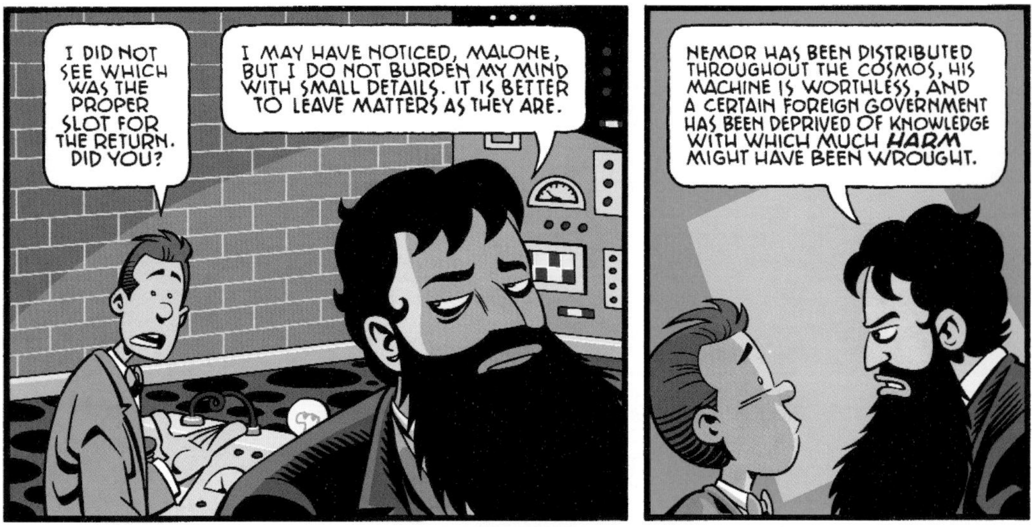
I DID NOT SEE WHICH WAS THE PROPER SLOT FOR THE RETURN. DID YOU?
I MAY HAVE NOTICED, MALONE, BUT I DO NOT BURDEN MY MIND WITH SMALL DETAILS. IT IS BETTER TO LEAVE MATTERS AS THEY ARE.
NEMOR HAS BEEN DISTRIBUTED THROUGHOUT THE COSMOS, HIS MACHINE IS WORTHLESS, AND A CERTAIN FOREIGN GOVERNMENT HAS BEEN DEPRIVED OF KNOWLEDGE WITH WHICH MUCH HARM MIGHT HAVE BEEN WROUGHT.

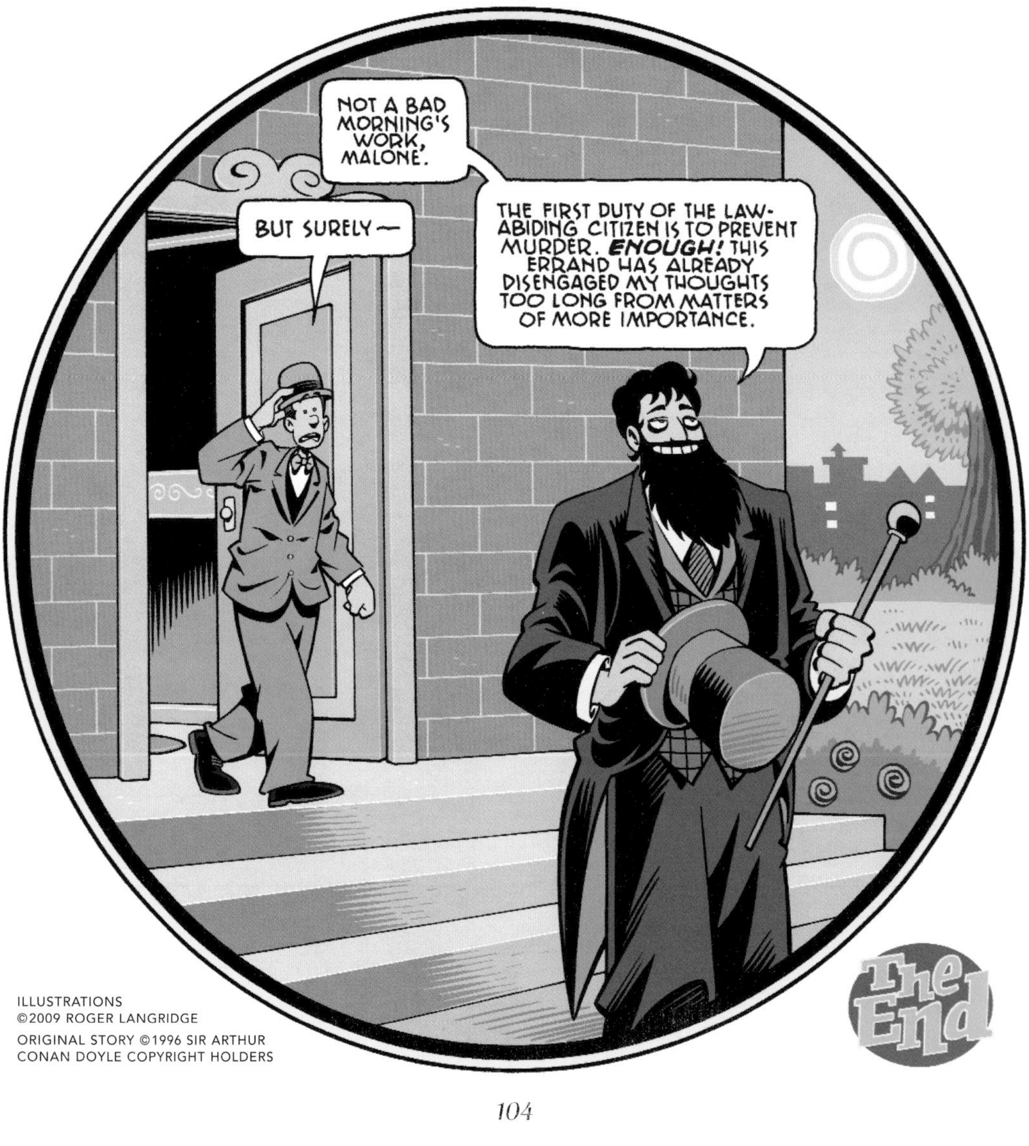
NOT A BAD MORNING'S WORK, MALONE.
BUT SURELY—
THE FIRST DUTY OF THE LAW-ABIDING CITIZEN IS TO PREVENT MURDER. ENOUGH! THIS ERRAND HAS ALREADY DISENGAGED MY THOUGHTS TOO LONG FROM MATTERS OF MORE IMPORTANCE.
The End

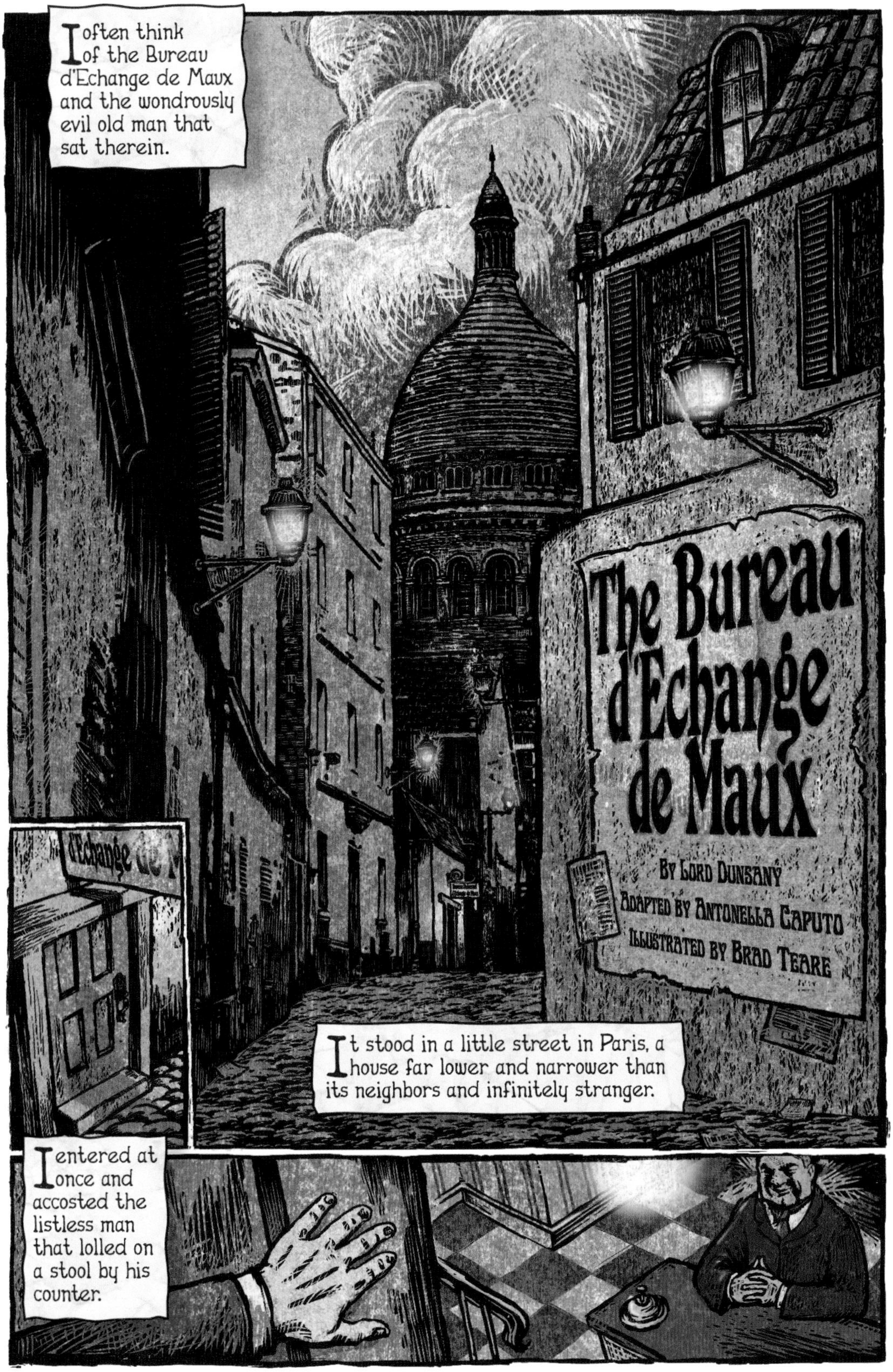
I often think of the Bureau d'Echange de Maux and the wondrously evil old man that sat therein.
The Bureau d'Echange de Maux
By Lord Dunsany
Adapted by Antonella Caputo
Illustrated by Brad Teare
d'Echange de
It stood in a little street in Paris, a house far lower and narrower than its neighbors and infinitely stranger.
I entered at once and accosted the listless man that lolled on a stool by his counter.

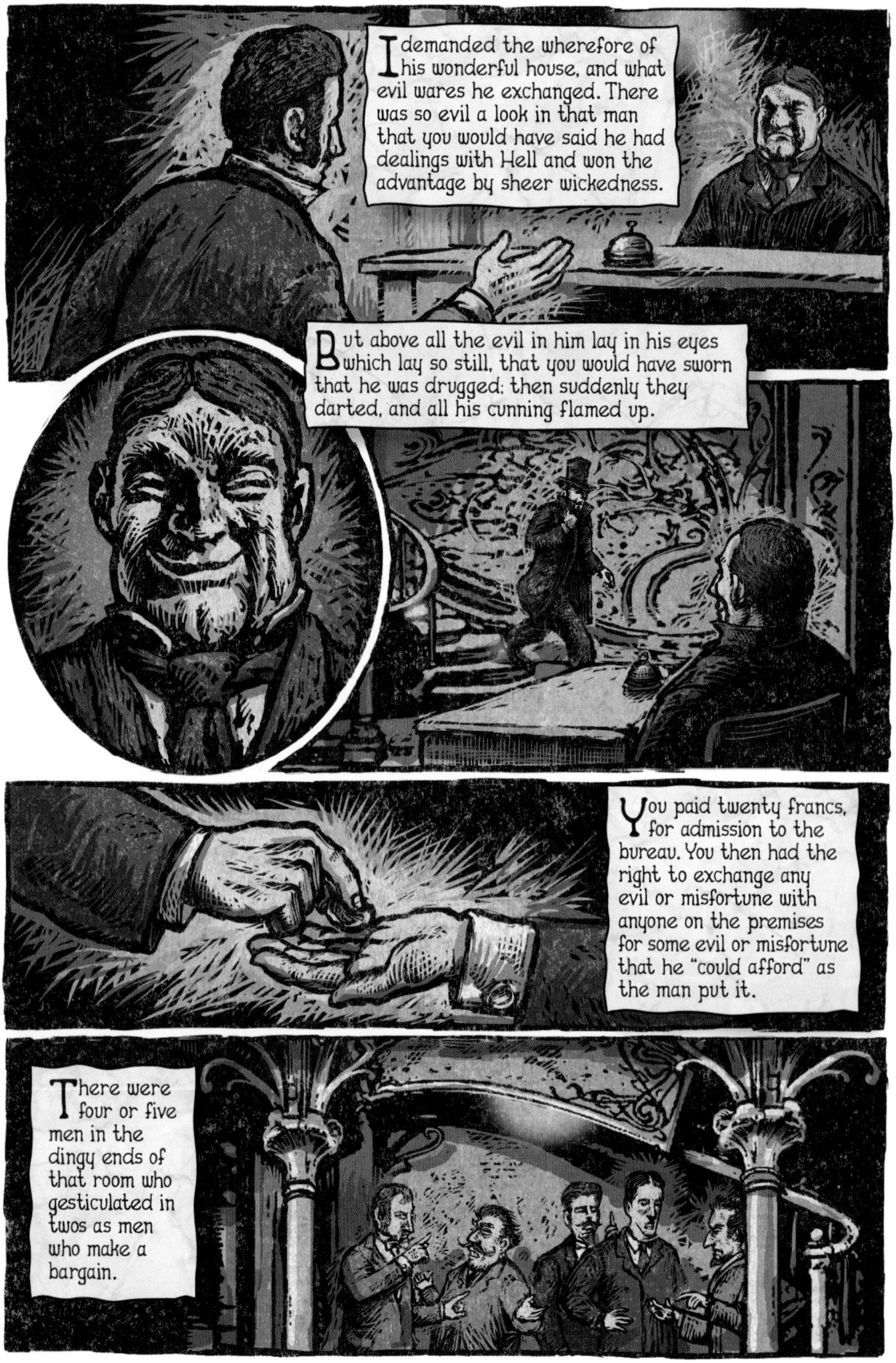
I demanded the wherefore of his wonderful house, and what evil wares he exchanged. There was so evil a look in that man that you would have said he had dealings with Hell and won the advantage by sheer wickedness.
But above all the evil in him lay in his eyes which lay so still, that you would have sworn that he was drugged; then suddenly they darted, and all his cunning flamed up.
You paid twenty francs, for admission to the bureau. You then had the right to exchange any evil or misfortune with anyone on the premises for some evil or misfortune that he "could afford" as the man put it.
There were four or five men in the dingy ends of that room who gesticulated in twos as men who make a bargain.

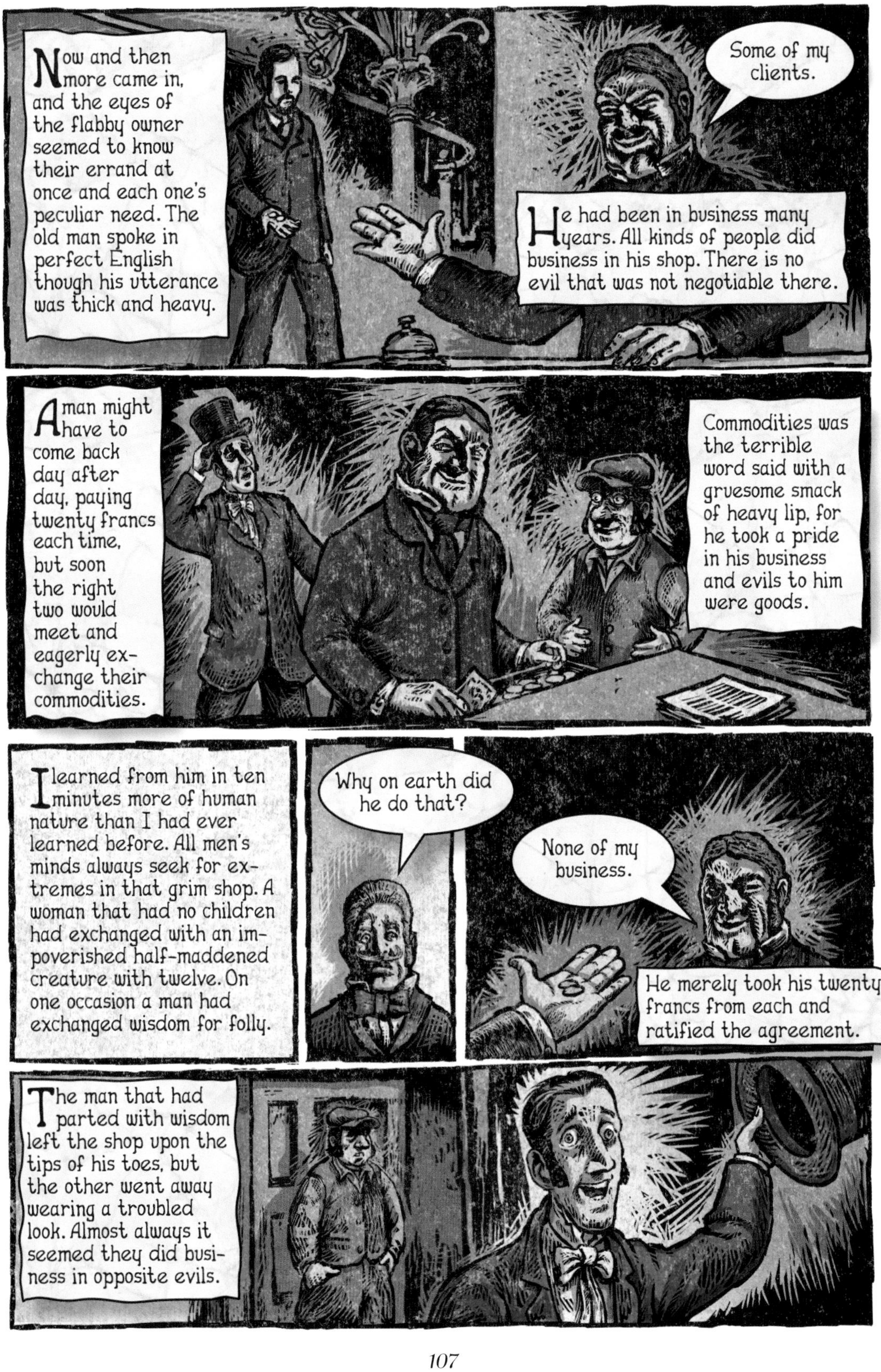
Now and then more came in, and the eyes of the flabby owner seemed to know their errand at once and each one's peculiar need. The old man spoke in perfect English though his utterance was thick and heavy.
Some of my clients.
He had been in business many years. All kinds of people did business in his shop. There is no evil that was not negotiable there.
A man might have to come back day after day, paying twenty francs each time, but soon the right two would meet and eagerly exchange their commodities.
Commodities was the terrible word said with a gruesome smack of heavy lip, for he took a pride in his business and evils to him were goods.
I learned from him in ten minutes more of human nature than I had ever learned before. All men's minds always seek for extremes in that grim shop. A woman that had no children had exchanged with an impoverished half-maddened creature with twelve. On one occasion a man had exchanged wisdom for folly.
Why on earth did he do that?
None of my business.
He merely took his twenty francs from each and ratified the agreement.
The man that had parted with wisdom left the shop upon the tips of his toes, but the other went away wearing a troubled look. Almost always it seemed they did business in opposite evils.

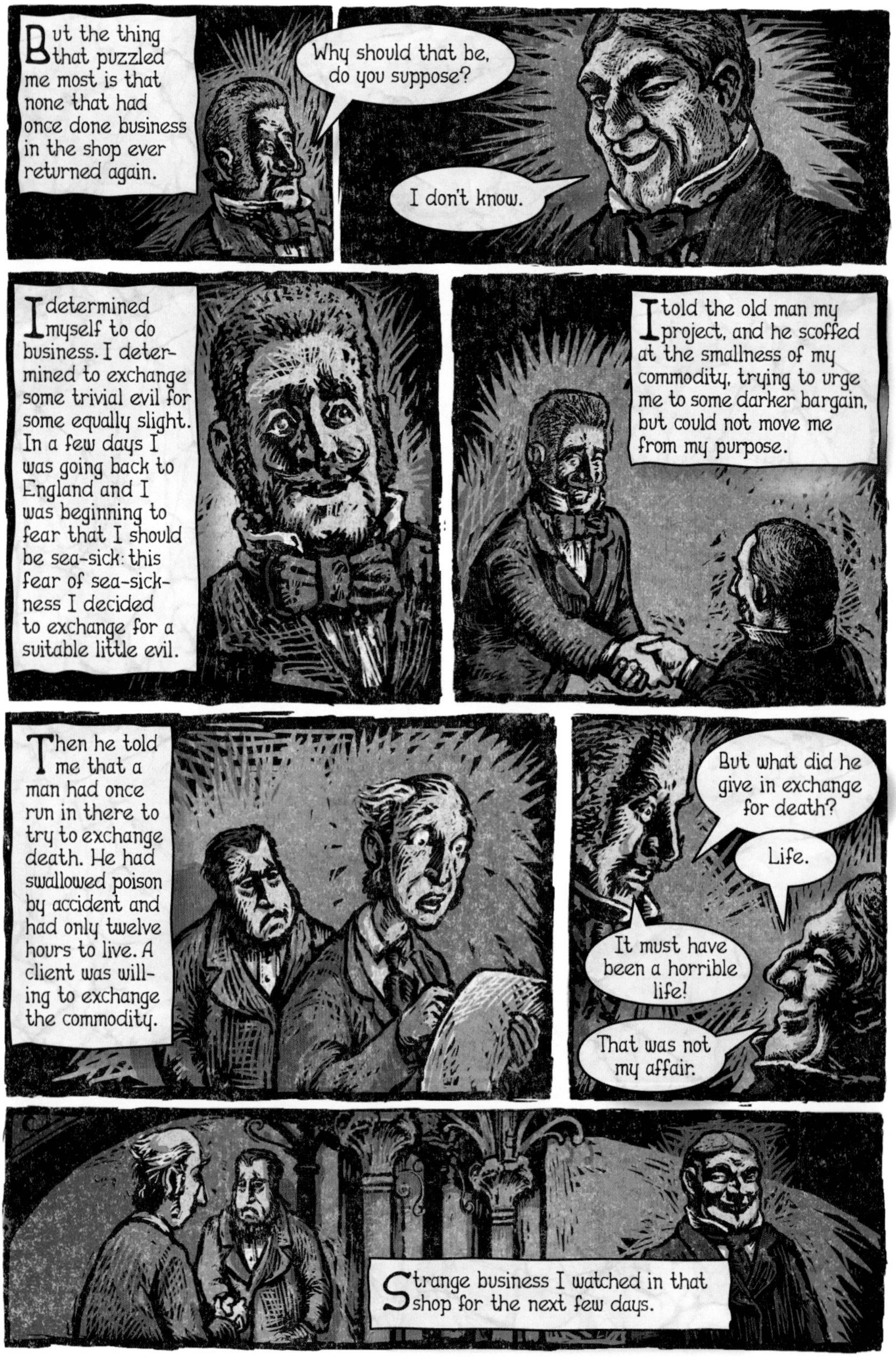
But the thing that puzzled me most is that none that had once done business in the shop ever returned again.
Why should that be, do you suppose?
I don't know.
I determined myself to do business. I determined to exchange some trivial evil for some equally slight. In a few days I was going back to England and I was beginning to fear that I should be sea-sick: this fear of sea-sickness I decided to exchange for a suitable little evil.
I told the old man my project, and he scoffed at the smallness of my commodity, trying to urge me to some darker bargain, but could not move me from my purpose.
Then he told me that a man had once run in there to try to exchange death. He had swallowed poison by accident and had only twelve hours to live. A client was willing to exchange the commodity.
But what did he give in exchange for death?
Life.
It must have been a horrible life!
That was not my affair.
Strange business I watched in that shop for the next few days.

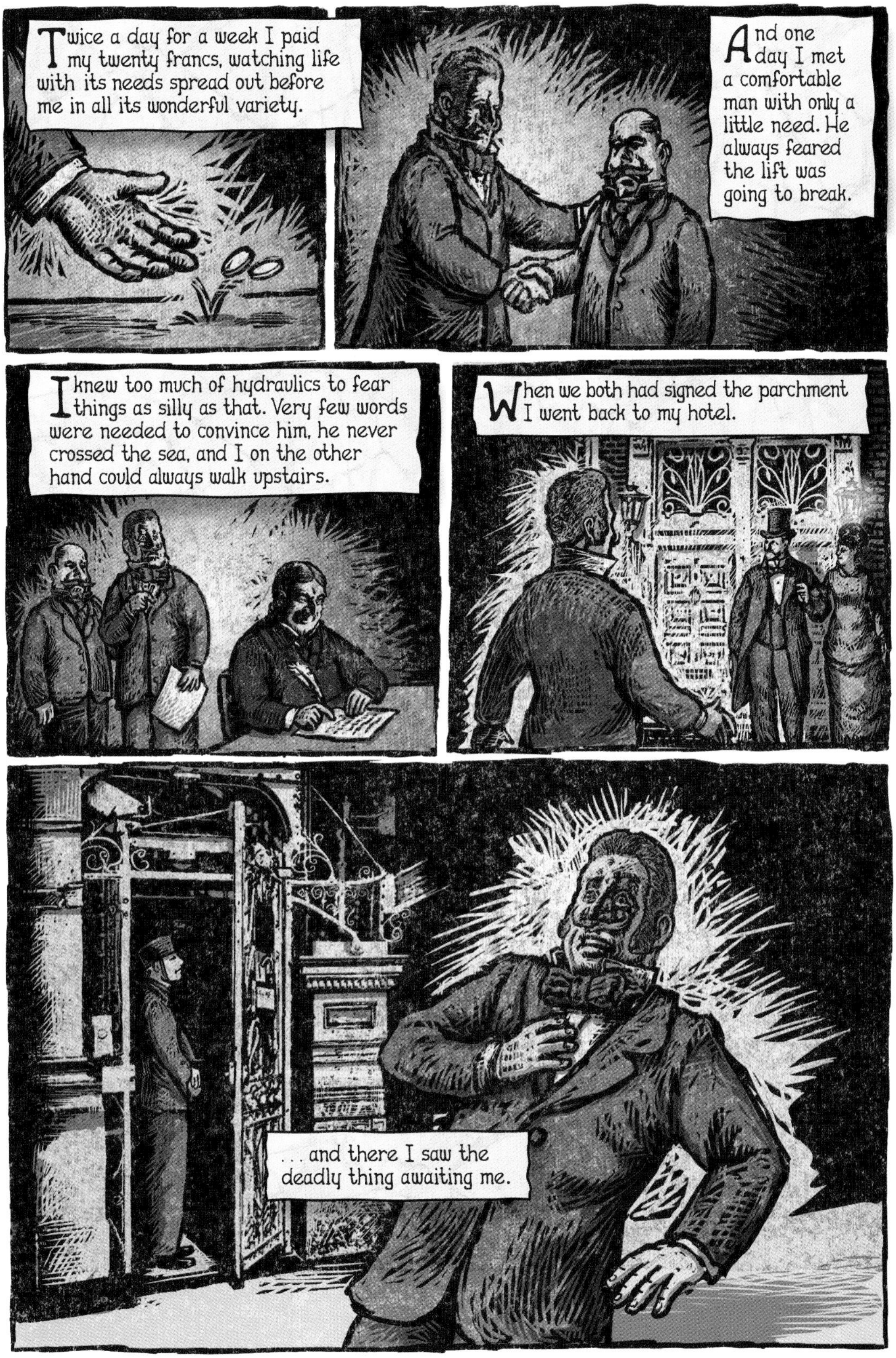
Twice a day for a week I paid my twenty francs, watching life with its needs spread out before me in all its wonderful variety.
And one day I met a comfortable man with only a little need. He always feared the lift was going to break.
I knew too much of hydraulics to fear things as silly as that. Very few words were needed to convince him, he never crossed the sea, and I on the other hand could always walk upstairs.
When we both had signed the parchment I went back to my hotel.
. . . and there I saw the deadly thing awaiting me.

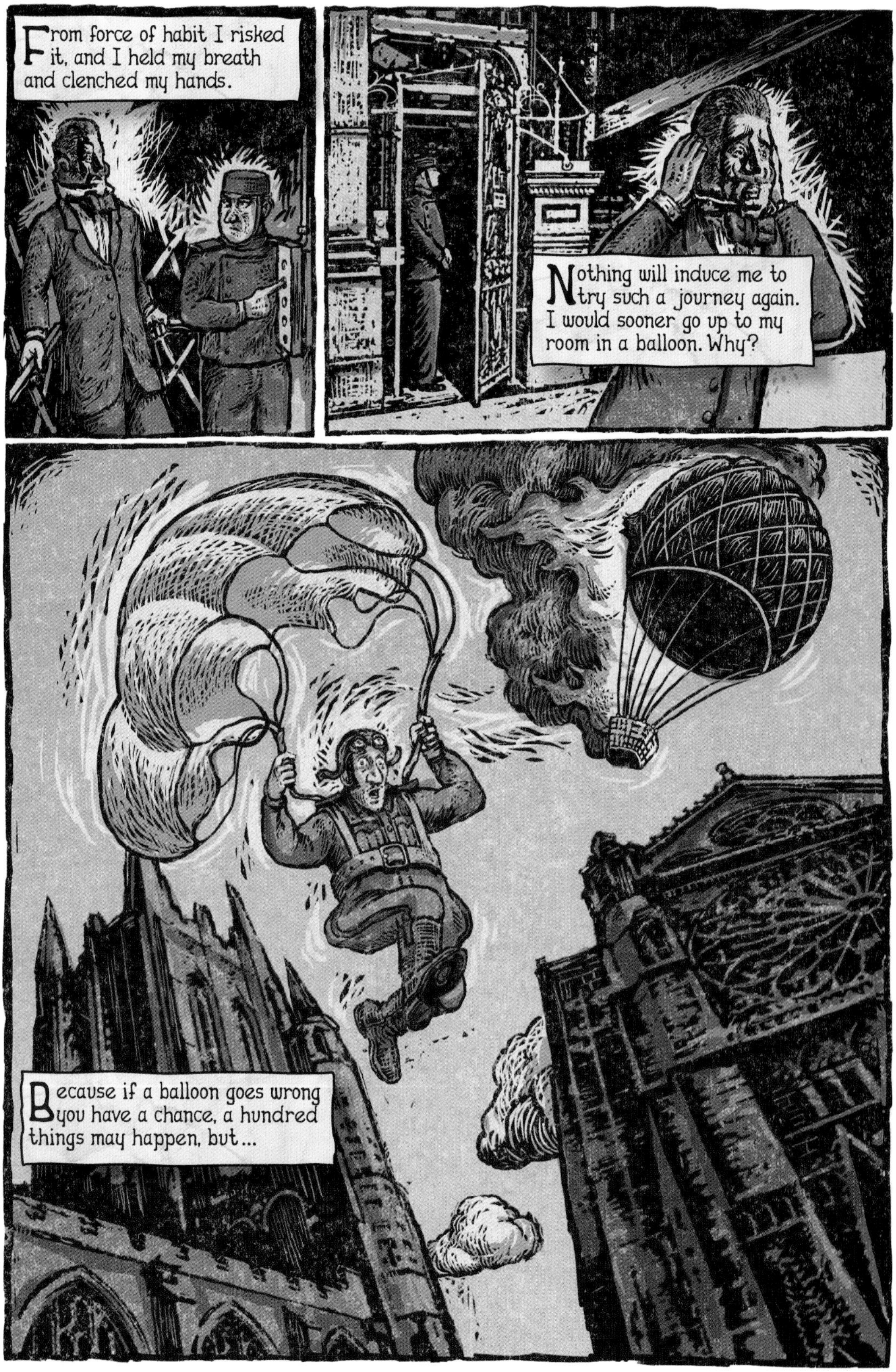
From force of habit I risked it, and I held my breath and clenched my hands.
Nothing will induce me to try such a journey again. I would sooner go up to my room in a balloon. Why?
Because if a balloon goes wrong you have a chance, a hundred things may happen, but...

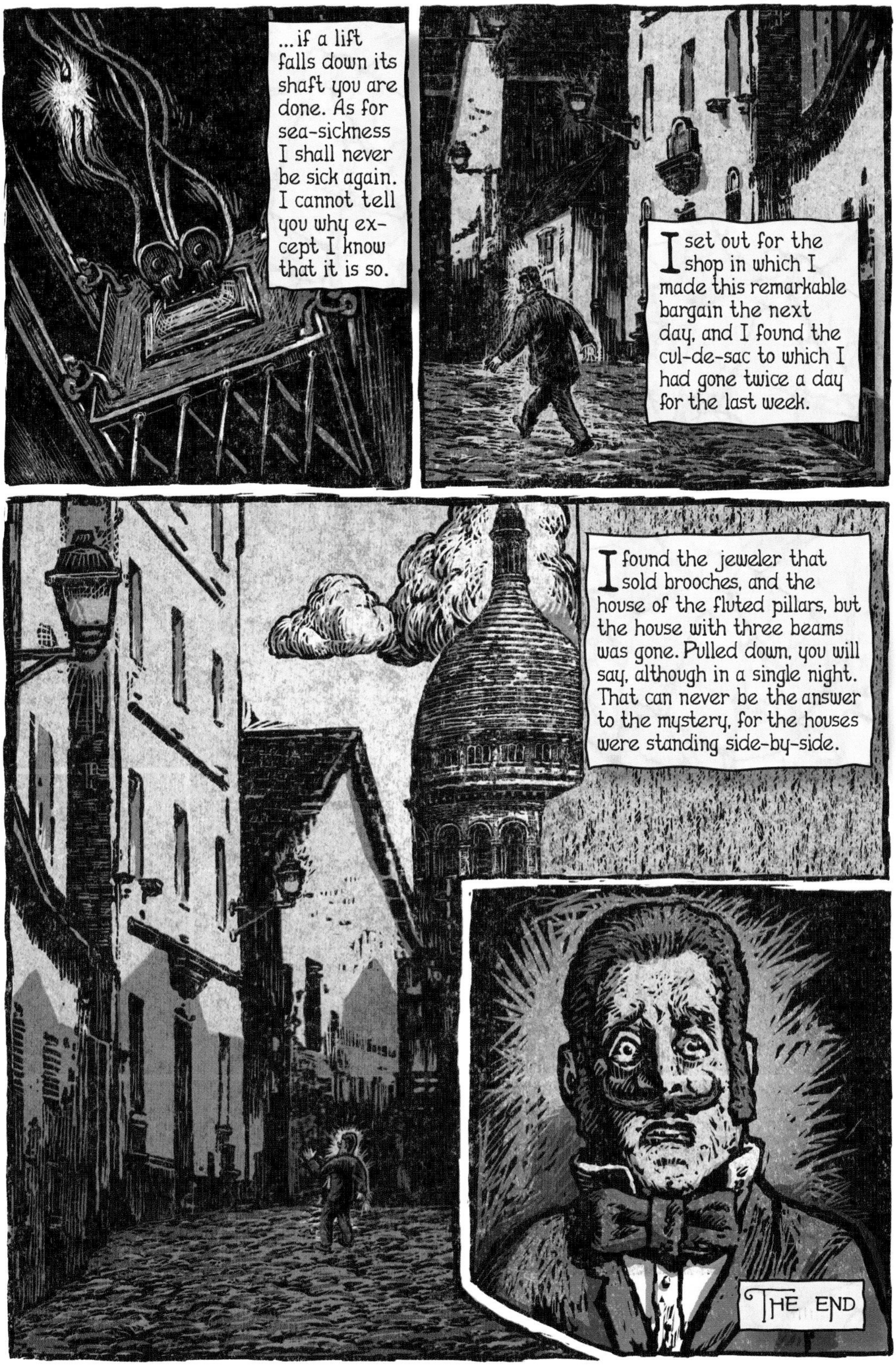
...if a lift falls down its shaft you are done. As for sea-sickness I shall never be sick again. I cannot tell you why except I know that it is so.
I set out for the shop in which I made this remarkable bargain the next day, and I found the cul-de-sac to which I had gone twice a day for the last week.
I found the jeweler that sold brooches, and the house of the fluted pillars, but the house with three beams was gone. Pulled down, you will say, although in a single night. That can never be the answer to the mystery, for the houses were standing side-by-side.
THE END

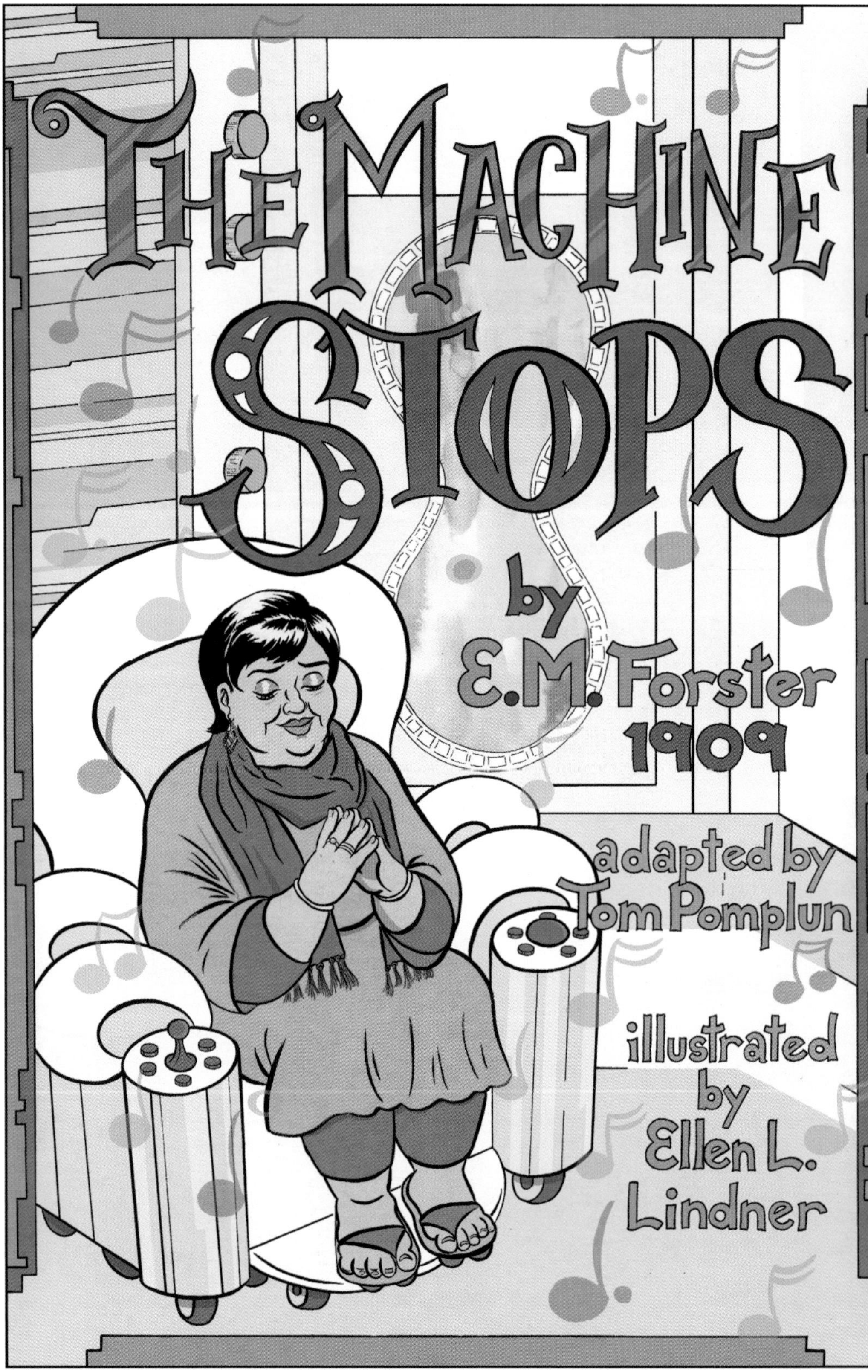
The Machine Stops
by
E.M. Forster
1909
adapted by
Tom Pomplun
illustrated
by
Ellen L.
Lindner

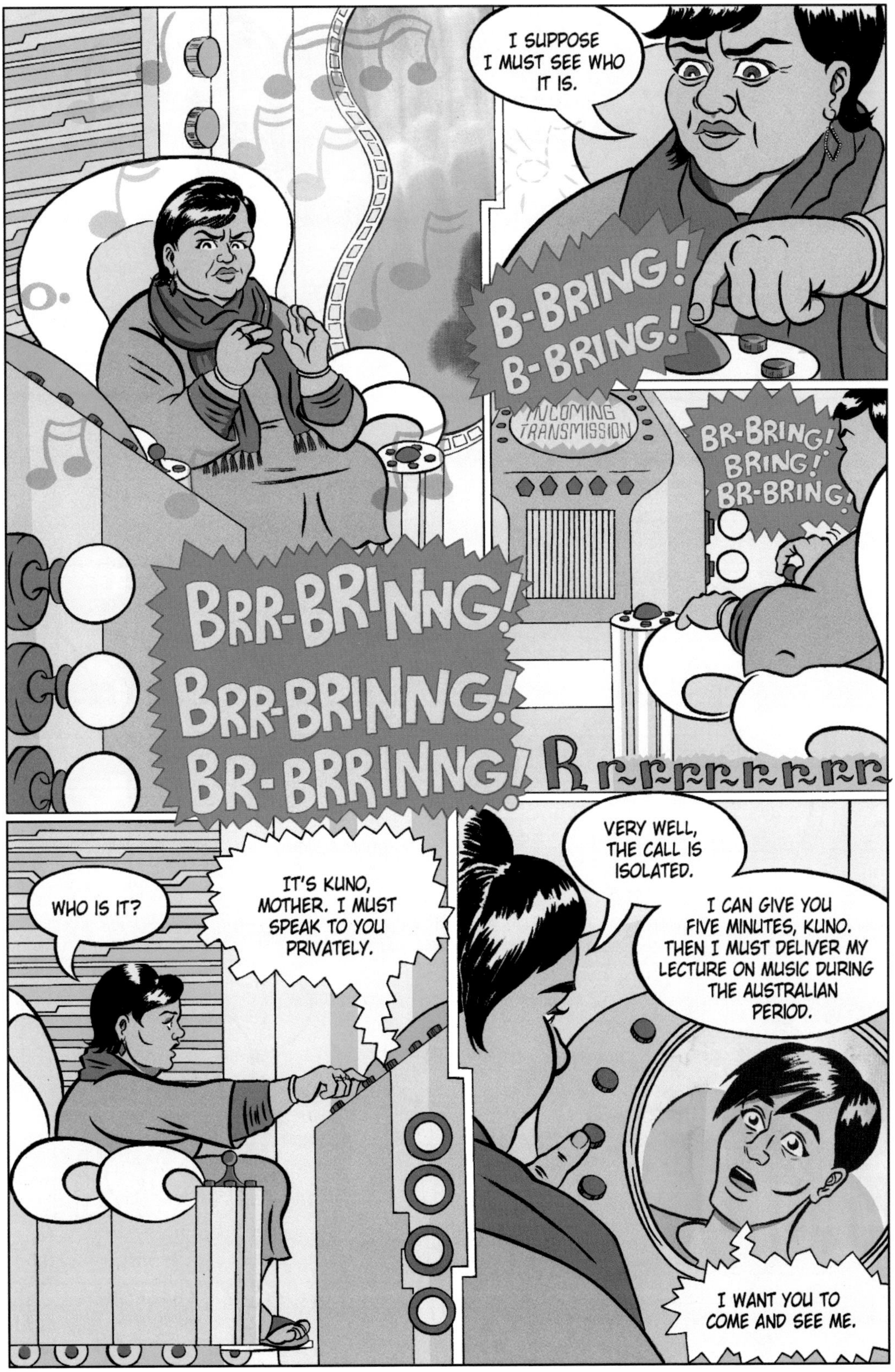
I SUPPOSE I MUST SEE WHO IT IS.
B-BRING! B-BRING!
INCOMING TRANSMISSION
BR-BRING! BRING! BR-BRING!
BRR-BRINNG! BRR-BRINNG! BR-BRRINNG!
Rrrrrrrrrrr
WHO IS IT?
IT'S KUNO, MOTHER. I MUST SPEAK TO YOU PRIVATELY.
VERY WELL, THE CALL IS ISOLATED.
I CAN GIVE YOU FIVE MINUTES, KUNO. THEN I MUST DELIVER MY LECTURE ON MUSIC DURING THE AUSTRALIAN PERIOD.
I WANT YOU TO COME AND SEE ME.

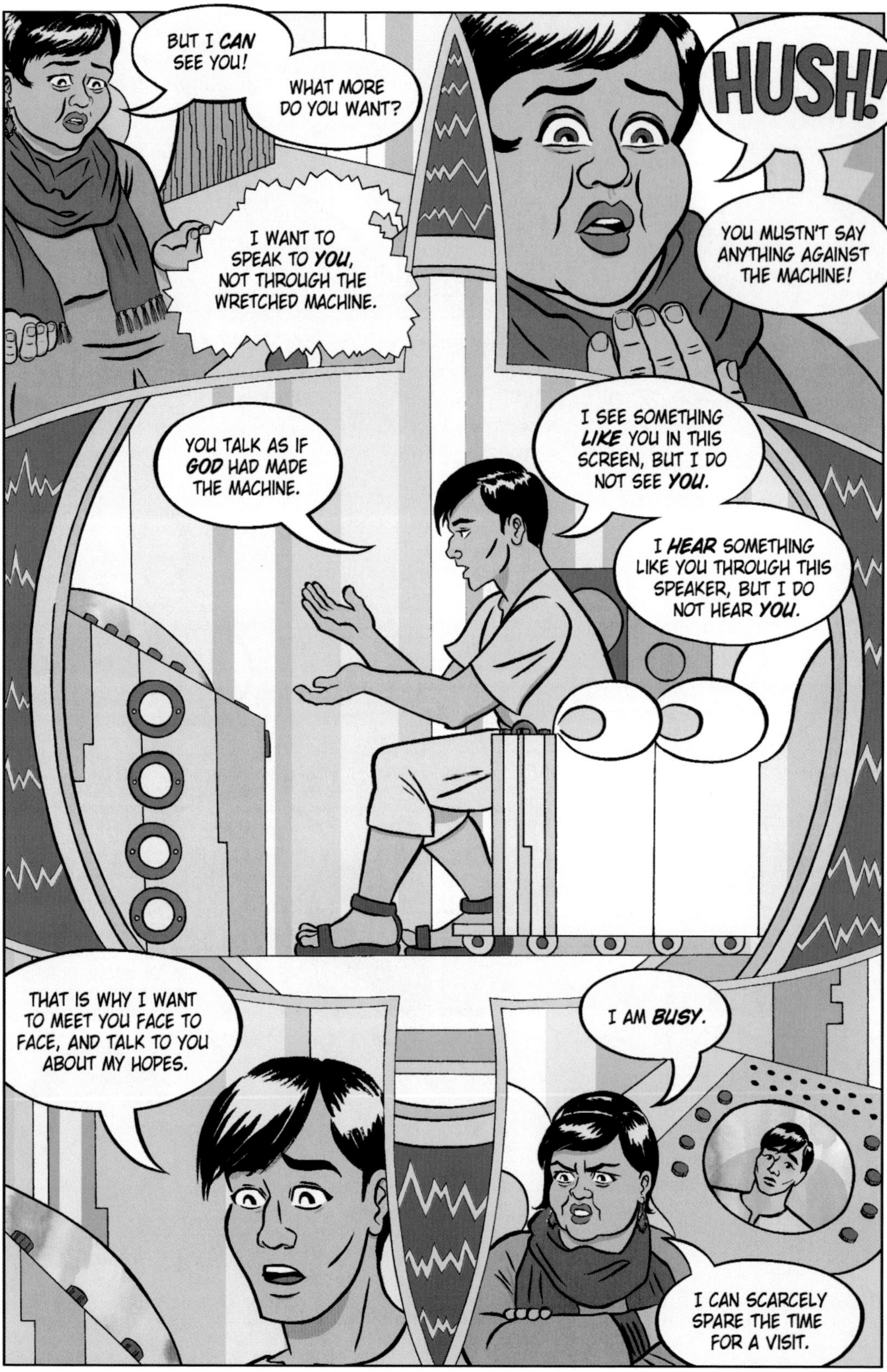
BUT I CAN SEE YOU!
WHAT MORE DO YOU WANT?
I WANT TO SPEAK TO YOU, NOT THROUGH THE WRETCHED MACHINE.
HUSH!
YOU MUSTN'T SAY ANYTHING AGAINST THE MACHINE!
YOU TALK AS IF GOD HAD MADE THE MACHINE.
I SEE SOMETHING LIKE YOU IN THIS SCREEN, BUT I DO NOT SEE YOU.
I HEAR SOMETHING LIKE YOU THROUGH THIS SPEAKER, BUT I DO NOT HEAR YOU.
THAT IS WHY I WANT TO MEET YOU FACE TO FACE, AND TALK TO YOU ABOUT MY HOPES.
I AM BUSY.
I CAN SCARCELY SPARE THE TIME FOR A VISIT.

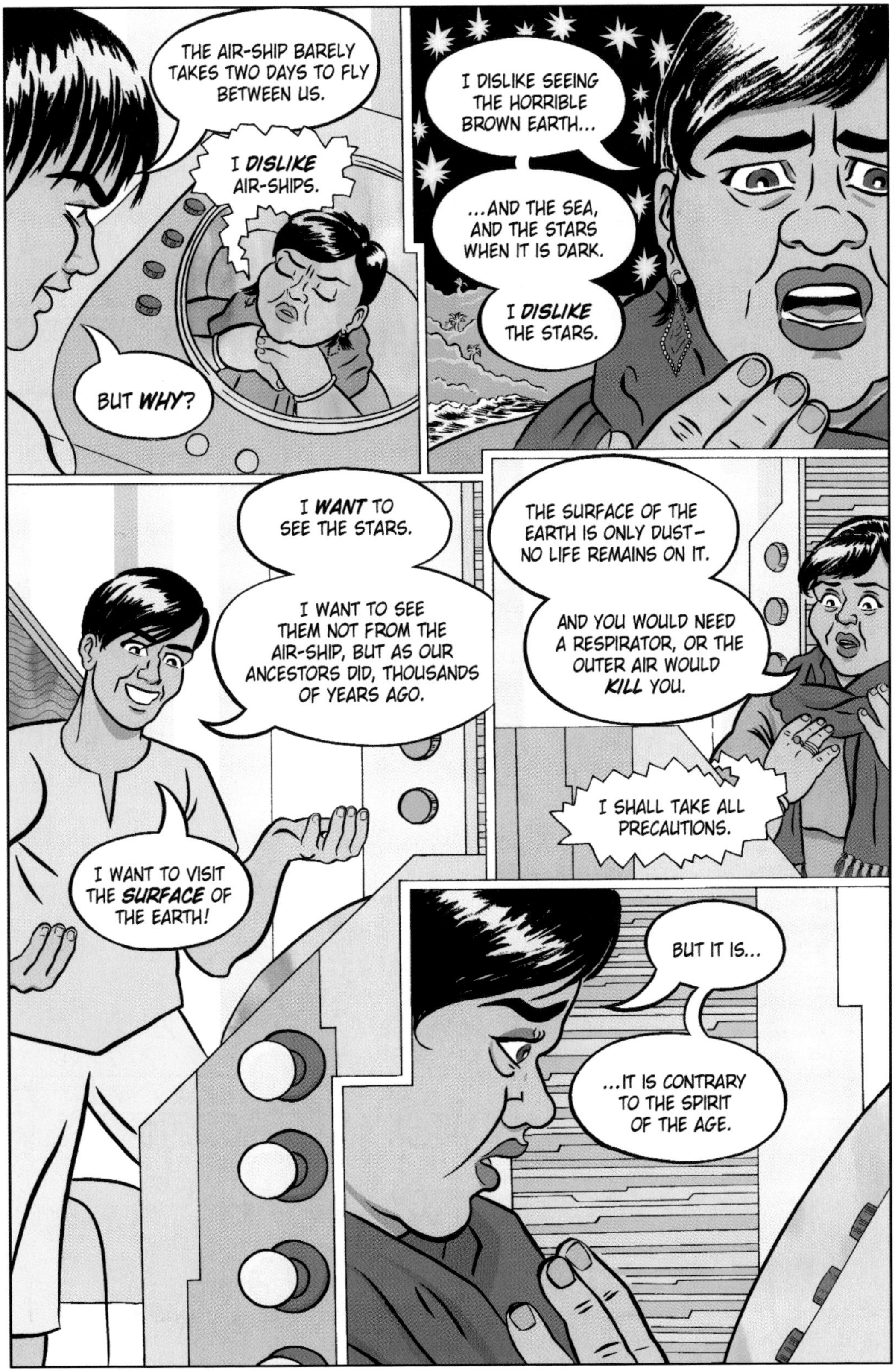
THE AIR-SHIP BARELY TAKES TWO DAYS TO FLY BETWEEN US.
I DISLIKE AIR-SHIPS.
BUT WHY?
I DISLIKE SEEING THE HORRIBLE BROWN EARTH...
...AND THE SEA, AND THE STARS WHEN IT IS DARK.
I DISLIKE THE STARS.
I WANT TO SEE THE STARS.
I WANT TO SEE THEM NOT FROM THE AIR-SHIP, BUT AS OUR ANCESTORS DID, THOUSANDS OF YEARS AGO.
I WANT TO VISIT THE SURFACE OF THE EARTH!
THE SURFACE OF THE EARTH IS ONLY DUST— NO LIFE REMAINS ON IT.
AND YOU WOULD NEED A RESPIRATOR, OR THE OUTER AIR WOULD KILL YOU.
I SHALL TAKE ALL PRECAUTIONS.
BUT IT IS...
...IT IS CONTRARY TO THE SPIRIT OF THE AGE.

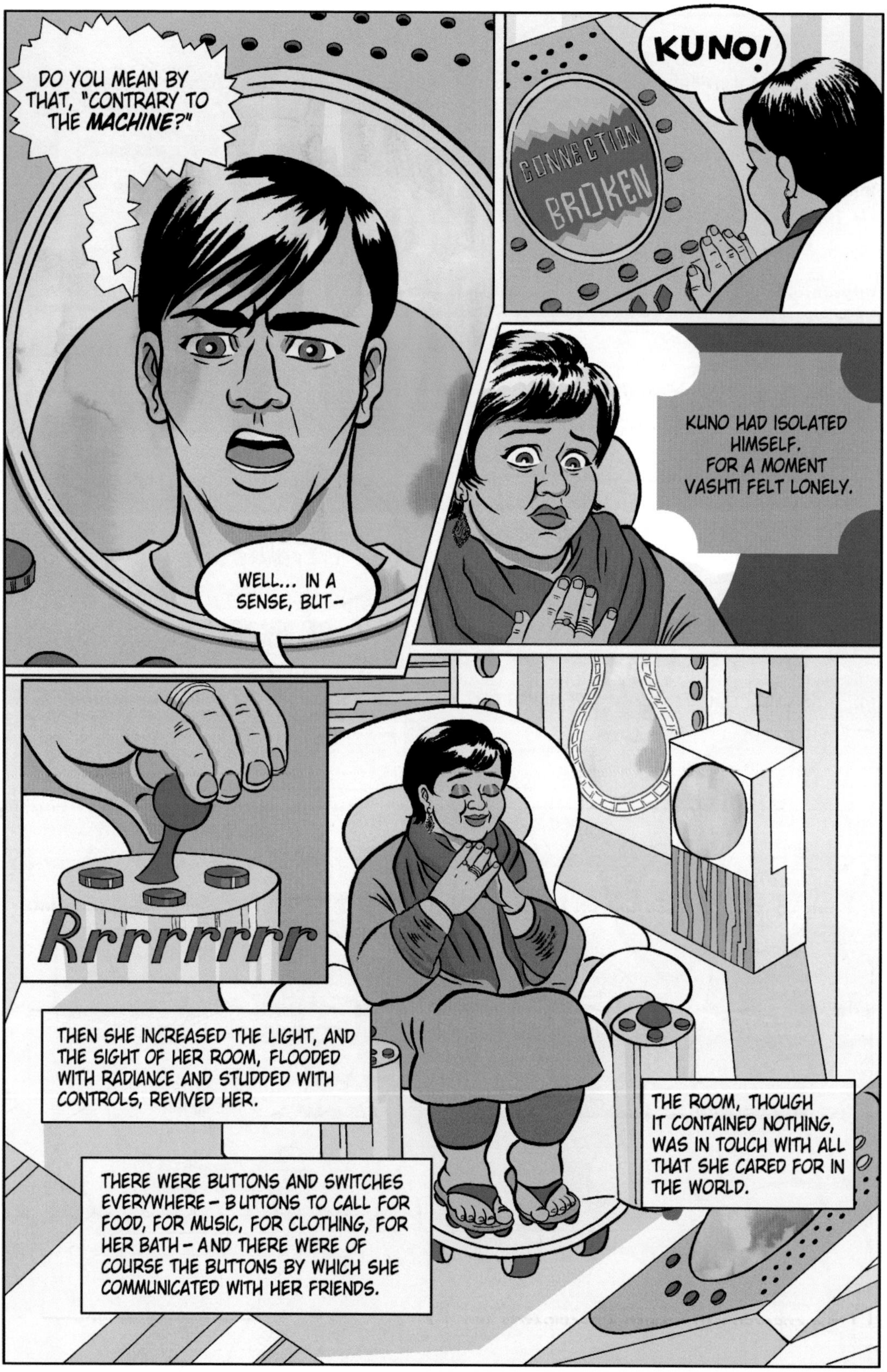
DO YOU MEAN BY THAT, "CONTRARY TO THE **MACHINE?**"
WELL... IN A SENSE, BUT-
CONNECTION BROKEN
KUNO!
KUNO HAD ISOLATED HIMSELF. FOR A MOMENT VASHTI FELT LONELY.
Rrrrrrrr
THEN SHE INCREASED THE LIGHT, AND THE SIGHT OF HER ROOM, FLOODED WITH RADIANCE AND STUDDED WITH CONTROLS, REVIVED HER.
THERE WERE BUTTONS AND SWITCHES EVERYWHERE - BUTTONS TO CALL FOR FOOD, FOR MUSIC, FOR CLOTHING, FOR HER BATH - AND THERE WERE OF COURSE THE BUTTONS BY WHICH SHE COMMUNICATED WITH HER FRIENDS.
THE ROOM, THOUGH IT CONTAINED NOTHING, WAS IN TOUCH WITH ALL THAT SHE CARED FOR IN THE WORLD.

VASHTI TURNED OFF THE ISOLATION SWITCH, AND ALL THE ACCUMULATIONS OF THE LAST THREE MINUTES BURST UPON HER. "WHAT WAS THE NEW FOOD LIKE?" "HAS SHE HAD ANY IDEAS LATELY?" "WOULD SHE VISIT THE PUBLIC NURSERIES?..."

INCOMING CALL

SHE REPLIED THAT THE NEW FOOD WAS HORRIBLE, AND THAT SHE COULD NOT VISIT THE NURSERIES THROUGH PRESS OF ENGAGEMENTS.

SESSION FINISHED.

GOOD-BYE.

Rrrr Rrrrr

THEN SHE SWITCHED OFF HER CORRESPONDENTS, FOR IT WAS TIME TO DELIVER HER LECTURE ON AUSTRALIAN MUSIC.

THE CLUMSY SYSTEM OF PUBLIC GATHERINGS HAD BEEN LONG SINCE ABANDONED; NEITHER VASHTI NOR HER AUDIENCE STIRRED FROM THEIR ROOMS.

SEATED IN HER ARMCHAIR SHE SPOKE, WHILE THEY IN THEIR ARMCHAIRS HEARD HER AND SAW HER.

HER LECTURE, WHICH LASTED TEN MINUTES, WAS WELL RECEIVED, AND AT ITS CONCLUSION SHE LISTENED TO A LECTURE ON THE SEA.

THERE WERE IDEAS TO BE GOT FROM THE SEA; THE SPEAKER HAD DONNED A RESPIRATOR AND VISITED IT LATELY.

THEN SHE FED, TALKED TO MANY FRIENDS...

Rrrrrr

Rrr

...HAD A BATH, AND SUMMONED HER BED.

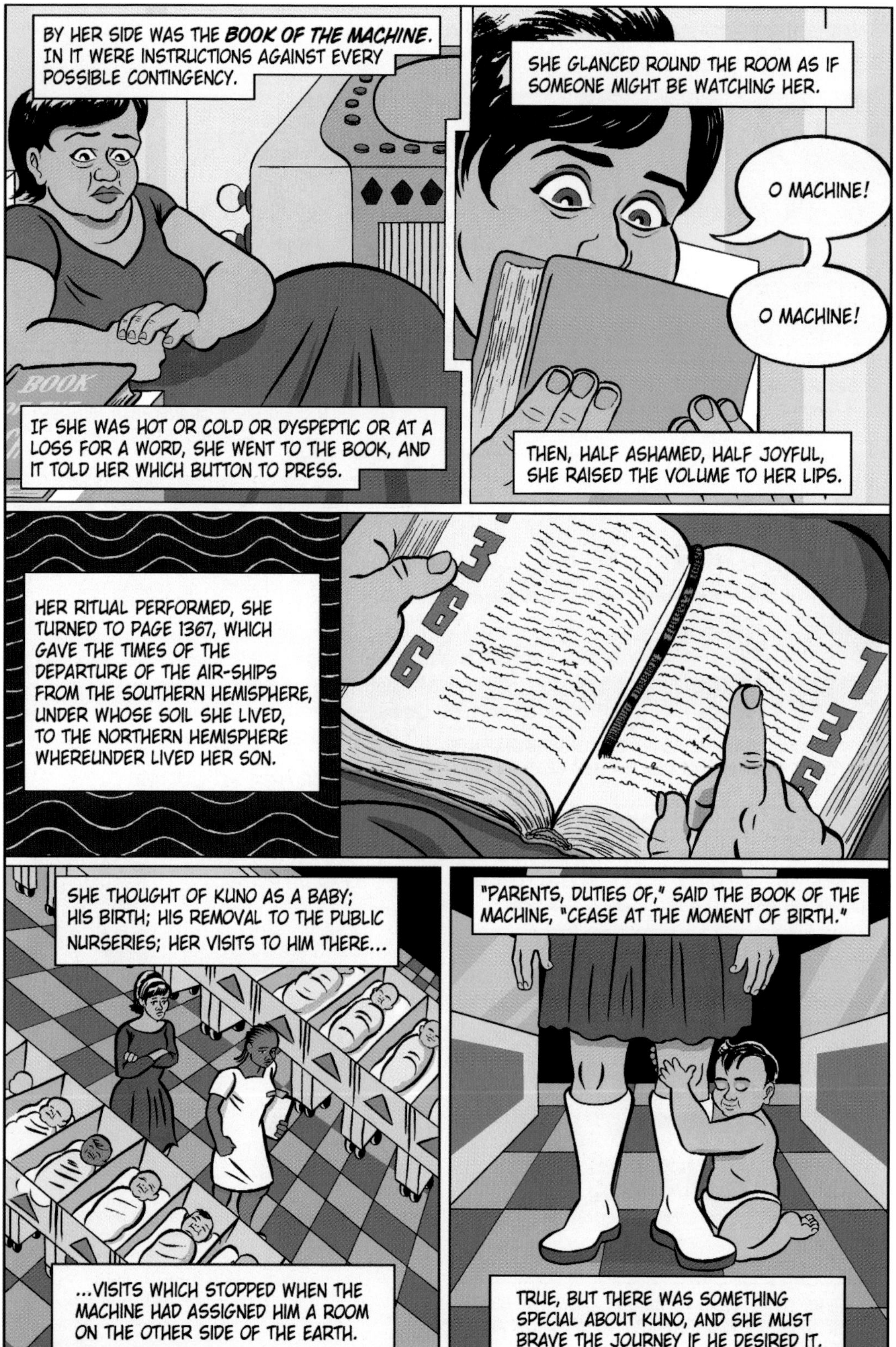
BY HER SIDE WAS THE ***BOOK OF THE MACHINE***. IN IT WERE INSTRUCTIONS AGAINST EVERY POSSIBLE CONTINGENCY.
BOOK
IF SHE WAS HOT OR COLD OR DYSPEPTIC OR AT A LOSS FOR A WORD, SHE WENT TO THE BOOK, AND IT TOLD HER WHICH BUTTON TO PRESS.
SHE GLANCED ROUND THE ROOM AS IF SOMEONE MIGHT BE WATCHING HER.
O MACHINE!
O MACHINE!
THEN, HALF ASHAMED, HALF JOYFUL, SHE RAISED THE VOLUME TO HER LIPS.
HER RITUAL PERFORMED, SHE TURNED TO PAGE 1367, WHICH GAVE THE TIMES OF THE DEPARTURE OF THE AIR-SHIPS FROM THE SOUTHERN HEMISPHERE, UNDER WHOSE SOIL SHE LIVED, TO THE NORTHERN HEMISPHERE WHEREUNDER LIVED HER SON.
SHE THOUGHT OF KUNO AS A BABY; HIS BIRTH; HIS REMOVAL TO THE PUBLIC NURSERIES; HER VISITS TO HIM THERE...
...VISITS WHICH STOPPED WHEN THE MACHINE HAD ASSIGNED HIM A ROOM ON THE OTHER SIDE OF THE EARTH.
"PARENTS, DUTIES OF," SAID THE BOOK OF THE MACHINE, "CEASE AT THE MOMENT OF BIRTH."
TRUE, BUT THERE WAS SOMETHING SPECIAL ABOUT KUNO, AND SHE MUST BRAVE THE JOURNEY IF HE DESIRED IT.

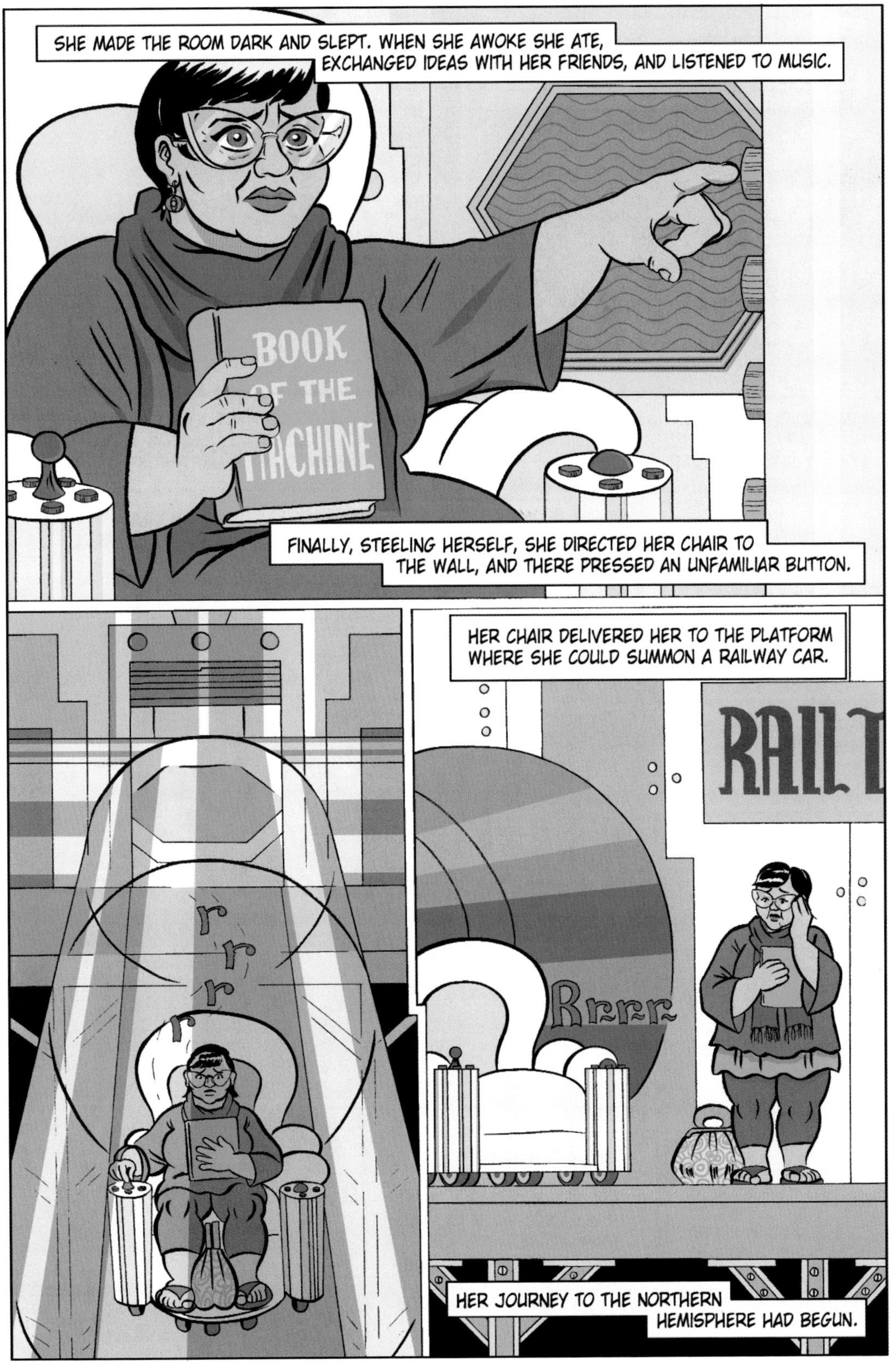
SHE MADE THE ROOM DARK AND SLEPT. WHEN SHE AWOKE SHE ATE, EXCHANGED IDEAS WITH HER FRIENDS, AND LISTENED TO MUSIC.
BOOK OF THE MACHINE
FINALLY, STEELING HERSELF, SHE DIRECTED HER CHAIR TO THE WALL, AND THERE PRESSED AN UNFAMILIAR BUTTON.
r r r r r
HER CHAIR DELIVERED HER TO THE PLATFORM WHERE SHE COULD SUMMON A RAILWAY CAR.
RAIL
Rrrr
HER JOURNEY TO THE NORTHERN HEMISPHERE HAD BEGUN.

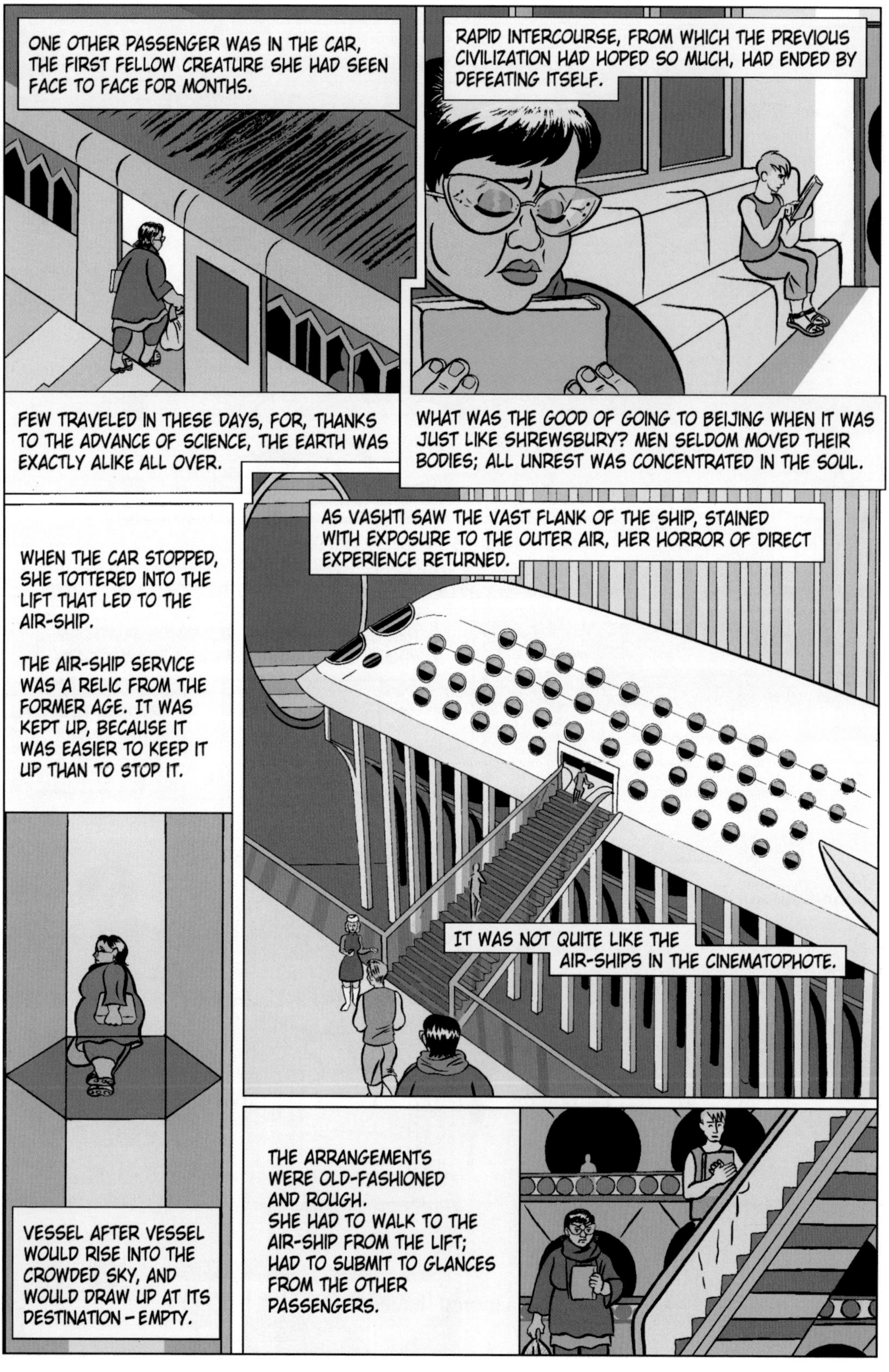
ONE OTHER PASSENGER WAS IN THE CAR, THE FIRST FELLOW CREATURE SHE HAD SEEN FACE TO FACE FOR MONTHS.
RAPID INTERCOURSE, FROM WHICH THE PREVIOUS CIVILIZATION HAD HOPED SO MUCH, HAD ENDED BY DEFEATING ITSELF.
FEW TRAVELED IN THESE DAYS, FOR, THANKS TO THE ADVANCE OF SCIENCE, THE EARTH WAS EXACTLY ALIKE ALL OVER.
WHAT WAS THE GOOD OF GOING TO BEIJING WHEN IT WAS JUST LIKE SHREWSBURY? MEN SELDOM MOVED THEIR BODIES; ALL UNREST WAS CONCENTRATED IN THE SOUL.
WHEN THE CAR STOPPED, SHE TOTTERED INTO THE LIFT THAT LED TO THE AIR-SHIP.
THE AIR-SHIP SERVICE WAS A RELIC FROM THE FORMER AGE. IT WAS KEPT UP, BECAUSE IT WAS EASIER TO KEEP IT UP THAN TO STOP IT.
AS VASHTI SAW THE VAST FLANK OF THE SHIP, STAINED WITH EXPOSURE TO THE OUTER AIR, HER HORROR OF DIRECT EXPERIENCE RETURNED.
IT WAS NOT QUITE LIKE THE AIR-SHIPS IN THE CINEMATOPHOTE.
VESSEL AFTER VESSEL WOULD RISE INTO THE CROWDED SKY, AND WOULD DRAW UP AT ITS DESTINATION – EMPTY.
THE ARRANGEMENTS WERE OLD-FASHIONED AND ROUGH.
SHE HAD TO WALK TO THE AIR-SHIP FROM THE LIFT; HAD TO SUBMIT TO GLANCES FROM THE OTHER PASSENGERS.

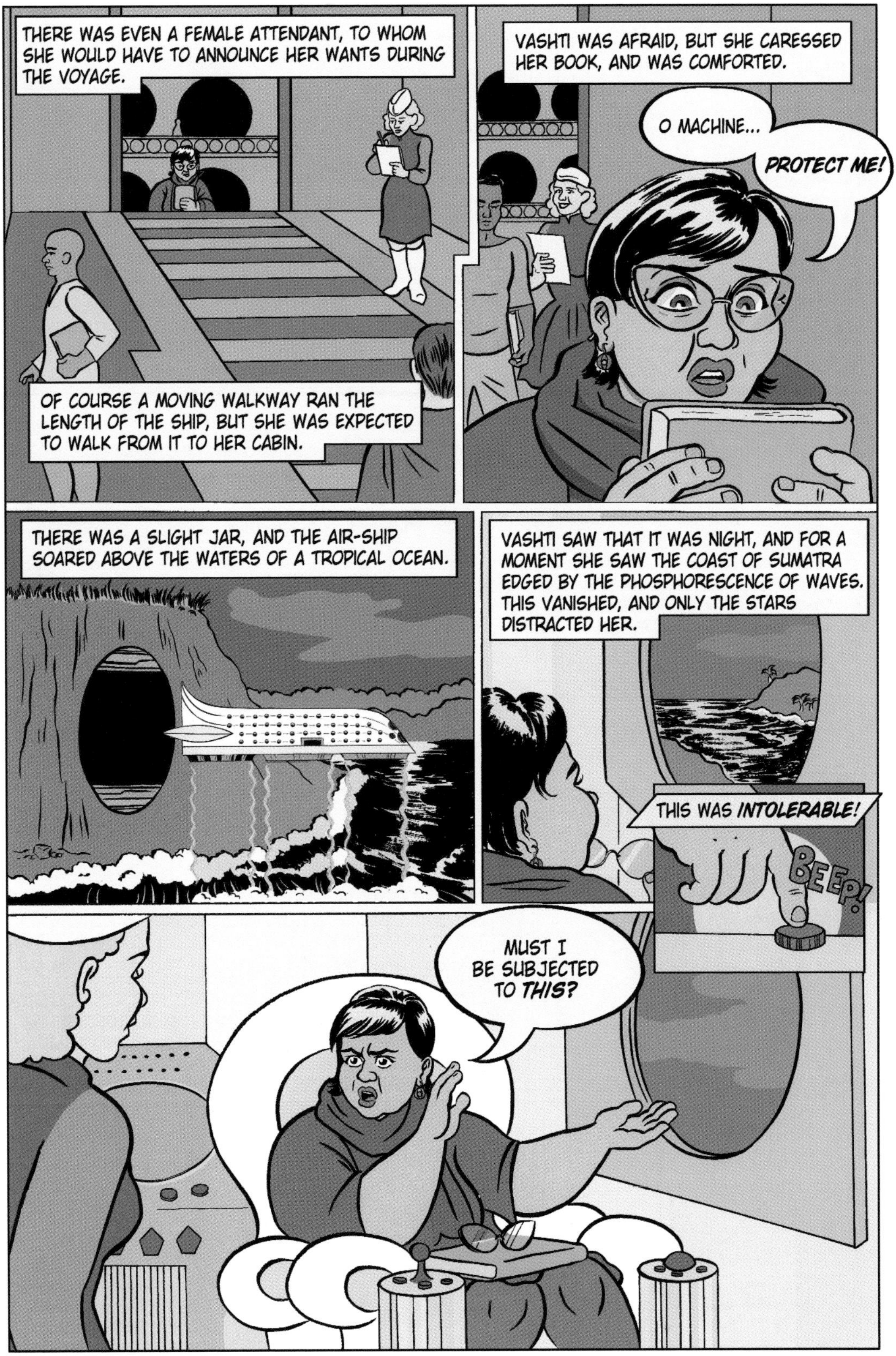
THERE WAS EVEN A FEMALE ATTENDANT, TO WHOM SHE WOULD HAVE TO ANNOUNCE HER WANTS DURING THE VOYAGE.
OF COURSE A MOVING WALKWAY RAN THE LENGTH OF THE SHIP, BUT SHE WAS EXPECTED TO WALK FROM IT TO HER CABIN.
VASHTI WAS AFRAID, BUT SHE CARESSED HER BOOK, AND WAS COMFORTED.
O MACHINE...
PROTECT ME!
THERE WAS A SLIGHT JAR, AND THE AIR-SHIP SOARED ABOVE THE WATERS OF A TROPICAL OCEAN.
VASHTI SAW THAT IT WAS NIGHT, AND FOR A MOMENT SHE SAW THE COAST OF SUMATRA EDGED BY THE PHOSPHORESCENCE OF WAVES. THIS VANISHED, AND ONLY THE STARS DISTRACTED HER.
THIS WAS INTOLERABLE!
BEEP!
MUST I BE SUBJECTED TO THIS?

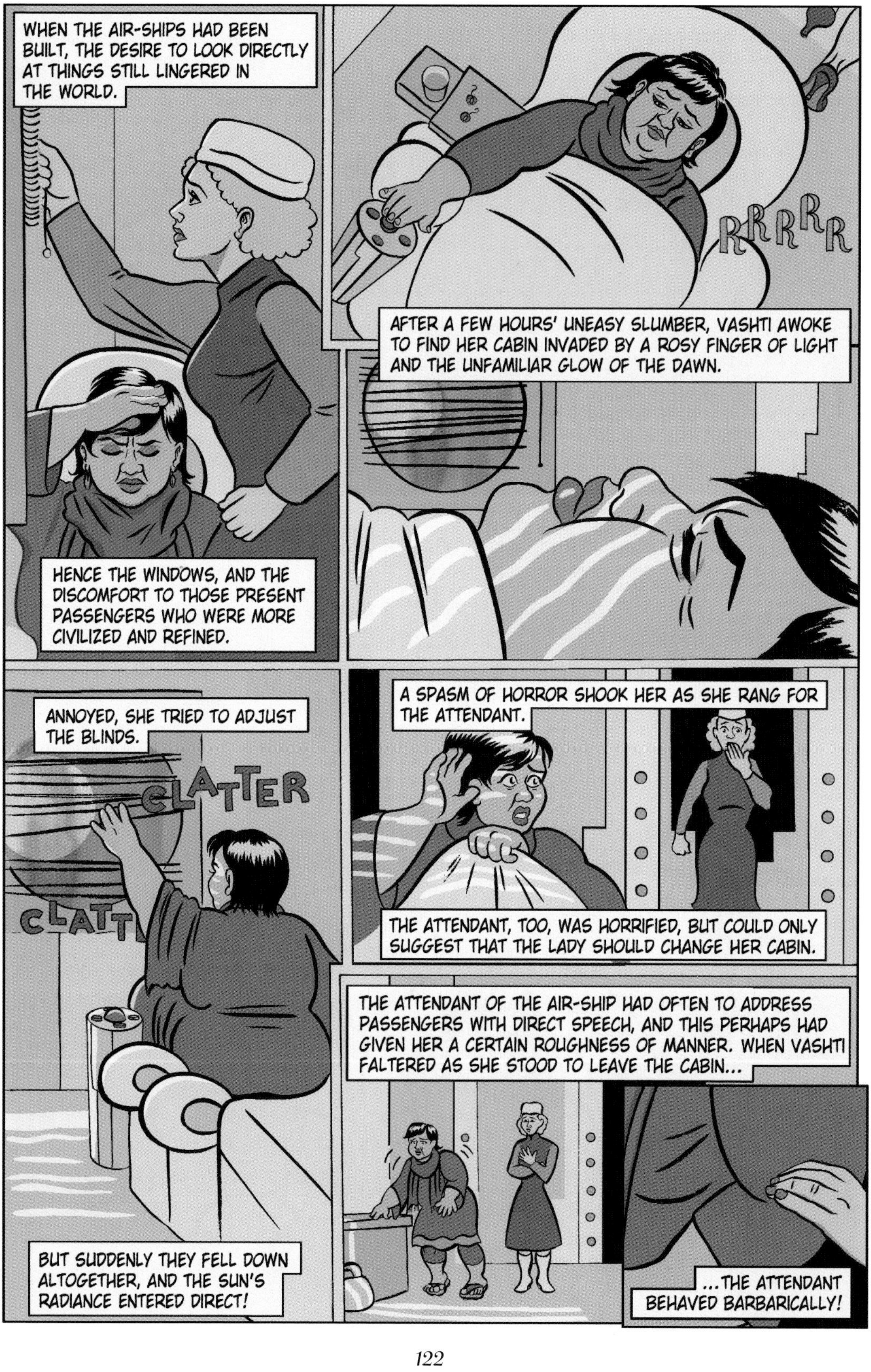
WHEN THE AIR-SHIPS HAD BEEN BUILT, THE DESIRE TO LOOK DIRECTLY AT THINGS STILL LINGERED IN THE WORLD.
HENCE THE WINDOWS, AND THE DISCOMFORT TO THOSE PRESENT PASSENGERS WHO WERE MORE CIVILIZED AND REFINED.
RRRRR
AFTER A FEW HOURS' UNEASY SLUMBER, VASHTI AWOKE TO FIND HER CABIN INVADED BY A ROSY FINGER OF LIGHT AND THE UNFAMILIAR GLOW OF THE DAWN.
ANNOYED, SHE TRIED TO ADJUST THE BLINDS.
CLATTER
CLATT
BUT SUDDENLY THEY FELL DOWN ALTOGETHER, AND THE SUN'S RADIANCE ENTERED DIRECT!
A SPASM OF HORROR SHOOK HER AS SHE RANG FOR THE ATTENDANT.
THE ATTENDANT, TOO, WAS HORRIFIED, BUT COULD ONLY SUGGEST THAT THE LADY SHOULD CHANGE HER CABIN.
THE ATTENDANT OF THE AIR-SHIP HAD OFTEN TO ADDRESS PASSENGERS WITH DIRECT SPEECH, AND THIS PERHAPS HAD GIVEN HER A CERTAIN ROUGHNESS OF MANNER. WHEN VASHTI FALTERED AS SHE STOOD TO LEAVE THE CABIN...
...THE ATTENDANT BEHAVED BARBARICALLY!

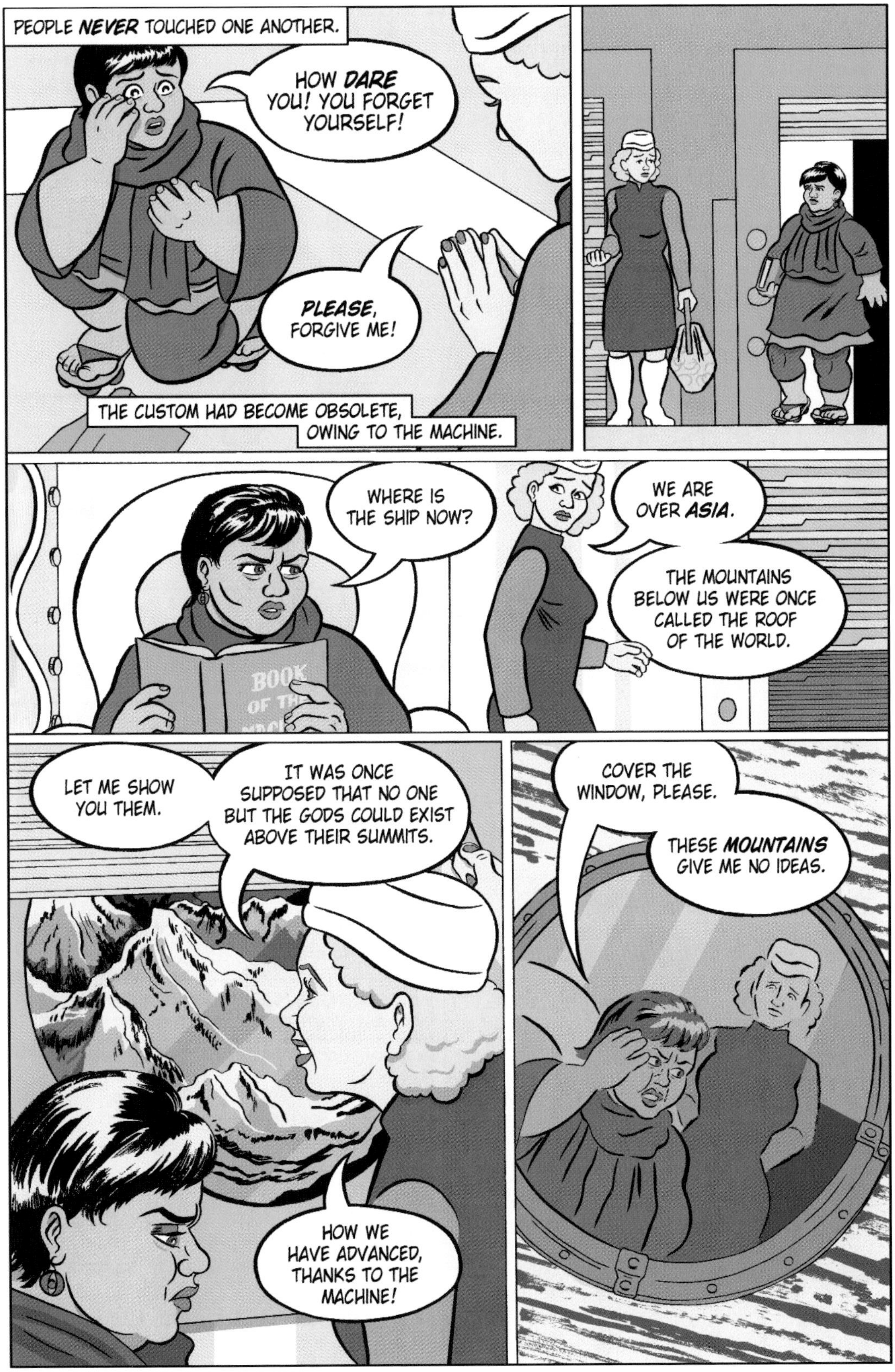
PEOPLE NEVER TOUCHED ONE ANOTHER.
HOW DARE YOU! YOU FORGET YOURSELF!
PLEASE, FORGIVE ME!
THE CUSTOM HAD BECOME OBSOLETE, OWING TO THE MACHINE.
WHERE IS THE SHIP NOW?
WE ARE OVER ASIA.
THE MOUNTAINS BELOW US WERE ONCE CALLED THE ROOF OF THE WORLD.
BOOK OF THE
LET ME SHOW YOU THEM.
IT WAS ONCE SUPPOSED THAT NO ONE BUT THE GODS COULD EXIST ABOVE THEIR SUMMITS.
HOW WE HAVE ADVANCED, THANKS TO THE MACHINE!
COVER THE WINDOW, PLEASE.
THESE MOUNTAINS GIVE ME NO IDEAS.

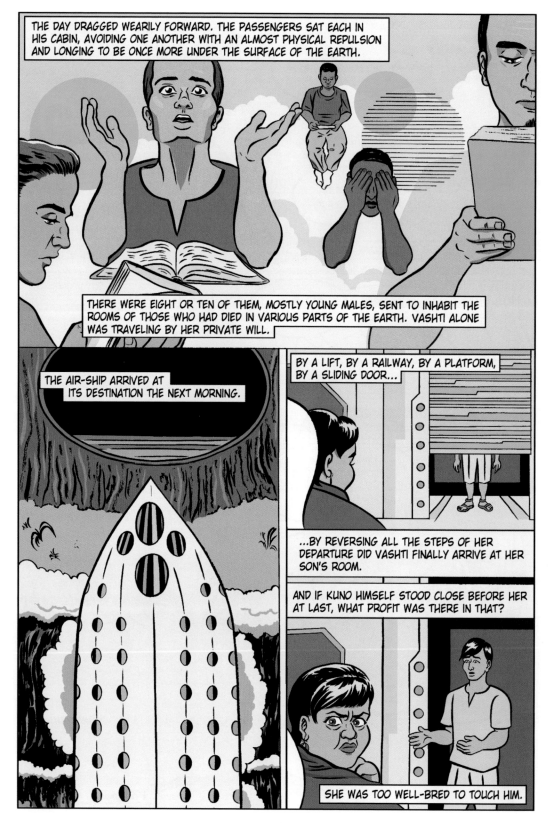

THE DAY DRAGGED WEARILY FORWARD. THE PASSENGERS SAT EACH IN HIS CABIN, AVOIDING ONE ANOTHER WITH AN ALMOST PHYSICAL REPULSION AND LONGING TO BE ONCE MORE UNDER THE SURFACE OF THE EARTH.

THERE WERE EIGHT OR TEN OF THEM, MOSTLY YOUNG MALES, SENT TO INHABIT THE ROOMS OF THOSE WHO HAD DIED IN VARIOUS PARTS OF THE EARTH. VASHTI ALONE WAS TRAVELING BY HER PRIVATE WILL.

THE AIR-SHIP ARRIVED AT ITS DESTINATION THE NEXT MORNING.

BY A LIFT, BY A RAILWAY, BY A PLATFORM, BY A SLIDING DOOR...

...BY REVERSING ALL THE STEPS OF HER DEPARTURE DID VASHTI FINALLY ARRIVE AT HER SON'S ROOM.

AND IF KUNO HIMSELF STOOD CLOSE BEFORE HER AT LAST, WHAT PROFIT WAS THERE IN THAT?

SHE WAS TOO WELL-BRED TO TOUCH HIM.

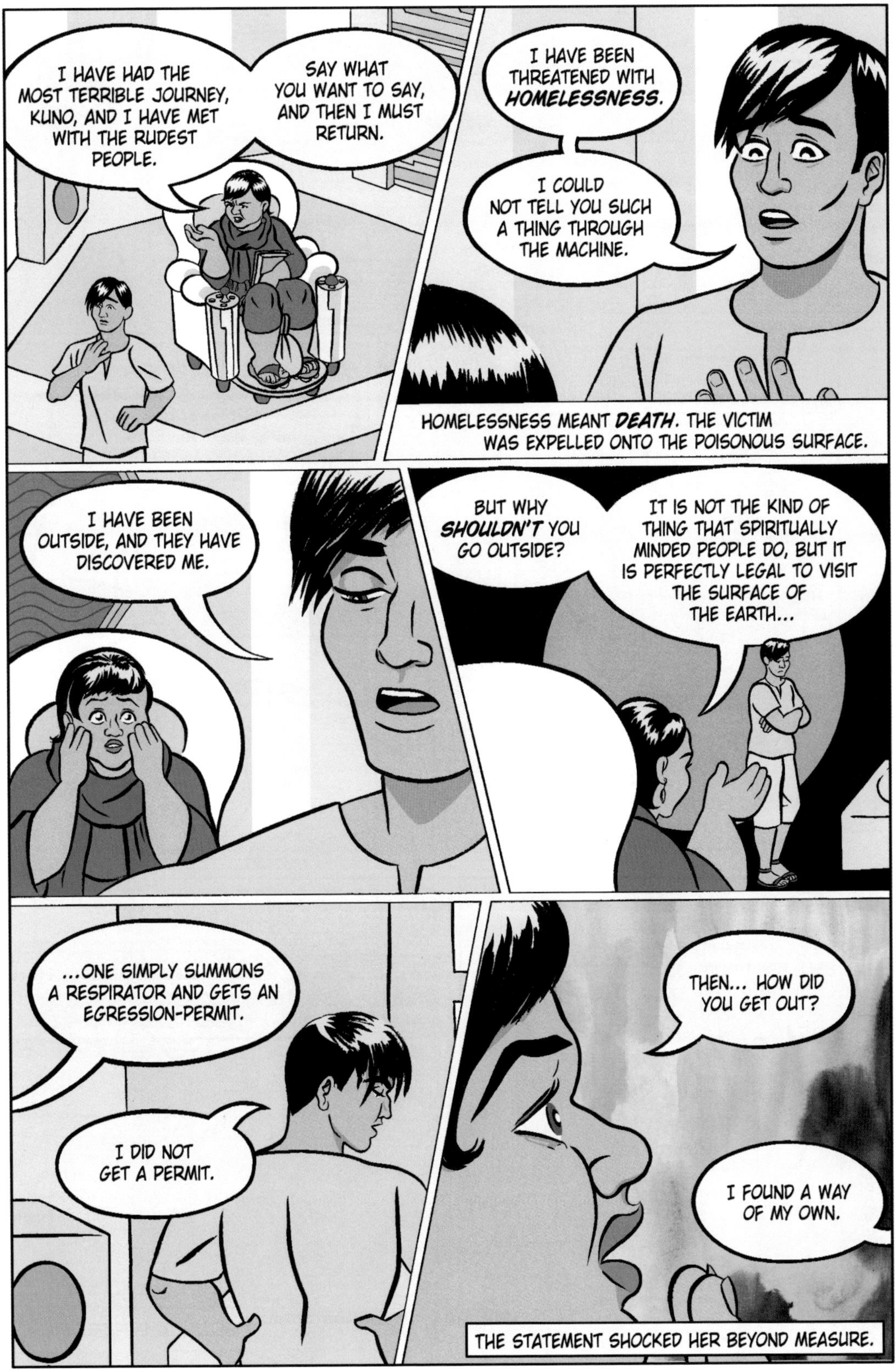
I HAVE HAD THE MOST TERRIBLE JOURNEY, KUNO, AND I HAVE MET WITH THE RUDEST PEOPLE.
SAY WHAT YOU WANT TO SAY, AND THEN I MUST RETURN.
I HAVE BEEN THREATENED WITH ***HOMELESSNESS***.
I COULD NOT TELL YOU SUCH A THING THROUGH THE MACHINE.
HOMELESSNESS MEANT ***DEATH***. THE VICTIM WAS EXPELLED ONTO THE POISONOUS SURFACE.
I HAVE BEEN OUTSIDE, AND THEY HAVE DISCOVERED ME.
BUT WHY ***SHOULDN'T*** YOU GO OUTSIDE?
IT IS NOT THE KIND OF THING THAT SPIRITUALLY MINDED PEOPLE DO, BUT IT IS PERFECTLY LEGAL TO VISIT THE SURFACE OF THE EARTH...
...ONE SIMPLY SUMMONS A RESPIRATOR AND GETS AN EGRESSION-PERMIT.
I DID NOT GET A PERMIT.
THEN... HOW DID YOU GET OUT?
I FOUND A WAY OF MY OWN.
THE STATEMENT SHOCKED HER BEYOND MEASURE.

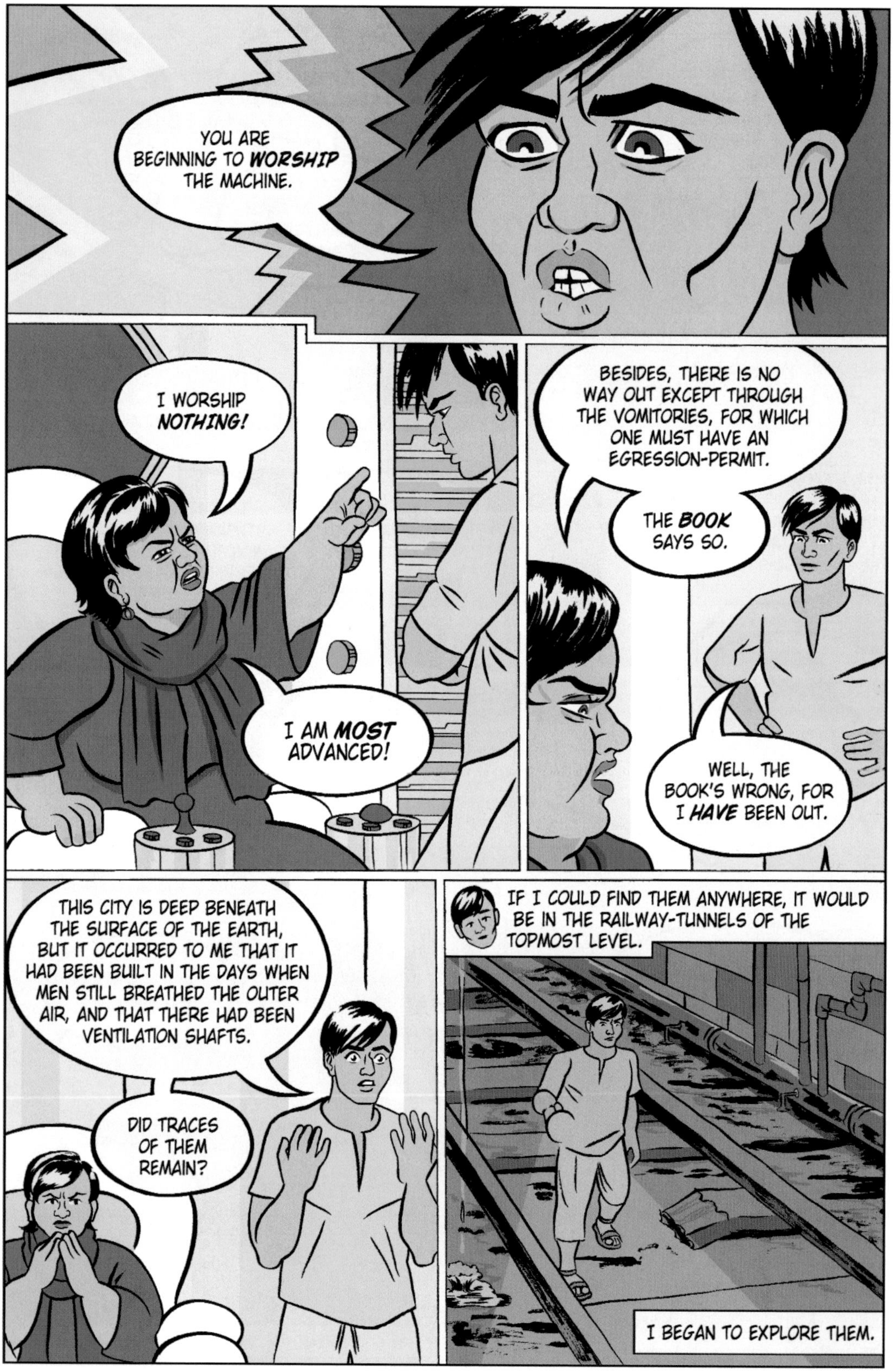
YOU ARE BEGINNING TO WORSHIP THE MACHINE.
I WORSHIP NOTHING!
I AM MOST ADVANCED!
BESIDES, THERE IS NO WAY OUT EXCEPT THROUGH THE VOMITORIES, FOR WHICH ONE MUST HAVE AN EGRESSION-PERMIT.
THE BOOK SAYS SO.
WELL, THE BOOK'S WRONG, FOR I HAVE BEEN OUT.
THIS CITY IS DEEP BENEATH THE SURFACE OF THE EARTH, BUT IT OCCURRED TO ME THAT IT HAD BEEN BUILT IN THE DAYS WHEN MEN STILL BREATHED THE OUTER AIR, AND THAT THERE HAD BEEN VENTILATION SHAFTS.
DID TRACES OF THEM REMAIN?
IF I COULD FIND THEM ANYWHERE, IT WOULD BE IN THE RAILWAY-TUNNELS OF THE TOPMOST LEVEL.
I BEGAN TO EXPLORE THEM.

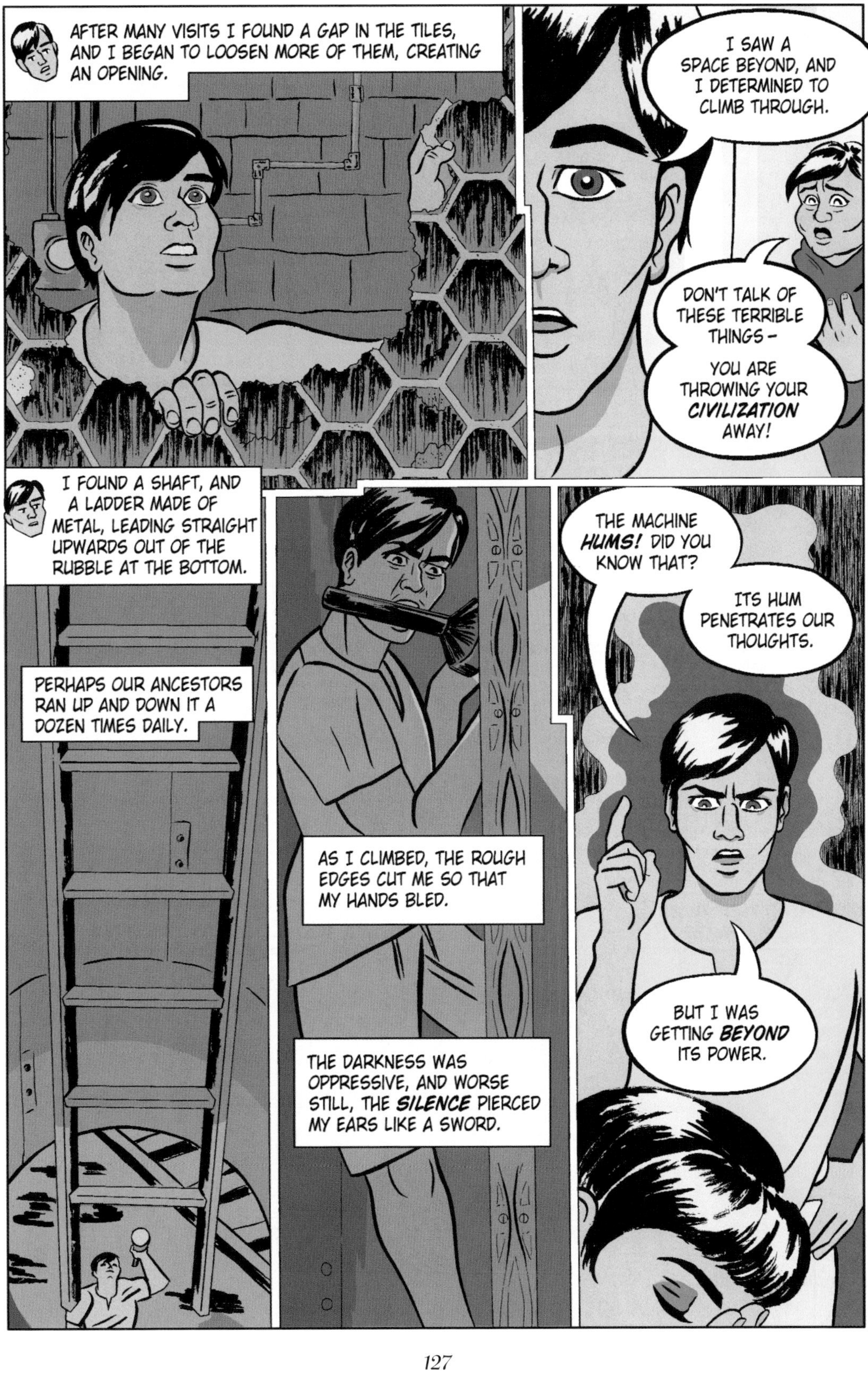
AFTER MANY VISITS I FOUND A GAP IN THE TILES, AND I BEGAN TO LOOSEN MORE OF THEM, CREATING AN OPENING.
I SAW A SPACE BEYOND, AND I DETERMINED TO CLIMB THROUGH.
DON'T TALK OF THESE TERRIBLE THINGS –
YOU ARE THROWING YOUR *CIVILIZATION* AWAY!
I FOUND A SHAFT, AND A LADDER MADE OF METAL, LEADING STRAIGHT UPWARDS OUT OF THE RUBBLE AT THE BOTTOM.
PERHAPS OUR ANCESTORS RAN UP AND DOWN IT A DOZEN TIMES DAILY.
AS I CLIMBED, THE ROUGH EDGES CUT ME SO THAT MY HANDS BLED.
THE DARKNESS WAS OPPRESSIVE, AND WORSE STILL, THE *SILENCE* PIERCED MY EARS LIKE A SWORD.
THE MACHINE *HUMS!* DID YOU KNOW THAT?
ITS HUM PENETRATES OUR THOUGHTS.
BUT I WAS GETTING *BEYOND* ITS POWER.

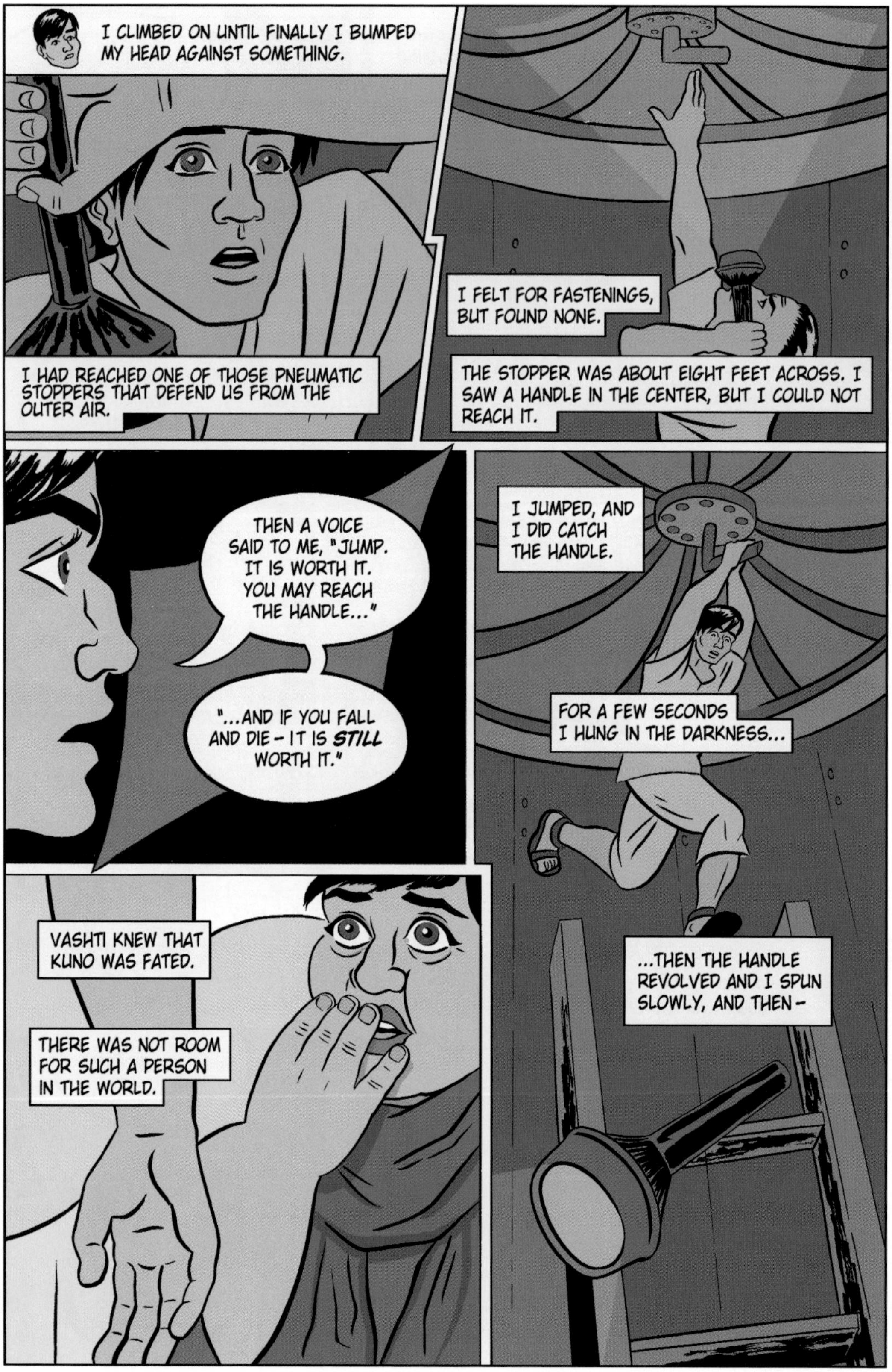
I CLIMBED ON UNTIL FINALLY I BUMPED MY HEAD AGAINST SOMETHING.
I HAD REACHED ONE OF THOSE PNEUMATIC STOPPERS THAT DEFEND US FROM THE OUTER AIR.
I FELT FOR FASTENINGS, BUT FOUND NONE.
THE STOPPER WAS ABOUT EIGHT FEET ACROSS. I SAW A HANDLE IN THE CENTER, BUT I COULD NOT REACH IT.
THEN A VOICE SAID TO ME, "JUMP. IT IS WORTH IT. YOU MAY REACH THE HANDLE..."
"...AND IF YOU FALL AND DIE - IT IS STILL WORTH IT."
I JUMPED, AND I DID CATCH THE HANDLE.
FOR A FEW SECONDS I HUNG IN THE DARKNESS...
...THEN THE HANDLE REVOLVED AND I SPUN SLOWLY, AND THEN -
VASHTI KNEW THAT KUNO WAS FATED.
THERE WAS NOT ROOM FOR SUCH A PERSON IN THE WORLD.

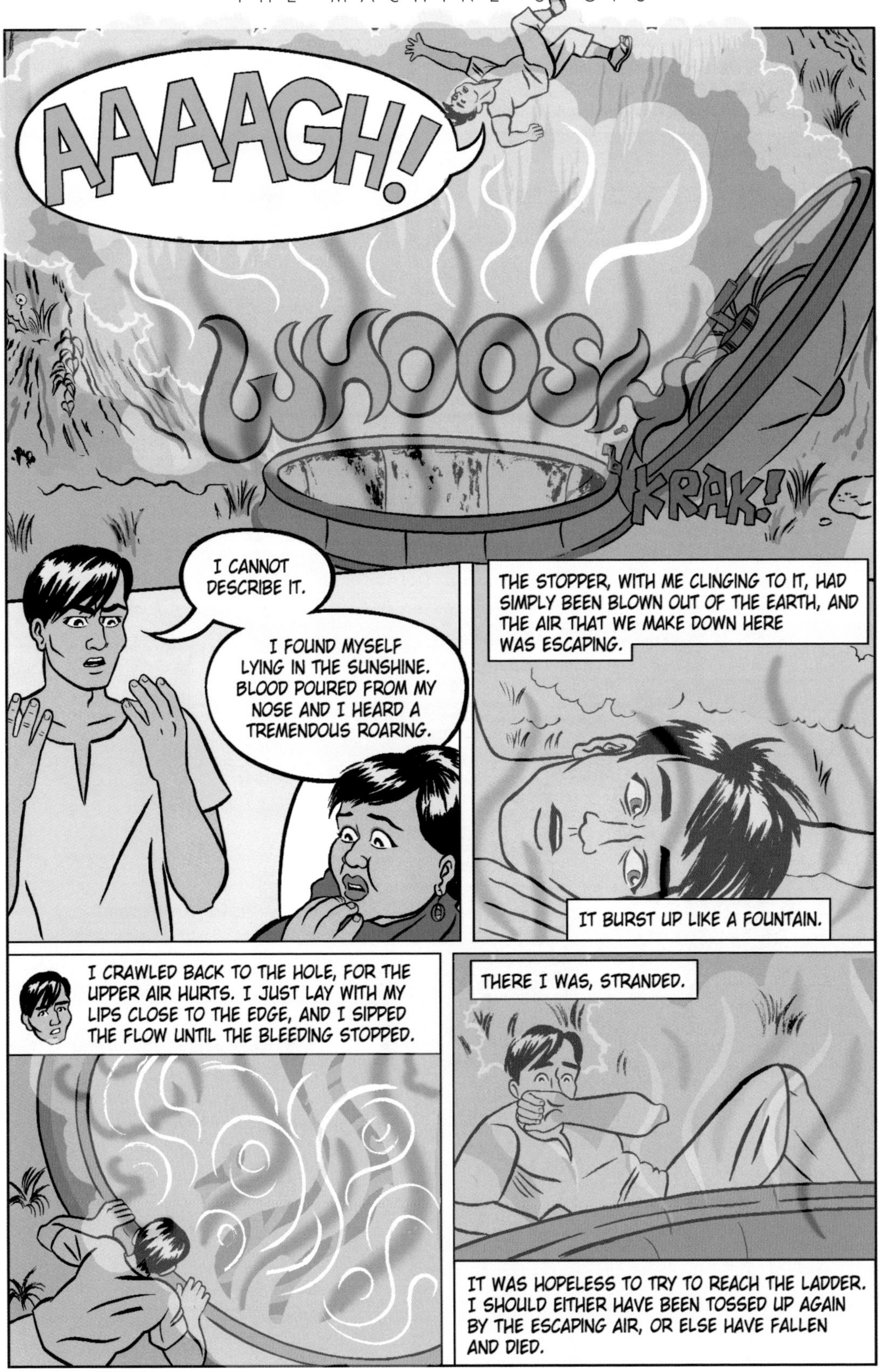
AAAAGH!
WHOOSH
KRAK!
I CANNOT DESCRIBE IT.
I FOUND MYSELF LYING IN THE SUNSHINE. BLOOD POURED FROM MY NOSE AND I HEARD A TREMENDOUS ROARING.
THE STOPPER, WITH ME CLINGING TO IT, HAD SIMPLY BEEN BLOWN OUT OF THE EARTH, AND THE AIR THAT WE MAKE DOWN HERE WAS ESCAPING.
IT BURST UP LIKE A FOUNTAIN.
I CRAWLED BACK TO THE HOLE, FOR THE UPPER AIR HURTS. I JUST LAY WITH MY LIPS CLOSE TO THE EDGE, AND I SIPPED THE FLOW UNTIL THE BLEEDING STOPPED.
THERE I WAS, STRANDED.
IT WAS HOPELESS TO TRY TO REACH THE LADDER. I SHOULD EITHER HAVE BEEN TOSSED UP AGAIN BY THE ESCAPING AIR, OR ELSE HAVE FALLEN AND DIED.

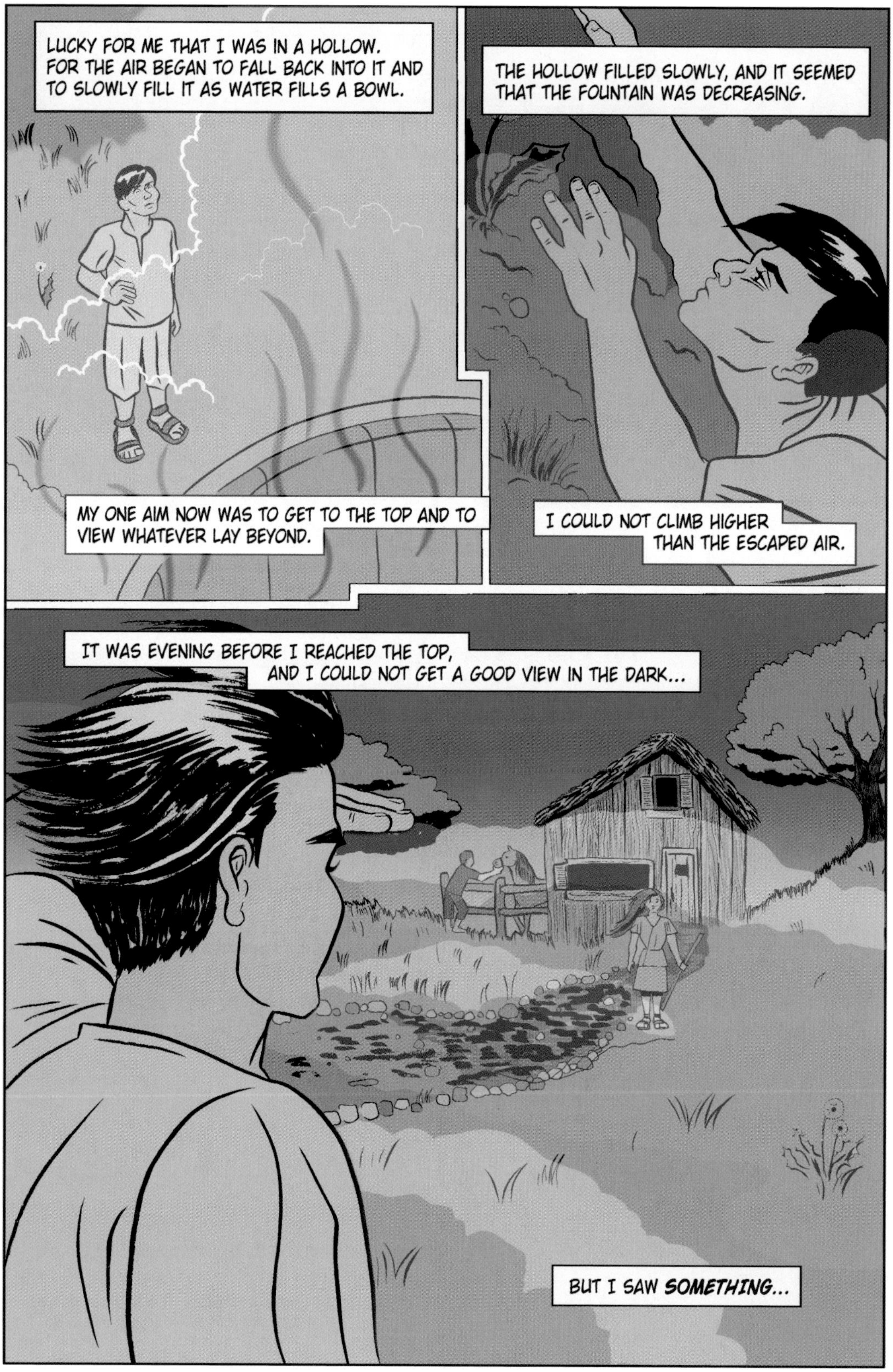
LUCKY FOR ME THAT I WAS IN A HOLLOW. FOR THE AIR BEGAN TO FALL BACK INTO IT AND TO SLOWLY FILL IT AS WATER FILLS A BOWL.
MY ONE AIM NOW WAS TO GET TO THE TOP AND TO VIEW WHATEVER LAY BEYOND.
THE HOLLOW FILLED SLOWLY, AND IT SEEMED THAT THE FOUNTAIN WAS DECREASING.
I COULD NOT CLIMB HIGHER THAN THE ESCAPED AIR.
IT WAS EVENING BEFORE I REACHED THE TOP, AND I COULD NOT GET A GOOD VIEW IN THE DARK...
BUT I SAW SOMETHING...

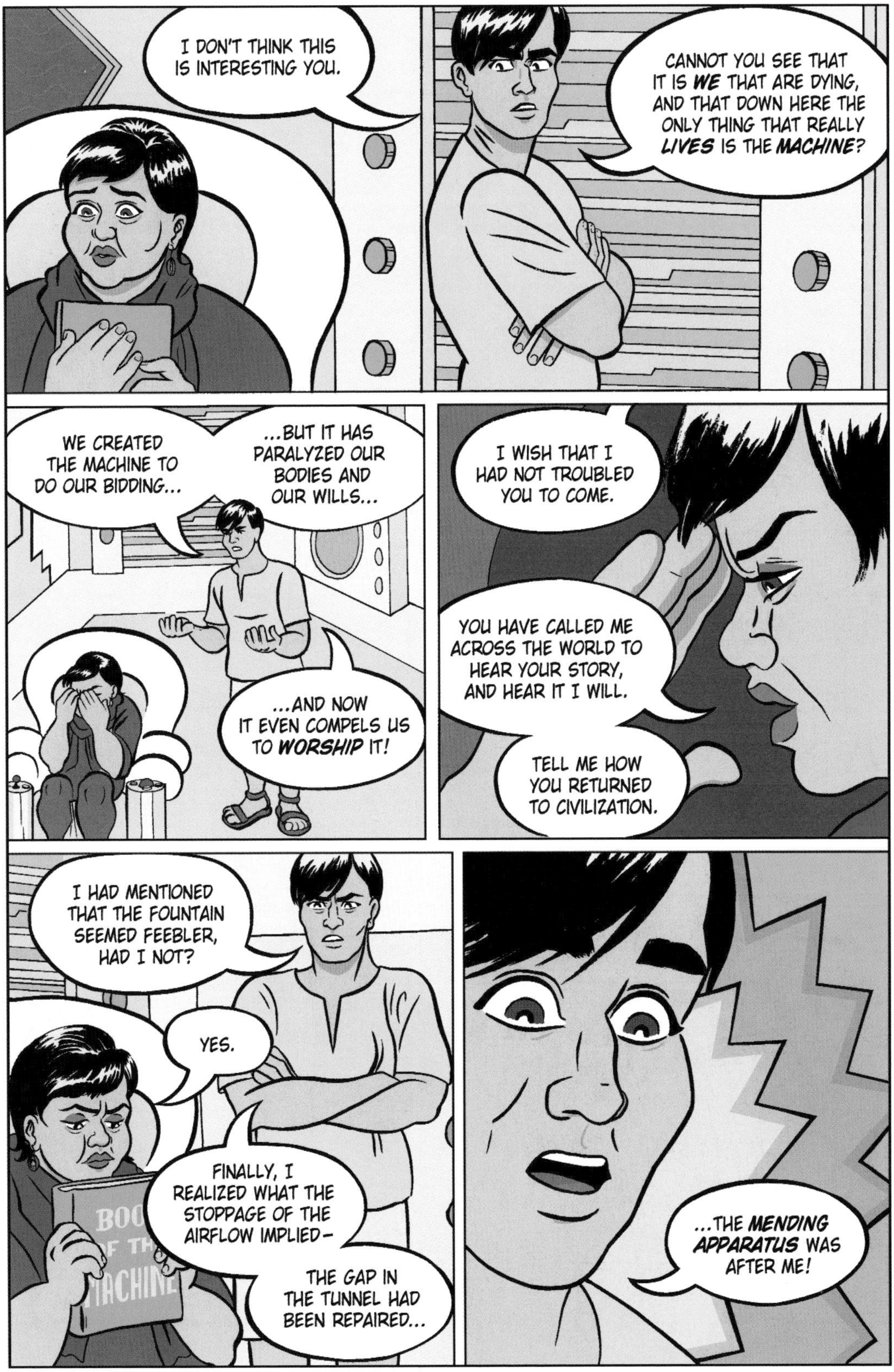
I DON'T THINK THIS IS INTERESTING YOU.
CANNOT YOU SEE THAT IT IS WE THAT ARE DYING, AND THAT DOWN HERE THE ONLY THING THAT REALLY LIVES IS THE MACHINE?
WE CREATED THE MACHINE TO DO OUR BIDDING...
...BUT IT HAS PARALYZED OUR BODIES AND OUR WILLS...
...AND NOW IT EVEN COMPELS US TO WORSHIP IT!
I WISH THAT I HAD NOT TROUBLED YOU TO COME.
YOU HAVE CALLED ME ACROSS THE WORLD TO HEAR YOUR STORY, AND HEAR IT I WILL.
TELL ME HOW YOU RETURNED TO CIVILIZATION.
I HAD MENTIONED THAT THE FOUNTAIN SEEMED FEEBLER, HAD I NOT?
YES.
FINALLY, I REALIZED WHAT THE STOPPAGE OF THE AIRFLOW IMPLIED–
THE GAP IN THE TUNNEL HAD BEEN REPAIRED...
...THE MENDING APPARATUS WAS AFTER ME!

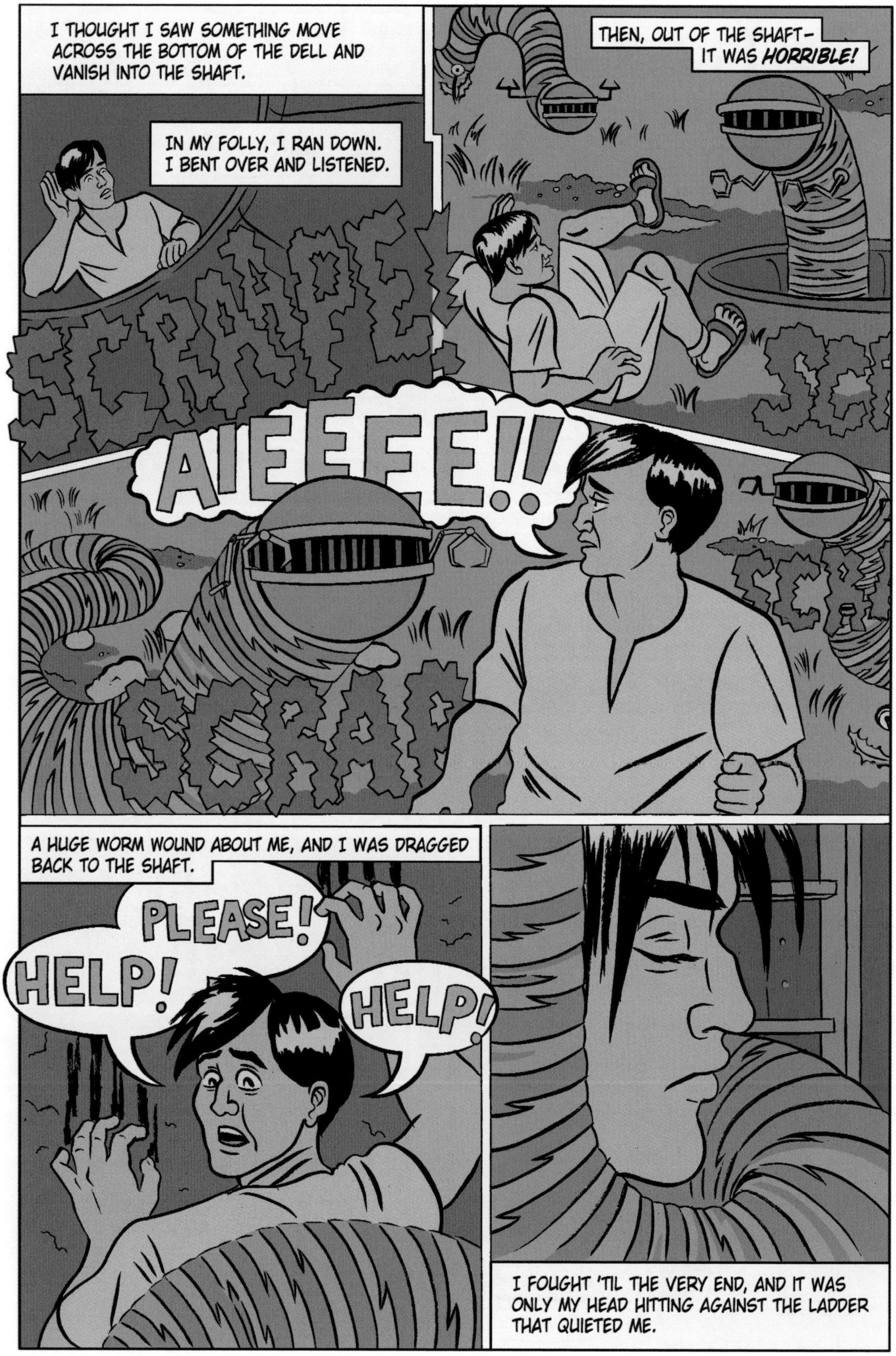
I THOUGHT I SAW SOMETHING MOVE ACROSS THE BOTTOM OF THE DELL AND VANISH INTO THE SHAFT.
IN MY FOLLY, I RAN DOWN. I BENT OVER AND LISTENED.
SCRAAPC
THEN, OUT OF THE SHAFT- IT WAS **HORRIBLE!**
AIEEEE!!
SCRAP
A HUGE WORM WOUND ABOUT ME, AND I WAS DRAGGED BACK TO THE SHAFT.
PLEASE!
HELP!
HELP!
I FOUGHT 'TIL THE VERY END, AND IT WAS ONLY MY HEAD HITTING AGAINST THE LADDER THAT QUIETED ME.

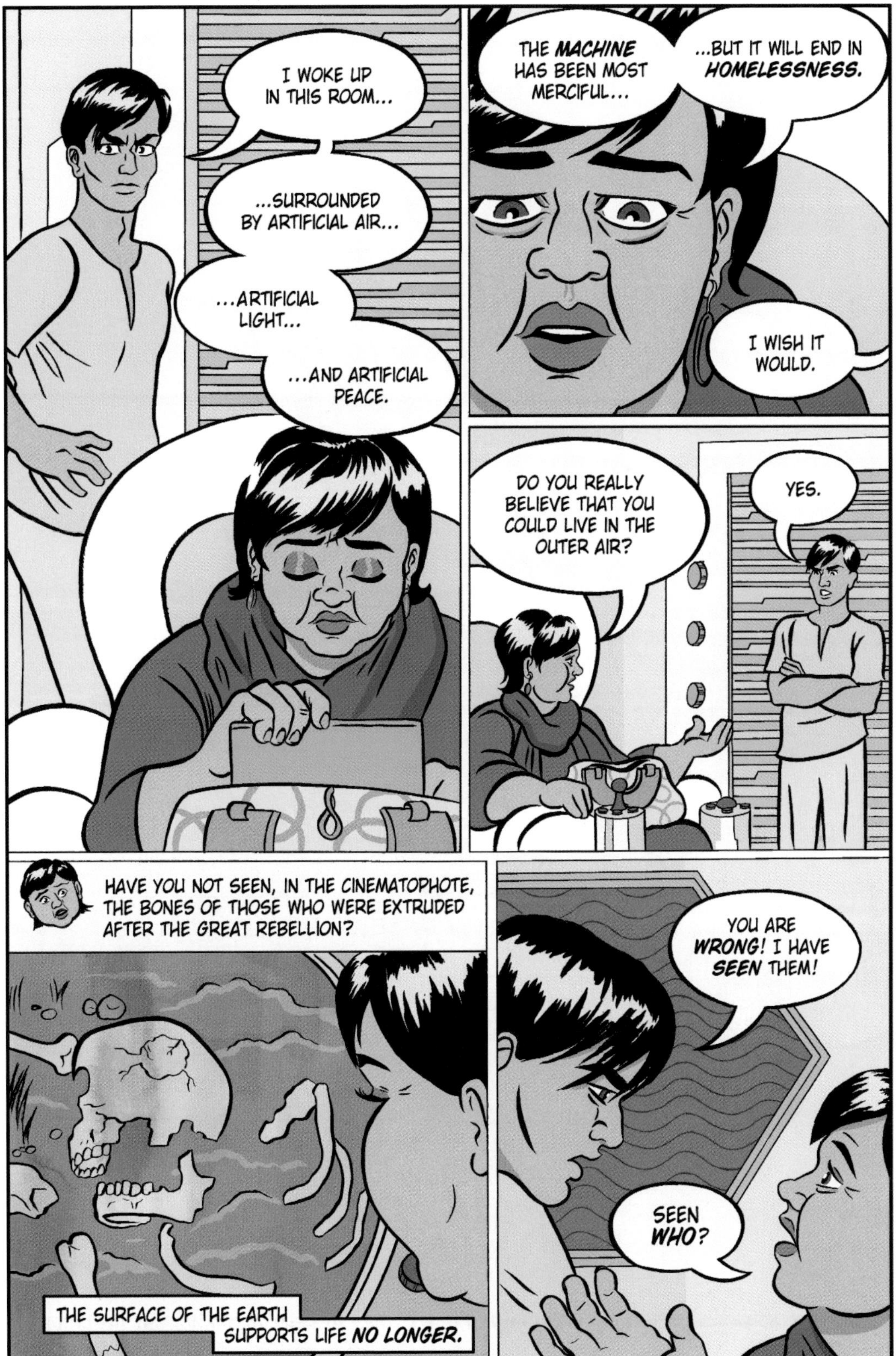
I WOKE UP IN THIS ROOM...
...SURROUNDED BY ARTIFICIAL AIR...
...ARTIFICIAL LIGHT...
...AND ARTIFICIAL PEACE.
THE *MACHINE* HAS BEEN MOST MERCIFUL...
...BUT IT WILL END IN *HOMELESSNESS.*
I WISH IT WOULD.
DO YOU REALLY BELIEVE THAT YOU COULD LIVE IN THE OUTER AIR?
YES.
HAVE YOU NOT SEEN, IN THE CINEMATOPHOTE, THE BONES OF THOSE WHO WERE EXTRUDED AFTER THE GREAT REBELLION?
THE SURFACE OF THE EARTH SUPPORTS LIFE *NO LONGER.*
YOU ARE *WRONG!* I HAVE *SEEN* THEM!
SEEN *WHO?*

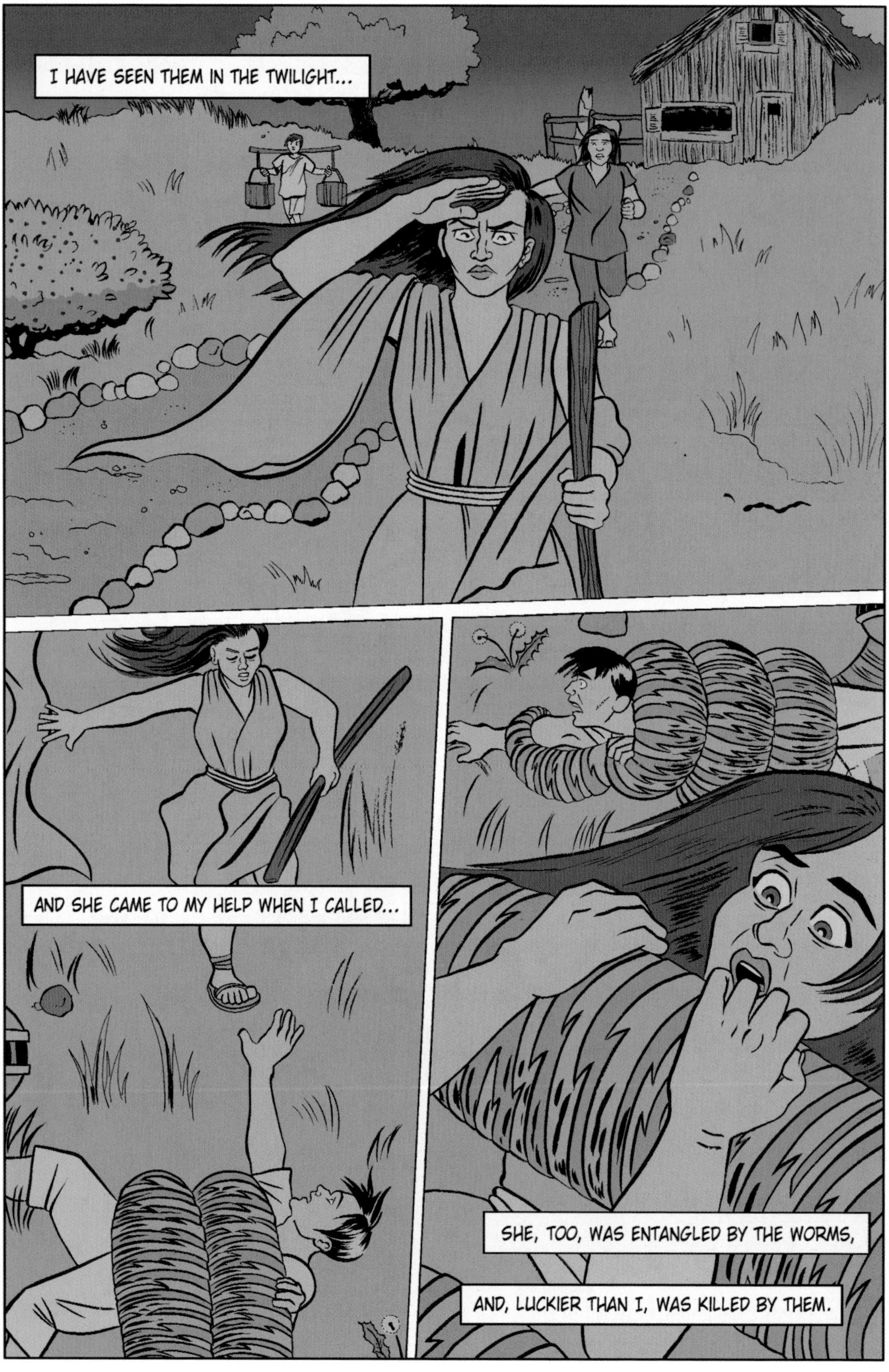
I HAVE SEEN THEM IN THE TWILIGHT...
AND SHE CAME TO MY HELP WHEN I CALLED...
SHE, TOO, WAS ENTANGLED BY THE WORMS,
AND, LUCKIER THAN I, WAS KILLED BY THEM.

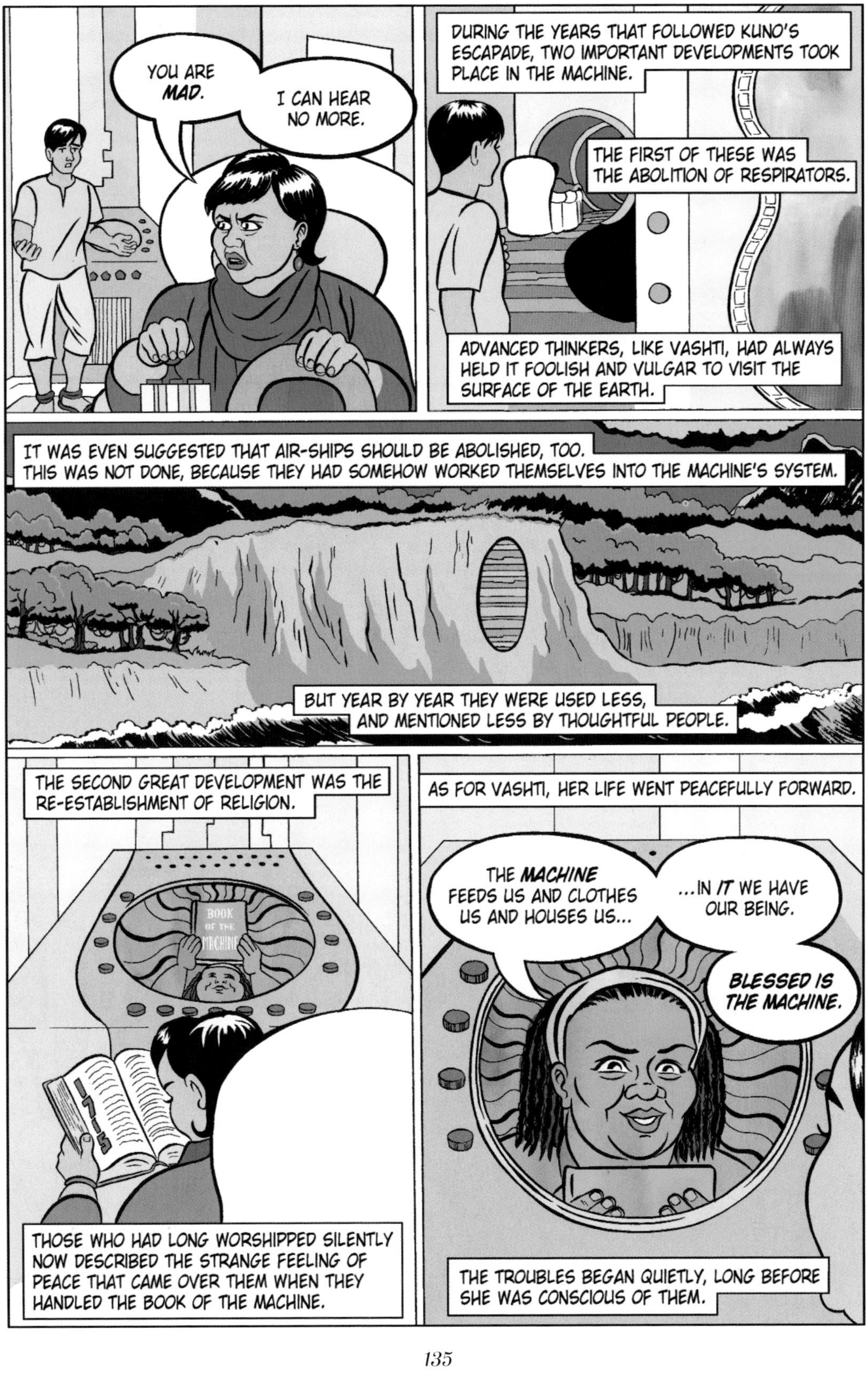
YOU ARE *MAD.*
I CAN HEAR NO MORE.
DURING THE YEARS THAT FOLLOWED KUNO'S ESCAPADE, TWO IMPORTANT DEVELOPMENTS TOOK PLACE IN THE MACHINE.
THE FIRST OF THESE WAS THE ABOLITION OF RESPIRATORS.
ADVANCED THINKERS, LIKE VASHTI, HAD ALWAYS HELD IT FOOLISH AND VULGAR TO VISIT THE SURFACE OF THE EARTH.
IT WAS EVEN SUGGESTED THAT AIR-SHIPS SHOULD BE ABOLISHED, TOO. THIS WAS NOT DONE, BECAUSE THEY HAD SOMEHOW WORKED THEMSELVES INTO THE MACHINE'S SYSTEM.
BUT YEAR BY YEAR THEY WERE USED LESS, AND MENTIONED LESS BY THOUGHTFUL PEOPLE.
THE SECOND GREAT DEVELOPMENT WAS THE RE-ESTABLISHMENT OF RELIGION.
BOOK OF THE MACHINE
THOSE WHO HAD LONG WORSHIPPED SILENTLY NOW DESCRIBED THE STRANGE FEELING OF PEACE THAT CAME OVER THEM WHEN THEY HANDLED THE BOOK OF THE MACHINE.
AS FOR VASHTI, HER LIFE WENT PEACEFULLY FORWARD.
THE *MACHINE* FEEDS US AND CLOTHES US AND HOUSES US...
...IN *IT* WE HAVE OUR BEING.
BLESSED IS THE MACHINE.
THE TROUBLES BEGAN QUIETLY, LONG BEFORE SHE WAS CONSCIOUS OF THEM.

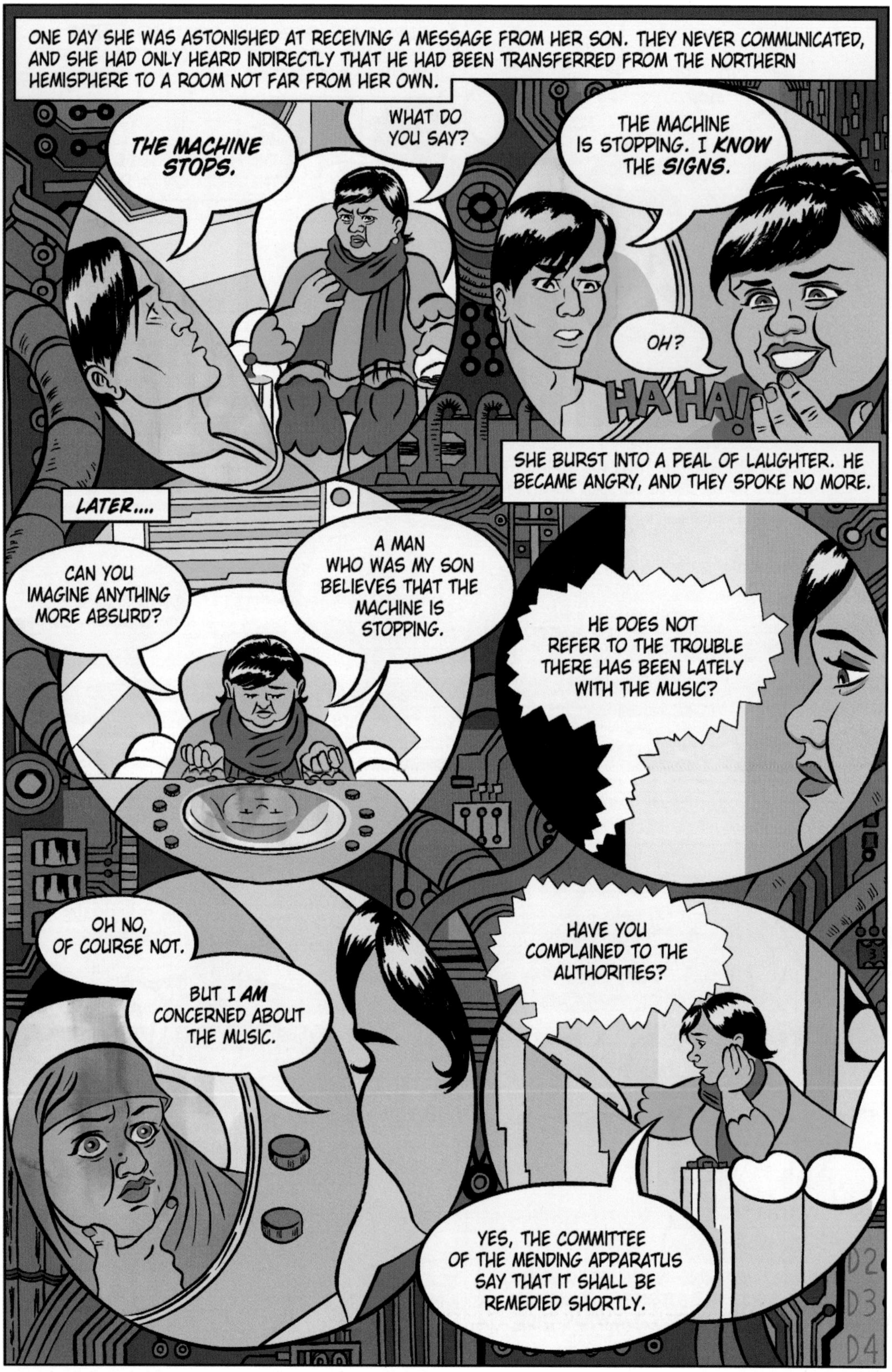
ONE DAY SHE WAS ASTONISHED AT RECEIVING A MESSAGE FROM HER SON. THEY NEVER COMMUNICATED, AND SHE HAD ONLY HEARD INDIRECTLY THAT HE HAD BEEN TRANSFERRED FROM THE NORTHERN HEMISPHERE TO A ROOM NOT FAR FROM HER OWN.
THE MACHINE STOPS.
WHAT DO YOU SAY?
THE MACHINE IS STOPPING. I KNOW THE SIGNS.
OH?
HA HA!
SHE BURST INTO A PEAL OF LAUGHTER. HE BECAME ANGRY, AND THEY SPOKE NO MORE.
LATER....
CAN YOU IMAGINE ANYTHING MORE ABSURD?
A MAN WHO WAS MY SON BELIEVES THAT THE MACHINE IS STOPPING.
HE DOES NOT REFER TO THE TROUBLE THERE HAS BEEN LATELY WITH THE MUSIC?
OH NO, OF COURSE NOT.
BUT I AM CONCERNED ABOUT THE MUSIC.
HAVE YOU COMPLAINED TO THE AUTHORITIES?
YES, THE COMMITTEE OF THE MENDING APPARATUS SAY THAT IT SHALL BE REMEDIED SHORTLY.

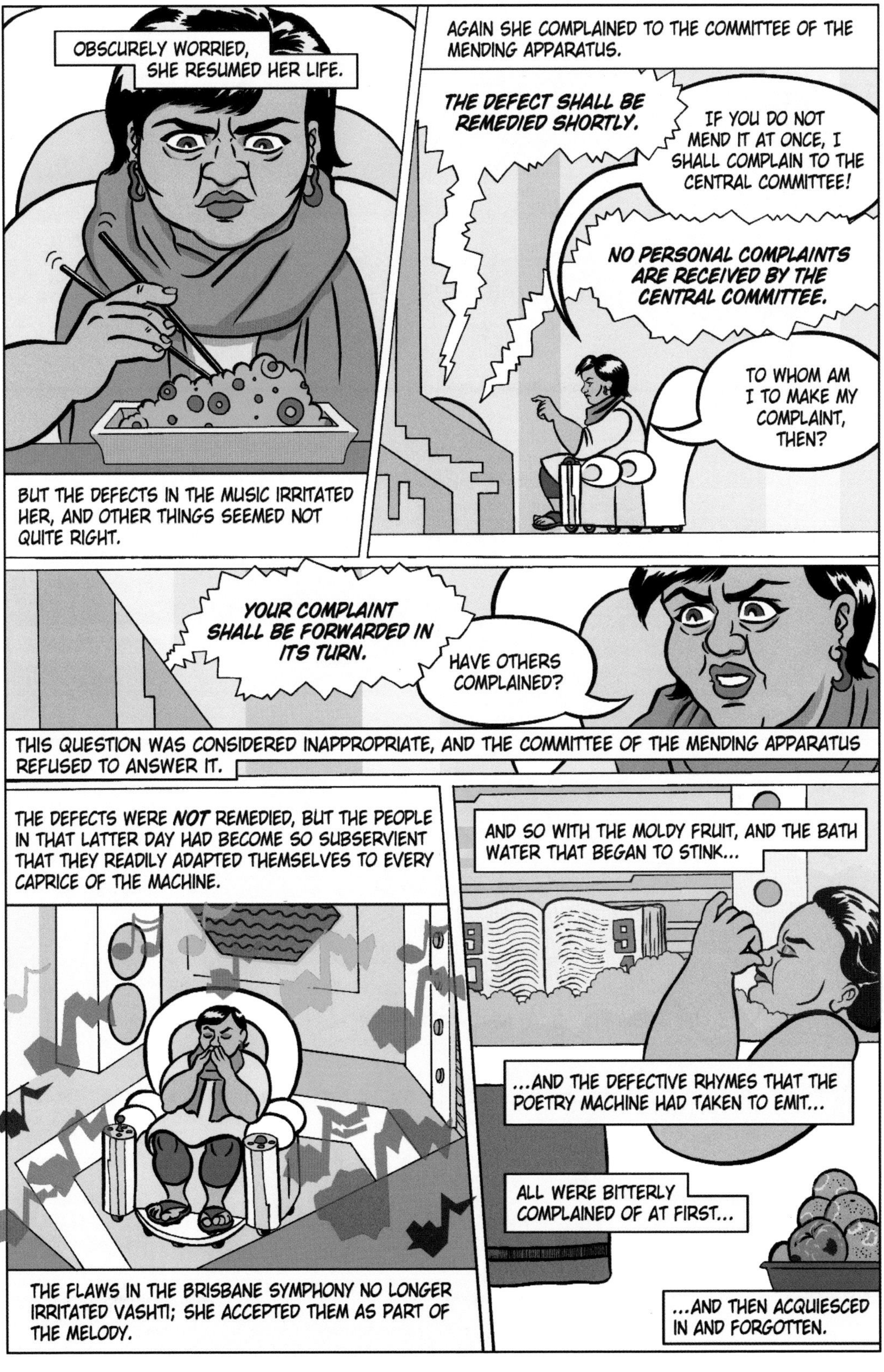
OBSCURELY WORRIED, SHE RESUMED HER LIFE.
BUT THE DEFECTS IN THE MUSIC IRRITATED HER, AND OTHER THINGS SEEMED NOT QUITE RIGHT.
AGAIN SHE COMPLAINED TO THE COMMITTEE OF THE MENDING APPARATUS.
THE DEFECT SHALL BE REMEDIED SHORTLY.
IF YOU DO NOT MEND IT AT ONCE, I SHALL COMPLAIN TO THE CENTRAL COMMITTEE!
NO PERSONAL COMPLAINTS ARE RECEIVED BY THE CENTRAL COMMITTEE.
TO WHOM AM I TO MAKE MY COMPLAINT, THEN?
YOUR COMPLAINT SHALL BE FORWARDED IN ITS TURN.
HAVE OTHERS COMPLAINED?
THIS QUESTION WAS CONSIDERED INAPPROPRIATE, AND THE COMMITTEE OF THE MENDING APPARATUS REFUSED TO ANSWER IT.
THE DEFECTS WERE NOT REMEDIED, BUT THE PEOPLE IN THAT LATTER DAY HAD BECOME SO SUBSERVIENT THAT THEY READILY ADAPTED THEMSELVES TO EVERY CAPRICE OF THE MACHINE.
THE FLAWS IN THE BRISBANE SYMPHONY NO LONGER IRRITATED VASHTI; SHE ACCEPTED THEM AS PART OF THE MELODY.
AND SO WITH THE MOLDY FRUIT, AND THE BATH WATER THAT BEGAN TO STINK...
...AND THE DEFECTIVE RHYMES THAT THE POETRY MACHINE HAD TAKEN TO EMIT...
ALL WERE BITTERLY COMPLAINED OF AT FIRST...
...AND THEN ACQUIESCED IN AND FORGOTTEN.

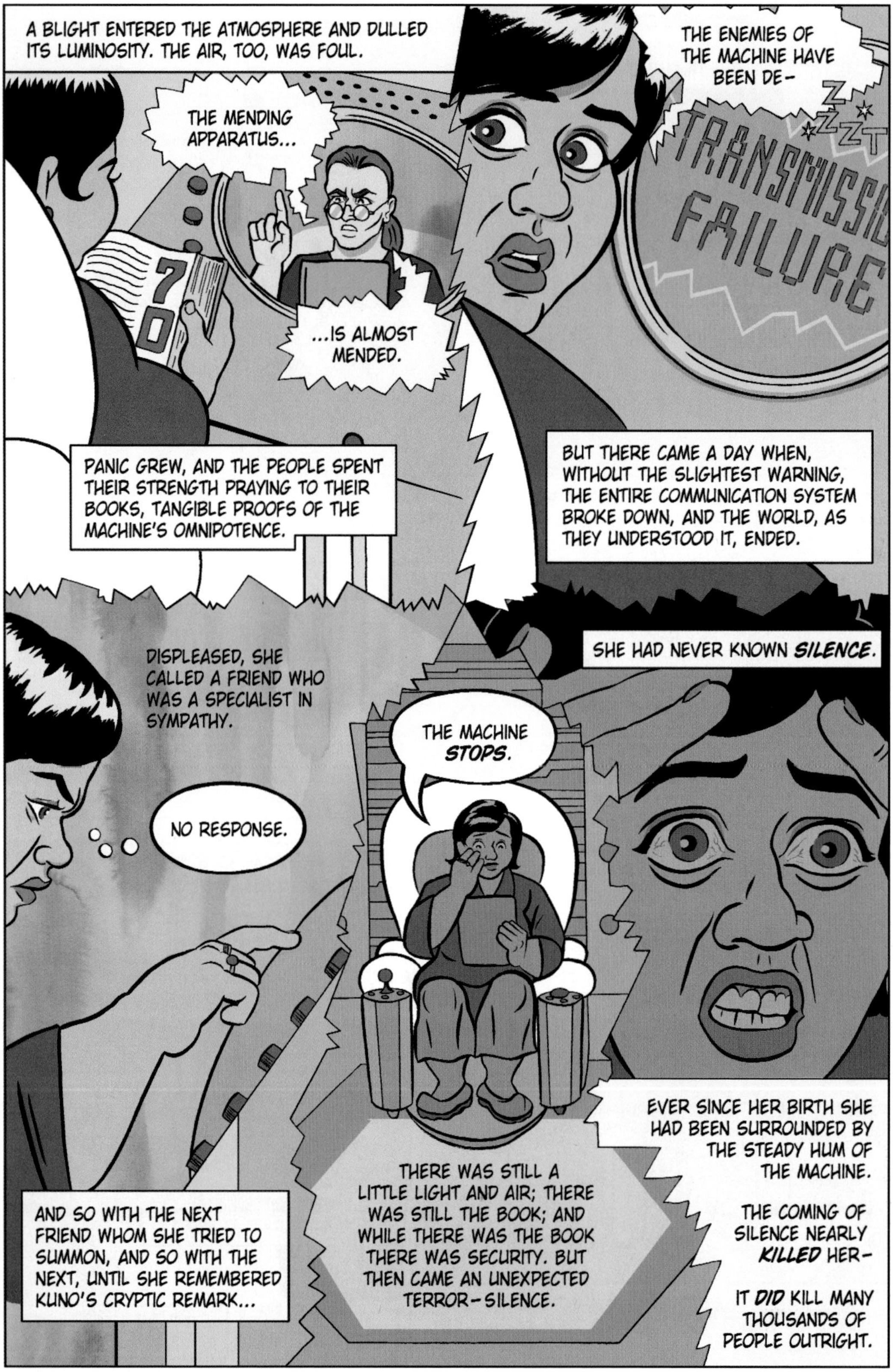
A BLIGHT ENTERED THE ATMOSPHERE AND DULLED ITS LUMINOSITY. THE AIR, TOO, WAS FOUL.
THE MENDING APPARATUS...
...IS ALMOST MENDED.
THE ENEMIES OF THE MACHINE HAVE BEEN DE–
ZZZT
PANIC GREW, AND THE PEOPLE SPENT THEIR STRENGTH PRAYING TO THEIR BOOKS, TANGIBLE PROOFS OF THE MACHINE'S OMNIPOTENCE.
BUT THERE CAME A DAY WHEN, WITHOUT THE SLIGHTEST WARNING, THE ENTIRE COMMUNICATION SYSTEM BROKE DOWN, AND THE WORLD, AS THEY UNDERSTOOD IT, ENDED.
DISPLEASED, SHE CALLED A FRIEND WHO WAS A SPECIALIST IN SYMPATHY.
NO RESPONSE.
AND SO WITH THE NEXT FRIEND WHOM SHE TRIED TO SUMMON, AND SO WITH THE NEXT, UNTIL SHE REMEMBERED KUNO'S CRYPTIC REMARK...
THE MACHINE *STOPS*.
THERE WAS STILL A LITTLE LIGHT AND AIR; THERE WAS STILL THE BOOK; AND WHILE THERE WAS THE BOOK THERE WAS SECURITY. BUT THEN CAME AN UNEXPECTED TERROR – SILENCE.
SHE HAD NEVER KNOWN *SILENCE*.
EVER SINCE HER BIRTH SHE HAD BEEN SURROUNDED BY THE STEADY HUM OF THE MACHINE.
THE COMING OF SILENCE NEARLY *KILLED* HER–
IT *DID* KILL MANY THOUSANDS OF PEOPLE OUTRIGHT.

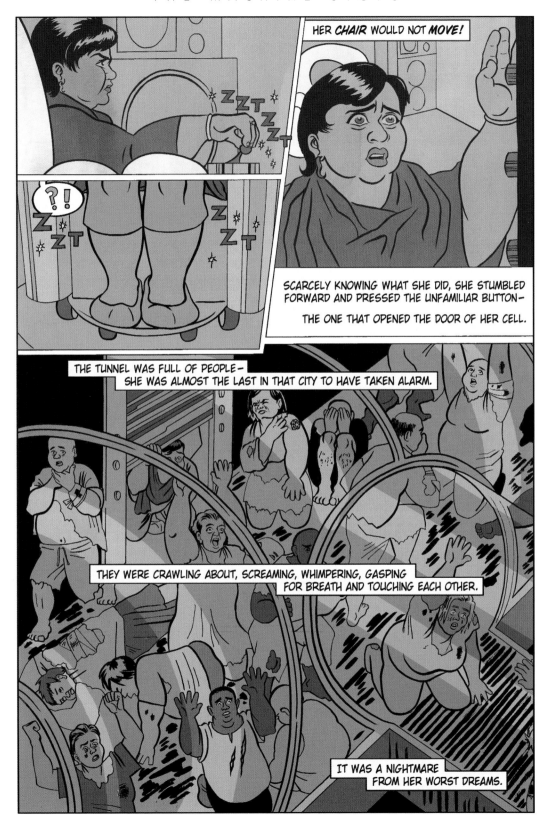

HER *CHAIR* WOULD NOT *MOVE!*

SCARCELY KNOWING WHAT SHE DID, SHE STUMBLED FORWARD AND PRESSED THE UNFAMILIAR BUTTON—

THE ONE THAT OPENED THE DOOR OF HER CELL.

THE TUNNEL WAS FULL OF PEOPLE— SHE WAS ALMOST THE LAST IN THAT CITY TO HAVE TAKEN ALARM.

THEY WERE CRAWLING ABOUT, SCREAMING, WHIMPERING, GASPING FOR BREATH AND TOUCHING EACH OTHER.

IT WAS A NIGHTMARE FROM HER WORST DREAMS.

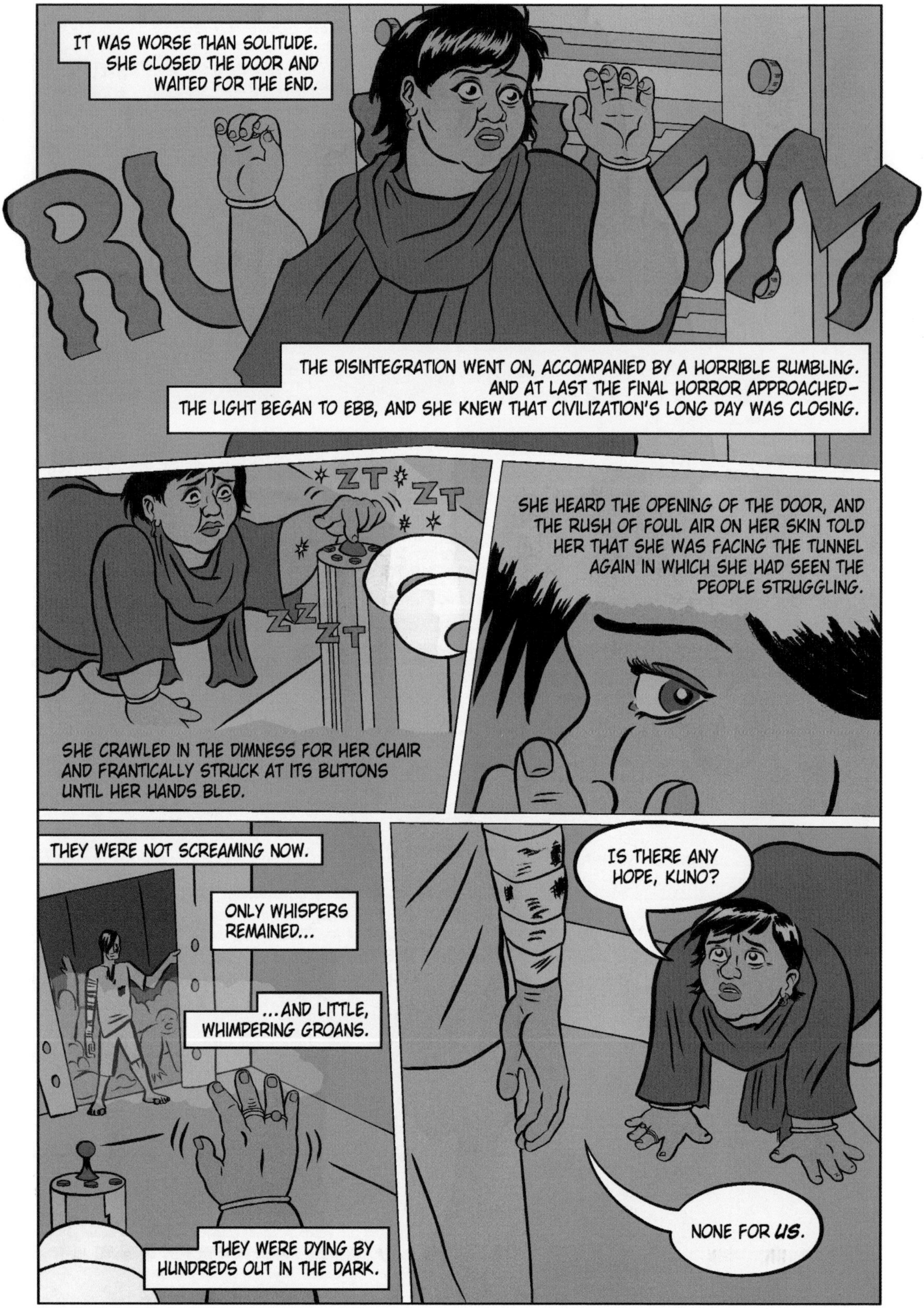
IT WAS WORSE THAN SOLITUDE. SHE CLOSED THE DOOR AND WAITED FOR THE END.
THE DISINTEGRATION WENT ON, ACCOMPANIED BY A HORRIBLE RUMBLING. AND AT LAST THE FINAL HORROR APPROACHED—THE LIGHT BEGAN TO EBB, AND SHE KNEW THAT CIVILIZATION'S LONG DAY WAS CLOSING.
ZT ZT
ZZZT
SHE CRAWLED IN THE DIMNESS FOR HER CHAIR AND FRANTICALLY STRUCK AT ITS BUTTONS UNTIL HER HANDS BLED.
SHE HEARD THE OPENING OF THE DOOR, AND THE RUSH OF FOUL AIR ON HER SKIN TOLD HER THAT SHE WAS FACING THE TUNNEL AGAIN IN WHICH SHE HAD SEEN THE PEOPLE STRUGGLING.
THEY WERE NOT SCREAMING NOW.
ONLY WHISPERS REMAINED...
...AND LITTLE, WHIMPERING GROANS.
THEY WERE DYING BY HUNDREDS OUT IN THE DARK.
IS THERE ANY HOPE, KUNO?
NONE FOR US.

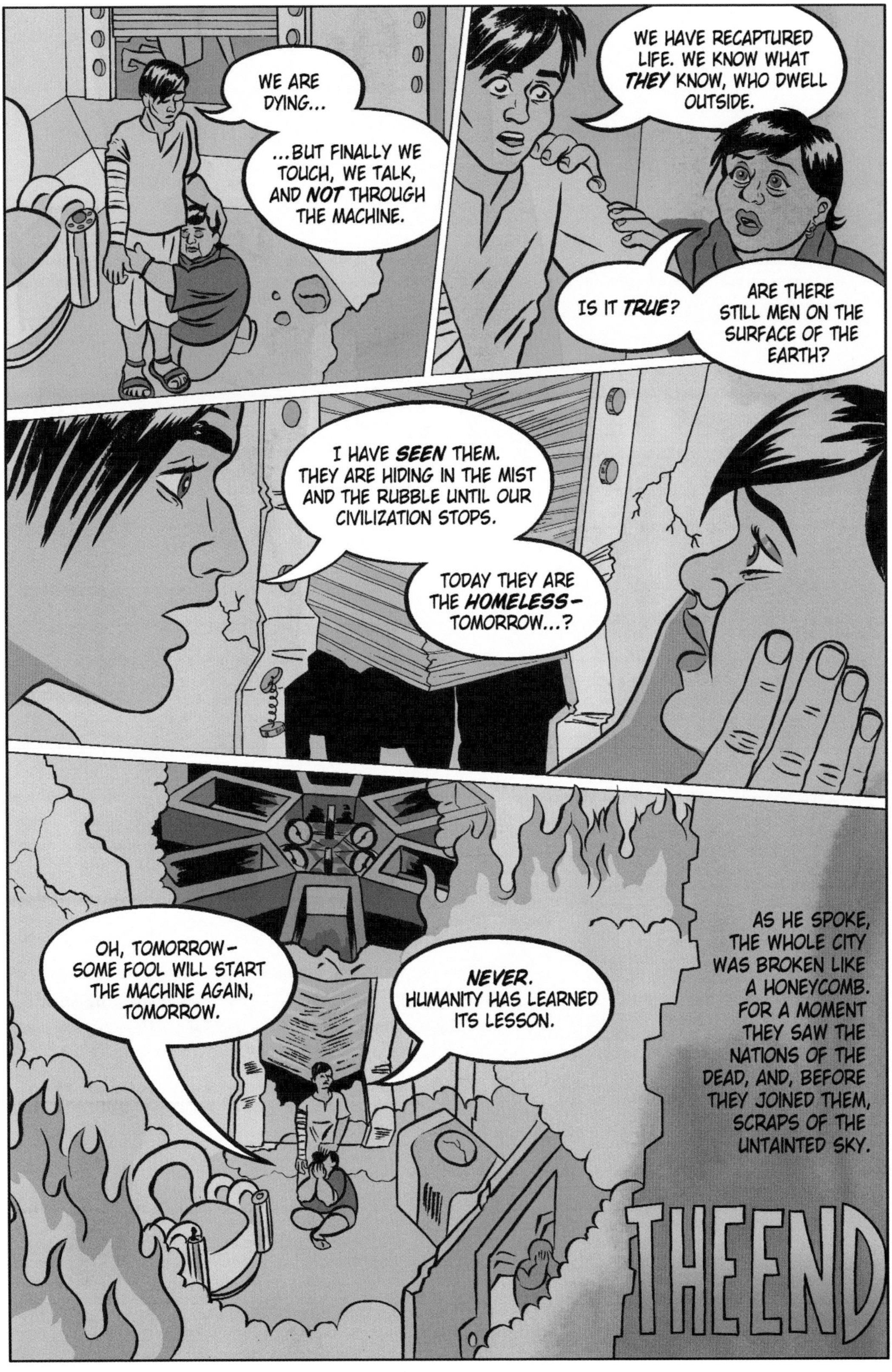
WE ARE DYING...
...BUT FINALLY WE TOUCH, WE TALK, AND NOT THROUGH THE MACHINE.
WE HAVE RECAPTURED LIFE. WE KNOW WHAT THEY KNOW, WHO DWELL OUTSIDE.
IS IT TRUE?
ARE THERE STILL MEN ON THE SURFACE OF THE EARTH?
I HAVE SEEN THEM. THEY ARE HIDING IN THE MIST AND THE RUBBLE UNTIL OUR CIVILIZATION STOPS.
TODAY THEY ARE THE HOMELESS— TOMORROW...?
OH, TOMORROW— SOME FOOL WILL START THE MACHINE AGAIN, TOMORROW.
NEVER. HUMANITY HAS LEARNED ITS LESSON.
AS HE SPOKE, THE WHOLE CITY WAS BROKEN LIKE A HONEYCOMB. FOR A MOMENT THEY SAW THE NATIONS OF THE DEAD, AND, BEFORE THEY JOINED THEM, SCRAPS OF THE UNTAINTED SKY.
THE END

MICAH FARRITOR (cover, page 4)

From his shadowy basement studio, Micah Farritor sketches, smudges, and works his pencils and erasers to the nub in his efforts to render a thousand words into each picture. He says he is proud to be in such good company in this volume, his first assignment for *Graphic Classics*. His other works include a contribution to the comic anthology of pre-war narratives, *Postcards: True Stories That Never Happened*, published by Villard Books, and *White Picket Fences*, from Ape Entertainment, an atomic-age comedy about youth, civic duty, and personal responsibility – with Martians. Beyond comics, Micah has worked with *READ Magazine*, illustrating literary works all the way from *Sleepy Hollow* to *Spoon River*. "Many thanks to Tom for inviting me to collaborate with Rich on the iconic classic, *The War of the Worlds*, to my wife, Jodi, for her unwavering support, and to little Ella, for being an inspiration every day." Check out more of Micah's work at www.mcfarritor.com.

GEORGE SELLAS (pages 1, 66, back cover)

George likes to draw. He claims he likes to draw so much that he sees everything in 2D, which can prove tricky when driving. George graduated from Paier College of Art in Hamden, CT with a BFA in Illustration, and after doing the "freelance slog" for a few years, went on to become an instructor and Studio Director at Guy Gilchrist's Cartoonist's Academy. Now he's back to the freelance slog again, creating characters, logos, labels, and lots and lots of caricatures. *A Martian Odyssey* marks his second full-length comics story, following *Tom Sawyer Abroad* for *Graphic Classics: Mark Twain*. George offers special thanks to "Misha, for her amazing love and support, and for putting up with all the late nights of work."

You can view an extensive gallery of George's illustrations at www.georgesellas.com, and find his work in:
Graphic Classics: Ambrose Bierce
Graphic Classics: Mark Twain
Graphic Classics: Robert Louis Stevenson

HANS CHRISTIAN ANDERSEN (page 2)

Hans Christian Andersen was born in Denmark in 1805, the son of a poor shoemaker. At age fourteen he traveled to Copenhagen, where he sought to become an opera singer. Failing this, he was admitted as a dancing student at the Royal Theatre. There he gained the notice of King Frederick VI, who sent him to the great grammar school at Slagelse. Before he started for school he published his first volume, *The Ghost at Palnatoke's Grave* (1822). Further writings gained little success, until his novel, *The Improvisatore*, appeared to wide acclaim in 1835. Less appreciated were his series of fairy tales, begun in the same year. He continued to write additional fairy tales through 1872, which led to the worldwide fame his work enjoys today. *In a Thousand Years*, a precursor to the science fiction story, was written in 1852.

HUNT EMERSON (page 2)

The dean of British comics artists, Hunt Emerson has drawn cartoons and comic strips since the early 1970s. His work appears in publications as diverse as *Fiesta*, *Fortean Times*, and *The Wall Street Journal Europe*, and he has also worked widely in advertising. Hunt has published over twenty comic books and albums, including *Lady Chatterley's Lover*, *The Rime of the Ancient Mariner*, and *Casanova's Last Stand*, and his comics have been translated into ten languages. Hunt is now working on an adaptation of *The Cremation of Sam McGee*, for the upcoming *Western Classics*. This is a companion piece to Robert W. Service's *The Shooting of Dan McGrew*, which he illustrated in 2005 for *Adventure Classics*.

You can see lots of cartoons, comics, fun and laffs on Hunt's website at www.largecow.demon.co.uk, and see more of his work in:
Graphic Classics: Jack London
Graphic Classics: Robert Louis Stevenson
Graphic Classics: Rafael Sabatini
Adventure Classics: Graphic Classics Volume Twelve

ROGER LANGRIDGE (pages 3, 92)

New Zealand-born artist Roger Langridge is the creator of Fred the Clown, whose online comics appear at www.hotelfred.com. Fred also shows up in print in *Fred the Clown* comics. With his brother Andrew, Roger's first comics series was *Zoot!* published in 1988 and recently reissued as *Zoot Suite*. Other titles followed, including *Knuckles, The Malevolent Nun* and *Art d'Ecco*. Roger's work has also appeared in numerous magazines in Britain, the U.S., France and Japan, including *Deadline*, *Judge Dredd*, *Heavy Metal*, *Comic Afternoon*, *Gross Point* and *Batman: Legends of the Dark Knight*. Roger now lives in London, where he divides his time between comics, children's books and commercial illustration.

See more comics by Roger in:
Graphic Classics: Edgar Allan Poe
Graphic Classics: Arthur Conan Doyle
Graphic Classics: Jack London
Graphic Classics: Ambrose Bierce
Graphic Classics: Robert Louis Stevenson
Graphic Classics: Rafael Sabatini

H.G. WELLS (page 4)

Herbert George Wells was born to English working-class parents in 1866. At age eighteen he earned a scholarship to Imperial College, where he came under the tutelage of Darwinian scholar T. H. Huxley. Evolutionary theory strongly influenced Wells' early "scientific romances." The first of these, *The Chronic Argonauts*, was serialized in his college newspaper in 1888. Seven years later he rewrote it as *The Time Machine: An Invention*, which became the first to be published in a series of popular novels including *The Island of Dr. Moreau*, *The Invisible Man* and *The War of the Worlds*. These "romances" became the foundation of modern science fiction. Their seminal influence in the field is challenged only by that of the French fantasist Jules Verne, who Wells once claimed "can't write himself out of a paper sack." Wells briefly joined England's socialist movement and in later novels promoted socialism, feminism, and free love, which he put into personal practice. He was a leading proponent of the League of Nations and chaired the original proposal. Wells wrote numerous short stories and essays and more than one hundred fifty books, including the nonfiction *Outline of History*, which sold over two million copies. But it is his early science fiction that remains his most enduring legacy. Before his death in 1946 Wells provided his own epitaph to an interviewer: "God damn you all, I told you so."

More Wells stories, including the story of Orson Welles' 1938 radio broadcast of *The War of the Worlds*, can be found in:
Graphic Classics: H.G. Wells

RICH RAINEY (page 4)

A ghostwriter who also writes about ghosts, Rich Rainey's nonfiction books include *Phantom Forces* (a history of warfare and the occult), *Haunted History*, and *The Monster Factory*, a book about classic horror writers and the real-life incidents that inspired their fiction. He's written over thirty adventure and science fiction novels and also created *The Protector* series about a modern day D'Artagnan in New York City. His short fiction has appeared in literary and mystery magazines, and numerous anthologies, including *Best Detective Stories of the Year*. In the comics field he created *Flesh Crawlers* for Kitchen Sink, *Antrax: One Nation Underground* for Caliber, and has written for *The Punisher* and Neil Gaiman's *Lady Justice*. He is now scripting adaptations of *Lost in a Pyramid* for *Graphic Classics: Louisa May Alcott* and Willa Cather's *El Dorado* for *Western Classics*.

Rich also adapted stories for:
Graphic Classics: H.P. Lovecraft
Graphic Classics: Bram Stoker
Graphic Classics: Oscar Wilde

JULES VERNE (page 52)

French author Jules Gabriel Verne (born 1828) was, along with H.G. Wells, the preeminent pioneer of the science-fiction genre. He wrote over eighty books, the best known being his novels *Journey to the Center of the Earth* (1864), *From the Earth to the Moon* (1865), *Twenty Thousand Leagues Under the Sea* (1870), and *Around the World in Eighty Days* (1873). Jules's father wanted him to be educated as a lawyer, and in 1848 he was sent to Paris to study law. There he began writing travelers' stories and librettos for operas. When Verne's father discovered that his son was writing rather than studying law, he withdrew his financial support and Jules was forced to support himself as a stockbroker and a law clerk. During this period, he met Alexandre Dumas, who offered him writing advice and would become a close friend. Verne's novels are noted for their startlingly accurate predictions of modern inventions including helicopters, submarines, automobiles, television, and the Internet. In 1885, James Gordon Bennett, Jr., owner of the *New York Herald*, asked Jules Verne to write a short story about life in the United States a thousand years hence. The resulting *In the Year 2889*, published in 1889, was credited solely to Verne, but was most likely co-authored by his son Michel.

JOHNNY RYAN (page 52)

Johnny Ryan was born in Boston in 1970. As a boy, he says, "First I wanted to be a cartoonist, then I wanted to be a physicist, then I wanted to be gay, and then a cartoonist again." He now lives in Los Angeles and is the creator of the award-winning *Angry Youth Comix*. His work has also been published in *Nickelodeon Magazine*, *Goody Good Comics*, *Measles* and *LCD*. "Comics used to be fun and crazy and weird and gross," says Johnny. "Now, they're a serious art form…it's as if everyone was having a big crazy orgy and then your grandparents walked in. They really sucked the life out of the party."

Johnny's decidedly unserious work appears in:
Graphic Classics: Ambrose Bierce
Graphic Classics: Robert Louis Stevenson
Graphic Classics: O. Henry

KEVIN ATKINSON (page 52)

"I've lived in Texas my whole life with the exception of 1985–1988, when I went to New Jersey to study with [famed comics artist and teacher] Joe Kubert," says Kevin. Since then he has created short stories and full-length comics for various publishers. He wrote and drew two series, *Snarl* and *Planet 29*, and collaborated on another, *Rogue Satellite Comics*. He's also inked *The Tick* comics, and illustrated Drew Edward's *Halloween Man*.

Visit http://zackgolem.deviantart.com to see more of Kevin's art. He has illustrated stories in:
Graphic Classics: H.P. Lovecraft
Graphic Classics: Mark Twain
Graphic Classics: Rafael Sabatini
Horror Classics: Graphic Classics Volume Ten
Adventure Classics: Graphic Classics Volume Twelve

STANLEY G. WEINBAUM (page 66)

Stanley Grauman Weinbaum (1902–1935) was born in Louisville, Kentucky. His romantic novel, *The Lady Dances*, was written 1933, but he is best known for his first science fiction story, *A Martian Odyssey*, which was published to great acclaim in the July 1934 issue of *Wonder Stories*. Isaac Asimov later described it as one of only three stories that changed the way all subsequent ones in the science fiction genre were written. It is the oldest short story selected by the Science Fiction Writers of America for inclusion in *The Science Fiction Hall of Fame Volume One*. Sadly, Weinbaum was dead from lung cancer within eighteen months of the publication of his most famous tale. He produced about a dozen more stories and several novels in his brief career, most of which were published posthumously in the next few years. His groundbreaking characterization of alien life was extremely influential to the field and established him as one of the great science fiction authors.

BEN AVERY (page 66)

Ben Avery adapted the script of the critically acclaimed graphic novel *The Hedge Knight* and its sequel *The Sworn Sword*, published by Marvel and based on the novellas by *New York Times* bestselling fantasy author George R.R. Martin. The writer of the *Oz/Wonderland Chronicles* from BuyMeToys.com, and based on the beloved fantasy characters, he has worked on Image Comics' *Lullaby* and *The Imaginaries* and his own all-ages series *TimeFlyz* (about time-traveling flies). Ben is now scripting an adaptation of Stewart Edward White's *The Honk-Honk Breed* for *Western Classics*. He lives in Indiana with his wife and four kids, but wishes he lived in a northern Ontario cabin (with his wife and four kids, of course).

Ben also adapted H.P. Lovecraft's *The Dream Quest of Unknown Kadath* for:
Fantasy Classics: Graphic Classics Volume Fifteen

ARTHUR CONAN DOYLE (page 92)

Arthur Conan Doyle was born in 1859, studied in England and Germany and became a Doctor of Medicine at the University of Edinburgh. He built up a successful medical practice, but also wrote, and created his most famous character, Sherlock Holmes, in 1887. Following a less-successful practice as an oculist, Doyle concentrated on his writing career. He was proudest of his historical novels, such as *The White Company*, and in 1894 introduced his second popular character, Brigadier Gerard. In 1912 he created Professor Challenger, who appeared in a series of science fiction-themed stories. But Holmes continued to be his most famous creation. Doyle felt that Holmes was a distraction and kept him from writing the "better things" that would make him a "lasting name in English literature." He killed his detective in 1893 in *The Final Problem*, only to resurrect him in 1903 due to public demand. Doyle wrote an astonishing range of fiction including medical stories, sports stories, historical fiction, science fiction, contemporary drama and verse. He also wrote nonfiction, including the six-volume *The British Campaign in France and Flanders*. His defense of British colonialism in South Africa led to his being knighted in 1902. By 1916 Doyle's investigations into Spiritualism had convinced him that he should devote the rest of his life to the advancement of the belief. He wrote and lectured on the Spiritualist cause until his death in 1930.

More stories by Arthur Conan Doyle appear in:
Graphic Classics: Arthur Conan Doyle
Graphic Classics: Special Edition
Adventure Classics: Graphic Classics Volume Twelve

ROD LOTT (page 92)

Oklahoma City resident Rod Lott is a freelance writer and graphic designer working in advertising and journalism. For twelve years, he has published and edited the more-or-less quarterly magazine *Hitch: The Journal of Pop Culture Absurdity* (www.hitchmagazine.com), and edits *Bookgasm*, a daily book review and news site at www.bookgasm.com. Rod's humorous essays have been published in several anthologies, including *May Contain Nuts* and *101 Damnations*.

You can learn more about his work at www.rodlott.com, and you can find more comics adaptations by Rod Lott in:
Graphic Classics: Edgar Allan Poe
Graphic Classics: Arthur Conan Doyle
Graphic Classics: H.G. Wells
Graphic Classics: H.P. Lovecraft
Graphic Classics: Jack London
Graphic Classics: Ambrose Bierce
Graphic Classics: O. Henry
Graphic Classics: Rafael Sabatini
Graphic Classics: Special Edition
Horror Classics: Graphic Classics Volume Ten
Adventure Classics: Graphic Classics Volume Twelve
Gothic Classics: Graphic Classics Volume Fourteen
Fantasy Classics: Graphic Classics Volume Fifteen

LORD DUNSANY (page 105)

Lord Dunsany, born Edward John Moreton Drax Plunkett, wrote more than seventy books, beginning with *The Gods of Pegana* in 1905. He is today one of the most popular fantasy authors in the English language and was also a poet, a successful playwright, and a competitive chess player. *The Bureau d'Echange de Maux* first appeared in his 1916 collection *Tales of Wonder*. Dunsany died in Dublin in 1957. H.P. Lovecraft was a great admirer of his stories, and wrote of Dunsany: "To the truly imaginative he is a talisman and a key unlocking rich storehouses of dream."

More poems and stories by Lord Dunsany appear in:
Fantasy Classics: Graphic Classics Volume Fifteen
Graphic Classics: Special Edition

ANTONELLA CAPUTO (page 105)

Antonella was born and raised in Rome, Italy, and now lives in Lancaster, England. She has been an architect, archaeologist, art restorer, photographer, calligrapher, interior designer, theater designer, actress and theater director. Her first published work was *Casa Montesi, a* fortnightly comic strip which appeared in the national magazine *Il Giornalino*. She has since written comedies for children and scripts for comics and magazines in the UK, Europe and the U.S.

Antonella works with Nick Miller as the writer for Team Sputnik, and has collaborated with Nick and others in:
Graphic Classics: Edgar Allan Poe
Graphic Classics: Arthur Conan Doyle
Graphic Classics: H.G. Wells
Graphic Classics: Jack London
Graphic Classics: Ambrose Bierce
Graphic Classics: Mark Twain
Graphic Classics: O. Henry
Graphic Classics: Rafael Sabatini
Graphic Classics: Special Edition
Horror Classics: Graphic Classics Volume Ten
Adventure Classics: Graphic Classics Volume Twelve
Gothic Classics: Graphic Classics Volume Fourteen
Fantasy Classics: Graphic Classics Volume Fifteen

BRAD TEARE (page 105)

Utah artist Brad Teare maintains a career as both an illustrator and a fine arts painter and woodcut artist. Clients include *The New York Times*, *Fortune* and Random House, where he illustrated for authors such as James Michener, Ann Tyler, and Alice Walker. Teare's comics creations have appeared in *Heavy Metal* magazine and the *Big Book* series from Paradox Press. He is the author of the graphic novel *Cypher* from Peregrine Smith Books (excerpted in *Rosebud 20*). Brad's work can be viewed online at www.officialcypherfansite.com and at www.bradteare.com.

His stories also appear in:
Graphic Classics: H.G. Wells
Fantasy Classics: Graphic Classics Volume Fifteen

E.M. FORSTER (page 112)

English novelist, essayist and short story writer Edward Morgan Forster was born in London in 1879. He is best known for his novels exploring themes of British imperialism, class difference, repression, hypocrisy and the attitudes towards gender and homosexuality in early 20th-century British society. Forster's first major success was *Howards End* (1910). Today, most people know of E.M. Forster due to the film adaptations of that and other works including *A Passage to India*, *A Room with a View*, and *Where Angels Fear to Tread*. When the first world war broke out, Forster became a conscientious objector. He spent the wartime years in Alexandria doing civilian work and visited India twice. After he returned to England, he wrote *A Passage to India* (1924), a novel examining the British colonial occupation. It was the last novel Forster published during his lifetime, but he continued to write short stories and essays until his death in 1970. *The Machine Stops*, Forster's only science fiction story, was originally published in 1909 in *The Oxford and Cambridge Review*, then collected in Forster's *The Eternal Moment and Other Stories* in 1928. In 1973 it was selected for *The Science Fiction Hall of Fame, Volume Two*.

ELLEN L. LINDNER (page 112)

Born on Long Island, illustrator Ellen Lindner studied art history and French at Smith College. As part of her degree Ellen spent a year in Paris, where she created her first comic book, an adaptation of *The City of Ladies* by Christine de Pizan. After graduation Ellen spent three years in the New York museum world before moving to London, England, where she earned her master's in illustration at Camberwell College of Arts. She has since published widely as a freelance cartoonist and illustrator. Ellen's latest project is *Little Rock Nine*, a graphic novel about the American civil rights movement written by historian Marshall Poe, out now from Aladdin Paperbacks. This spring she'll be self-publishing *Undertow*, a tale of Brooklyn in the early '60s. You can see more of Ellen's comics and illustration online at www.littlewhitebird.com or take a peek at her sketchbook at http://ellenlindner.livejournal.com.

TOM POMPLUN

The designer, editor and publisher of *Graphic Classics*, Tom has a background in both fine and commercial art and a lifelong interest in comics. He designed and produced *Rosebud*, a journal of fiction, poetry, and illustration, from 1993 to 2003, and in 2001 he founded *Graphic Classics*. Tom is currently working on *Graphic Classics: Louisa May Alcott*, scheduled for October 2009 release. The book will feature a new comics adaptation of Alcott's most famous novel, *Little Women*, by Trina Robbins and Anne Timmons. Also included will be seven of Alcott's lesser-known tales of mystery and horror, illustrated by Mary Fleener, Shary Flenniken, Lisa K. Weber, Toni Pawlowsky, Arnold Arre, Pedro Lopez and Molly Crabapple (in her GC début).